To Bob,

Every Other Four

The Journal of Cpl. Matthew D. Wojtecki,
Weapons Company 3rd Battalion 25th
Marines, Mobile Assault Team Eight

Cpl. Matthew D. Wojtecki

Bloomington, IN  Milton Keynes, UK

authorHOUSE®

AuthorHouse™
1663 Liberty Drive, Suite 200
Bloomington, IN 47403
www.authorhouse.com
Phone: 1-800-839-8640

AuthorHouse™ UK Ltd.
500 Avebury Boulevard
Central Milton Keynes, MK9 2BE
www.authorhouse.co.uk
Phone: 08001974150

First published by AuthorHouse 10/23/2006

ISBN: 1-4259-5400-6 (sc)

Printed in the United States of America
Bloomington, Indiana

This book is printed on acid-free paper.

For my Father,
who would have been very proud.

A Note to Readers

For the protection of the troops presently fighting in areas of the Al-Anbar province, specific areas, locations, and movements have been changed and/or modified. Troop movements, operations, classified units, and grid coordinates have been altered for reasons of operational security. After action reports that are presently classified have been omitted from the final copy of this work. Such changes, however, do not change the validity of these volumes.

Last Transmission
A preface by:
Pamela Montgomery, Gold-Star Wife of LCpl Brian Montgomery
WPNS Co. 3/25 – Snipers, Akron, OH.

"To the Family,
This is the hardest thing I have been asked to do but most likely, the most important thing. I never meant for things to turn out as they have. They have, so in this letter, I will try to give you the peace and comforts that I myself believe in... Anyone who really knows me can tell you that I consider myself an American above all else, and now an American who serves his country in the United States Marine Corps. After what had taken place on September 11, 2001, there was not a day that went by where I did not regret the fact that I had not served my country... We (the United States Marine Corps) are the most respected, and the most feared of all the armed forces in the world. Our honor, courage, and commitment to Country, Corps, Family, and Self are above all else and that is how I wanted to live my life. I have no regrets of the choices I have made. I also take nothing for granted. I know now more than ever how good life in the States really is."

-LCpl. Brian P. Montgomery in his own words from excerpts taken from his last letter he wrote to his family

LCpl. Brian P. Montgomery, upon arriving in Iraq, volunteered to fill an opening within 3rd Battalion, 25th Marine Regiment's Scout Sniper Platoon. On August 1, 2005, LCpl. Brian P. Montgomery's three-man sniper team alongside another three-men sniper team all perished in an ambush. The ambush occurred outside the Euphrates River town of Hadithah. Contrary to popular belief, Hadithah is not a small town. It actually consists of around 100,000 people, and is a main stopping point along the smuggling route from Baghdad to Syria. Also located just north of Hadithah on the Euphrates River is the Hadithah Dam. This Dam provides an enormous amount of Iraq's power and is an integral part to rebuilding Iraq's infrastructure.

The Marines of 3rd Battalion, 25th Regiment left 29 Palms, California for Iraq within the first few days of March 2005. The families of this reserve battalion based mostly out of Ohio, only knew that their Marines were en route to Iraq's most deadly province, Al-Anbar. No one knew where his or her Marine would be stationed. Whether it would be the hot spot of Fallujah or Ramadi, or if they would be stationed at the relatively safe Marine base of al Asad. By midmonth, all Marines of 3/25 had arrived safely to their destination, Hadithah Dam. The families were notified of their location. By that point, these reservists' families began to research the location of their Marine. Using mostly the Internet, Hadithah and the surrounding areas seemed to be one of the more quiet spots in the Al-Anbar Province. 3/25 replaced 1st Battalion, 23rd Marine Regiment, and 1/23 suffered limited casualties during their seven-month deployment. This information eased the worried wives, parents, children, girlfriends, and fiancées. But by this point, 3/25 Marines knew that this deployment would not be easy and that the Hadithah-Hit corridor could turn into the next Fallujah.

By March 25, 2005, 3/25 suffered their first casualty; Cpl. Bryan Richardson, a Kilo Company Marine, was on patrol when the Humvee he was riding in was hit by an IED in the town of Hit. I remember that day so clearly. I had always been a news junkie, but when my husband deployed, it almost seemed to turn into an obsession. I hungered for any information about what he and his brothers were doing and where they were. I was constantly searching the Internet for any type of information, and that afternoon, it popped up. The DOD briefings tend to go like this, "Today a Marine assigned to the 3rd Battalion, 25th Regiment was killed in Al-Anbar Province when the Humvee he was riding in was hit by an IED. The name is being withheld pending notification of next of kin." The minute I read that, my stomach dropped, and I just thought, please don't let there be two Marines waiting for me at home. I was frightened, and I couldn't think about getting any work done. All I could think about was how to avoid going home. I finally made it home that night. There were no Marines waiting for me. As soon as I saw that, a sense of relief came over me. The next day, the name notification was released. My heart ached for that family, but at the same time I was thankful that it wasn't mine.

As soon as we had suffered that first casualty, I began to pray harder and more frequently because the realities of war and what it takes to defend our freedom finally hit home. Before 3/25 deployed to Iraq, my heart always went out to those who lost a family member in Operation Iraqi Freedom or Operation Enduring Freedom, but even though I hate to say it, the faces always turned into numbers. The media is very good at making you look at the numbers. Three thousand (3,000) were killed on 9/11, over 2,300 killed in Iraq, and over 18,000 have been injured. The media portrays it wrong. They are not just numbers. They are men and women with deep convictions, courage, and commitment. Each has a unique story. On March 25, 2005, I finally understood that. My life was changed forever.

I was working twelve to fifteen hours a day while being a full time mommy taking care of our infant son. My husband and I were entrepreneurs. We had one business, but even though we had just had our first son in August 2004 and knew he was being deployed, we proceeded to open up our second company. I was swamped with work, responsibility, and worry. I was very productive, but I could never get the worry out of the back of my head. I was constantly thinking about my husband and his safety. All I wanted more than anything was to see and embrace him. Many nights I went to bed late and then laid awake for hours thinking about him, our dreams, and what it would be like to see him again. Then he would call, and every time he'd call, it was like Christmas morning. It felt so good to hear his voice. His voice would melt my fear and worry away. We would laugh, joke, and talk about our son. My husband never wanted to talk about Iraq though. He said that he was living in Iraq and that he would much rather hear about what was going on at home. Phone conversations were always too short. I know I could have stayed on the phone with him for hours because just being on the phone made it feel like he was home. I couldn't touch him, but through his voice, I could visualize his facial expressions, his smile, and his laugh, and I longed just to see that smile again.

As soon as I would get off the phone with my husband, I'd call his mom and dad. I let them know that my husband and his brother were doing well and in good spirits. I was the liaison between our Marines in Iraq and our family. During the deployment, I spent many hours on the phone and in person with my wonderful in-laws. We have a great relationship. Everyone understood why my husband called me more often than him or her. Then April 13, 2005 happened. A 120mm mortar round killed Cpl Michael B. Lindemuth. My husband spoke very highly of "Muth" and I remembered meeting him once at the pre-deployment briefing. This one hit close, real close to home.

The 3/25 Marines had control of their AO, area of operations, for barely one month, and they had already suffered their second casualty. My heart couldn't handle what my brain was telling it. I knew that the road ahead was bound to be long and tough but not just for the families but for the Marines, too. I just didn't know how tough it could actually get.

My family and I continued to go on with our everyday lives, just as if our Marines were still here. Day in and day out, we went to work, completed our tasks, and went home to sleep. 3/25 Marines did almost the same thing except they were not sleeping at home. Families continued their prayer vigils, emails, motomails, and kept sending out weekly care packages. My husband, his brother, and their fellow Marines knew that there were many people out there who cared and were pulling for them. I continued to receive many phone calls from my husband. It seemed as if he had more access to the phones than some of the others. I cherished each phone call and sometimes begged him to not get off the phone with me. I never knew when he would get another chance to call. Besides the unknown, my husband was very good at easing my fears and worries. He always let me know when he was going out and for about how long. As soon as he got back from a mission or an operation, he'd call and tell me everything was all right. Those particular phone calls were an integral part in keeping the family together and easing our worries. We all had so much on our minds and on our plates; we could not afford to spend all day worrying.

Most families whether reserve or active duty have to completely adjust to the sudden change of their Marine or Soldier being deployed. Wives not only have to take care of the kids, but they have to do the yard work, housework, bills, and work or go to school. It's a big change to go from two people splitting the household responsibilities to one person. Single Marines and Soldiers rely on their parents or a sibling to make sure that their bills are paid, their pet is taken care of, and even their house is taken care of. Families must adapt and overcome when they are presented with this situation. For some it is harder and takes longer for them to adjust, especially on the first deployment. Marines and Soldiers in relationships, regardless of whether they are married, would realize that the distance and time apart could take its toll on the relationship. The husband may worry that his wife is cheating. The wife may worry about her husband because war can change a man, and she may be left at home wondering what it will be like when he does get home. The emotional strains put on a relationship during deployment are great, but if you stick through it, the end reward is always greater.

As the deployment drug on, I began to worry about my husband and if he would be the same man when he got back home. May and June were very tough months. 3/25 suffered more casualties. Most days, it wasn't just one casualty, but it was many. May was a particularly terrible month. Within the span of four days starting on Mother's Day, we lost twelve Marines. We lost twelve husbands, fathers, sons, and brothers. On May 11, 2005, an AAV carrying a platoon of Lima Company Marines hit an IED. This hit the news wire before it hit the military wire. An imbedded reporter wrote in about the tragedy, and in her article, she used nicknames of Marines that were killed in action. There was a chance that one of these Marine families may have found out about their son's death on the Internet before they could have officially been notified. That day was a disaster for the families. I was glued to my computer all day. I was scared for my husband and my brother, but even more furious with that embedded reporter for the lack of respect she showed these families.

I didn't hear from the Marines or my husband that day. Sometimes not hearing anything at all is the best that can happen. The old adage of "No news is good news" is really, what you have to live by during a wartime deployment. Even though it was a devastating week for our Marines, their families, and the state of Ohio, I realized that I am a Marine wife, and I must push on as my husband is doing. I must not let the worry overtake me. I must not give up because my husband and his brothers who are in harms' way cannot and will not give up. As time went by, the days and weeks went by slower. My husband had been gone for six months, by the time July rolled around, but it felt like he had left home years ago. 3/25 had suffered 22 casualties by July. June was particularly hard for my husband because he lost three more of his good friends. Three fellow Marines in his old mobile assault platoon: Cpl Brad Squires, LCpl Thomas Keeling, and LCpl Devon Seymour. He was heartbroken and told me he could not talk about it until he returned home. He was in combat and there is no time to feel or grieve because he had to keep his head in the game.

For the end of June and beginning part of July, a banged up knee sidelined my husband. He was furious. He wanted to be out there with the rest of his brothers "fighting the good fight," as he would say. My husband was disappointed that he couldn't go down to Hit with the majority of the battalion to participate in a large-scale operation. To be honest with you, I was relieved. Staying at the Dam made him safe. It kept him out of danger, and that let me breathe a sigh of relief and not worry as much about him. The family and I continued to worry and pray for my brother-in-law and the rest of the battalion, but we were all relieved. I hoped it was something more serious like a torn ACL, so he would be kept on light duty the rest of the deployment, but boy, was my husband furious with me when I told him that. He told me that his people needed him, that he was making their lives safer, and that he wanted to be out there alongside them. I quickly apologized to him for my comment, and he did too. He understood why I said what I did. By early July, he was taken off light duty and back in the action.

As July progressed, I started to worry more. I didn't understood why I was worried more, but I was. Things at home with the businesses had been tough. It was hard not having my husband here to give advice when needed. It was getting harder and harder to keep up with all the responsibilities, and all I wanted was five minutes with my husband. I just wanted to hug and hold him. That was all I needed to know that everything would be okay. Of course, I couldn't get that hug. Little did I know how much I would really want that hug and embrace.

Last Transmission:
"Deuce, Deuce. This is Ace. Over.
Radio Check. Over-
Lima. Charlie.
Ace Out."

-LCpl. Brian Montgomery's (Ace) last mock radio transmission to his brother (Deuce) as written in his last letter.

It was August 1, 2005. It was early evening, and I had just left Wal-Mart. I just bought my husband all new underwear and t-shirts for when he would come home. We were about two months away from 3/25 coming home, and I was really starting to anticipate it. I missed my husband and my brother-in-law more and more each day. Sometimes the pain of being away from my husband was unbearable. That evening my son was with my father-in-law because I had some work to do with one of my businesses. After leaving Wal-Mart and en route to the other store, my father called me. The minute he started talking I could tell something was wrong. My dad kept telling me that I needed to come home, but he wouldn't tell me why. We argued over the phone for ten minutes. Frustrated, I even told my dad that if he was sick to call 9-1-1 because I had responsibilities to take care of. That's when my dad realized that the only way to get me to come home was to tell me the one thing I never wanted to hear. My dad told me that there were two Marines waiting for me, and that they wouldn't tell him why they were there. I was driving at the time and about ten minutes away from home. I told my dad I would be there as soon as possible. I threw my phone down. That was when my world shattered.

I knew what they were going to tell me. They were going to tell me that my husband was dead. I lost it. I was hyperventilating and sobbing uncontrollably while speeding down the road. I really don't know how I made it home that evening. I walked into my house to find two Marines: Sergeant Major Mark Brokaw and Staff Sergeant Paul Clements waiting for me. They asked me if I was Mrs. Pamela Montgomery, and I said yes. Then the Sergeant Major told me, "The President of the United States of America and the Commandant of the Marine Corps regret to inform you that Lance Corporal Brian P. Montgomery was killed in action while conducting dismounted operations in…" I will never forget those words. They have been etched into my memory forever. My husband was dead. The father of my child was dead. Brian, my husband, was dead two days before our son's first birthday. This could not be happening to me. It wasn't real. I asked those two Marines not very nicely if my brother-in-law, LCpl Eric Montgomery, was coming home. They were unsure, so I told them that I don't care what they did, but get him home because I needed him here. The family needed him here. Those two Marines promised me they would find out Eric's status and orders and that they would let me know as soon as possible. Upon notifying a family of a casualty, the notifying officers are not to leave until the next of kin is not alone. Because my father was with me, Sergeant Major Brokaw and Staff Sergeant Clements each gave me a business card and told me they would contact me the next day. They then left.

At that point, all I wanted to do was go to my father-in-law's and hold my little boy. I was distraught, but I had to call and tell my mother-in-law, that her oldest son was dead. That will forever be the hardest phone call I ever had to make. I don't even know how she understood the words I was saying because I was crying so hard. As I told her, she screamed so loudly. Soon after that, we got off the phone, and then the Marines called me. We had to go over to my mother-in-law's and officially notify her. I couldn't go hold my boy yet. I had to be strong and go with the Marines to my mother-in-law's. Upon getting there, the Marines told me that not just Brian was killed, but four of his fellow snipers were also killed and one was missing. Two Marine sniper teams were ambushed. The news kept getting worse. I asked them if they were sure that Brian wasn't the one that was missing and if he was really dead. They confirmed my worst fear again. Brian was dead. After relatives of my mother-in-law arrived at her house, I knew she would be okay because somebody would be there with her. I left and began to make my way to my father-in-law's.

By this time, the family knew, and our friends were all finding out. I made it to my father-in-law's and saw my son for the first time after hearing the tragic news. It hurt to look at Alexander and know that he will never have the chance to know his Daddy. He'll never know how much Brian loved him and how proud he was to be his daddy. My heart shattered into a million pieces for the second time that day. The first time was for my loss, but the second time it shattered, it hurt more because my heart was hurting for Alexander. Eventually, the family and my friends made their way over to my house. We sat in the driveway, drank, and talked. We were numb and in shock. It wasn't real. I was barely 24, and I was going to have to bury my 26-year-old husband. Our dreams and aspirations would never come to fruition. I was lost, empty, and alone, even though so many people surrounded me.

I didn't go to sleep that night. I couldn't. My mind was racing all over the place. The next day we started the mass amounts of paperwork and decision-making. The Marines didn't even know when Eric would be home or Brian's body would make it home, but I had to pick out a funeral home, a cemetery, and a casket. The paperwork was never ending. I don't remember what any of it really was. The next day I found out that all six snipers were dead and accounted for, and I found out that 3/25 lost another Marine too that day. That Marine was killed by an IED in Hit. We lost seven Marines in one day. 34 Marines were killed in five months from one Ohio reserve battalion. I convinced myself that nothing else could happen to 3/25. They had suffered enough. We had suffered enough. The job needed to be completed, but our suffering was over. That day, an influx of people stopping by the house brought food and cards. The flow of people never seemed to stop. I needed to get out of that house. I needed a break. I needed a beer. So my sister and I snuck out of the house. Brian's name had not yet been officially released to the public, so I was fairly safe from the media. We proceeded to go to Brian and mine's favorite watering hole. It was happy hour, and it was quiet. That was perfect. I was able to hide and keep to myself. This bar was where I was working when Brian and I first started dating. I knew everyone there, so it was really comfortable to be there. The manager asked me what to put on their sign outside about Brian. That was the first of so many amazing gestures my family received. I had them turn the news on because I knew that one of the local channels had been at my father-in-law's house. Living in a relatively small suburb of Cleveland, word traveled fast, so the local media knew even before the names were officially released. I made myself watch the news thinking that it would make it real, but it didn't. I sat at that bar crying. Watching the news and the pictures of Brian, I heard the words, but I could not comprehend them. It was not real. This was not happening to me.

My family was a disaster on the inside, but we put our game faces on. We remained strong for our friends, for each other, and for Brian because that's what he would have wanted. Finally, that evening, my father-in-law received a call from my brother-in-law, Eric. He was out of Iraq and in Kuwait. He would be home in a few short days. It was so good to know Eric was okay and on his way home. It let us all breathe for a moment. It let us be a happy for a split second because Eric would be home. I was able to get a few hours of restless sleep that night, but I awoke to more terrible news.

3rd Battalion, 25th Marine Regiment had garnered the attention of the media, not just locally, but nationally and worldwide. Because of the amount of casualties, the battalion had suffered and the circumstances surrounding the deaths of those six snipers, the media was hounding us at home and the Marines in Iraq. Then the unthinkable happened. An AAV filled with fourteen 3/25 Lima Company Marines hit an IED. They were all dead. The media was again reporting this before any families were notified. As the families of those six snipers and one other Marine were trying to grapple with their own loss, they had to grasp that fourteen more of their Marine's comrades were dead too. I remembered thinking it was my fault. I thought those Marines were out trying to find the insurgents that killed my husband, so it was my fault that they were dead. I now realize that that was skewed thinking. Anyone could have hit that IED. My heart hurt and still hurts for those fourteen families. Now 48 Marines from 3/25 had been killed in action. That meant 48 new Gold Star families, 48 grieving wives, girlfriends, sisters, fiancés, brothers, moms, dads, and children.

To this day, the thought of those first couple of days and those emotions and realities can lead me into a panic attack. There are days where I don't want to get out of bed because reality hurts too much. There are also days when life seems *normal*. Normal is such a weird word for me to use. There is nothing normal about being a 24-year-old war widow and raising my son on my own. There is nothing normal about losing a loved one in combat. The process drags on, and the media will not let you grieve in peace. While you are grieving, the media tries to get you to denounce the war and admit that your loved one died in vain. My husband did not die in vain. He believed in the cause and so do I. These Marines believed in what they were doing, so how do you put words in their mouths when they are dead, when they can no longer speak for themselves? It is despicable. These men fought and died for this country and its freedoms. One of those freedoms protects the media, but yet, the media believes it is okay to disgrace and dishonor these valiant men. There is also nothing normal about dishonoring men and women who believed in this country and its people so much that they were willing to and did die for her and them. So there really is nothing normal, but like all people who have suffered a loss in their lives, we move forward. The pain never goes away, but it does get easier to live with each day.

For not just 3/25 Gold Star Families and Marines, but for all who have a lost a loved one in combat, I keep you all in my prayers everyday. I pray that over time you find strength and comfort in their sacrifice. I pray that the hole in your heart will close one day, and I pray that you will never forget and not let the rest of America forget the sacrifice made. In closing, I leave you with my husband's last words in his last letter to me, to our son, to his brother, mom, and dad that comforts me each day.

"Family and friends, I leave you with this. My death is not a tragedy. It is an ending, and every ending must have a new beginning. So take this new beginning and run with it. Never look back, stand up, and be proud because I am. For I have walked through the shadows of the valley of death, and I fear no evil. I will be there whenever you need me, and someday we will all be reunited. I love you all.

Sign: LCpl. Brian P. Montgomery; Ace; American and Patriot
USMC 3/25 Weapons Company Team Death

-Love-
Brian

VOLUME ONE

JANUARY 8, 2005

Today 3/25 had prepared a sendoff at North High School gymnasium next to our small reserve center on Dan Street, in Akron, OH. I felt indifferent today, not knowing what to expect as the Marine Corps always had its share of surprises. As a Marine at Weapons Company, I had grown accustomed to long nights of staying after drill and cleaning heads and offices as a PFC. All Marines went through this when they first got to the unit from Parris Island. There was still much to be done in preparation for deployment, such as issuing new ID cards. Each ID card takes about ten minutes to make because of a smart card chip that has to be filled with our basic medical records and information necessary for the government to keep track of our information. Normally this would have been a hassle if records had been on paper, but add the electronic version, and it became even more time-consuming. Unfortunately, making electronic cards still did require paperwork just to get the ID cards made.

At 1430, we were to report to North High School. LCpl Dinkelman and Dmytriw walked with me to my car and I drove them two blocks to a ceremony. Close to 3,000 people waited for our sendoff inside the large high school gymnasium

As we walked inside, eager parents that were constantly thanking us for our service welcomed us. I was anxious to see my fiancée and parents, but I had to wait because we had to line up in formation and march onto the gymnasium.

Food from the local USO, radio stations selling Red Bands of Courage, and two TV stations were there waiting to wish us good luck or get some kind of response out of us. As the band from North High played, we marched out to a crowd of thousands of parents, wives, children of servicemen, and loved ones who wished that once we were gone that *all* of us would come back home soon, so they could greet us upon our return as heroes. The Mayor of Akron spoke and brought up the fact that many of the troops that served in the Vietnam War were not treated as honorably as we were. He assured us, in his short-winded speech, that despite many of our opinions on the war, that we would be welcomed home generously upon our return.

The ceremony was very brief. We said a short prayer and they allowed us to spend one more night with our families before we shipped out to our first training area. I rushed to look for my parents and my fiancée, who were sitting in the top section of the gymnasium. Angela, my fiancée, had a small American flag and her Marines t-shirt on. My mom and dad looked happy to see me, and we hugged for several minutes. I wish the sendoff could have lasted for a lifetime. As we talked, a reporter from Fox 8 wanted to interview my mom and I. At first I didn't know what to say, but then I remembered what we were here for and explained to the reporter that we had a job to do. He asked me if I was scared. I agreeably said that anyone would be scared and uneasy if they were in a Weapons Company heading to Western Iraq to support a line company and that it was ok to be scared. I think that I was trying to convince myself of this fact as much as I was trying to convince the local viewers of the nightly news.

As we walked out of the gym, there was a banner with signatures and messages that made me feel like I would make it through the whole ordeal. My fiancée signed the banner, "God bless you and keep you! I appreciate all you do. I love M.W."

That day I had not expected so much support. I think about those who appreciated us no matter what their political opinions they held regarding the war. In a way, I wish other countries would look at America and see that, despite our differences, we are still able to live together without killing each other. This is why I believe I am fighting.

Later that night, Angela, my brother Rudy, my parents, and I went to a nice restaurant. My favorite restaurants always have some kind of theme behind them. This time we ate in a jungle-themed one that had fountains spraying water in colorful patterns as the lights reflected off the ceiling. The food was great, but I still wondered how I would be able to say goodbye to my family and the love of my life. I love her smile. The way she laughs and how she tells me she loves me all the time. Dinner was great with a few beers and my dad's stories lightened the mood a little. I almost forgot I was leaving for a long time and didn't know if I would be coming back.

We watched the sendoff on the news on one of the last nights I would spend at home. Although there was a lot of time spent covering our send off, the reporter seemed like he was in a routine, because there was always something bigger to report. Angela and I sat together for hours talking about our future plans. I never wanted that moment to end. Just for one night, the moments where we looked at each other and said nothing, seemed to matter. This is how we said goodbye.

JANUARY 9, 2005

The morning came fast and my breakfast never tasted better. Newspapers scattered across the kitchen table about our unit's deployment reminded me that today was the day I was supposed to leave.

Talking to my dad at the kitchen table over breakfast made me feel good. He always had something positive to say. My mom was cooking the eggs and potatoes, which was probably the best food I would taste in a while, and asked me if anything else had to be done before I left. We left my house around 1330 to leave for the drill center.

Few words were said. The car ride brought back memories of my childhood. I thought about my brothers and how they always argue with me, just like brothers do. We passed through our hometown that I would not see again for at least a year.

Starbucks had always been my favorite coffee and it was nice to have an espresso before leaving to put me at ease. As my mom parked in front of dozens of other Marines saying goodbye to their wives and parents, a feeling of nothingness came over me. Somehow, my greatest fear was coming true. It was hard to say goodbye to my family. My Mom took it pretty hard, but I knew she would take care of me. My fiancée could not come and if she would have, I probably would have broken down in the parking lot.

It was almost like the first time that I went to pre-school when I was four. My parents said everything was going to be okay and that this was supposed to happen. I wish I could have stayed home that day.

Time seemed to creep by today. Most of which was spent waiting for nothing. They probably wanted to make sure we were all here and that no one would have to be chased down and arrested for being AWOL.

LCpl Dinkelman was rather riled up. He was writing in his journal. Most of it was probably none of my business, but he did tell me about a girl named Ashley that he hoped would wait for him while we're over there.

The majority of the day I spent showing off our new toys. I brought a camcorder, a laptop, and several books that I could use to entertain myself during those down times that the military is notorious for having. I was restless and my feelings were not going away, no matter how hard I tried to hide them.

JANUARY 10, 2005

The plan today was to bus us up to Cleveland Hopkins Airport where we would catch a commercial airline to *Victorville, CA*. At this point, I just wanted to get out of Ohio. I knew that the sooner I left, the sooner I would come home. We made final gear checks and were allowed to have two sea bags, one carry on, and our new ILBE packs we were issued. The ILBE packs were lightweight and combat ready. I carried my gear to the bus, which happened to be my pack and carry on. All sea bags were already packed by a working party an hour prior to our leaving. As I got on the bus, I was given a card that appeared to be written by a kid no older than ten. Everyone got a card, but despite that fact, it made me feel good and I hope I get to meet him when I come home to thank him. The card read, "Dear Marine, thank you for your courage and helping to protect our freedoms. I will be praying for you and greatly appreciate you sacrifice, from Ben."

The slow ride to the airport began with a movie, *"Full Metal Jacket"* in which a platoon prepares for Vietnam. A young reporter tells his story of the Marine Corps recruiting process and what Marines went through during the Vietnam era. I respect Marines who served during Vietnam and I believe they went through so much and were given so little credit. I hope and pray that my experience will not result in my instability and I can go home to my family and appreciate them with full emotions and normal feelings.

Boarding the plane seemed like a dream. I was flying away from my dreams and my life temporarily. This was not something I wanted to go through, but it was not negotiable. The four and a half hour flight was very comfortable and the flight crew expressed great admiration for us as they made an announcement over the loud speaker.

We arrived in California at 1300 and the jet lag instantly kicked in. I knew that I would not be sleeping until sometime after 2300 that night. Another bus was there waiting to drive us to Camp Pendleton. Enclosed deep within the Mojave Desert, Camp Pendleton is one of the largest Marine Corps bases. We ended up staying in the most primitive of accommodations on base. Our barracks were made of thin metal, which got extremely hot during the day and very cold at night. We drove through the desert as rain clouds came over the mountains and created disappointment. I felt my hope disappear knowing that this ride would not end in a place we could call home.

Getting into the spirit of things our platoon assembled a working party to unload our sea bags and packs and settle into our new homes for the next 45 or so days.

JANUARY 11, 2005

Things were pretty relaxed, but the thought of home and things I could normally do freely, like take long naps or talk on the phone, seemed like a crazy dream. They gave us a brief in the chow hall, as the wind whipped over the roof outside. The wind caused the most God-awful noise. It sounded like nails against a chalkboard. The man inside kept saying, "Safety is paramount in a training environment," which is why we went over basic safety rules and procedures, I guess. A brief was also given on an endangered species of tortoise, which many Marines just disregarded. The 7-ton trucks we drove on training patrols would often have pictures of tortoises painted on the doors as a joke. All I could think about was taking a shower and calling home.

I introduced myself to my new squad. It was great talking with the other Marines and hearing a little bit more about them. There were four of us in all: Corporal Lindemuth, Johnson, LCpl Knox, Steel, and me. Cpl Lindemuth is 27 years old and came from a rural background. I feel comfortable with Cpl Lindemuth being with us and I think others did too, because he has been over to Iraq before and always told us stories about his experiences. Cpl Johnson was the city type Marine that loved music and worked at a window factory in Cleveland. He was very friendly and he motivated me with his commentary on movies and R&B hip-hop music. LCpl Knox, who I had been acquainted with prior to our deployment, is 21 years old. Knox loves talking about the one thing that we really have in common, our interest in money. LCpl Steele is a nineteen year old from Oklahoma attached to us from a TOW platoon in Broken Arrow, Oklahoma. He is computer savvy like me and is a two year exploratory major in college. I think I will talk him into declaring one.

I showed the small scrapbook that Angela made me with our pictures in it to the guys. Cpl Johnson thought it was a good thing to have. It was great to finally get to know some more people and it made me feel like I could identify with them more. From this day forward I knew the only way to come home safe was to put my confidence in these Marines and rely on them to get me through.

JANUARY 13, 2005

In training, it seems like everyday is never ending. Physical exertion is the main thing we have to worry about, especially dehydration. I forced myself through a two-click hump to the gas chamber from Camp Wilson. The gas chamber is a requirement every year for the Marine Corps. We have to adjust our gas masks and crowd into a room where they release CS gas into the room. CS gas is a riot control agent that burns, but after a few years of doing it, I didn't feel much, just a tingling in my lungs and on my skin. When I attended the school of infantry about three years ago, some Marines thought it would be funny to put Vaseline on some unlucky PFC and throw him in the gas chamber. We heard screaming from inside as it intensified the effects of the gas. The chamber was pretty much a routine, all except that this time we were training to be equipped to handle a VX nerve agent attack. If the insurgents got a hold of anything and decided to put it into rockets or mortars it would definitely be a bad day for us. A gas attack would probably be the worse case scenario, but that is why we were in training; to prepare for the worst. No one knew what to expect a few months from now.

I felt so out of shape and I knew that I ate too much during the Christmas holiday. They say that humping is 95% mental attitude, and for the most part that's true. Most of the two clicks (a short walk in the Marine Corps) I thought about Angela and I on the beach in Cancun, a place I could go in my mind to get away from the aches and pains of reality. I had to face the expectations of preparing my mind for war and accepting that I would be away from home for a long unforeseeable period.

Inside the foggy gas chamber, we pulled off our masks together and began coughing. I tried to keep myself under control. I exhaled, put on my mask, and inhaled somewhat clean air. If this were VX, the gas would have affected the central nervous system and sent the victim of the horrid gas into convulsions until someone used a three-inch needle on that unlucky bastard, sticking him in the thigh until he was able to recover from the gas or get medical help.

I talked to my sweetheart after we returned to base and let her know that I could not do this without her. Angela is such a wonderful girl and often times when I am thinking of home, I think of us married. We are together in a beautiful house and have a great life together. As the line went dead my mind raced back into reality. The smell of the hot phone center and dozens of Marines on pay phones surrounded me.

After several hours of EMP (a training program designed to prepare us for firefights in combat) outside of our hooch / tin can, I finally fell asleep with my earphones on, tuning out the world.

JANUARY 14, 2005

I had my last can of espresso from home while attempting to clean up around my area. It was rather difficult. The sand floors kicked up dust every time someone walked by and a lot of the dust was causing Marines to have coughing spells. Rumor had it that there was something in the sand that caused lung cancer, because it built up in your lungs and had nowhere to go. I didn't know what to believe, although I thought now was a good time to introduce myself to my faith again. The living conditions were, as Cpl Lindemuth said, "worse than Iraq."

We BZOed our rifles today on the shooting range not far from Camp Wilson. They issued me an M249 Squad Automatic Weapon, which can become very heavy and annoying at times. Somehow, I knew it would be an advantage in Iraq. I let others know this too. I was always being a smart ass about things. Sighting in the weapon is rather difficult, I had to break one of the 5.56mm links and shoot one round at a time as I adjusted the front sight post on both barrels. Sometimes I feel left out because everyone else has an M16-A4 and I am one of two people who is a SAW gunner in the platoon, aside from LCpl Boreo, a loud an obnoxious Marine who always seemed to be on some kind of weight gain / muscle formula and worked out constantly. He always complained about how this deployment would make him lose weight.

We prepped for tomorrow's training evolution. Roll call was at 2200 and the Sergeant Major gave us a talk about safety, because of one Marine from Lima Company accidentally expended a round into the air after it was improperly cleared. The battalion seemed to be still motivated, although I'm sure that will change after a few months of this routine. *They are going to make us wish we were in Iraq*, I thought.

JANUARY 15, 2005

Fire watch made the mistake of waking us up a half an hour late this morning at 0530. The company went to range 105a for more of the EMP training program. LCpl Dinkelman and I sat on the hard ground and complained about how we would probably never use this training the whole time we were in Iraq. This new form of training has been created from the experiences of the Marines who served in OIF I and II. The majority of the training focuses on the speed of firing the weapon at close distances from 0-50 meters on human targets.

Our squad seems to be getting along very well together. I was assigned to be a gunner in the turret on one of the Humvees. It was great because I could see everything from the turret and it made me feel somewhat happy. Tonight we would prepare for more EMP training and would be out in the field for three days. "The field" was the worst place to be. It seemed to be where every grunt lived. Everyone bitched about being outside for extended periods of time, but being at Camp Wilson was like being in the field. It couldn't get much worse. I shoved a few shirts and socks in my pack next to the three MRE's that I would probably force myself to eat out of pure hunger.

I hope that others will see me as a hero and respect me when I get back. I often think of walking into work in my dress blues and everyone shaking hands with me, telling me it will be okay. A lot of thought has gone into what I want to focus on when I get back home, but mostly today I just thought of my fiancée and being happy with her forever.

There could have been better days. A lot of the negative attitude comes from us, the LCpl's and PFC's, who have to do the shit work for the NCO's that make us do stupid shit for no reason or to hurry the fuck up when we have our weapons apart and are cleaning them. Knox and I are friends and I think we share the same feelings about the transition from civilian to active duty.

The time does seem to go by faster when we are moving around and doing things. We need some time to shower and take care of ourselves, because many Marines are still spreading the awful illness that is going around. They always say that mission accomplishment in the Marine Corps comes first and then in a close, but not too distant second place is troop welfare. I think that is becoming very evident these past few days, although I'm sure I will get used to living in my own filth.

I hope that I can motivate myself more and hopefully start working on some self-education. At this point if there would be a better place to go better than Camp Wilson, it would be Iraq.

JANUARY 16, 2005

Weapons Company went to the field for three days for the EMP qualification course. It consists of drills at close range to the target, maneuvering properly in a combat engagement, and at night with NVG's on. Many Marines got pretty close to the person next to them when they expended rounds. The hot brass would eject from the chamber and lodge itself in between the flack and clothing of the unlucky Marine. This caused disruptions in the line of fire when Marines attempted to remove the lodged rounds. It must have looked crazy from a distance. LCpl Dinkelman has a huge scar on his neck and we always give him crap because it looks like a hicky. "Who did you get with Brett?" I said.

He didn't find it very funny because the scar was deep enough that it would probably stay on his neck for his entire life. "My tan line is ruined," Dinkelman said. He went to the tanning booth four to five times per week back home in Kent, Ohio. I'm not sure whether he just went there to hook up with chicks or if he was actually going to work on his tan. One time at drill, he came in and looked like an Arab. "Shoot him," I said jokingly and he started laughing.

I still miss home and hope we will get to Iraq soon. I think they attempt to make training more intense then combat. There is a saying, "The more you sweat in training the less you bleed in combat." I'm not sure that will prove true. When studying for tests in college it's always good to study everything, but usually a lot of it never appears on the test.

JANUARY 17, 2005

We woke up with frost covering our sleeping bags at range 105a. I did not want to get out of the rack and I'm glad I did not have fire watch last night. Tonight was a night fire, so I prepared myself for a long night without sleep. Some of the down time between relays was spent talking about football, politics, and finance. I have to think seriously about my life when I return if I want to focus on a particular area of business. Many other Marines aren't worried about that, but the college kids have their little cliques as well as the "blue collared" boys and the "hillbillies." The Corps is different from the real world. Even though I am a college kid I can still talk to a redneck or the city folks because we all have one thing in common, we are going to war no matter who we are. I have found it easier to talk to people too. Thoughts constantly come into my head about Angela and how much I love her. The little things she does and how she listens to me thinking aloud, even though sometimes I can be boring. Our training was moved up to get ready for shipment to Iraq.

Rumor was that the Vegas liberty package was cancelled, which wasn't really that much of a disappointment to me until I thought, *what if it was the last time I would ever get to spend in the U.S. and what if something happened to me in Iraq?*

Cpl Lindemuth talked for hours about some of the stories he had from his combat experience and early memories of 80's culture. Most of the Marines sitting around us weren't even born yet or were just getting out of grade school.

The night fire was a cluster fuck, everyone was firing every which way and trying to get used to firing using NVG's and PAC2A's, which mount on the rifle and when used properly will allow you to engage a target at night. The training staff blamed a lot of it on us being reservists and there was a lot of tension still between the active duty Marines and the reservists. Sgt Tate almost got in a fistfight with a Sergeant that mumbled, "God damn reservists," under his breath. They were not going to Iraq, we were. I loaded my weapon slowly and began to fire on a target. The bright green glow of the NVG's lit up the target and the loud sounds of firing continued for at least four hours into the cold desert evening.

The next morning we began firing to complete the EMP training course and Cpl Lindemuth seemed happy. He always liked to keep the Marines on his team happy. We shot side by side together as we advanced one by one onto the dog-targets. Cpl Lindemuth thought it would be a funny idea if he drew a smiley face on his target. The silhouette now looked as happy as he was, grinning from ear to ear. We went back to our original positions and waited for the signal, "ready…" The whistle blew loudly letting us know to turn and do a 180 from our stance and then bring up our M-16's and fire. One of the active duty sergeants noticed Cpl Lindemuth's drawing,

"Who the fuck drew on their target! I wanna know right now! So we have a fucking artist in the group?" The Sergeant scowled at Cpl Lindemuth.

"I was just trying to have a laugh Sergeant," Muth said.

"I bet you don't hit anything," the Sergeant replied.

"Aye, Sergeant."

I tried to hold back the smile and I think he saw me, but didn't say anything. You could hear the Sergeant walking away, and as he did, you could hear him under his breath say something like, "fuckin' reservists." Cpl Lindemuth and I walked to the target areas to take down our old ones and staple up new targets. He pretty much hit every single shot into that smiley face's head. "Good shooting Corporal," I said.

"Thanks Wojtecki," Cpl Lindemuth said as looked at me through those ridiculous aviator sunglasses that he always wore.

We walked back to our area and started the drills over again for four more hours. I hated EMP training and I'm sure Cpl Lindemuth wasn't too fond of it either.

Everyday it is hot during the day and extremely cold at night. Weather here is extreme in the Mojave Desert, but I'm sure residents of 29 Palms are used to it.

As we were forming up to get in the vehicles, Doc Hernandez was talking about Jesus and how he should be in our lives. He was a preaching man and would always say something religious any time of day, no matter what kind of shit sandwich we seemed to be in. I wanted to get in touch with my spiritual side if it gave me hope and let me somehow get through this. Somehow, I think I will need God to help me through this as much as sometimes I haven't always been faithful. They say, "There is no atheist in a foxhole," and when it really comes down to it, I should accept God rather than fight him.

It felt so good to get to sleep at 0030. Coming back from the field is always a relief, no matter where you come back to.

I still had been thinking seriously that the life I so carefully planned is not just a dream. My thoughts sometimes garble and often, I cannot straighten them out. Sometimes I fade in and out of reality, staring into space sometimes in the rack. It sometimes hits me really hard and it's like I can't breathe and need to come up for air. Reality to me right now is sort of like when I was a kid. It was one of the first times going swimming out in a lake near my house, I dove down into the water and spun around. Eventually I tried to come up, looking at the sun and the reflections. I swam towards the ground and laid upside down thinking the moment would last forever and that I could breathe, but started choking on water and eventually came up. Sometimes I don't know if no matter how hard I try I cannot get out of this situation. The pain is terrible sometimes.

Life here has been very different. So many people came together from different professions and different ways of doing things. A good person with intellect would be able to adapt to every personality and be able to talk and communicate with everyone. Under the circumstances however, I look for someone to talk to that may share a piece of my life. As our relationships become closer, I'm confident we'll hang on to these personalities and value them when we return.

Experienced Marines from 3/8 talked to us today about their time in Iraq. They said that the insurgents in Iraq were barbarians and would do anything for their cause—- even blow themselves up. Some Iraqi militants are hesitant to go out on patrols for fear that their baby's eyes may be plucked out and their wives raped in their own houses only to be slaughtered in an instant. After hearing this I think that it will be easier to pull the trigger on them when the time comes to do so. Although I think the value of human life is important morally, these people seem like a waste of life and according to the Gunnery Sergeant from 3/8, all deserve to die.

The people of Iraq consist of 80% Shiites who believe in a modern form of government and a small minority, the 20% Sunnis, who believe that rule and power should be handed down to someone who is a direct descendent of Mohammad, the prophet of the Islam faith. The last known leader, Ali was the brother-in-law of royalty and was the last to be elected from the holy bloodline. From what we were told, our mission is to stabilize the government and bring peace to the Middle East. Regardless of political turmoil and pressure in America along with the constant bickering, our nation should enforce freedom in any country, because we are a world power. I am sure that in my grandfather's time, when he was in World War II, there were probably Americans who felt we should have stayed neutral longer while the Japanese bombed our soil and the Nazi's swept across Europe. After I am in country for a while, I have a feeling that I will care less about the Iraqi people and more about fighting to survive.

JANUARY 18, 2005

A Marine always keeps his weapon spotless and clean. The maintenance today pretty much just involved making sure every piece of grime, carbon, and sand was off our weapons. A dirty weapon in Iraq could mean the difference between one second being alive, trying to fire a jammed weapon, and being dead the next. Many people were just sitting around listing to music and cleaning. It reminded me of the movie, *"Platoon"* where people were just hanging out.

I woke up feeling miserable and could not eat anything. There was a long line at the chow hall. The little coffee shop that sat off in the distance looked so out of place as I stood there and stared at it like it was a mirage. It was so different from the rest of the shit-hole camp that got worse everyday. I couldn't even use the head because there was always a line wherever I went.

Being homesick for me is still a problem, but I didn't want to forget about home and always keep it close in my mind. In some way, doing something so horrible for a period could make the quality of life much better back home, at least in theory. I had no idea what it would be like when I got back. I was just starting out and as I reminded myself of that. I fell back into a miserable slump again. There were so many things I took for granted like freedom and going to college. It all seemed to be distant to me now.

As we came closer together as a platoon, it became easier to get through the time we spent together. For one, we could complain about everything together and that was the best part about it. Knox is always bitching about doing mindless stupid shit around the camp, Steele is always talking about being Asian in Oklahoma and how weird it is, and our fearless leader Cpl Lindemuth is a big history buff and is always talking about famous wars and battles. We all sat there trying to think of call signs for Cpl Johnson. *"DJ CJ spins the best beats!"* Johnson chuckled in his chair, still cleaning his M16.

JANUARY 19, 2005

I feel happier because I received two letters from Angela and one from my parents. Angela's letter had perfume on it and Sgt Tate wanted to smell it. He kept bugging me about it so I read some of it too him as we stood in line at the armory. I dreamt last night I was lying next to her and woke up to a cold, dark hooch. The wind was making a very odd sound as it whipped through the tin can and out the door on the other side.

I had an MRE for breakfast. The four of us pretended we were at a four star restaurant.

"Would you like any more water Mr. Knox? Or perhaps some Tabasco sauce?"

"No, thank you that will be all," Knox said in a funny accent and we both started laughing historically.

The company had some information to pass and said that someone called home the other day and said something stupid over the phone like, "I gotta check off this net." It's funny because now it's the butt of every joke around here. We had some ideas on who could have said that. "It could only have been a COM (Communications) guy that said that!" I told Knox.

"Shut up Wojtecki," Knox had that look on his face as if he was ready to hit me.

I called home and my dad said that everyone back home thinks that we are heroes already. When we go to Iraq, if we don't come back with any medals I would be fine with that. I just want to make it home in one piece and with all four of my extremities. It's hard to think sometimes what I would do in combat. Most Marines hope they would do the right thing.

We are attending a school on the Blue Force Tracker, which is a computer tracking system installed inside some of the Humvees in Iraq that were used for navigation and communication on the battlefield. LCpl Dinkelman, Leach, and three other Marines came with me. I like it already because we are going to main side, away from Camp Wilson. Heated buildings are not something you get to hang out in everyday, so I considered myself lucky.

The four-hour class was just an overview and focused on the communication aspect of the program. For example, in convoys the system would be used to communicate with other units approaching that position. Dinkelman, Cpl Bauer, and I represented our platoon. An independent defense contractor from Washington D.C. led us through the short 4-hour course. He was probably being paid three times what we were and that is something I envied. We managed to stop and make ourselves sick from eating chilidogs from the main side PX. I also shopped around for Valentine's Day and Dinkelman looked over my shoulder most of the time. Other than trying to find out where the class was being held for about two hours in the morning it was a very good day aside from the usual bitches and complaints that Marines always seemed to have.

Many of the Marines at the BFT School were COM people and snipers who had learned about a system that is actually still top secret at the time. We caught a ride in a white van and a guy named Sgt Boskovitch said he was learning how to use it. Everything sounded pretty cool to me and he looked exited about it. The rest of our platoon had been doing convoy operations in preparation for the majority of the work we would be doing in Iraq. However, half the Humvees being used were equipped with the BFT system, so it was our job to come back and show others just how things worked. Most of them didn't see it that way and Knox was pissed that he didn't get to go so he could get away from the monotonous routine of training, day in and day out.

My Grandma wrote me a letter today. She said that she couldn't believe I had grown up so fast. She said that she feeds the morning doves from her front porch where we used to come over and play when we were kids. We would always go over for Christmas and watch cable TV while eating my Grandma's homemade chocolates that she would make by the pound. She said she goes to Wal-Mart a lot and she is usually on the inside looking out at all the snow falling. Sometimes she sits there for hours and watches the birds. The letter really cheered me up and got my mind off training for a while. It made me think of my Grandpa and what a guy he must have been like. Around the year I was born, he died of cancer. His time during WWII made him a hero to me and I always wonder what it would be like to sit around and listen to his war stories.

We decided to squeeze in another two hours of training before we hit the rack, sitting in on classes involving the new PVS14 night vision scopes, which were probably already obsolete once they were purchased. I did not have any problem getting to sleep tonight and wished that I could wake up and it would all be over.

JANUARY 20, 2004

It became a normal routine. Wake up at 0530, walk to the head, wait in line to take a piss, brush my teeth and wash up, and come back to the hooch where I would drink either water and eat part of an MRE or be lucky enough to have bought some POGY Bait from the PX.

Another group trained on the BFT today so I had to get back to convoy ops training. Think of the bumpiest ride that you have had and multiply that by ten and that was our convoy. I was in the back of the high back with nine other Marines. It was a tight ride, especially when someone has not taken a shower in a couple of days.

LCpl Morgan, an economics graduate from Ohio University had been talking to me about starting a real estate company when we got back to the real world. Morgan also listens to me babble about finance for hours on end.

We trained on standard convoy procedures until we were sick of it. Sgt Tate liked what he was doing and for some reason I don't think this was his first deployment. I was assigned to the 240G turret. Rough and bumpy terrain sent us on a ride. Morgan was in a nearby vehicle when we hit a large bump and his door popped open, sending him almost flying out of the vehicle. He was not hurt, but it scared him shitless. Morgan stayed quiet for most of the day and Marines joked around while he sat in the Humvee, "Your not going to jump out again are you Morgan?" Laughs and snickers of Marine humor filled the cold desert air. Following the training in the field and a flat tire on one Humvee, we attended a UXO and IED class covering the basic types of IED's and how Hajji sets them off. Hajji is kind of like Charlie in Vietnam, but just like Charlie, Hajji is everywhere.

Cordless phones explode remote detonators. Popular misconception will have you believe that cell phones set off the Improvised Explosive Devices, but in reality, the majority of IED's are set off using Motorola talk-on's and cordless phone base stations. In Iraq, there is a lack of RF pollution, so a cordless phone can have a range of up to five clicks.

It seemed unreal that the very large 120mm and 155 mortar rounds would be set off at us. I started thinking about what it would be like. Reality really kicks in and you realize that there are people that hate Americans and their way of life and would do anything to destroy democracy and our culture even if it meant destroying themselves in the process.

"The plague," as we call it is still floating around. Cpl Lindemuth stayed back because he has been sick. Several others received the shot to the ass, a concoction of antibiotics as far as we all knew.

Many times when we were just sitting around I think of the MTV show, *"Boiling Points"* that Angela made me watch. NCO's and the leadership are very discouraging and it pisses me off that someone that was just put on active duty just a few weeks ago could throw their weight around. Of course, I guess that's life and right now I guess I would just have to suck it up.

JANUARY 21, 2005

Rustling sounds came from the seventh hooch down from the heads. The sound was coming from MAP 3. We were packing for the field, the place where grunts belong, although I thought on many occasions how we were already staying in the field where we were, and I'm not sure how it could get worse. Although we were a Mobile Assault Platoon, we still would be integrating into an 81's platoon, which was short for the 81mm mortar MOS, one of many jobs you could be stuck with in the Marine Corps. I remember telling my recruiter I wanted to be in the infantry and they pretty much stuck me in a mortar platoon because that is what was available. That is how a lot of us ended up in 81's and I don't think anyone specifically "applied" for the position.

I packed enough for three days in the field. I had no idea what to expect, but I was already miserable having to get up so damn early in the morning or late at night depending on how you look at it. Gun team 1 was ready to hit the ground running. I had been with Gun 1 for three years as an ammo man, which was supposedly a very important job, but was another way of saying, "We don't know where else to put you, so we'll make you hump ammo to the gun line." Other jobs were the gunner and A-gunner. One Marine controls the data on the gun and the A-gunner fires the rounds on the mortar system so it requires some team effort. This particular morning however, I did not feel like being a team player. Dan and I were about to be ammo men for three days of training in the field that we would probably never use which was even more aggravating. Everywhere you looked in this place, there was always something to bitch about, but I remember someone had once said, "A bitching Marine is a happy Marine."

We loaded the Humvees with all of our gear, packs, and enough MRE's and headed to range 104. A few of us have been on a first name basis just for a laugh and to raise our spirits. Dan Dmytriw, Brett Dinkelman, and I have been pretty good friends before the deployment so we felt quite comfortable together.

Most of the day went by smoothly because when we got to the range, our platoon Sgt decided to put Dan and I on a gun by ourselves, which meant I was a gunner and Dan was an A-gunner. It was quite a surprise, since I have not been on the gun in two years, that our gun was fast, if not faster than the other guns. The gun line consists of four guns in a section. Large 81mm steel tubes fire a mortar / projectile that can be either high explosive illume or white phosphorus. This information we considered vitally important, especially since all of us went through SOI in the lovely town of Jacksonville, NC and forgot just about everything every weekend because of the bar scene and because Marines always have a tendency to drink and get into fights when together.

Tonight we fired coordinate illume missions and what they called the "shake n' bake," a mix of WP & HE rounds that shook the ground and baked everything in sight with no way of stopping the burning. The government uses mortars because they are cheap at only twenty dollars a round and because they do not require a battalion level authorization to engage the enemy like an air strike would.

We set up our sleeping systems right next to our gun and prepped for the next full day of firing. The platoon has 600 some odd rounds to hump to the gun-line and fire in the three days that we will be at 104.

JANUARY 22, 2005

It was so cold waking up this morning in a sleeping bag. I hoped and prayed for the sun, but unfortunately, we had about three hours until heat would dry our wet gear from the dew that settled all over the desert. Hot chow was on its way from Camp Wilson en-route to the range. Dan and I hoped we would get coffee and hopefully something good to eat. A typical Marine Corps breakfast consisted of crappy green or brown eggs that held the shape of the pan, some burned potatoes, and bacon. I truly missed waking up at home and cooking myself the world's greatest omelets with onions, peppers, and tomatoes. All I could think about was getting back to the rear. I felt so dirty and nasty.

A Regimental Gunner gave us a motivating talk on the employment of the 81's in Iraq. This guy had so much energy and never quit. We were pounding in the most training we could for our time on the guns. The heat rush hit at about 1400 and I felt like I was going to pass out. The gunner went on and on wildly about firing the guns in Iraq. He talked about an FPF, or Final Protective Fire, which was executed when the shit hit the fan and people were dying. The Gunner said that he would be coming back tonight at 0300 to wake us up to fire. Little did we know that he would come back around 2300 and we would have to jump out of our sleeping bags. Keeling was the funniest person to get out of bed for fire watch, "I'm awake!" He moaned in agony as he fell back asleep and I had to wake him up multiple times. LCpl Keeling and

Uzukawu are funny characters when they are together. Keeling grabbed his blanket and took it to the gun with him for watch. About ten minutes after I got in my back, "Fire the FPF! FIRE THE FPF!" I hadn't even gotten my boots on and gun teams were dropping rounds in their underwear.

After that, I could not really get to sleep. Apparently, when I woke up I was mumbling some obscenities to my relief on watch. Lack of sleep really set me off for the remaining time in the field.

JANUARY 23, 2005

The Colonel and the Regimental Sergeant Major stopped by the range today to speak to the Marines of Weapons Company. They complimented us on our training efforts and the usual speeches intended to blow smoke up our asses that officers usually give. The Regimental Sergeant Major was an older fellow, probably in his 50's and he reeked of Aqua Velvet, which instantly gave me flash backs of swabbing the deck at boot camp and the endless hours of cleanup we went through that I can remember trying to avoid. He talked to us as if we were his kids, which came as a relief in a weird way compared to most generals and Sgt Majors who just gab off orders and can be assholes at times. The Colonel does not just come out to see us for no reason. He came out to tell us where we would be going in Iraq, which was still somewhat classified. Although there had been some rumors about exactly where we would be shipped, we knew exactly where after a few minutes of the Colonel talking. According to him, "I want you to know exactly where you are going so that there is no confusion and you get it straight from the horse's mouth. Weapons Company's mission will be to secure a Dam near the city of Hadithah, a 70 mile stretch of roads in the western portion of Iraq just North of Fallujah, in an area known only as 'The Sunni Triangle.'"

It came as a surprise to me, reminding me constantly that there was a chance of me dying and that I really didn't like that, in fact I hated it. I keep telling myself on a daily basis that we will all come home safe and then I can live my life as normal.

To top it off today, a British Royal Commando came to visit as well. We were like a regular Mr. Rogers' show. This guy was locked on and it sounded like he was very knowledgeable. Commandos were the first Royal Marines founded in Britain and were known to be hard asses. Major Catalano, our Commanding Officer, told us a story about his Commando friend, who after a night of heavy drinking wanted the Major to go on a three mile run with him. After his story, I knew for a fact that you had to be crazy to be a Commando or at least have a screw loose.

The Commando passed some word to our company. Apparently, he said several operations had found out that keeping our nametapes on any visible place was a bad idea. The CIA found out that al-Qaeda hackers had taken footage of Marines in cammies and one Marine's name tapes were visible. They used the last name to look up personal information, which they then used to terrorize the family of the Marine. According to the Commando, this Marine was hunted down and slaughtered in his own home and in his own country. Believe me, my name tapes came off almost instantly after the formation ended.

We finished the shoot with some direct lay in which we would set up the guns without the use of the FDC, which was the Fire Direction Center for the 81's platoon and controlled commands on the gunline, and team leaders would have to use range estimation to plot the targets.

We finally got back to the rear and it never felt so good. I dropped my pack and as soon as I had permission, ran to the phone center. I didn't get very much sleep so my conversation was very dull. It was always very stuffy inside the small trailer, which housed about 35 phones, all of which usually were full, aside from the four or five that Marines insisted on trying, but never worked. I was just happy to hear her voice. Angela seemed so sad and didn't know what to do. She was crying and then I started to cry and tried not to let anyone see me. I talked until my phone card expired and then went to the Warriors Club for a few minutes. I'm still pissed because they still charge two bucks for slice of pizza, although I'm sure this wasn't really a time to be stingy. I remember supply and demand from economics, but this was the deep end of that concept.

I talked to Cpl Lindemuth out by the generator while he proceeded to cut my hair and we talked as he buzzed my head. I told him I was growing my hair long for Angela. He said he was trying to grow his long too and he was working on a "combat stash." I took a shower about 30 minutes later and tried to avoid getting my clothes wet in the changing area. There just happened to be a large puddle of water in the crowded room where I was standing.

Major Catalano is our company commander and is really quite motivating. When everything sucks and we are absolutely having the worst time, he always has a way of keeping our spirits high just by talking to us. He took his shirt off and turned around while talking about something. The huge tattoo covered his back. "What does that say?" A Marine from our company asked.

"Well I got drunk one night and the next morning I got this huge tattoo on my back that says 'CUT ABOVE HERE' in Arabic inscribed on my back. I'm not sure how it got there, but my wife was ready to kill me when she saw it," the CO said.

"That's motivating sir," a voice from the crowded shower room shouted.

I was proud to serve with the CO because he was about the only officer I could talk to that treated me like a person.

I proceeded to my rack after an ice cold shower and then passed out thinking about Vegas and somewhere, anywhere but here.

JANUARY 24, 2005

The days seemed to go faster and faster. MOUT was on the schedule for today. Casualty percentages they told us in an urban combat environment are 80% or higher. I was not in the mood for this shit today. I was tired and just wanted to get to Iraq already. I climbed up onto the 7-ton with others in our platoon. The training involved how to maneuver in a city environment on foot while carrying a combat load and flack jacket. They told us if we were on a convoy and we ever took fire from buildings in nearby cities, squads in the Humvees would have to assault through. The major difference between us and other branches of the service is that in our infantry we never leave or retreat, we stay and assault through no matter if it means dying or not. It was a scary thought as I watched groups charge into the fake buildings, built out of aluminum crates similar to that of what trucks hull.

Several times today, I found myself drifting off into space and thinking about the great times I had at home in Ohio and all of the things that I normally took for granted.

The MOUT Training area consisted of a town in a secluded part of the base that if you were not looking for the place, you would never know it was there. It was rather secretive and I could only think for hours why it would be. Signs were written in Arabic and buildings were similar to the structures in Iraq. MOUT is very exhausting, especially with sappy plates and a full combat load. *When we get to where we are going I hope that we do not have to assault through buildings and I hope it is only as a last resort*, I thought. I read about situations in the papers and books about what happens over there, but really couldn't think about what I would be doing. I just hope it was something productive and that it would at least be worth the sacrifice.

We received more speeches from another General that just drove down from our headquarters at Camp Lejeune, NC. It seemed like we were a big deal, especially since this has been the third important person that has talked to us in the last few days. The General of 4th Marine Reserve Forces said, "I am transferring command to the 3rd Expeditionary Force, which we will be attaching ourselves to once we get to Hadithah Dam." I caught myself a few times almost falling asleep to his long-winded speech. He was also an older fellow and was one of those crazy people who decided to devote his whole life to the Marines. I could never be that person, no matter how much they paid me. I guess you could say that this was not really my calling, but regardless I was here to defend freedom and I would do it willingly and with courage.

I got a letter from my parents today and pictures of the last meal that we had together. The fourteen-ounce New York Strip steak sounded really good right about now. I thought about how delicious it was, how juicy and flavorful every piece tasted. I would probably be thinking about that steak the entire time we were here.

Another day closer to getting the hell out of here and accomplishing the mission we were deployed to accomplish.

JANUARY 25, 2005

Second Platoon worked on vehicle patrols today. Lt Haunty briefed us on the training order and we stepped off at about 0900, after a full breakfast with eggs, corn beef, cereal, and orange juice. Usually we bitch and complain about the food, but the breakfast this morning was better than others were and certainly better than eating MRE's. Supposedly, the patrols we did today in Humvees with machine guns and automatic grenade launches is what we would be doing the majority of the time when we got to Iraq. Eat, breathe, sleep, and drive in Humvees. The purpose of vehicle patrols is to make certain that the enemy does not set IED's in the roads and disturb the population, which we strived to make peaceful. Once we get off a patrol, the next section goes out to replace us and it is a continuous cycle so that the insurgents do not have time to make us react to them. Attached to our section were some scout snipers that needed to be extracted about 30 miles south of our position. Snipers are very much respected in the Marine Corps. They are tough, hard, and have to be able to sustain long periods of time on foot in the desert and in one position for days on end. Snipers also have to be able to navigate using the grid system, which is now used on most modern GPS's. I rode up in the turret with the 240G machine gun, Cpl Johnson was driving, and Cpl Lindemuth was the Vehicle Commander. Roads out at Camp Wilson weren't exactly a smooth ride and being up in the turret doesn't help much either, especially when the 240 is not on a mount and just strapped on with a bungee cord. Cpl Johnson took a sharp turn and the 240 barrel fell down on my hands cutting the area between my thumb and forefinger wide open. "Shit!" I screamed.

"What's wrong, Wojtecki?" Cpl Lindemuth was trying to concentrate on the road and at the same time see what the hell I was yelling about.

"I busted my hand open on this damn 240! Piece of shit!"

Cpl Johnson slowed down a little and looked up at my hand that was now bleeding all over the turret. "Well, we haven't even gotten to Iraq and you've already fucked yourself up," Cpl Lindemuth tried to yell over the loud exhaust as we sped around corners of the back roads in the training area.

Our main objective was training on vehicle dismounting and formation drills such as a "Mad-Max" which is a code word for, "get the hell out of the vehicle and provide security while support elements move up to the front lines."

Talk around the platoon always had something to do with the liberty we were supposedly getting in Las Vegas, Nevada or "Sin City." We were going to be released into Vegas the end of February. I just wanted to get out of Camp Wilson to avoid working parties and visit the excellent seafood buffets at Cesar's Palace. The thought of staying in a nice hotel and getting a private shower without everyone standing around you was very nice. Just having a soft bed to sleep in was a luxury right now, but it was something to look forward to even though it seemed so far away.

JANUARY 26, 2005 (0000-2200)

An admin stand down started at 0730 this morning for miscellaneous paperwork. One of the final checks for deployment was making sure that all of our health problems were worked out on paper and that almost every shot that could ever have been given to someone and still make them a human had to be accounted for before we left the States. The downside of probably every branch of the service and the government for that matter is that its admin procedures were very bureaucratic and forms had to be filled out to do the simplest things.

We all marched down to the chow hall where Weapons Company had to complete an admin audit consisting of a small pox release form, life insurance forms, and our BIR's. If something was not right on a particular form, we would have to complete the entire form over again by the numbers or as the Gunny in charge put it, "breaking it down Barney style." It was very hard to hear in the chow hall so the Gunny was practically screaming at the top of his lungs so that the entire company could hear him. I was more focused on getting free snacks from the chow hall, like the cereal and the tea packets.

It was a very cold rainy morning. There were still plans for training patrols today with blank rounds to simulate actual combat. None of us are looking forward to what we have ahead of us, only the insane. The maintenance and admin stand down would last long into the afternoon, which for most of us who were still among the sane, was fine with us.

In a way there was a burden lifting slowly off my shoulders. There were often long endless nights at home worrying about deploying and going to Iraq. Maybe I was falling off my rocker, but somehow I felt relieved by all of this mess. I was going to be in the shit and for most people this would be (staying in freezing cold and extreme climates in the California Mojave Desert), but somehow I felt comfort in finding God or maybe everything has suddenly opened up my eyes to the reality ahead of me. I had a dream last night that I had a son and that I talked to him about the time I was in the war. He looked at me with the widest eyes and looked up to me. Somewhere in the middle of my dreams I found the comfort I needed, but woke up to an unfamiliar face waking me up for a radio watch, the usual shift from 0000-0100.

I got a card on my rack that appeared when I woke up. It was from Angela and it said that she missed me very much and that I am her hero. It was great to hear from her. It made me very happy and I looked at it almost daily. There are not many places to hang things up here, but I moved both of my sea bags together and then put my books on top near the edge of the can that we live in to have a shelf for my stuff. I don't think anyone here is as organized as I am, other than LCpl Morgan and of course, LCpl Dinkelman.

We are using NVG's tonight and turning all the lights off for our patrols. Then, using brevity codes, we can maneuver accordingly through the darkness. I am going to go to sleep while I can. In the back of my mind though, I know that this training is necessary and I try to keep a positive attitude, because I know the more training I get, no matter how useless I think it may be, it may save my life and I can't screw around with that. I have no idea how the war will change me and I am really scared. Before I left at the sendoff, I told the reporter from Fox 8 news that everyone was scared and that a brave man, even though he is scared, will still be able to do his job and come home. It's still difficult just working up the courage to go on, but knowing I have a great family at home and people that love me, that makes me want to fight.

JANUARY 27, 2005 (0000-1300)

I threw myself into further training on convoy and patrolling drills. Mounting and dismounting the vehicles in the event of an enemy attack by small arms was something I got used to. PFC Stroh, a metal-head from Cleveland, who works in construction, LCpl Gurgol, a pipe fitter from Cleveland, and Cpl Johnson were all part of the second vehicle's first squad. There was a long sleepless night ahead of us. We were told that we would probably not be sleeping, so my motivation was usually pretty low, since I loved to sleep (that meant being in this shit hole less, at least in mind). At 2200, we drove to our makeshift firm base where we dug into our positions after assaulting other members of our platoon that were acting as enemies. While driving along I looked out the right side of the vehicle and just started firing with my weapon, "There he is!" I shouted with intensity. I exited the vehicle, opening up my door and then slammed it shut. I started laying down machine gun rounds from the M249 SAW. I continued firing on top of the ridgeline at a figure with an antenna. An enemy was at an observation post. The Marines inside the vehicle were going ape shit, "He's right there on top of that ridge!" I said.

"I don't..." Cpl. Johnson squinted at the ridge, which is blocking half of the sun, "Oh there he is!"

"Finally you see it, I'm going to assault to that mountain over there and lay down suppressive fire." I ran out of the vehicle like a mad man trying to keep my SAW upright.

The rest of the vehicle soon followed and the driver moved the Humvee into position.

I was so filled with adrenaline. I almost forgot my spare barrel. It wouldn't be the first time I've been bitched at for not having it. I got a real ass chewing from Cpl Lindemuth for that one, but I found it. In a matter of minutes, everyone shot everyone else up. It was like a game of guns that I used to play when I was little with my brother. "Hey, I got you! NO you didn't, I got you!" I would always argue. It was soon over and I caught myself dozing off on road watch while Stroh's insane metal blared over his headphones that looked like they came straight out of the 1980's, out of a *"Saved by The Bell"* episode or a *"Back to the Future"* movie. We seemed to be getting very acquainted with the Humvees. Tonight was like no other, a cold miserable one I'll never forget. 2100 passed, then 2200, 2300... We were in charge of guarding a roadblock and were instructed to open fire in the event that a vehicle tried to bypass our razor wire and flare obstacle. Sitting in a vehicle for twelve hours is one thing, but being on alert all the time can be quite nerve racking. I can only imagine what it would be like when rag heads were shooting at us. The night was long and very cold.

At 0400 in a daze of confusion, we were instructed to escort a makeshift casualty vehicle for a ground MEDEVAC, where later we were lit up by enemy fire and we had to return to our previous position. At this point, running on zero hours of sleep was really getting to me, but we got some good training and it allowed me to get to know the Marines around me a little better.

JANUARY 27, 2005 (1300)

We are still on the oddest of schedules. Other platoons call us the Nazi platoon, because we train harder than anyone does and some say that our platoon Sergeant has lost it. I would rather not be part of this platoon, but the fact that there are people like Cpl Lindemuth and LCpl Knox, that when shit gets tough you can bitch together and somehow laugh about everything. We would always make a joke out of everything bad that has come our way. I feel much better now having stuck it out with this platoon.

When we got back to Camp Wilson, we were allowed a few hours of much needed rest. A good shower, a shave, and doing my laundry made me feel like a new person. I think about home a lot and it still never escapes my mind. I am so close but so far away from it.

JANUARY 28, 2005

Last night they allowed us to drink two beers at the chow hall. Cpl Lindemuth and I walked down through the soft sand to the chow hall, which Knox had commented on several times for being a shit hole. He worked there one time during the cycle and I guess everyone got their turn to scrub pots and pans, but it was in order of seniority of course. Cpl Lindemuth spotted me and bought me two drinks. We sat down at the hard metal picnic tables. I listened to him talk about combat tactics and his past wartime experiences from his first tour of Iraq.

I got a good night sleep. The beer was a tease and it was just enough for us to want more than that. I could see some people going back in line two or three times in a row. There were always limits to good things though. I was just glad to get a taste of alcohol. God only knows when we would get it again. I woke up at 0630 this morning feeling dazed. The mail clerk handed me two letters from my parents and from my company that I had interned at before I left. At my feet, there was also a big box of stuff, magazines, and lots of junk food.

I managed to sneak my way into the phone center. It was pretty crowded and stuffy as always. I talked to Angela, who seemed worried because of a recent report on the news where fifteen Marines were killed in western Iraq on a helicopter. I told her to be strong and not to worry, that nothing would happen to me. *God I hope I was right*, I thought as I leaned forward with my head against the pay phone. It made me think of where we were going and how it seemed to be the worst place on earth to be right now. It was good to hear my fiancée's voice again and to hear what was going on back home.

After a long formation outside under the light of a small generator next to the hooches, we reorganized into three sections of our platoon——by blood type——- for administrative purposes. It made sense because if anything happened to us we could always use blood from another Marine to restore our wounds if it got that bad. I was now in first squad first section alpha team with Cpl Johnson, Steele, and four other Marines from other platoons. I had a feeling this wouldn't be the last time we would be rearranged. The ten hours that followed were very slow and it was good to use the time to relax and grab a quick coffee with Knox at the coffee shop, which was the oddest place to have a café that served lattes and mochas. It reminded me of my obsession for espresso in college. I remembered how I would survive through finals week by pounding down the caffeine and cramming the books.

Knox had just returned from COM training at Camp Lejeune, North Carolina. They flew him down there and he got to stay in a hotel and party his ass off while everyone here was freezing in the rain. He said he got a lot of free time and liberty almost every day. *That lucky bastard,* I thought. I was ready to kill him. I was so envious. He seemed happier than the rest of us. I talked about finance as usual and how privatizing social security was a great idea with some downsides and how my portfolio was doing over the past year according to one of the *U.S. News* magazines I got in one of my care packages. Down time is a good thing, but it always seems that when we get it, that thinking about the real world always catches up with us. They say that, "Idle hands are the devils play toy." I think a serial killer wrote that and I think it rang true even outside of prison, especially in the military. To our knowledge, the next thing on the training schedule would be a three to five day RCAX. This would be where all small arms coordinate their firing into one movement. Officers got a kick out of these exercises because they were logistically exciting, as well as fast paced in the field as well. TOW Missiles, machine guns, grenade launchers, mortars, tanks, snipers, and vehicle-mounted weapons were just a few weapons that would be used throughout the evolution. This also meant extensive time in the field. I hoped that time would go fast, which it often did when we were not sitting around waiting to be shipped out. I made the mistake of hoping that the weather would cooperate with the training, but I knew it would pour on us, and if, *"it ain't rainin' we ain't trainin'."*

JANUARY 29, 2005

Iraqi elections begin in three hours. Analysts and political correspondents expect a 50% turnout and over 137 candidates / parties are supposed to be on the ballot. A U.S. Embassy was bombed just after the 7pm curfew was put in place in Baghdad. For 3/25 it was a pretty relaxing day just getting ready for the field for five days or so. Dinkelman, Dmytriw, and I are with the 81mm mortars and plan to repeat what we did just a week ago. A lot of complaints and gripes came from team alpha, but then again what would a day be like without its complaints and interesting comments? I knew we would get through the time we had by sticking together and laughing about things. I think that without amusing ourselves that I would probably dive into insanity.

It was rather windy today. It began with the mystery chow and drawing out weapons from the armory, which was a fenced in area of quad cons not too far from the chow hall. It was as if we were always marching over here to put weapons in and take weapons out. I felt so dirty here and I haven't taken a shower in the past few days. My books still lay on top of my sea bags and I was thinking about making a bookshelf out of old MRE boxes. My area is as organized as it can be and I cannot think straight without an uncluttered area. Sand always blows in my eyes and gets in my lungs; especially when people drag their feet in the barracks. Today I mostly zoned out, making phone calls on Steele's cell phone and listening to the occasional gossip and rumors about girlfriends and wild stories that are probably made up about how smooth some guys are and how they got their game on in the clubs. Our gear is loaded on the Humvees and we are ready to fire some 800 rounds of mortar ammo tomorrow.

JANUARY 30, 2005

We prepped for the field. All 81's were to report for another three-day training evolution on top of the normal five-day field operation and another trip to range 400. I was up until about 2000 and after we were packed, we pretty much just sat around until a formation. It occurred somewhere around 1900 outside of our hooch with full combat load and plenty of junk food for the field. We prepped our gear while we listened to the COM guys give class after class on the PRC119 radio. It was such an ancient piece of equipment. Even Knox said that it was out of date, but whatever was cheap and worked was what the military used. At zero hour, we formed up with the mortar systems and ran dry mortar missions until it was time to depart. I can't say how frustrated I was over the past seven hours from 2000 to 0300. I guess I was going to get used to half days and whole nights. I was going to kiss my eight hours of sleep I got at home goodbye.

The formation was a complete cluster fuck. We could have driven across the entire state of California for the time it took to sit in the second high back from the rear while 37-degree winds whipped into us from behind. The issue was finding our grid position, not to mention loading up some 700 HE and White Phosphorus (Shake & Bake) onto 7-tons only to use 100 or so of them. Dan and I huddled in the corner of the high back with my sleeping bag and Brett curled up in the fetal position. The Marines up front got a constant supply of heat from the air vents. I could feel some of it, just slightly, if I positioned myself right. After eight hours of sitting in the Humvee, I passed out. My bones were cold and my blood felt frozen. We coordinated SEAD and artillery with our missions, which meant having perfect weather for the F-15's to fly over and drop bombs on old rundown tanks that had been rusting in the desert since the Gulf War.

I was drained of all my strength by the time we were unpacked from the canvas-topped vehicle. They managed to squeeze over ten people in one vehicle, but at least it was somewhat warmer than if I had just been by myself, although I envied those who got to sit up front. What motivated me was that when we were loading up ammo, Captain Macintyre helped us in the working party. He was an officer that wasn't afraid to work and I respected him more than any of the other officers. The others, who normally were known for just making other people do the manual labor while they relaxed in their makeshift offices, in tents, and in old buildings that always seemed to have heat when it was cold or A/C when it was hot.

That night we slept fairly well considering we were only getting four and a half hours or so of sleep after setting up the gun line and covering the tubes with ponchos. We just bedded down right next to the vehicles. We were so tired. Pulling out my sleeping bag inside the freezing cold Humvee seemed like the best idea I have ever had.

JANUARY 31, 2005

We stumbled out of the rack at 0600 and quickly made sure our gun was ready to fire. From the time we got up until around 2100 we fired SEAD's. The F-15's and rotary wings flew in and dropped bombs on training targets. The brass said that 81's were very accurate and right on target, but than again they were probably just blowing smoke up our asses like they usually did. I saw the impacts though and they were pretty damn accurate. I heard it from the FO's who were down near where the target area, so I could believe it. It was a slow, boring day of firing on the mortar range. The wind here in 29 Palms is *very* cold, in the 30's. I still managed to somehow get sunburn, be dehydrated, and cold all at the same time. This sucked. Because of our long romantic evenings of humping ammo last night, we got to hit the rack tonight somewhere around 1930. That was like a miracle sent from above. More than four hours of sleep was a blessing and a record since we've been here. Some Marines had to stay up for fire watch, but I was to get the mortar ready for tomorrow's hip shoot. That's where we would get a grid and would have to hop out of the vehicles and set up the 81's as quickly as possible in that given location. It seemed like a more logical use for the mortar system since we would not be staying in the same location if we assaulted an enemy target.

Somehow, even after eleven hours of sleep I still felt tired. I ate some granola bars from one of the care packages I got and then quickly mounted the mortar system on the high back for a day of driving, stopping, setting up, shooting, mounting up, and then driving again. We had 100 some odd rounds and only fired about fifteen. We drove to the first designated area and set up our guns.

The Platoon Sergeant, Sgt Williams, only had the first three guns in his section firing at a time. We were done shooting by 1400 because of some range violation and range control, or coyotes as they so cleverly named themselves, would not allow firing after a certain time. It took us until 2330 to get out of that hellhole, a small crevice on the side of a mountain that we were firing out of. I rode back to Camp Wilson with the first stick of Marines returning and then was somehow "volun-told" to come back to the field as an A-Driver to pick up more Marines. When we got there, we were instructed to wait about three hours until the 7-tons finally came and ammo was loaded and ready to bring back. Luckily, SSgt Venerose snatched me up and we left again in the 7-ton to the motor pool. The Staff Sergeant seemed irritated that he had to sign out the vehicle and turn it back in. There was a whole process to signing out vehicles on papers called, trip-tickets, and then marking exactly where you went and how long you were gone so that the military could keep record of its fuel expenses. The remaining Marines that were out there, mostly second section mortars stayed until 0230, those unlucky bastards. The thought of re-enlistment at this point certainly would never cross my mind and all I could think about was that this must have been up there with one of the worst three days of my life.

FEBRUARY 1, 2005

I had just returned from the field. Just my luck, there was a 0830 formation. I was ordered to prep my gear for another night in the field with the heavy machine gun platoon. *This wouldn't be so bad,* I thought because we were going to actually do something worthwhile. Our training would consist of a warning order, which was a brief that went over, in detail, the mission at hand and how we would accomplish it. Three platoons of machine gunners mounted in Humvees would participate in a live fire engagement with the .50 cal as well as the MRK19 automatic grenade launcher. Lima Company had some eleven vehicles as well and we were to cover the line company as a CAAT with our three Humvees from Weapons Company. Our route consisted of some simulated villages and non-hostile engagements as well as what to do in the event of an IED and roadblock situation. The convoy also had a full team of combat engineers that would disable bombs. Air was also on station for the operation that consisted of F-15's and apache / cobra helicopters. Members of the Korean military were also there to observe and learn about how U.S. forces trained. It seemed kind of weird to have Koreans there observing us, but South Korea is commonly mistaken for North Korea, which often appears in the news for possessing nuclear weapons. It could have been North Korean military for all I knew. I was just a grunt and my job was to mind my own business and follow orders.

After we completed the warning order with Lima Company, we were to step off at 1300. It was amazing that with all the technology we have, we are still doing warning order briefs using maps made out of sticks and rocks in the sand. I was still out of it at the time. Our first engagement was a contact right. We opened up with small arms fire at eight green pop-up targets that were all coming up at random locations around our field of view. I tried to help Cpl Johnson as much as possible. Handing him up boxes of .50 cal ammo was all I could do and if I saw something, I would call it out right away so that the radio guy could call it in and we could get clearance to engage with live rounds at the target. We called in a few bogus targets like rocks and old rusted out tanks that I think we mortared a few days earlier.

Through the course of the convoy, we engaged three targets; a squad sized enemy element, a roadblock, and a 1974 Chevy Corsica that we managed to blow the hell out of. The car simulated a roadside vehicle born improvised explosive device or VBIED for short. The C-4 explosives were pretty impressive when the technicians ran up on the vehicle, which would have been quite nerve racking had it been an actual VBIED. They slapped two sticks of plastic explosives attached to a DET cord lasting only about five minutes. The blast shook our Humvee. I could see the glass vibrating and time seemed to go in slow motion as the explosion rocked the entire area. We were a good 400 meters from the controlled blast. Cpl Johnson hunched down in the turret shortly after Cpl Kustra and I ran back in the vehicle. I still was lugging around a SAW, so I was running as if though I had a cross on my back. In a way, I guess that I did. "Shit, that was huge!" Cpl Kustra panted out of breath as he put his M-16 between his legs and looked at the remains of the car.

The CAAT vehicles were the first to leave the area for refueling and then spending yet another night in the field. I'm thinking it's only to toughen us up and make us hard. I think there would be no way in hell that we would spend the night out under the stars in Iraq, for the simple fact that we could be snatched up at night and find ourselves on Aljazeera with a knife at our throats the next day. The night in the Humvee was cramped and cold. It was like an icebox. I slept with the Christmas blanket that Angela gave me before I left and the airplane pillow I picked up when we arrived here. My legs were so cramped up and it was very uncomfortable sleeping. I opened up my care package my parents sent me when we stopped for refueling and made a quick fifteen minute stop at the hooches. I was assigned fire watch from 0500 to 0530, and had to wake everyone up for reveille that morning.

I talked to Angela over a cell phone on top of a Humvee and she was worried about me. I was worried about her too and I love her so very much. It felt better to hear what was going on back home and what I am missing out on. I just wanted to go back to the rear and rack out for three days straight. I feel so sick and weak and may be developing what we call, "the plague."

FEBRUARY 03, 2005

Saying goodbye to the field didn't bother me much at all. I felt dirty, sick, and tired. Luckily, higher ups were staying in the field to complete the mission's second wave with Kilo Company. About an hour of sitting around and we were clear to go back to Camp Wilson, which wasn't much of a sanctuary, but it was a place to get a shower and at least relax for a while.

Most of the heavy guns and the odd man out, the mortarman who had to fill a COM guy's spot (me) went back to the rear. We could see the Cobra helicopters over our heads as we got back to Wilson. I unloaded my gear and organized it as neatly as I could. Organizing helped me escape reality and I could think about other things while I straightened up my cot and the area around me. I got another care package again today from Angela. It had a huge picture of us together laying on top of a box full of goodies. We took that picture on Christmas with me in my uniform hugging her by the Christmas tree at her house. We went to JC Penny's this year to get our photographs because one of her friends worked there and we could get a better deal than at the ball. Also, a card from Evan, a kid that she baby-sits on Thursdays that read, "I hope you come home safe. I'm proud of you." Kids always had a way of making you feel better. I hung the picture by my bookshelf, which still sat on two sea bags. Today I got a chance to unwind. We always hated second and third platoons because they were probably sitting in the rear for the past two days.

Somehow, I didn't think that those making the schedule had everything planned out and that most of the time we spent here in California was for the most part, tentative. I woke up feeling very angry at the world. I probably would get the prize for being the most disgruntled in my platoon, although Knox is also up there with me. We had to do a round robin. This involved some simple training classes that we would each spend about twenty minutes a piece on and then switch to the next station. Our leadership did not feel satisfied so we ended up double timing to some empty buildings near the camp and doing some extra training on MOUT.

I felt like I was being buried alive and could not escape. The thought of going to Iraq seemed like a dream and the two months of training we were getting couldn't prepare us for it. I don't think things would sink in until we landed in Iraq.

The feeling that we had done everything came over me. Somehow, it was never enough to train us for what would happen next.

FEBRUARY 04, 2005

Revile sounded at 0530. A warning order went out around 0730 and the formation lasted hours in the cold morning wind as we stood there and waited for the world to end. I took about a half an hour to get out of my sleeping bag and drank a double espresso that I managed to ration from what was left of my care packages. I brushed my teeth and washed my face. I don't know why I bothered to everyday. I looked at myself in the mirror. My eyes were red and had large black circles under them from lack of sleep. It looked like someone had punched me. The smell of urine came from twelve or so Marines taking their morning piss scrunched into a ten-foot urinal on the other side of the wall where the sinks were. Duty platoon was usually in the head cleaning it out. If you didn't get high from the household cleaning products they were using to clean out the place, then it wasn't clean. I rubbed my eyes and walked out of the head into the soft moist sand that had absorbed two days of rain.

I was told to operate the 240G again in the turret despite the last accident I had. I took some pictures with my old 35mm camera that everyone in my platoon made fun of me about. "Hey Wojo, ready to join us in the 21st century?" Knox yelled so I could hear in the turret.

"Shut the hell up, I'm getting a digital camera in the mail," I said, noticing that I was getting a bit of an edge since we had left a month ago.

The mountains were very surreal in the midst of our training. They were always there even after we would leave and would be there for a million more years despite our ever-changing lives and the sacrifices each of us would make. We left at 0900 or shortly after. We were working on more patrolling as a platoon; similar to the rotations that we would supposedly do in Iraq. Getting up to the training area was a bumpy ride. I didn't want to cut myself again on the sharp turret so I held the machine gun underneath my arm. The dust was not making my cough any better. This morning I woke up coughing and I had the worst a sore throat. It felt like I was coughing up sand paper and the dust just made it worse.

In our patrol, we were ambushed by other members of our platoon and were to react accordingly, assaulting through to our objective with the .50 cal and 240 firing while coordinating with dismounted troops. You had to be careful where you were firing because there might be ground troops out, and God forbid you aim in the wrong direction. There were several points that we could have improved on such as just working on our SOP's. Everything we learned with our old platoon had to be redone to fit the needs of the new Platoon Sergeant. It was adapt and overcome I guess, but who knows, I think I was just along for the ride.

FEBRUARY 05, 2005

This morning we have a company forced march to range 108. It sucks because we have to hump the .50 cals and 240G's because our platoon SSgt said that they were filthy the other day and, "what if you were in the shit and Marines were dying and your weapons jam up because you were a lazy ass and didn't clean them?" We ended up splitting up the weapons into pieces. I carried my SAW and a 240 A-Bag and switched off with others that had heavier things to carry like the .50 cal barrels. We squad rushed on a range that was more than 800m long. Definitely an exhausting run, but it allowed us to get used to our new squads and adopt new tactics. I carried the SAW, so my job was laying down the suppressive fire. The only problem was that rushing with the SAW was a real bitch. Sgt Jenkins, a Marine who served two tours in Afghanistan led our team. We rushed nearly 800m during the dry run without ammo, which involved getting down when you were fired at, getting up and moving while firing and maneuvering on the battlefield. It was harder than it sounded. "I'm up, they see me, I'm down." I would catch a face full of dirt when getting down. The next person would rush, I would fire, and it would go on and on like that until we were at the 800m mark. The course kicked our asses and Cpl Spencer said he could hear me breathing loudly from across the range. "It was as if you were having an asthma attack or something," he said. The bad part was after the dry run and the live run were finished we would have the hump back to look forward to, which was more than two clicks away.

All the training we did today was worth it, because everyone looked forward to the liberty we were going to have on Super Bowl Sunday. I wasn't one for sports but if it meant getting free time, I was all for it. It turned out that we didn't end up having to walk. A loud cheer could be heard as the 7-tons pulled up to pick us back up and take us back to Wilson.

Lately, I have been feeling emotionally numb and I try to look back to when I cried during sad romantic movies and laughed with Angela at the mall or over coffee. We used to go to coffee shops almost daily. I missed expressing myself, and being on a free and clear schedule.

The debrief following the range was very positive for first Alpha. Sgt Jenkins said that the SAW did a great job of suppressing pop-up targets.

We were shuttled back to Camp Wilson by 7-ton and the game as usual was "how many Marines could we fit into the vehicle?" We managed to get all of second onto five vehicles and it was back to the hooches to clean weapons and pray that sometime before 0000 we would be turned-to, to take showers and make phone calls. I snuck out later and used Brett's cell phone to talk to

Angela. The thing about the SAW was that no matter how much I cleaned it, I could always make it cleaner and carbon always got into very small places that couldn't be reached unless I scrubbed for hours, especially after firing a few hundred live rounds. I decided that I couldn't wait to talk any longer and had a feeling in my chest like I needed to talk to her. She seemed to be keeping herself busy. She was babysitting her cousin Nick for the night.

After I used up Brett's cell phone minutes, I made a bet with Knox on what time we would get turned-to. He said 2300, but I said we would be here all night.

Lt Haunty today told us about a classified after action report of a company of LAV's who were attacked at Hadithah Dam. He said the enemy was getting smarter, but luckily U.S. Forces killed 23 Arabs and none of the Marines were hurt. It opened my eyes to the threat that these terrorists posed and that we were to be going to that area in a little less than a month.

FEBRUARY 06, 2005

Cpl Wyman is yelling at Kuznick for not getting up on time. Its 0630 right now and he was supposed to wake up for the clean up / working party of range 108, but I guess he was the only one that didn't get up. Falling back to sleep was difficult after I was awakened by Cpl Wyman's loud and very disturbing voice. In fact, it was impossible. I lay in my sleeping bag with a runny nose and sore throat until about 0730 when it finally got a little warmer out. The hooches that we lived in were often called "Ice Boxes" because they hold all the coldness in them from the night before and until the sun reaches almost to the overhead position at about 1200, I was pretty much screwed and have to force myself out of the rack into 30-degree weather and extreme cold.

Today was not that bad because it was as close to liberty as we would ever get. For a long time we had looked forward to just being able to have some free time and tomorrow that would be possible. We were all allowed to visit main side Camp Pendleton to do our laundry and mail some of the stuff home that we would not need to take with us to Iraq, like woodland cammies. I read about 100 pages of my John Grisham novel, which I had been reading occasionally to get my mind off the deployment and where I was.

I felt very depressed today for some reason. I guess that's what a lot of down time will do to you. I managed to send out some film and video to my house for my parents to develop and watch. I also wrote a few letters to Angela, which mostly were about plans for what we would do when I got back. A cruise was on my mind, but we were not sure what we were going to do. Being at home would be fine with me just relaxing in my own home and eating good food would be vacation enough. Still I am always worried constantly about being forgotten when people move on with their lives and they forget that I am protecting their way of life that they cherish.   Morgan has a magazine which I read today about planning for the future. As much as I could, I tried desperately to stay as clean and organized in these conditions as I could. I read a few pages and couldn't stand the dust clouding up in my face when someone would walk by me. I went outside, sat in the sun, and read half an article before chow.

I thought about some things today. Finishing college was my most important priority. *What if I forgot everything I learned and somehow did not get my degree? Would I still be successful when I got back? How would I deal with my life after having been at war?* These were all questions I had no idea how to answer in my mind and naturally, they kept reoccurring through out the day, repeatedly like a broken record.

The mess hall served nachos, steak, and potatoes for dinner. It really hit the spot compared to what we were eating day in and day out. Nothing tasted better. Tomorrow we were to prepare for SASO at March Air Force Base for God only knows how long. I think they said something like two weeks. I had my doubts about any set length of time, especially how things were going around here. A few of us had a saying that 3/25 stood for "three things change two times every five minutes" and so far, that proved true. I looked forward to getting through this training, because the closer it got me to getting home the better. Home now seemed now to be no more than a distant memory. I would sure miss this country especially after we touched foreign soil and the reality of war would hit our minds.

Following the steak and potatoes, I walked outside and could not believe my eyes. A huge Budweiser truck pulled in outside of the chow hall and a few employees began setting up tables. The super bowl party was about to begin. Several of us would wait in line to get beer for one dollar a glass and then get back in line still having a full glass so that by the time we got up to the front of the line, we could then purchase another beer. A female Gunnery Sergeant got wind of our plan and stopped us, "this is bullshit," she said, "get your drinks, go back, eat some nachos, and then when you're done drinking that beer come back and get another one."

You should have seen Cpl Lindemuth's eyes light up when he saw that truck. Knox couldn't drink and neither could Dan because they were under 21, but between a few companies of Marines, we managed to clean out the entire truck and the beer was gone by about 1800. Disappointed faces waited in the line to get nachos. I sat there and stared at the TV screen for a few minutes before going back to the hooch.

At 2000, we had a mission to accomplish, code named "Irene." There was an abandoned building next to our barracks and the Marines of second platoon were tasked with a special mission. A Corporal from our platoon passed the word that there were two cases of left over beer behind the skids out back. Our mission, if we chose to accept it, was simple. To finish and dispose of the ordinance and get the fuck back to the barracks. When our platoon entered the building, there were comments about how luxurious this building was compared to our hooches.

"We should be living in here, there's carpet and everything in here," A voice said coming from the back of the room.

"Yea, there are even electrical outlets in every room," I said as we proceeded into the inner rooms of the old rundown luxurious Battalion Aid Station. I think what was on most people's minds was the alcohol and they didn't care where they drank it. We all got one beer a piece and the toasts began that bound us together in the midst of a war, a bond that could never be broken.

A Marine from the platoon in Broken Arrow, Okalahoma quoted Psalm 91, the warrior's prayer:

Though a thousand fall at your side and ten thousand at your right hand, the pestilence will not reach you. You will only see it with your eyes and witness the punishment of the wicked. Because you have made the lord my refuge, the Most High- Your dwelling place, no harm will come to you; no plague will come near your tent. For He will give his angels orders concerning you, to protect you in all your ways. They will support you with their hands so that you will not strike your foot against a stone. You will tread on the line and the cobra; you will trample the young lion and the serpent.

Others toasted to their families and friends. We all wanted to come home and knew that the Marines we were standing next to right now would go to war with us, and some might not make it back.

It was amazing how Marines from all areas can come together and fight for one cause. It is a bond that no one at home could ever understand. Things we find funny, to others at home would seem sick and disgusting, or some how would make them insane. Among us brothers, we could talk about anything and laugh about nothing.

Another Marine interrupted the loud talking, "When we are old, and grey we will always remember moments like these where we come together and follow those who have gone before us, in the cold, extreme hot, and adverse conditions we will be together and we have each other."

He pulled out a Listerine bottle full of what looked like a mouthwash, which he later informed us, was full of Ever Clear, which is almost pure alcohol and tasted so foul when mixed with Listerine. The horrible taste went down well with others beside me and the words that were said here tonight.

Today was a day for second platoon to have a few beers among just us men and be together headed towards an inevitable war. We realize that those who fought before us, because of us relieving them, were permitted to go home and see their families.

Cpl Stocker stumbled out of the old building that still looked like a mansion compared to what we were staying in and said a few words before he turned in, *"I am really glad and honored to serve with you guys and I would do it again in a heartbeat if I had to. When I was little, my uncle told me about how he was in the Vietnam War. He was drafted and pulled out of school when he was eighteen. He said they took him to the base where they stood in line. They told everyone to line up and count off; every other fourth person they selected was assigned to the Marine Corps. They kept calling people, 1 Army, 2 Air Force, 3 Navy, 4 Marines, all until the last person in line. He shipped out to Vietnam that day."*

A cold feeling came over me as the wind blew and the lights from the generator shined off our iceboxes and we hit the rack half drunk and praying we would make it home once we left.

FEBRUARY 07, 2005

The thought of eight days in the field 60 miles away from camp didn't really seem all that appealing to me, but getting my ass out of Wilson should give us a break from sleeping in cold barracks with dirt floors and no heat.

Second Platoon had a formation at 0745 and then they released us to do whatever we need to do to get ready for the movement tomorrow. That meant packing a gear list with plenty of clothes and supplies for our training.

I was not really in the best of moods today. I sat outside, watched the sunrise, and then went to the PX for a while with LCpl Morgan. He reminded me that we should start on our business plans, but I really didn't feel up to doing anything right now. I curled up in my rack for another two or three hours. Marines were being shuttled to main side. I stood and waited for the bus while a huge crow with black feathers picked up a piece of meat someone had carelessly dropped from the Roach Coach. That was a nickname we gave to a truck that came out on the clock before chow and sold candy, pop, hot burritos, and burgers. Everything junk food, they sold at an elevated price. I talked to my dad on the phone and he said he got my letters and said that he missed me and to have fun at the Air Force base. My dad was in the Air Force during the Vietnam era and was a flight technician for the SAC. I figured he had probably been to March at some point in his military career.

A chess game and several movies were going on in the background as I read the business section of the newspaper dated from a week ago that was mailed to me yesterday. Doc Baronehernandez (probably the longest name put on a nametape) was giving haircuts, so I managed to sneak my way in and save five bucks before taking a shower and packing up my gear for training.

Soon we would say goodbye to California and this horrible training would be a memory as reality set in and we left the land of the free into a completely different world of chaos and conflict.

3

FEBRUARY 08, 2005

I had fire watch this morning at 0000. I have just gotten to the point where I am totally relaxed and I'm ready to fall into a deep soothing sleep and then someone comes and wakes me up to guard the barracks full of sleeping Marines from the coyotes that usually rummage through the trash by the heads looking for food. It is quiet and all I can hear is the wind whipping through the hooches and the howling coyotes under a half moon. The dark half of the barracks is exposed to the desert and it's difficult to walk around in the dark. The generator roars and there is a small light off in the distance by the chapel. Sometimes I look at the mountains on the horizon and try to guess how far away they are. I dared my fire watch buddy to run to one of them and I'd give him ten bucks if he did. I kept looking down at my watch and woke up my relief fifteen minutes early.

Revile was at 0600 this morning. I lay in my rack for a good half an hour or so before getting up and starting the morning routine. 3/25 was preparing to move to March AFB today for our SASO training package. We packed everything we would need for ten days of what we thought would be shitty, but maybe not as bad as where we were staying right now. Busses loaded up at 1000 and it took us what seemed to be hours to move out of this place.

God only knows how long the bus ride was. I slept the whole way there as small houses, huts, and farmland went by our tour bus. I woke up as we pulled out into the training area. I could hear plains flying overhead, the sound of their engines whined above us. The slower and larger C130's were probably carrying a full load of warriors to a far away land. Second alpha stepped off the bus and were greeted by swarms of sand flees. As if there could not be a worse place on earth, naturally the Marine Corps could find it and call it home. This was worse than Wilson and probably the worst shit hole I have ever laid eyes on.

We sat on our packs and waited for highers to do accountability while swatting the sand flees off us. They were biting my hands and any place open and exposed on my body. For one reason or another, we did not stay in the abandoned rural community of slums and sand fleas but crammed on another bus and traveled a few miles down the road to some barracks that were used by a local sheriff's department, probably a police academy or SWAT training center. We stopped briefly at some very nice barracks with what looked like all the amenities of a hotel. *Yea right,* I thought to myself and sure enough, we were relocated to some rundown slum, our barracks. Windows were broken off and paint chips were chipping off the sides. It was a regular crap hole.

"That's more like it!" the bus shouted almost in unison. We unloaded into our new home for the next ten days. Climbing to the second floor with all my gear gave me flash backs of boot camp, when my senior drill instructor made me carry both my sea bags, my leaking laundry detergent, my pack, and all of my loose gear up four flights of steps to my squad bay. The place looked like it had been abandoned for a good 40 years or so. I picked a spot on the floor with the rest of my squad and did some exploring. Electricity, running water, carpeting, and stalls in the heads were just a few amenities that set this place apart from Camp Wilson. The building was a typical government installation, although nothing was up to code and if this were a piece of real estate in the civilian world, it would have been shut down and condemned in a heartbeat.

A change of scenery would do me some good and as anything new, it made me feel anxious of what was ahead. Only tomorrow would tell.

FEBRUARY 09, 2005

This morning I felt strangely warm. The rooms we were now staying in were like the Holiday Inn compared to Camp Wilson. We were going to a school, an actual elementary school or at least using the main auditorium of the Riverside California elementary school. Little kids would have their plays and moms and dads would watch their kids be stars, pumpkins, and knights saving the world from the dragon's evil breath. There was to be no swearing, weapons, dipping, or smoking near the school, so we had to try very hard to be on our best behavior. Classes were given by a Lieutenant who took information from classified after action reports of units that have deployed to Iraq in OIF I and II and basically lectured us on what they did wrong, their mistakes, and how we could improve our SOP's to be more efficient and lessen casualties. We would receive some of the best training in the U.S. here. To make it that much more realistic we were given live SESM rounds, which are rounds loaded up with paint so shooting people would be real and add to the training experience.

It was very odd how an elementary school would be integrated into a simulated combat village. There are actually Marines here that are assigned to this area and their sole purpose is to grow their hair and beards out and be props in a training simulation designed to be as close to Iraq as possible. Most of them have AK-47's and look like the commoners of Iraq. Their clothes, right down to their turbans, looked very believable.

Today we trained on clearing rooms and satellite patrolling, a technique that the British had invented and proved effective during the later parts of the Chechnya conflict and parts of the Gulf War. We used the live SASM rounds and while I was clearing a room, I was shot in the arm through one of the windows. Damn did it sting! It left a quarter sized welt on my arm and I'm not sure how long it will be there.

I got a few letters in the mail, which finally caught up to us in our new location. Mail call was so typical of the military, "Knox!"

"Here Corporal!"

"Wojtecki!" The Corporal shouted.

"Here Corporal!"

"Johnson!"

"Right Here!" and right on down the list until the pile was completely empty. There must have been letters in there from a month ago just piled up waiting to be handed out at the most inopportune time. I sat outside the porch of an abandoned and asbestos ridden shack and read my letters. I thought about life back home. *I wonder what everyone is doing right now. Are they thinking about me?* The chow made me almost want to throw up. It reminded me of one of the letters I read from my dad. He said that my Uncle Bill was in the Army in the South Pacific and enlisted together with my Uncle George. The funny part about the letter was when he told me the story about the two of them and how they used to steal food from the chow hall. Well, one day they stole some crackers that looked very good, but it was dark. They got into the light while they were chewing on the mushy crackers and Uncle George said, "These crackers are very mushy!" My uncle Bill just looked at him with wide eyes. They were eating crackers with maggots crawling all over them! I held the puke in and went back inside to sit on my pack.

Today happened to be Ash Wednesday and a lot of Marines went to sermons in the evening. The Sheriff's Department of Riverside was conducting PT drills for the academy. A warning order commenced at 2130 for tomorrow's training cycle so the day ahead looked busy. A feeling of fading in and out of reality seemed to be more evident today than any other day. The longer I could stay inside my mind while days passed by, the faster I would get through this hell. However, I knew things would get worse once we got in country. Sometimes the waiting for something is worse than actually doing it.

FEBRUARY 10, 2005

I rolled over on the moist ground and remembered where I was. I had the most awful taste in my mouth. I ate one of the energy bars that Angela sent me while trying not to get out of my sleeping bag. It was fucking freezing out. It didn't make sense that we got up at 0500 because our warning order specified 0700. I bypassed this mornings chow. I just figured that anything left over from yesterday's feast was used to make today's breakfast. I almost puked that shit up yesterday, so there is no way in hell I'm eating it today. I did have some coffee, which kicked in about a half an hour later.

The basic concept of vehicle patrols- similar to vehicle convoys, but not to be confused with them- is to either protect or assault an area, conduct SASO, and interact with the local populous to gather intelligence. Role players and SESM rounds were to be used in the patrol that kicked off at 1000. Don't ask me why we got up at 0500, but then again if it didn't make sense, I guess we would be doing it.

An Army Psy-Operations unit trained with us today. Their sole purpose is to break down the enemies' will to fight using a loud speaker, similar to what the Nazis did during World War II after the Normandy invasion. It was proven effective and therefore used to communicate to the enemy that as the speaker clearly put it, "Eitibhy'a eitibhy'a! (Attention) You are outmanned and outgunned! Hand yourself over to Coalition forces or face the full firepower of the United States Military!"

Another of their more cheerful recordings that got annoying really quick went something like, "Eitibhy'a Eitibhy'a! Citizens of a free Iraq, you have the power to save lives by reporting any terrorist activity to coalition forces."

The loudspeaker played repeatedly and depending on the situation, would play a different set of instructions such as don't get near the vehicles or surrender now to coalition forces. Although later on while I ate my cheese tortellini MRE that was revolting, they were using the Psy-ops vehicle to have a *"Rage Against the Machine"* concert that played right near us. It was like an Ozz-Fest on wheels, but the lower half of the music was cut off leaving only the treble and it sounded worse than screeching nails on a chalkboard. I would say it would probably irritate and even piss off some of the locals in Iraq.

Second Alpha stepped off at 1030 and we began our patrols. We pulled out of the long driveway leading up to the sheriff's department, which doubled as our barracks onto a main civilian road. So there we were driving down an interstate on the outskirts of River Side California for just a brief moment. We got a few looks from the people as we continued driving with masks on and weapons in hand. As we pulled onto an unmarked government road leading up to barbed and razor wire fence that appeared to surround the entire training compound, several media trucks from the Air Force and other Marine units started filming us. Soon after, a gold Toyota pulled up and we were given the command "contact right!" We stayed out of the vehicle most of the time, which wasn't that realistic to what we would actually do, but for the purpose of searching an area and exploring a small village, it was an ideal move.

In Iraqi culture, it is a custom for a senior ranking officer to talk to a village elder when traveling through a village. We trained on this with the actors and the elder told us about an IED up ahead. They were probably thinking that we wouldn't ask them. I think the point of the exercise was to remember to attempt to get intelligence from people, because it could save Marine's lives. As part of Iraqi culture, it is also not acceptable to shake with your LEFT hand, because it is believed to be dirty and realistically it is the hand that they use to wipe with when defecating.

Other unacceptable things that set Iraqi people apart from us are things like showing the bottom of your foot. It is a sign of disrespect. You cannot give the "OK" sign because it is the sign for the Eye of the Devil and it also means asshole or fuck you. When greeting an Iraqi, put your right hand over your heart and make eye contact with him. If it is a woman, you should NEVER make eye contact with her or shake her hand. Women are regarded as being lower than men because Muslims believe they are the cause of original sin and the reason that it was brought into this world. Marriages are arranged for women and there is no dating outside of what the father allows. Men also hold hands in public and kiss one another as a sign of respect. Several of these customs and curtsies we used when controlling the crowd through the training village.

Several Iraqis / actors came up to me and pointed to a pack of Camels he had in his hand, which probably meant he wanted cigarettes. They were getting excessively close for comfort and so I said, "agaaf," which means, "stop!" We then pushed through the town and marked two more IED's until we had contact in a small ravine and several casualties were taken. At that point we had to call in a nine line MEDEVAC transmission, which was a set of instructions to tell the bird how many how bad and our location.

The Psy-ops vehicle kept playing that annoying message and we kept assaulting through until end-ex was called. We then went back to the base and de-briefed the mission. It was warm inside the building, so I stayed there until the last possible minute, until they kicked us out. I really wanted to make a phone call and desperately needed a shower.

FEBRUARY 11, 2005

Every bone in my body was sore. Looking outside at the rain at 0600 didn't make me feel any better. Our training focused on cordon knocks and searches. A quadrant knock is a polite way of searching an Iraqi's house to win over hearts and minds and to make sure no insurgency was taking place. De-briefing the scenario showed that you should always do a detailed search because we missed two pounds of C-4, which was taped under the coffee table and the suicide bomb strapped to one of the women in the household.

The planned attack was horrible. Second Alpha took 90% casualties before the end-ex was called. We sent too many guys into a kill zone at once. All the while, the sky pissed on us, and it made me feel even worse. I saw some letters spray-painted on the side of one of the rundown houses near our camp where we were staying. It read, "Allah Travel Agency. Cheap Rates"

Second Platoon, after completing the training evolution around 1300, went back to the firm base to work on room clearing and attempted to get out of the rain.

Last night after my radio watch I got a letter from a fifth grader named, Courtney, who thanked me for serving our country. She wanted to know if the Marines were difficult. I think if I wrote her I could not describe the difficulty or the mental strain of trying to finish college and deal with the reality of war.

Do you know that feeling that you have when you are riding roller coasters all day and then that night, you feel like you are still on the rides and you can actually hear screaming or just random voices? Lately, I have been feeling a lot like that at night or the few minutes I have to relax, except it's a feeling of being constantly on the move, the screams of joy are machine gun fire, and the cries are of the dying.

I mentioned to Dmytriw how we quickly regress to lower ends psychologically according to Maslow's Hierarchy of needs and that we would not be able to fulfill one thing until we were certain that another was taken care of. Although several professionals have disagreed on these theories, there was some truth to them in this case. The basic needs were at the bottom of the pyramid. Then love, accompaniment, gratification, all the way up to self-actualization, education, civic organizations, and appreciation for the fine arts. It was obvious where we were on the Maslow hierarchy. I felt that now more than ever I stopped thinking about bettering myself and started thinking more about my own basic needs like survival.

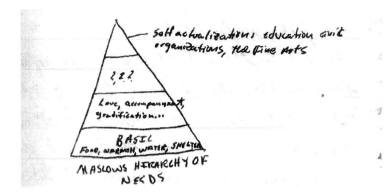

In Angela's letters, she wrote about hoping that I wouldn't change or be a different person when I came back. It's a fear I have that the war will change me for the worst and I will not be able to love or appreciate anything the way I used to. Sometimes I daydream that we could live happily and have normal lives where we could buy a house, live together, and love each other forever.

I cuddled up on a concrete floor next to a broken out asbestos filled wall and pieces of drywall were everywhere. I imagined a world where I was safe and happy and I went there.

FEBRUARY 12, 2005

Breakfast was a cup of coffee this morning as it usually was for me. The coffee here sucks worse than the kind you get at a used car lot and it tasted like sludge. Doc Barone gave me something that would help me sleep last night and it seemed to work well. I woke up getting only six hours of sleep and feeling refreshed. I know I couldn't bitch about six hours of sleep. That is actually the most sleep I have gotten in a while.

We went to the school auditorium again for more classes, this time on evading capture and what to do in a hostage / POW situation. We are supposed to give nothing to the enemy but our name, rank and serial number. Beyond that, we are instructed to act oblivious and not give direct answers. I kept thinking about all the people that were beheaded and tortured on television and videos posted all over the Internet. I kept wondering why they would put such a thing on television. *Were these people human?* Our instructor was from the school for interrogation in Maryland. He seemed to know what he was talking about, being retired from the Navy after twenty years and then going on to be an instructor.

I tried to think of what I would do in that particular situation. *Would I crack or would I retain my honor?* I guess that I would never really know the answer to that question until I was put into that situation and I hope to God that I never would be.

Towards the end of the class, my eyes got heavy and before you knew it, we were running back to the vehicles and heading back to firm base five. Later on that day after several hours of sleep, three Iraqis that were U.S. citizens that live and work here on this base for the government as linguists gave us a short culture class on some of the customs and courtesies that we should know before we go over there. They seemed like very nice people and thanked us several times for being away from our families to soon take part in freeing their country. Some of the interesting points that they mentioned were that after the fall of Sadaam, several of the Bath party members were out of jobs and positions of power after the coalition forces liberated Iraq. They formed an insurgency because they had nothing left of their riches and were forced to sell everything they had. Their only recourse was to cause death and destruction and threaten the lives of Iraqis and their freedoms. This could be why we were still in Iraq and continuing to battle enemies for a free Iraq. This group is however only a minority in the country because most of the Republican Guard were killed or captured in OIF I.

They showed me a lot of signs like to halt or how to say hello in Arabic. It was a very interactive period of instruction and something that was well needed for us to see some real faces that were actually from that country and could tell us about it first hand. Many of the people back home wonder if the Iraqi's appreciate what we do and the answer is, yes they do. This was evident with the gratitude that these people showed us and the fact that they could not thank us enough for what we were doing.

After the class, we formed for chow and had something resembling sweet and sour pork. Dmytriw was talking to me about my M249 SAW, "I can't wait until I see the day when you will open up with that bad boy," His evil looking grin almost scared me.

"Don't worry, Dan, I'm sure that day will come really soon here."

"Yea, no shit," He agreed

We got our chow and sat down on the concrete next to our building. I had lost my appetite and felt sick.

Tomorrow there was word that we would be conducting a mock war where we would break up into teams. One side would act as the enemy and the other team would act as the coalition. It sounded interesting or at least more interesting than focusing on repetitive shit that we would never use.

FEBRUARY 13, 2005

Sgt Tate formed us up at 2100 and said that we would be leaving that night at 2300 and to pack up. About an hour later "the word" changed and the next thing you know we were unloading our packs and staying at the firm base that night. I was ready to kill someone, but I was happy to spend another night in a building where I could be warm.

0600 came quickly and I made a routine of bypassing chow. Since we had our gear packed already, we loaded up the vehicles. I was in a high back with Doc Barone, Lt Haunty, Knox, Kroft, and PFC Truthan. Our team was led by Cpl Kustra and our mission was to support Lima Company on their convoy with our extra firepower and personnel. When we got to Lima Company's firm base it made me feel like the place we were staying in just the other night was a Hilton. This place was a complete and utter shit hole in every sense of the word. Mud was everywhere from thousands of boots trudging over the damp, rainy ground. It looked like something you would see on those charity commercials that are always asking you to donate money to them. The best part about it was that these old houses were littered with lead based paint and asbestos. As Dan Dmytriw put it so well, "This place leaves much to be desired." I even hesitated to go to the head. It was so nasty. Lt Haunty set up a terrain model and we had a brief before going out to train with Lima. We had three checkpoints, a café, a school, and the Mosque.

The area we were to cover was very small and we spent most of the time, "running the rails," a technique used in cities to keep crowds away from the vehicles. This tactic was supposedly supposed to control the crowding of people up against the vehicles by dismounting the whole team except the driver and the gunner and having them run alongside the vehicle. It was extremely exhausting to say the least and several of us joked about always running the rails and how we would have to all of a sudden stop using common sense.

There was a myth in the Marine Corps, that "Charms," which are a square shaped hard candy found in MRE's were, when eaten, supposed to make it rain. I always throw mine away anyway and I think it is just because when we are in the field, the weather always takes a turn for the worst and somewhere along those lines, some smart ass opens up a package of Charms candy.

The fact that things change was a good thing today. After Doc, Kroft, and I were sent back from the convoy to guard the gear we lucked out because we got to sit around and talk about the war, politics, and religion. Doc always loved to talk and even preach about religion.

Rumor had it that we were staying the night tonight at the Iraqi police station where 2-B was also staying. The place was not half bad compared to what we had stayed in for the past several days, all except for the rats the size of my fist that crawled underneath my cot when I slept.

I knew things were too good to be true when we got back from convoy patrols at 2345, got about an hour of horrible sleep before getting a wake up by Sgt Young at around 0145 to pull a four and a half hour watch until 0430. By the time I got to sleep, I had about two hours until reveille. The shift was ridiculous and I often times found myself dozing off on post only to be awoke by the guy sitting next to me telling me that our shift was over and we could go onto the next post for another hour to relieve those Marines that would then go to the next post and so on.

When first section second platoon went out on their patrol, they said that Kilo Company had opened fire on one of the head Sheiks in the Mosque, which caused the role players to riot and become especially hostile around the ING.

Today sort of blended into tomorrow, seeing as I didn't get any sleep and the caffeine pills wore off after only a few hours. It seemed like they were the only small round pills that would keep me alive for the next week or so. Hopefully pulling 24-hour shifts wouldn't be something we would do a lot in country. No one had any idea what we would be doing or what it would be like over there other than to just expect the worst and hope for the best.

FEBRUARY 14, 2005

I woke up to the sound of Sgt Tate's voice, "You have 20 minutes until we leave on this convoy!" I was still in shock and couldn't believe I was here. It was a confused feeling like, *what's going on? Where am I?* I ate half an MRE and then put my fleece, Kevlar, glasses, and weapon on. At this point, I was so exhausted and everything hurt all over. We really did not have a specific training mission today other than showing our presence in the Iraqi village and preventing IED's from happening. After an entire day of driving around, not firing a single round, and running a lot of rails, we moved our location again because Kilo had a shoot out with some of the corrupt police there and it was not a very safe place to sleep anymore. One of our missions involved extracting snipers from their POS that were being mobbed by angry locals. Later that night I talked to Angela and wished her a happy Valentine's Day on someone's cell phone, which had barely any reception. It sucked being here. Every minute of it for me was a living hell. I sat in the vehicle and watched over the weapons with Dmytriw while the Colonel rambled on about the rules of engagement.

"If you did what you did here in Iraq, we would be in a bad situation," He said as he tried not to look at any one person or company. The three Iraqi national guardsmen also talked about being nice to people and respecting them. "If you treat them respectfully and smile at them they will like you and admire you," The Iraqi man said thinking about how to say things in English.

The only thing that made today a good day is the fact that we got a full night's rest, which many of us needed very much.

I had a dream that I was taking a walk with my dad in our yard and just talking and looking at the trees and the leaves blowing in the wind. Fall was always my favorite season. I loved how the trees changed colors and the cool breeze blew on my face. The cars went by down my street. I thought in my dream about how I have my whole life ahead of me and how so many things are now to be desired now that I am away from them. I looked at my dad and he smiled at me. I woke up and stared at the holes in the walls and the sounds of sirens and SESM rounds being shot into the night.

Doc said something I think is true. "Wake up every day thanking God that you still have your arms and legs and that you're still alive."

FEBRUARY 15-16, 2005 0700-0600

I spotted a few more scurrying rats around the area where I slept and I couldn't fall back asleep. Holes in the walls of the houses let the cold air and the rain inside where we stayed. The thought of reacting at a moments notice to the hostility in the training area was not pleasant. Our mission today was to switch off with Bravo section and occupy an Iraqi police station. From firm base four, we patrolled into town with weapons drawn at condition one. We were also ready to collect Intel from some of the Iraqi role players.

Shots were fired from what looked like the police station and about nine people were killed and had to be MEDEVACed out in a 7-ton. My job, Sgt Jenkins said, was to lay down suppressive fire with the SAW while our squad rushed all the way through to the police station, and illuminated the terrorist threat. Somehow, I was tasked with standing post from 1130 to 1700, until someone finally realized that we were still outside the police station.

During that time, we were to defend the base and maintain fire superiority. I was on post with Cpl Leachman who had five and a half hours to sit and tell me about his college career as a civil engineer. I told him about my dad and how he was a Professional Engineer and we talked politics and guns until we were relieved. Cpl Leachman is an avid gun fan and hunts a lot. Together we held down the post and observed an Iraqi funeral take place, where Iraqis mourned the death of a sheik that was killed just a day earlier.

The scenario was supposed to result in chaos because of an IED planted in the area. Lt Haunty crazily rushed out in front of the funeral and picked up the IED before it exploded. The controllers said they had never had the exercise turn out non-fatally. Weapons Company was good for following ROE's and winning the hearts and minds. Although, if anything ever got out of hand there was always "two in the heart and one in the mind."

The police station was a little better than our previous night's position, although the area smelled of mold and dust. The rats seemed to have moved in right along with us too.

That night we were sent out on a patrol to enforce a curfew at 2200-0400. There had been reports of "the teacher," a bomb maker that had been hanging out in the mosque area that needed to be destroyed. Our squad was the outer cordon, providing security in a nearby house we had cleared of enemies. I found a perfect spot using my NVG's. A small hole let a small amount of light from the street into the house. It was perfect for resting a SAW on and observing activity outside. I had to report anyone who went by passed the curfew. There was some suspicious activity, but most of the time it was just the normal crowd of people that we always saw gathered for prayer hour. Iraqi Sunni Muslims gather for prayer five times a day, during which time there is a prayer call in Arabic that sounds every time and becomes rather annoying. I couldn't imagine listening to this horrible wailing for seven months and I'm not sure how I could deal with it.

After our three-hour patrol, I slept for about three hours until I was put on a five and a half hour watch until reveille. It seemed like the other night all over again. Absolutely nothing happened during that time, but I had a chance to tell Cpl Leachman my entire life story about my fiancée, my career, and about my family. The best spot in the house was the heated .50 cal Humvee post that I dozed off in until morning. The watch was set up in a circular fashion. Each Marine in the section would pull an hour at each station. There were five stations: Post one was at the front gate, post two was the .50 cal vehicle, post three was the MRK19 mounted vehicle, post four was an abandoned building about 200m from the firm base, post five was a bunker next to the front gate, post six was radio watch in a trapped door room inside the police station, and finally, post seven was the 240G overlooking the road. Each post lasted for 45 minutes. I barely could stay awake by morning. It was like the worst fire watch I had ever pulled in my life and I guessed it would be getting much worse.

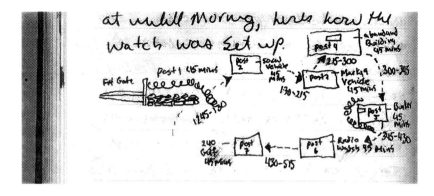

FEBRUARY 16, 2005

No one came to relieve us this morning on watch. I had no complaints about staying in a heated Humvee. That was a complete luxury aside from the no sleep part. The sun came up fast and I could almost watch it moving into the sky to warm up the air and kill the freezing cold and frost now settling on the grass. I managed to shut my eyes from 0515 to 0630 until everyone started packing up stuff. It was the end of the exercise and the role players were to report for a formation just as we were. I could hardly move and my legs cramped up easily. I was definitely in need of some R&R and we hadn't even gotten in country. Looking forward to being in a nice warm hotel in Vegas made me happy and put a smile on my face. It's like when you can't control yourself in public when your thinking about something and you burst out laughing and everyone looks at you like, "What the hell is wrong with you, why are you laughing and smiling?"

We turned in our vehicles and then humped back to the area where the buses had dropped us off about seven days ago. There was no sense of time in this place. As we were walking, we saw role players getting out of abandoned houses and headed towards a tall building near the end of the training area. It reminded me of the movie, *"Dawn of the Dead"* where the creatures would come out of their hiding places and start attacking living people to make them part of the dead.

We stood in the area where we first came in, which always seemed to be swarming with mosquitoes and sand fleas. I saw this as an opportunity to catch some Z's. I could hear two Marines playing the harmonica as I zonked out, until I woke up an hour later when we were loading the buses to go back to Camp Wilson. I was glad to get out of this place and it had been one more training evolution closer to going to war.

The ride back was peaceful. I ate some of the food that came in my care package and had an apple that Dan gave me. I fell asleep to passing mountains and the roar of C130's taking off overhead, probably taking some unlucky bastards to war. We passed a very nice casino and club that gave me thoughts of Vegas and sent my mind wondering into a world of music, heated rooms, fluffy beds, and hot showers. That time was coming and it was only a week away from us.

When we got back all I wanted to do was get a shower. At this point, I had not taken one in roughly nine or so days, since we left. I had to scrub extra hard to get all the nasty grime off me. Waiting in line to get in the shower though was always fun, but feeling the lukewarm water on me woke me up to reality. *Who are you Matt? Why are you here? What the hell is wrong with you?* I asked myself as steam rose from the shower and condensed on the open metal pipes just overhead. I dropped my pants in the water accidentally while trying to change in the crowded room outside the showers and managed to get dressed. I stumbled out onto the soft damp sand into 40-degree weather.

Later that day after we settled into the cans, Dmytriw and I went to main side to get some food and just to get away from people. I bought some more stickers and stationary for writing and wanted to make some phone calls. We passed by a small retail store and a stand was set up with strange red books. An old man stood there crazily promoted his book, "It's an action adventure novel and most of the main characters are Marines!" as if to say, "Why the hell aren't you buying this book, come on what have you got to lose?" Dmytriw just looked at me with a puzzled sort of look and we quickly walked passed the coffee kiosk, making a break for the exit. We spent about two hours there and then took the bus back, which ran every hour until 2000.

Not much went on that evening. I talked to Angela on the phone, who had not been feeling very well over the past several days and could not talk very well. Her voice sounded raspy and she was trying to talk normally. She told me how she got a scholarship for teaching just last week and I was so proud of her. She seemed like she was still upset at me for leaving. Somehow, I could blame myself for signing the contract, but if I was never in the Marines, I probably would have never found her in that crowd at *The Boot* that day and would have never met her. I knew everything was going to be okay and we would get married and spend our lives together.

Tomorrow we are supposed to be vaccinated with small pox in preparation for Iraq and finish some admin paperwork. In desperate need of sleep, the day drew to a well-deserved end.

4

FEBRUARY 17, 2005

I felt relieved that today was supposed to be a relaxing day with only a battalion formation planned and some classes going on at the chow hall. I felt sad today, but at the same time somewhat relieved. We had finished the bulk of our training as the Colonel said and we were prepared for war.

"All of you will return, although some of you may come back in a box," the Colonel said as he quoted the General of 2nd MAR Div. I didn't think this was motivational at all, which I expected from a gathering formation, but the Colonel liked to give it to us like it was, no smoke or mirrors, just straightforward. Sometimes reality was hard to deal with and I still think it hadn't really sunk in yet with me. It's like when you hit your head really hard by accident and then suddenly you see things differently for a brief moment. The Colonel's speech hit hard and I just wanted to go and get it over with.

Our classes today dealt with combat stress and medical issues such as viral illnesses, diseases, and infections caused by insects and spiders in the Iraq area. It was quite interesting to a point, such as the seven types of scorpions and five kinds of venomous vipers, including the infamous camel spider, which despite the myths floating around in emails only runs 10MPH and does not chase people it just runs at you to get in your shadow and get some shade to cool itself. Other diseases like malaria and small pox were mentioned as well. I was listening, but was more concerned with getting some hot tea and snatching up cereal boxes from the chow hall.

After the break, a doctor got up and gave a presentation on Iraq's climate. He showed the temperature scale for Iraq month to month:

Jan	Feb	Mar	Apr	May	Jun	Jly	Aug	Sep	Oct	Nov
76	82	87	96	102	105	110	100	96	87	76
27	33	40	55	70	84	86	77	65	54	27

The Doctor teaching the class went off on a few tangents while Marines dozed off, about how small pox vaccinations were actually a weakened strain of cow pox virus injected into us that could spread to others if we came in contact with anyone within 72 hours, which happened to be when we were in Vegas. This ought to be interesting, to see a battalion of Marines infect Sin City with a deadly virus. The hooker population of Nevada would be wiped out completely.

Later in the evening after Knox, Steele, and I ate at the warriors club, Lt Haunty came in and said we were going to Hit, Iraq just north of Fallujah and that it was a real hot zone. This I would believe once I saw it, because there were so many rumors floating around and probably for a good reason, to prevent others from knowing who we are relieving over there. It was some kind of info that no one was supposed to know about. I made a few phone calls today and reserved my hotel room for Vegas.

FEBRUARY 18, 2005

Rain hit the top of the metal hooch making a loud popping sound like a machine gun spraying a cyclic burst at a known target. I knew that somehow the weather was affecting me. The Starbucks coffee and Pop-Tarts from my care packages were a pleasant treat on such a crappy morning. I had fire watch last night from 0400-0500 and managed to be volunteered for a post at 0700 for an hour in the morning. The more senior you were the less you had to do. I guess it was the way of the Marine Corps rewarding you for all those years of doing fire watch and working parties. 0341's stayed in the rear today as the machine gunners went to the 240 range. The expert rifle shooters in all platoons qualified for ACOG's, a scope mounted on the M16A4 that magnifies your target and allows for more accuracy than open sights. I guess I did not have it half bad not being out in the rain pulling the trigger all day for two days in the horrible weather. Although digging trenches to keep the water from running off into the barracks wasn't exactly fun either. It was all they had planned for us today. We had some classes to fill time, but Knox, Perry, and Turner were tasked with washing the platoon's laundry at the Laundromat not far from our hooch. This took up half the day because the advanced party was leaving for Iraq in 24 hours and needed to do some last minute washing. I sat there for about five or six hours and read a book or two. I talked on the phone and tried to get the day behind me as fast as I could. Sitting for more than four hours I noticed is dangerous for the mind because I start to think that time is standing still and that I want things to start moving as if I could get home quicker. It was sort of like riding in a car to a place far away. I wanted to put my foot on the gas and get to where I had to go and get back. It was aggravating just sitting around and it played with my head.

I ate my first meal at the chow hall in quite a while. Chili on top of rice and some kind of fruit drink mixed up in a big jug and served lukewarm. I chowed down half of it as quickly as I could to avoid the taste. Usually there would be containers of salsa or some kind of hot sauce to block the awful taste of preservatives in the tray rats. I missed the taste of a home cooked meal and my Dad talking about his day at work and saying the blessing before meals.

I went back to the hooches. It always takes me a while to orient myself and maneuver through the soft damp sand walking to where we live. Sometimes I think aloud while I'm walking or I'll be talking to Knox most of the time. I think I just wanted to be by myself. I organized my woodland uniforms I would not be taking to Iraq and packed them up in a box to send home.

FEBRUARY 19, 2005

There have been rumors in the civilian world about the small pox vaccine and its affects on the reproductive system as well as other side effects. After 1977 smallpox was officially eradicated from America so the government stopped supplying the vaccine, however after the Cold War and the fall of communist Russia, several scientists still had knowledge of the vaccine once held in Russia and its implications to terrorist organizations. Several weapons were reported to have traces of the virus and after Russia's fall, the small pox strain just "disappeared" from the labs, making it lost and unaccounted for by American intelligence officials. This is why the military personnel of 3/25 were ordered by the Commanding General to receive the vaccine today. The vaccine is not actually the *real* virus, but a weak vaccine designed to have the same reaction and build up your immune system.

I was nervous, as I am sure anyone would be about getting stuck with a needle. I had no idea what it would do to me or its long-term effects, but we didn't have much of a choice. The vaccine is a series of three shots poked into the left arm. After two days, a discoloration develops across the effected area, flu like symptoms develop, and then in five to seven days the sore welts up into a nickel shaped discoloration. As if that were not enough after about fourteen days, we will develop a red ring the size of a baseball on our arms and soon after a scab falls off and we are left with a scar for the rest of our lives. *I guess that's better than having small pox though, right?* Unfortunately, being exposed to anyone and the wound will result in cross contamination. That is why the entire company is going to Vegas for two days, "Do you see the logic in that Knox?" I always joked.

"Of course I do, Wojo, and I'm sure the wives and girlfriends will appreciate that little tidbit if we decide to tell them," he said.

"Yea, sure," I mumbled and stood in line while I froze my ass of in the cold wind beside the Battalion Aid Station.

I personally think that what it does to us is worse than the actual threat or the likelihood of us actually encountering the virus. Suddenly I envisioned the entire battalion being wiped out after insurants found out we were vulnerable to the small pox virus and then it made sense. Despite the likelihood of it happing, it was better that we were safe going in than sorry.

The majority of the day I spent laying in the rack, listening to music and trying to make time move faster. Morgan and I also made a vision plan for ourselves. When we got back, we wanted to make sure we knew what we were going to be doing with our lives. When I get back to the real world, I'm going to thank God every day that I am as fortunate as I am.

"Maybe this is God's way of punishing us for taking things for granted," I told Morgan.

"That could be, man."

"Hey I gotta take a shower, this sore is killing me, and I feel contaminated." Dmytriw told me to stop being so paranoid about the whole, "small pox" thing. I couldn't help but worry and feel even more weak and sick than I ever have. I went to bed wondering what I had just infected my body with and what I would wake up with the next morning.

FEBRUARY 20, 2005 LAST DAY OF OFFICIAL TRAINING

I don't know how to begin writing today or how to express the deep emotions that I feel right now at this very moment. It is as if I am looking inside a looking glass and can walk forever, but no matter how far I walk towards where I want to go, I keep looking through and walk towards a light in the distance. Nothing seems to get closer.

I spoke with Angela today and broke down crying on the phone. There is no real way to express how I really felt, but I am sure this will affect me for the rest of my life. Putting my hands over my face to cover up my emotions, I tried to hide myself from the crowded phone center. Nothing seemed to work, although I was glad that I was on the phone. I talked briefly and told her it was the last day of training today and wasn't sure what would be happening in the next couple of days or when I would speak to her again.

I made a video today to send home that shows my family and fiancée what Camp Wilson is like and where I was staying. It made me feel a little better to give them a message and know it would be delivered and they could see me on television.

Dmytriw, Knox, Kroft, and I shoved ourselves in a van that normally supposed to seat eleven now seating seventeen. Its like that one time in the late 70's where all those people fit themselves in a Volkswagen Beatle to raise money for charity. I remembered seeing that on television once. We rode to main side, where we got pizza. The service was horrible and the pizza was greasy, although why the hell was I complaining? It was better than most chow hall food and was the best that we had given where we were.

My cough is getting worse, I think I should see someone about it, but I really don't feel like sitting at BAS for the whole day. I asked a couple people how you know if you have pneumonia. Most of them weren't sure and neither was I, although once when I was five I got pneumonia and was pulled from kindergarten class for about a month. I loved being in the hospital because I got candy and I remember getting a balloon with one of the characters from Sesame Street on the front of it. The priest from The Immaculate Conception Church in Ravenna came in to visit me. All I could remember from having pneumonia that time is getting a chance to play with a black kid named Patrick a bed over from me, and that month I got to spend out of school. I probably had it and my lungs would fill with fluid, get infected, and I would die before I got to Iraq. Something inside me just didn't really care.

Most of today I spent thinking about home and how we were leaving for Iraq in less than two weeks. I knew as much as I did not want to go that it was the only way to get home and hopefully the time would go by fast.

FEBRUARY 21, 2005

The never-ending rain pounded on the top of our aluminum hooches. My cough bothered me all through the night and I didn't get much sleep. Come to find out, we only woke up in the morning to stand in the rain for five minutes while Sgt Tate passed word, something about cammies, and a class we had at 0800 today. "Okay that's it, just form it back up here at 0800," he said loudly.

I fell asleep on top of my sleeping bag for another hour after chow. It was about the most restful sleep I had all night. The class was somewhat interesting about calling in F-15's and rotary wings on selected targets. A Captain gave the class in first platoon's hooch. Cots were moved out of the way to make room for a hasty terrain model. I sat in the back, letting out a hoarse cough every five seconds making others look back at me. Everyone was looking forward to Vegas, which was only three days away. Most people were having loved ones come out, but I couldn't stand the thought of saying goodbye to Angela again. If I saw her, I would probably have a nervous breakdown, run away, go AWOL, and never look back. I wanted to be a hero and I had trained to do so for the past two months. I just wanted to get on the plane and get out of California. The rain came down and never stopped. It was as if 3/25 was cursed with the fact that no matter where we went, the rain would follow us. Well, I had an idea of where we could go where rain would never follow us, 5,000 miles away from here. I promised Angela I would pick her up some souvenirs from Vegas and had to pick up a hard drive for my laptop. For some reason they told us that they would be erasing everything if we carried laptops with us as well as searching ALL of our personal gear for contraband. Before we left, they said that they would also search us to make sure that we did not take any pictures or have any information in our possession that would be classified or violating Op-Sec. This was apparently a big risk for the vets that returned before us, trying to sneak home weapons and ammunition as souvenirs. One Marine even tried to smuggle home an RPG. I guess ignorance is bliss.

Since our cammies had been sprayed with promitherin to keep bugs and infections away, we wore our PT gear the entire day. In a way, it felt good to get out of uniform for a day and I felt a lot like white trash, walking around in sweat pants everywhere. I sewed glint tape on the shoulder pockets of my digital cammies, which we are required to attach so that air will pick up the tiny panels on their thermals in the dark and in daytime and will be able to distinguish friend from foe. I guess they had a big problem with that during the first Gulf War and this was a quick and easy way to prevent friendly fire.

I fell asleep for most of the day and tried to remember little things like driving to school, getting coffee at Starbucks not far from the campus, and going out to dinner at new restaurants on Friday nights.

FEBRUARY 22, 2005

A bus came from main side to pick us up near the heads. We were told to mail all excess gear and clothing that we wouldn't need home. Up until that moment, I was still a bit under the weather and went on coughing for most of last night. I felt so sick and I convinced myself that I had pneumonia or bronchitis. I didn't feel like going to BAS, because if I went before Vegas I might have to stay there while everyone was living it up and gambling their hard-earned money away.

Since training was over I just wanted to spend money on food from the PX, Rice King (Chinese food), and the coffee shop. I did manage to get some coffee before taking a big box to the post office to send home, which hardly seemed worth paying $37.50. It seemed like the money made here was harder to spend. I had to go through a lot more than just a summer job or working in an office to get it. Nevertheless, not having to lug all this extra gear around will be nice. I was still ready to chuck the box into the dumpster and spend the money on Subway or pizza.

The small pox is getting worse, it feels like something is growing on my arm, more rain is pouring down now, the chow still sucks, and my cough is driving me crazy.

I had pretty much settled into a constant routine of thinking and obsessively worrying about Iraq. My dreams are filled with long walks with Angela, perfect sunsets, *and snow.*

I passed out for about an hour after chow and watched, *"Lost in Translation"* on the small screen of my laptop. It made me think about how much I wanted to live in the city and all the places I have been so far. I was so lucky, luckier than most people here were. Iraq would be the only place they would go out of Ohio and for some, the best thing that would happen to them in their lives.

I finished making my video to send home. Doc Barone gave a sermon from John 5:13 while Dinkelman said hello and several others gave an occasional curse word or two to the camera.

As I walked back from the PX, I saw a perfect rainbow appear and ten minutes later it started raining on me. Something about being in the Marines, it didn't matter if it rained on me, I didn't care anymore. I woke up for mail call after dozing off on my cot, took a shower, and listened to Cpl Bauer's cello concerto in G-major.

It's amazing what a full week of R&R will do to a person. Vegas snuck up on us, it was only a day away and it seemed like someone left the schedule blank. It was nice to take a breather before heading in country and the small pox had made us so weak everyone just felt like sleeping all the time.

The less I thought about the logic of things and the more oblivious I was, the better I felt. I had permission to feel good for a while.

FEBRUARY 23, 2005

I was not motivated to get up at all today. At 0615, Sgt Tate got up in front of the formed up third platoon in sweat pants. Sgt Tate wasn't feeling well either and in a loud voice explained what needed to get done:

We need to get these 604 forms filled out. They're fucking for your cammies that a lot of marines haven't got yet. You "mother fuckers" better be on your toes and better not be getting complacent. After action reports are saying that there have just been seven different engagements in the Hit area of Iraq, where we are going. Small arms fire and RPG's, okay. No reports of anyone killed. 1/23 remains optimistic in us relieving them shortly. Everyone should be focused and keep their game faces on, this is real and we are going, there's no doubt about it.

I would be optimistic too, if I knew I was getting the hell out of Iraq, I thought. We hadn't even started yet and I could sense that almost to the point where I didn't even believe the Sergeant. Gambling, booze, and women were on everyone's minds, but there was a special place in my mind for Iraq and it was driving me crazy.

I took another bus ride to main side today just because I was so bored back at Wilson. Knox, Kroft, and I visited the Internet café and got some real food at Subway.

It became obvious which Marines had attended college and were pulled out to fight this war when an argument broke out about designer cloths and trends vs. southern culture. Most of us come from middle class households and our lives were suddenly interrupted by activation. PFC Dawson decided to wear combat boots with his jeans to Vegas and Cpl Conjemi filled him in on how stylish "metro" types dressed. Brett didn't have a problem dressing himself. He already had his brand new clothes mailed to him, all of them totaling probably a grand. I pulled my wrinkled clothes from my sea bag and attempted to iron them out. "It doesn't matter if I wear these boots!" Dawson yells from across the hooch.

"You fucking idiot! Look at my shoes, their Italian. At least I know how to dress myself you fucking redneck," Conjemi screams.

"Shut the hell up!" Dawson got really mad and we almost had to pull him off Cpl Conjemi.

It was amazing how the Marine Corps could all get us together in one place and expect every one of us to get along despite our obvious differences. Most of the time we didn't have a problem unless it was about fashion, money, being a "city slicker" or a "hillbilly" or going to college versus not going to college. I could imagine how close we would become after only a few months at war.

We were called out soon after Dawson stopped arguing with everyone about God knows what. I stopped paying attention after a while. They split us up into sticks for Vegas, rows of ten or so that were responsible for each other, and if that person screwed up, then we all paid for it. The First Sergeant got up in front of us and got our attention, "Okay listen up! These are your fucking sticks for Vegas and guess what? They are also your flight sticks to get on the bird to Iraq," The First Sgt said and basically told us not to screw up in Vegas because we would pay for it or get NJPed.

My dad seemed optimistic on the phone today and he read some of the current events out of the paper to me. He said the price of oil had caused the S&P to fall slightly and he read a few lines out of the M&A section that were worth reading.

Lt Haunty said that Marines stationed in Fallujah had been pushing the insurgency up into 1/23's AO. They were really stirring up the hornet's nest for us. The recent election had caused some turmoil as well, but it showed us that the majority wanted a democracy and it was evident from the reports from cities around Fallujah and Baghdad.

I watched the sunset, cleaned off my civi's, and went to sleep. I couldn't wait to put them on in the morning. In a few hours, we would be leaving and we would do most of our sleeping on the bus to Nevada. I served a fire watch at 0100 with LCpl Vella and we talked about how he was in fourth recon and how he never expected to be here training with us. Reveille was at 0430 and before you know it, we would be on the bus to Vegas.

5

FEBRUARY 24, 2005 LAS VEGAS, NEVADA

A voice woke me up from the end of the hooch, "We need someone who's not in their civi's to come clean the head," Steele told everyone. LCpl Steele was put in charge of gathering a working party to clean the heads before we left. If we cleaned them last night, we wouldn't have to be doing it. *That would have made sense.* I looked at my watch and it was a little past 0400. Scurrying around in my sleeping bag to get my civi's on, I hurried as fast as I possibly could. The last thing I wanted to be doing was cleaning the head right now. Knox and I made a quick getaway down by the fitness center and we stood there and talked for about twenty minutes until it looked like the coast was clear. *Welcome to the life of a Lance Corporal,* I thought and couldn't kid myself. This wasn't the first time I had avoided working parties. Knox talked about his movie he wanted to make called, *"Shitbags"* where he would show how disgruntled Marines dealt with day-to-day obstacles. One story he told me was about a guy that enlisted and really hated being in. He hated it so much every day and tried to think of a way to get out. So, he came up with a plan. Everywhere he went he would dribble a basketball when in fact no basketball existed. He would dribble an imaginary basketball everywhere, especially in front of his command. When someone asked him, "Hey what are you doing, Marine?" he would say, "I'm dribbling my basketball." Months went by and he finally convinced everyone he was crazy. Finally, the moment he had been waiting for, he got his chance to stand in front of the man and explain himself. The Colonel looked at him and said, "Son, we can't be having crazies in the Marine Corps. It gives us a bad name, so we decided to give you your separation papers." The Marine was thrilled. He set his imaginary basketball down on the table, signed the papers, and walked out. The Colonel had a puzzled and very surprised look on his face, "Hey Marine, you forgot your basketball."

"I know," he said, "Game over." I started laughing when I heard Knox tell me that and I thought his movie was a good idea.

It was unbelievable that Vegas was already here, which marked the absolute end of the time we would spend training at Camp Wilson and we would soon begin flying to our new home. Confusingly enough, highers now juggled around three places that we would possibly be going to so our destination for sure was still up in the air. It was either al-Asad, Hit, or Hadithah Dam. I grabbed my duffle bag and Knox, Dmytriw, and I ran in front of the rest of the company to stand and wait for ten buses to get there in a matter of a little less than an hour, which I of course more than expected. I knew this would take forever and couldn't help dozing off in the wet sand near my gear. It was not long until the first bus finally showed up around 0800, then the second, and a third, and so on until the tenth bus showed up. We had to wait until all of them got there to board. I got on the bus that I was assigned to with Dmytriw and I tried to put the seat back. I was sitting near the back of the older charter bus. Some movie blared over the loud speakers. At least four hours went by and we stopped at a rest area where Marines got out and huddled almost like zombies in front of a heated area where everyone pulled out cigarettes and fed their nicotine addictions. I decided to check out the head, since I had been used to carrying on a conversation with the person next to me while relieving myself, this came as a luxury. Soon enough we continued on our trip as everyone made their way back on the buses and we pulled out of the rest area as if we had invaded it and then eradicated the place.

I was somewhat exited as I saw Vegas for the first time since last year. Looking out the large windows of the charter bus, we watched as cars zoomed by. People stared at us as if we were something of a rarity in the great Sin City. The truth was this was the place to come if you were a Marine stationed at Camp Pendleton or if you were a reservist training at Camp Wilson. My first time was with 3/25 about two years ago at our two weeks of training per year and part of the speech that you always hear, its just one weekend a month and two weeks in the summer, that's it. You have a better chance of winning the lottery than being pulled from college. My recruiter's voice still rang in my head and I thought what a bunch of bullshit that was. If I met a Marine that did not want to kill his recruiter because he lied to him I would be very surprised. I don't think any of us knew what we were getting into, but at this point, we didn't care. We were about to be released into the world and most of us did not know if this would be the last time we would ever see America again.

A good Marine considers himself already dead as he marches into battle. These few little words kept popping into my head as we formed it up for the Sgt Major's liberty brief. A deep raspy voice emerged from the crowd, "Don't get into trouble or else guess what will happen to you? N-J-P!" He seemed to answer himself with confidence. Marine's wives and girlfriends waited impatiently as the Sgt Major talked on and on about if we got caught and numbers to call in case we found ourselves in jail and the whole rundown. We were dismissed and told to be back in this auditorium at 1500 to check into our hotel rooms.

The first thing Dan and I did was go to a buffet and eat until we almost puked. I had never seen so much food all at once and I don't think I ever ate as much either. I filled my plate with pizza, rolls, deserts, ice cream, chicken, sushi, salads, and cakes. It was a real pick up compared to eating chow in a chow hall where all I could hear over and over again was that fucking fan making a loud squeaking noise as I tried to woof down the horrible tray full of food. I faded back into reality and took a big gulp of iced tea.

Dan and I checked into our hotel room sometime after 1500. It felt good to get in a room and relax for a while. There was no hope or excitement, just the fact that we could stay here for a while was good enough for me.

I walked around the hotel for a little while. Puffs of smoke loomed in the air and blurred the flashy lights of the slot machines and games that lured you in with fancy sayings, "Win a Jaguar! This could be yours! You could be a millionaire!" I made a quick run around the hotel as if to inspect the place. All I saw were people being happy, on vacation or just having the time of their lives. Who knew what they would be doing after this. They would go back to their jobs, to their golf games, and to their wives. We would be going to war.

I opened the door to our room and then jumped into bed for the night. The pillows were so soft and I sunk deeper into the bed. Casino lights flickered outside of room 306 and thousands of people gambled their lives away three floors below.

FEBRUARY 25, 2005

Just down the hall from us near the pool area of the Tropicana Hotel there was a nice breakfast buffet that Dan and I ate at after rolling out of bed at 10am.

We decided to go shopping for a while and Dinkelman wanted to show Dan what to look for in a new outfit. I thought it was somewhat gay but Dan insisted that we go and pick out his 90-dollar pants and 100-dollar shirt. I joked with him and said he looked like a flaming homo in those tight jeans and brown shoes, but he actually got a lot of compliments. For that kind of money, I hope someone would at least admire my outfit too.

The air was thick with smoke from the city, which is something you notice right away when you have been in isolation for nearly two months. I loved that smell and it was good to be back in a concrete jungle again. In Vegas, there were lights everywhere and a huge sculpture, a giant lion made out of gold displayed itself at the MGM Grand. The city was full of money. I could feel it and see it all around me. It was great.

That night we went to a very nice restaurant, which was perfect for crazies who thought that this might be their last real actual day alive in America. I didn't know if at this point, I would be a very different person after my tour, but for once I was in a tasteful place surrounded by good people and that was all I could really hope for.

Brett lives in room 1680 in the Paradise Tower of our hotel. We stopped by there before heading to our room and somehow were sidetracked when we ended up riding the roller coaster at the *New York New York*. It was a great view, but I was about to puke and it made me dizzy and nauseated.

Dan and I finally made it back to our room, watched some television for a while, and backed up some files on my laptop, saving them from involuntary deletion. I decided to put a movie on and I fell asleep after the first five minutes. I remember what the Warrant Officer, a friend of my brother's wrote me, "They can do whatever they want to us, but they can't stop the clock." There were no complaints about today and I wish I could stay here forever. Time got closer and closer until we had to go to war, suffering, and waiting for that one day that we would all appreciate when we stepped off the plane and made it back alive.

FEBRUARY 26, 2005

I automatically woke up on instinct this morning at 0600. It was programmed into me. I passed out until 0900 taking one of the last normal showers I would get for a while. Hot water ran over me and I closed my eyes hoping to wake up in my shower back home. I was far away from my life and there was no way to get back. Our plan was to have NO plan today. Dan and I checked out of our room and met Brett for breakfast at the buffet again. The best thing there was the chocolate ice cream and the fresh made omelets cooked right in front of you. Cpl Lindemuth stood in line with us, I think he was coming from a Karaoke party and he said he couldn't remember most of last night. We talked with him for a while and then Brett and I went to the pool and sat there in lounge chairs trying to get his wireless Internet to work. He was good at taking pictures on his digital camera and putting them into slideshows.

I decided to find the post office, which was next to the game room in a secluded area of the Tropicana. I was going to mail out some souvenirs to Angela. A shirt I picked up for her, a frog statue holding a heart, a Las Vegas key chain, and some papers from our hotel. Dan got a massage by some guy while we laid around waiting. "Never mention this to anyone that I got a massage from a guy that was probably gay," He told me as he smiled and I told him my lips were sealed.

Somehow, the thought of infecting the entire city of Las Vegas was not really much of a concern as I laid in the hot tub and almost fell asleep.

We walked the strip for four or five hours just soaking up the atmosphere and putting the occasional quarter or two into the slot machines. Another popular thing here in Nevada and in California was the Oxygen bar. I never saw anything like it before so it was pretty amazing to me. A straight shot of oxygen will defiantly revitalize your mind and body, not to mention help a hang over in a hurry. The guy at the desk was very polite and said that a lot of Marines come through here all the time. I felt light-headed but very focused as I tried to listen to what he was talking about. Walking back to the hotel depressed me to the point where I felt numb. It's a feeling that could only be felt once and that I cannot really explain to my loved ones, although I have tried.

At the formation at 2100, being sober was optional and 90% of Marines were drunk which made for an interesting ride back. One Marine had to be kicked off the bus because he threatened to kick the shit out of the driver and then proceeded to go into the back of the bus and puke his guts out in the middle of the aisle. Unfortunately, I was sitting about five seats up from the spill and had to smell it all the way home.

FEBRUARY 27, 2005

Almost everyone slept in today. I woke up around 1100 and started packing for Iraq. I made some last minute phone calls and formed it up near the hooches at 1330 so the Docs could check our small pox shots. It was absolutely repulsive. I could hardly believe it. A quarter sized wound was living on my left arm. I guess that meant that it was working. Others who did not have a discoloration had to get the shot over again because it didn't develop right and that meant the vaccine wasn't working. I was checked off the list with others that stood around in formation with their blouses off and left sleeves rolled up. I couldn't stop sleeping and after I was dismissed, fell asleep for a few more hours. They told us we would be leaving for Iraq on Wednesday, March 2. Everyone drew their weapons from the armory and then slept a little more until chow time at 1700. A real shock was eating this shit after we just got back from eating in four-star restaurants. On the way back from chow, Cpl Riddle passed the word, "Formation at 1800. We are leaving tomorrow morning for Iraq at 0300!"

I had to call home after packing my gear for the last time. I'm not sure when I would talk to my family and fiancée again. My dad seemed to be well, but had just got home from chemotherapy and was resting. One of many thoughts I had was that he would be alright. My fiancée talked about our wedding and I told her that we would be leaving at 0300 in the morning. Supposedly, our location was still classified and Sgt Tate said that it was only for us to know and no one else to find out. Second MAP was going to Hit, Iraq and would be on the plane for twenty hours with a layover in either Ireland or Germany. It was interesting getting to stop in Europe, but what really worried me was that most of the VC's and platoon commanders from 1/23 had been MEDEVACed for injuries just recently. This made me a little more open and emotional about making my phone calls. It's like that time everyone fears when you are in a plane and all of a sudden it goes down. You know you're going to die so you say what's on your mind to the person next to you, because that's the last interaction you will have with a human before you perish and burn up in the fiery rubble of plane parts and engine fuel. To be honest, I did not know what to expect, but it was a reality check and would probably not sink in until we left this shit hole. Six more hours until God knows what, was something I thought about as often as I could take a breath.

6

FEBRUARY 28, 2005 0300 SHIPPING OUT

I loved how they told us we were leaving on Wednesday and then just sprung this on us. Like a jack in the box, "it's turning, it's turning, it's turning, surprise you're going to Iraq tomorrow morning at zero dark 30!" It was freezing cold inside the hooches without any blankets at 0200 and I was told at that moment by a voice in the dark that we had fifteen minutes to move our gear down to pickup point one. The hooch was silent and not a word was said. I hauled my gear down to the site one piece at a time. I carried down one ILBE Pack with oversized carry-on strapped to it, two sea bags stuffed with care packages, a flack jacket, and a daypack with Kevlar. It took me about twenty minutes to carry everything down. From there we began waiting around for about two and a half hours until shortly after 0430 when we loaded our packs, trying to shove everyone's pack into the small containers towards the bottom half of the bus. The Marine Corps was all about making a lot fit into little spaces. From here we had about a three hour bus ride to March Air Force Base near where we trained for SASO. I slept through most of it. I remember someone telling me, "Grab sleep when you can," which would be on and off for the next seven days or so. The staff at March Air Force Base put us up in a hanger where we had to be weighed with all of our gear on. I stepped up onto the weight pad and the red digital numbers ran up to 207.

The hanger was like an auditorium with chairs spread out and a big screen TV with DVD's no one wanted and volunteers from the VFW that gave us a nice lunch. Peanut butter and jelly sandwiches with juices and coffee were carefully set out on tables.

I stuffed cereal bars in my cargo pockets for fear that somehow we would not get to eat and MRE's would be handed out to us. There were free books sitting in a corner along with miscellanies items that people had donated for us to have. Up on the walls were articles of Marines who flew out to Fallujah and other areas of Iraq. The paper turned a dark yellow color and looked like it had been there for a year or so.

After a few hours and four PB&J sandwiches later, we were still here. I tried to keep myself entertained by reading some books and listening to my headphones. I could not make a phone call today because I would probably break down and cry and would spend more than the ten minutes allowed on the cell phones that were donated for use from the USO. A grey haired man who looked as if he had been in ten wars passed out phone cards that would work anywhere in the world.

Weapons Company 3/25 left at 2:30pm on Monday, February 28 in flight to Frankfurt, Germany and then to Kuwait city. When talking to Corporal Lindemuth, who had been there, and said it is a very rich city because of Kuwait's oil contribution to the world. People drive Escalades, Mercedes, and BMW's. They were always on cell phones and wearing rags on their heads along with 2,000-dollar Armani suits.

We boarded the plane in a huge single file row from Junior to Senior Marine, which stretched across the tarmac to the hanger. Marines struggled to carry all their gear at once. I said goodbye to America for the last time and hoped to return home soon. There were 5,745 miles left and ten hours and seven minutes to Germany.

MARCH 01, 2005

We landed in Frankfurt this morning around 1200 local time and lost some sleep along the way. I always wondered where the time went when we lost it. The jet lag was far worse than our departure from Ohio to California. We were only here in Germany for about an hour to refuel and somehow twenty hours had disappeared into thin air. I watched five or six movies on the flight and fell asleep again. The business class section of the plane was full of officers, first class was full of higher ranking enlisted Marines, and then there was us. We were in coach sleeping with our rifles tucked underneath our seats and in the compartments above us. A few independent contractors rode in the back and hitched a ride.

The flight crew was very helpful and most of them were twenty-year Air Force veterans including the Captain. The plane was a Boeing 777 so it was enormous and held the entire Weapons Company and part of Headquarters. The Captain sounded exited, because he was going to Iraq to pick up his son, who was stationed in Baghdad and coming back from a one-year tour in the Army. I admired the Captain and his son, he was on a mission to get to where we were going and would be there in no time.

I had a very realistic nightmare about half way through the flight that the plane crashed over the Pacific and landed in the water. I couldn't breath and my lungs filled with water. Gasping, I woke up shaking and sweating. Turning one of the vents towards me, I tried to cool myself off and get some fresh air. I looked at the clock that read 0200. *Where was I? What was I doing?*

We spent the entire day and night flying. I wrote a post card in Germany to my family and used a cell phone the USO gave us for a few minutes. I must have woken up my parents, since it was 3am in Ohio when I called, but they were glad to hear from me and I told them where I was.

It didn't appear as if Germany liked us very much, which is why I think we were confined to a hanger for an hour or so when we stopped there.

7

WENDSDAY MARCH 02, 2005 - KUWAIT CITY, KUWAIT 0100-0300

We landed in Kuwait somewhere around 0100. It was very difficult to get used to or even write about the time changes and my body was growing very tired.

I was on a working party along with 40 other Marines to unload seabags and packs from the plane. It seemed like it took forever. While we were there, I got a look around the place and realized we were no longer in our country and had to constantly watch our backs. We loaded our packs onto an old big rig truck with an enormous trailer. The Arabic driver stood outside and watched us as we loaded up packs and seabags one by one. The sand blew up in front of us and surrounded the truck. The blackness bothered me, all around us it seemed like there was nothing and I could feel it. It took forever to load the packs. After we were all done, the truck drove off to where we would later meet it at our destination. I stood in line and got two full drums of live ammo. It was weird having it on me, seeing as the Marines only issued us ammo when we were on the shooting range. We loaded the buses and I gave up trying to sleep after just a few minutes. The adrenaline pumped inside of my body. We closed the curtains on the bus. I looked outside through a bullet hole that hadn't been there too long and it scared the shit out of me. We were headed to Camp Victory, an Army base just an hour from where we landed. The air smelled dry and arid and the wind wouldn't stop blowing.

WENDSDAY MARCH 02, 2005 0300-0700

We arrived at the camp around 0300 and received a brief from a female Army Soldier. Camp Victory had amazing amenities that were a hundred times better than that of Camp Wilson. The chow hall food is excellent, and it has an Internet café, Pizza Hut, heaters in the tents, and wood floors inside.

Since Camp Victory was so nice, I knew we wouldn't be staying there for long. Our tents looked like something out of a movie, like an opium den right down to the odor, or as LCpl Boreo put it, a circus tent. There were hundreds of these tents just set up everywhere, waiting for Marines and Soldiers to arrive and occupy them, while waiting to fly out to their AO's after acclimating.

MARCH 02, 2005 0700-1100

Most of the time on the plane was spent sleeping. *Get as much sleep as I can*, I thought, although that really wasn't going to happen because of the time changes. I would be getting used to it after a few weeks, but now, it felt funny looking out the plane window and flying into darkness. It was 12:30am back home in Ohio. I hoped I could make a phone call before we left for al-Asad Air Base. We were now at Camp Victory and would be flying into Iraq by C130, although when we did not know yet. They were rough, rugged aircrafts that were good at hauling anything: Tanks, Humvees, cars, trucks, everything except for human cargo. The flights are hot and are most often bumpy.

Four of us went to chow from my gun team, not far from our tent. We were greeted by two Iraqis who served us omelets and whatever else we could think of. We drank sodas or pop depending on where you are from (the south or from the east coast), ate ice cream, cereal, eggs, and bacon. As we Americans would say, "I'm lovin' it!"

"We won't be here for long," Leachman scowled, "the food here is too good." He reached to the other end of the table and grabbed the salt and pepper.

"You know what? You are probably right, Corporal," I said with a mouthful of ice cream.

It was almost like a paradise on the way to the worst hell we would ever experience. We stepped out of the chow hall and took a look around. Absolutely nothing for miles, just open desert and sand.

No telling what we would be doing today. I just wanted to lay on my cot forever. We found some old mattresses lying outside and I used one of them to put on my cot to make it more comfortable. Who knew what was growing on these things, I thought, but I didn't care, I just plopped my sleeping bag right down on it and I was out like a light. I still felt sick and the small pox on my arm looked like a bullet wound.

MARCH 02, 2005 1100-2359

I slept for most of the day and eventually wondered out of the tent around 1600 to go eat chow. Going outside was interesting. A sandstorm almost knocked me off my feet as it swept through the camp. I spit out sand and continued walking, although I couldn't see where I was going. It really looked strange the way the sun and the sand colored the sky. I was still in a daze. Our team met up with Captain Macintyre, whom I have to say I have great respect for. The man leads by example and I would feel confident going to battle with him, which in other cases I could not really say with conviction.

I held my drum of 200 rounds and my SAW close to me. It was a pain in the ass to carry around, although I would rather be carrying it, than an M-16 if we were caught in a difficult situation. I thought about how long I would have to carry it and it scared me. I was used to coming in on weekends and than going back to college on Monday. "Adapt and overcome," I guess the Marines always say.

We had chicken and wings for lunch and of course, everything was excellent and filling. Cpl Kustra went with me and after we got our fill, we made our way to the Internet tent. This place was a regular party camp. Whoever was lucky enough to be assigned here was entitled to use the Internet, play volleyball, basketball, eat fast food, and sleep in the opium tents. I knew we weren't so lucky. I would be glad just to get on the Internet and email my family. Cpl Kustra, I think, among a minority of others in my platoon, really saw the humor in this whole ordeal. "How fast do you think our tour of duty will go by?" I asked him.

"I don't know, but if it went as fast as our training went, I will be very happy," Cpl Kustra signed his name to the Internet roster and we sat down together. While we waited, it seemed like an entire training evolution to use the computer. I guess I would have to get used to waiting in line for everything worth using.

We waited about an hour to get on the one of the slowest computers in Kuwait. I sent out my mailing address to Angela and my parents so that they could send me care packages; in the hopes some goodies would be waiting for me when I arrived at our final destination. The place was crowded and mostly soldiers were in the tent, laughing and having a good old time. Despite the military's efforts to make all of us equal, Marines crowded together in one corner while soldiers were in another corner of the room. In the middle of the room, it looked like a card game with a lot of money riding on the winner.

Cpl Kustra and I met the rest of our platoon at the tent where we were staying on the far edge of the camp, tent 4-20, by the bottles of water. Showers were nearby, and always ran out of hot water, so I always ended up always freezing my ass off, while still trying to get as clean as possible.

I couldn't stop sleeping. All I'd been doing was using the Internet, eating chow, and sleeping. I wasn't alone. Everyone slept around me, too. I'm not sure why, but I've never been able to sleep for twenty-four hours straight. I thought it was because of the time change, but then I let my mind wander and had thoughts that it was the small pox making me ill or I had some final stage of pneumonia and would soon perish in this no man's land.

I had a dream that I was at a funeral and that one of my uncles had died. It made me cry to think about how young I was, and how young my family members usually are when they die. Most of my uncles died in their sixties and my grandpa died in his fifties. I just prayed that God could give me an extension.

MARCH 03, 2005 CAMP VICTORY - KUWAIT CITY, KUWAIT to AL-ASAD AIRBASE, AL-ASAD, IRAQ

"Lord Jesus, thank you for dying on that cross to pay the penalty for my sins. You promised to come into my life. I know you don't lie, so I thank you for coming into my life as you promised. From this point forward, I'm going to believe your word that you now live in me. Amen."

—Chaplain Jeff Struecker, SGT Task Force Ranger, 82nd Airborne

We woke up at 0500 and had the last good chow we'd see for a while. The chow here was good, so obviously we couldn't stay here long. We packed up our shit and left around 0750; right on time for once. The bus would take us to Ali-Asalem and then land at al-Asad air base in Iraq, where we would then convoy out to our AO's. I was on a working party (that I always seemed to be on) that helped with the gear as it was loaded onto the bus. We always formed chains in the Marine Corps to pass off gear from one person to the next, which at times worked better than carrying 100 or so packs to the bus individually. Everything here was a team effort and you had to learn to work together to get simple things done.

The bus ride seemed to go smooth until I smelled clutch and our bus driver stopped on the side of the road as traffic whipped by on MSR 8. People got out and voluntolds posted security around the perimeter of our bus while the driver got out and radioed some other hajjis to come look at our bus. *It's broken asshole*, I wanted to butt stock him so bad, but I kept holding the SAW close to me, just in case.

Our driver looked scared as security exited the bus and took the perimeter. About 30 long minutes went by. Doc was sleeping next to me. He was the only guy I know that could be sleeping at a time like this. I was just staring into space until they came up with the bright idea of switching our bus. I got off with other Marines and got onto the next working bus that pulled up next to us. We were now headed to the airbase where we would wait for departure.

I saw the C130 and just looking at it, I felt uncomfortable. We headed onto the tarmac in sticks and loaded up into the C130. My gear was weighted off to one side and I had to run to keep up. I am a short guy compared to everyone else so it takes me twice as many strides to catch up. I loaded all my gear onto the aircraft with the rest of the packs and sat down. The seats were uncomfortable as hell and we all crammed in tight. I'd ridden on planes like this before, to Quantico, Virginia on a drill weekend, but never for two hours.

The load commander, an Air Force Airman, took a picture of us before we got off at al-Asad. Maybe his intentions were sentimental or maybe he just wanted to have a keepsake because he knew some of us probably wouldn't be coming back. It was so hot on the aircraft with everyone piled in it. Sometimes I think the Air Force just tries to fuck with us, so they turn the heat up, hoping that one of us will spill the beans. Other Marines had to use the head and were pissing in bottles. I looked out the window several times just to make sure that there was nothing for miles.

We landed about two hours later at al-Asad airbase in Al-Anbar, Iraq. The gate on the C130 opened up to the worst sand storm I have ever seen. I had my Wiley-X's (goggles) on that my mom sent me and they worked pretty well. I was still trying to get used to the extra load of flack, kevlar, and SAPI plates. We got there and again unloaded our gear into another set of tents. It was becoming a routine. Sometimes I wondered if we would even reach our permanent home. Several Marines were leaving for Hadithah Dam tomorrow, but no word on when our platoon would be leaving for Hit.

Right now, my favorite thing in the world was eating chow and it happened to be very good here too. I was going to get fat in a hurry, I thought, but the walk to the chow hall from the tent area was about a mile and with all of my gear on, I got a real workout. I looked around and asked myself, *why are we fighting for this piece of shit? Is it even livable?* I talked to Angela this morning at 0230 Ohio time. I can't help but think how much I love her sometimes and I don't know how I would get through this without her help.

MARCH 04, 2005

The brief this morning at 1000 was given by the Commanding Officer of 1/23, the unit we are replacing. He went over what our AO in the areas surrounding Hit would cover, the city of Hit of course, and about five to six MSR's that were named after the periodic table of elements, and oddly enough, American NBA teams such as Nuggets and Raptors.

The Major drank from his gallon jug of water while he described the types of mines and IED's we would be seeing, such as the South African 155 mortar rounds rigged to explosive devices and double stacked mines that would blow a Humvee sky high. It was all in all disturbing and killed most of the morale that we had.

A lot of us jokingly talked about kicking the ass of whoever selected our missions over morning chow this morning.

"Hey, make sure you watch out for those double stacked, South African 155, MAP Killing IED's!" I said to Cpl Kustra and he started cracking up.

"That guy pretty much said we're fucked," Cpl Kustra said.

"Yea, pretty much." I laughed and thought about how no one else in the civilian world would ever get or appreciate our dark humor, but sometimes you just had to laugh it was so ridiculous.

Nothing really went on today other than the brief and classes. It was as desolate as the area outside of Kuwait. There were miles and miles of sand wherever I looked and no place to run. No attacks or taking fire at al-Asad yet, but I'm sure when we go outside the wire that we would see some action. It pisses me off because a hit by an IED or mine strike is not followed by small arms fire, the Major of 1/23 clearly pointed out. Those cowards, "The Muj" which was short for Mujahadeen terrorist cell that was prevalent in these areas and Zarkowi's organization did not even have the balls to fight us. We just go out and look for mines to blow up our vehicles and hopefully we will get lucky sometimes and find them first. I guess I will find out first hand how things go in Iraq. The best thing to do is plan for the worst. A bitching Marine, they say, is a happy Marine and "if you ain't bitchin' there's somethin' wrong."

We are supposed to be flown in by Helo on 06 MAR to our AO. I hope that it is not all that it is cracked up to be, for our sake.

I drifted off at 1800 and woke up at 0300 with an incredible urge to urinate before passing out for a full twelve hours before going to chow again. I was sick or coming down with something, I just knew it, and it scared me.

MARCH 05, 2005

I was supposed to be packed up to leave at a moments notice. We never know when we would leave and our retrograde into the AO was tentative. Yesterday I woke up with a drum of SAW ammo and just today, I was issued two drums and 60 loose rounds of M-16 ammo. I guess we were preparing for the worst-case scenario, but right then, I thought that getting some action would be better than sitting around, looking forward to the next time chow came around.

I didn't feel right today. I was a wreck. The depression was setting in and the thought of doing absolutely nothing gave me more time to think about what would happen once we got to our AO. Doc Barone and I stopped by the phone center and I made a phone call home. My parents seemed quite concerned and asked if I needed anything else. I could really use some cough syrup and more phone cards I told them. In the middle of the conversation, I saw some graffiti on the walls written in permanent marker, "OIF= Oil Isn't Free." *I just hope,* I thought, *that we are fighting here for the right reasons.* I guess everyone who has just landed in a combat zone would have similar thoughts running through their minds. It wasn't like I was trying to be anti-war, it's just a shaky feeling that I had every time I breathed. I just wanted to forget about this whole mess and wake up in my own bed. I wanted to have the ability to go to the mall, attend college, and spend late nights studying for finals. At the same time, I was glad to pay my debt to society, and be one of the few that would step up and actually do it. I'm not a coward and I will defend my country if it is necessary.

Most of the talk today was about the lack of up-armor on Humvees. Previously, we were told that issue was resolved. In addition, we were promised high-speed gear, but when it came time to deliver the gear, it was nowhere to be found. This apparent lack of proper equipment scared the shit out of me, especially when we were patrolling without up-armored Humvees.

I've noticed there is much inter-service rivalry here too. It's below the surface and provides hours of entertainment. For example, we laughed when reading it scrolled all over the shitter walls. You could read things like:

"Why did that helo crash, killing 30 people? It was the air winger's fault!" and "Reservists suck!" followed by the classic comment "Stop writing on the fucking walls."

The al-Asad gift shop is a small incense-filled room with gifts from Iraq—- things you can take home to your wife or family members like Persian rugs and Iraqi flags. Most of the workers here look Pakistani and are trying to peddle marble and jewelry for cheap prices. It reminded me of the guys in Mexico that would come up to you on the beach and try to sell you fake gold and silver. "No! No fake! Real! You buy now!" they would say and try to suck you into haggling with them. I figured it was too early to be thinking about souvenirs, but eventually I would probably get a few for Angela and my parents.

Here I was sitting and waiting on top of my packed up gear. Waiting to leave while finishing 100 or so pages of a book I started before I left Ohio and listening to Knox talk about his new movie he was going to make. I knew Knox had an overwhelming passionate hate for Muslims, particularly ones that would crash planes into our buildings. Before eating chow, I took a shower for about a half an hour (even though the limit was two minutes) and slept another thirteen hours after chow until I found myself, here, waiting again. The anticipation of suddenly moving into a death zone littered with IED's and mines was slowly killing me inside.

8

MARCH 06, 2005 CONVOY TO HIT, IRAQ - MAP 3 AREA OF OPERATIONS

I staged my gear inside the tent and ate my last bit of chow before step-off at 1000. Rushing back from chow, figuring I'd have to load up in a hurry; they then told us that we were stepping off at 1400 because of a delay. My thoughts were empty and meaningless, but my faith grew stronger every day I was in country. Rumors ran wild about Hit, Iraq. They said it gets mortared every three hours, that a form was to be filled out every time we opened fire, and that there was no electricity. When we finally saw the Humvees roll in at 1300 a lot of the Marines from 1/23 cheered up a lot and started giving us tips on little things we could do to survive here.

Before I knew it, I had all my gear on and was sitting on a seven ton truck with twenty other Marines waiting to convoy up to what would soon be our new home for the next seven months.

I saw some Freedom Fighters, which are similar to Iraqi National Guard, but trained by Marines. They were waiting to convoy up too and were standing around bull shitting. One of them had a cigarette in his hand and was waving it around and laughing at the other Freedom Fighter. We were told these guys were hard chargers. They fought in Fallujah, had superior fighting skills, and actually had the guts to stick around and not desert. They wore the old Desert Storm style camouflage.

Several of us were saying our prayers and others were just looking off into space or trying to catch up on sleep. People talked about writing a book and how it would be nice if someone published one. I told them I was planning on it.

It took us three hours to roll out of the wire and get to condition one (bolt forward, round in chamber, magazine inserted, weapon on safe). I was nervous, but kept my eyes pealed. LCpl Vella sat next to me and we propped our rifles up against the walls of the seven ton, looking through our open sites, just waiting for an enemy to pop out and challenge us. I looked around as we soon left al-Asad Airbase. I was looking at absolutely nothing. A complete abyss for miles, nothing but sand, mud, and some high frequency power lines running into Ramadi, south of Fallujah and up into Hit city. We stopped 30 long minutes later and finally arrived at FOB Hit. It looked like a typical Middle Eastern hotel that you see in the movies and it was rumored to be an old morgue. MAP 3 threw its gear off the trucks and saw the Marines we were replacing from 1/23. They were cheering and they looked so happy, as I would be if I was being replaced. I wish I were those Marines. I knew then that I had a long seven months ahead of me. SSgt Braun picked a temporary room for our platoon to stay for the nine days until 1/23 moved out and rotated back to al-Asad in sticks and the relief in place was complete. The rooms were not all that bad compared to some of the other places we stayed. I had a cot right by the wall and managed to snag a few old mattresses. I was starting to believe the morgue rumor because the room had square concrete blocks about the size of bodies.

I hesitated to take my stuff out because we would be moving again eventually. I just wanted to settle down and pull stuff out of my sea bags. I loved setting out my books and my laptop, because it reminded me of my room where books would be scattered everywhere at times and my computer was always within reach. We finished putting things in their places and then had a formation for a delightful MRE chow. They had pop, which was all I cared about drinking and some sort of big screen projector with videos from a computer for entertainment. The floor was tiled and there were crude tables and chairs, but never enough room for everyone. A voice from the back shouted, "Welcome home gents, welcome home!"

MARCH 07, 2005

I sat in the chow hall starring at the fridge full of pop while I listened to the instructors teaching the classes from 1/23. "The purpose of these classes you are going to get today is to prepare you to do a full RIP with us," the officer said. The Relief in Place, or RIP as they called it, was a complete change of command and personnel. The trick was to do it without a disruption, as one unit left and one unit stayed. Operations would continue at full force and continuance, 1/23 would leave and 3/25 would take over without the insurgents' knowledge.

The sun rose and was blocked out by clouds and the frequent sandstorms that seem to be so prevalent around here. MAP 3 stood outside and listened to a Sergeant talk about IED and mine threats. Following the short class on how to find IED's and mines along roads without hitting them, we walked a small stretch of dirt road and attempted to spot simulated IED's and mines that had been set up to see if we could spot some of them. We found A 155 mortar round inside a sand bag with a remote detonator, a double stacked Italian anti-tank mine buried in discolored earth (I almost stepped on that one), and an antenna actually wrapped around a small twig the size of your finger next to the road. This was a wake up call at most but showed us that the threat was real. The Sergeant teaching the class was blown up by an IED previously, so the eyewitness account made the class even more convincing.

At one time during the Gulf War and during OIF I, II, and then just recently in OIF III, the Army had housed an entire brigade here. They handed over the FOB to 1/23 rather abruptly from what I'm told, just a brief rundown of mortar hits and observation posts and then it was, "See ya!"

Luckily, 1/23 had prepared all day classes to orient us to the new area here at FOB Hit. They showed us the mortar positions that they had fortified over the last few months, observations posts or OP's and Vehicle Check Points or VCP's; they told us inside the CoC, their headquarters, "Believe it or not this area has been motared over 175 times and just recently with 155 rounds which shake the earth and scare you shitless." The Captain described the facts vividly almost as if it reoccurred for him at that moment.

"Yes, we are i0n the shit boys! Now you gotta look at it this way, not many people get to do what you do. You get to get into firefights, drive Humvees and shoot at cars, and call in CASEVAC's on your best friends!" I don't think that Cpl Kustra and I could believe we just heard what he said but I knew it would be the butt of every joke for months on end.

"CASEVAC's on your best friend, hah!" Cpl Kustra laughed hysterically as we walked out of the CoC.

We had an MRE lunch and the majority of the afternoon consisted of more classes. We learned about coordinating the JCC, the Joint Control and Command of Iraqi troops, which was our secondary objective, to train the Iraqi forces so we can get the hell out of here. There are three types of Iraqis: The IP (Iraqi Police), the ING (Iraqi National Guard), and the IFF and ISF (Iraqi Freedom Fighters and Iraqi Special / Security Forces). The IP are mostly corrupt and work for the Mujahadeen. The ING who for the most part are somewhat dependable, but are lazy and only show up for work when they need money, and the IFF, which are a cell imported from Saudi Arabia. They are supposedly trustworthy and have saved Marines' lives before. I saw some of them and they play soccer all the time and are friendly to me. They are the first hope of training forces towards a self-sustaining government. I'm sure we will come in contact with these Iraqi's in some form or another while we are here. The JCC team leader made a good point, "If these mother fuckers are too cowardly and scared of defending their own country and its freedom, then we will outsource Iraq's security to other forces that will."

The PX comes here every two weeks and mail comes about every week from al-Asad. The phone center is located in our building and Internet is available too, all the way out here. It was amazing to see computers and network cables running to the room full of Marines waiting to communicate with their loved ones. I want to eventually get down there and make a phone call to let everyone know I'm ok and doing well. This place more than ever made me miss home, but I think of it as a test of faith.

After a full day of classes and orientation to the new FOB, we settled down for the evening. Tomorrow we would do a left seat / right seat and go out on a patrol with 1/23. They would be in the drivers seat (left seat) to show us where everything is and what proper procedures are and then they would turn it over to us (right seat) to allow us to show them that we knew what we were doing before they would complete the RIP.

I learned that two people were killed and several injured from mines and IED's. As anyone would be, this put me in a bad mood and I just wished I could catch a little shuteye. I hoped that the time would go quickly here and I could be that Marine smiling at the other Marines as I head home.

MARCH 08, 2005 WAKE UP CALL

A SSgt from Charlie Company 1/23 took us outside the wire to BZO our weapons. I sited in my SAW with three single shots at a makeshift spray painted black target. I shot high and needed an adjustment on the front site post. The BZO area was a 100-meter area where the enemy could not see us, but could definitely hear us. The Staff Sergeant said that they know we are here and "the Muj are always watching."

From the looks of the black marks in the dirt next to where we laid down to shoot in the prone, the area had been mortared before and they knew what we were doing. BZO was the only thing on the schedule for today. I just had a bad feeling about shooting in that area, it defiantly wasn't the smartest place to shoot, and make loud sounds because the palm groves were a few clicks north of us and that is where the Muj love to lob mortars from.

I was outside eating an MRE and joking around at about 1400 when I heard a loud, "Boom!" and a crash from the south side of the AO on Route Bronze by one of the vehicle checkpoints. I didn't know what it was. I think it was mortar fire, I told myself and quickly ran inside the building and put on my flack and kevlar. The blast shook me and my heart sank into my chest, *what was that?* Corporals and other NCO's immediately took accountability, "What the fuck was that?!?" I screamed.

SSgt Braun came in and had an answer, "That just now was a VBIED, Vehicle Borne IED."

"BOOM, BOOM, BOOM…."

"And those were mortars!" he shouted.

Everyone laughed at him, but considering the situation, it wasn't that funny at the time. We dropped to the deck as soon as we heard the three loud booms that shook the concrete walls of the small hotel morgue / FOB. I stayed inside for a good hour or so, it was the first time I had witnessed a mortar and VBIED attack so you could imagine the shock I was in. Others in Charlie Co. 1/23 casually walked around. They were used to it.

The after action reports from the attack on the checkpoint on Route Bronze had described the Muj driving a white four door Sedan as very nervous and suspicious looking. Two Marines were severely injured and CASEVACed with shrapnel wounds and the bastard in the car, all that was left of him, was brains and two feet stuck where the clutch and gas petals used to be.

It's incredible that someone could hate us so much that he would kill himself to hurt us. It angered me and I wanted to go and shoot someone. We ended up police calling the area after the attack, which really made sense, and most of the day was spent nervously discussing the issue and waiting for another attack to take place. I knew now that this was real and I was relieved that I was still alive and uninjured. It was definitely a wake up call. We were in the shit, a war zone.

I passed out again early. The phone center was closed because of the injured Marines and because of operational security. Issues with us telling the public before the families were notified were to be prevented by cutting all means of communication until this could be taken care of. I'm guessing this would be the SOP every time we were involved in an attack.

Other MAP's were out on patrol for the night and we took part of the day shift. They switched me to MAP 8 again which I'm sure would change several times over again as soon as I was getting comfortable.

MARCH 09, 2005 DRIVERS-ED

I had a dream that someone was calling to me from the darkness and woke up in a sweat in the middle of the night. *I was in a morgue*, I thought, as I laid on the concrete block big enough to lay a stiff on. At 0800 a few of us that had not received our drivers permit were supposed to go through a series of classes today so we know what to do if something should happen to our driver. I was still a little out of it from yesterday. A Gunnery Sergeant from 1/23 motor-T and some mechanics were there to teach us everything there was to know about Humvees. The mechanics at motor-T taught us the basics of automotive maintenance. I was thinking about sleeping and got my chance to around 1200 when Dmytriw and I snuck out of the class. Most of the classes, I think, were required because there were many auto related deaths, 53 deaths to be exact within the last six months. The thought of being a driver just did not sit well with me, but if it came down to saving our ass, I would do it.

Later on in the day, we continued fortifying our room with sand bags. I finally got on the phone for a few minutes and got a hold of my brother Rudy. He had just gotten back from a conference in San Francisco. He was there for some kind of political science association at Hiram College in Hiram, Ohio. I was tired of living out of a sea bag and wanted to at least get some stuff organized. Tomorrow the word was that we were going out on our first patrol. Parts of our section would be going out with 1/23 to get accustomed to the new AO. I told my brother I would appreciate it if he would send me a one-way ticket to the States. I passed out again shortly after 1900, after a rather uneventful day, another day that I was still alive and one more day closer to getting the hell out of Iraq.

9

MARCH 10, 2005 OPERATION RIVER BRIDGE - HIT, IRAQ.

The primary mission of Operation River Bridge is to follow up from previous operations like Operation River Blitz, which was created and put in place to push insurgents out of the cities so they could be dealt with and destroyed and the local populous could resume peace. We are dealing with an enemy that moves in and out of a population quickly, whose aim sometimes is not even known and may sometimes be as simple as destruction of the American Infidels. Foreign fighters such as Chechnyan rebels who despise Russia's peace efforts and even Syrian mercenaries and Iranians, who kill for money to feed their starving families, often play a part in the terrorism. Other threats forcing recent operations to take place have been the Mujahadeen and terrorist cells in the area that pay townspeople to plant IED's and mines along local MSR's and reek havoc among the small communities, threatening their way of life. 1/23's goal in River Blitz was to flush cities of this problem by conducting raids on cities and VCP's to stop insurgents from running away and moving to other lawless towns in the surrounding area.

3/25's task of completing Operation River Bridge brings the full force of our company including; a full line company dispersed to ASP's and frequently into the city of Hit for patrols, two tanks to provide support, OP's manned by the line companies to watch for Muj (that think they can get away with planting IED's on roads in our AO), and snipers who are punched out to local areas to keep watch on suspicious activities. In addition to this arsenal, a Weapons Company with MAP's that will conduct VCP's and provide security as well as supporting all elements with heavy weapons and mobility of light armored assault vehicles.

Over the next several days beginning tonight with a trip to Hit City by selected volunteers, Operation River Bridge will be in full force and a 1/23 – 3/25 Relief in Place will be completed.

Several Marines from 1/23 were selling off things that they didn't want and couldn't carry home like TV's, VCR's, and DVD players. Soon we would move to where 1/23 was and they would be on their way back home to Texas.

I had a lot of time to think today and felt myself breaking down. The civilian I am will be so much more appreciated when I get back home in now close to six months. By breaking down, I guess I mean that part of me that expresses itself, that longs and loves for now until I return, seems so distant. I don't know what will happen to me. Several Marines have gone as far as beating the shit out of the first person that says one word to them. Like I said, it is hard to explain and it's a feeling that only a grunt at war will understand.

MARCH 11, 2005

Weapons Company did a gear change over with 1/23 today. We using the gear formerly used by 1/23s gear for the next seven months and then we'll in turn pass it on to the next group of Marines. To me it made absolutely no sense because we bought all new gear at the drill center. New PVS14 night vision goggles, CLU's, and other optics were left patiently waiting for us at the drill center in Akron and we were stuck using these pieces of shit. Ammo for machine guns, grenades, flash bangs, and fuel cans were among other things littering the sidewalks of the FOB as 1/23 prepared its Marines for movement to al-Asad. The Marines themselves were selling TVs, DVD Players, and other appliances. It looked like a flea market.

MAP8 was supposed to patrol MSR Uranium today and do snap VCP's off Route Bronze. Ops were given to the line companies and MAP3 was put on a 30-minute strip alert. They were to be ready to go within 30 minutes of us calling for support if something should happen to us.

Last night, I woke up by mortar fire and illume missions supporting Kilo Company. This lasted long into the night, which made me restless and irritable for most of the day. Eventually MAP 8 would have to "pop its cherry" and go out on patrol. I was happy because my platoon had all of my friends from my old gun team. Dmytriw and Dinkelman were there and it made it easier to deal with going out, knowing there were people that I could trust by my side. I'm sure after a few months in country I would come to trust everyone in my platoon and everyone would be close to me.

Rumor has it that the folks in Hadithah Dam (the other half of our battalion) were doing room and gear inspections and several Marines have already gotten written up for unacceptable uniforms. From what I heard they were taking bets on when the Sgt Major would actually go out on a dangerous mission and God only knows how long it would take before people would snap and fire off live rounds. It was a good thing that we were here in the Hit AO. It was out of the way so it was not as stressful as areas where higher ups constantly are up your ass and turn everything into a boot camp.

Today was also disbursement day, the day where Marines could get money and buy things from a mobile PX that only came around once in a while. I didn't feel like waiting in the line that stretched out into the courtyard of sand that separated the first two-story hotel building from the second. I just wanted to go to sleep. I watched the tanks roll by our room doing rehearsals for Operation River Bridge. When tanks were sent out you know there was something going on and troops were in contact. They were a great show of force. It showed the enemy that we were more powerful and were not going to be easily defeated.

I really needed a bookshelf to put my things on and was aggravated that my gear was unorganized and shoved in my sea bag any which way. I talked to Angela on the IP phones. They have something called Segovia here. It is an Internet IP phone service that charges about ten dollars for ten hours of talk time. It was so much better than buying phone cards and using an entire 800-minute card in twenty minutes because of the international charges. Segovia was a place that we could go to talk, but couldn't talk forever. We were limited to an hour on the phone per Marine and there was always a list and a line of people to get on right when the phone center opened. The person on the other end of a Segovia phone always complains about the two-second delay that takes some getting used to. I have to talk and then wait a few seconds for them to hear it until I can talk again. Segovia was pretty much my life when we were back in the rear.

MAP 8 is going out on patrol tomorrow night, although word could change again as it often does here. Cpl Stocker talked to me about our patrols, "It's just us out there so don't be afraid to pull the trigger if you feel anything is suspicious, alright killer? Welcome to MAP 8," he said in that southern drawl that he was known for. Cpl Stocker was from Southern Ohio and grew up on a farm. We always screw with him about life on the farm, he always gets defensive about it, and ends up saying something like, "Say that again, I'll punch you in the fuckin' eye."

I knew I could pull the trigger if I had to, but no one really knows what will happen at that very moment when you have another human being in your sights. That was a good thing for me because we weren't killing humans; we were killing savage uncivilized terrorists that deserved to die. I probably could not live with myself if I hesitated and my fellow Marines were killed. I'd rather it be some Hajji then a life of a fellow Marine.

The rules of engagement are given to us in a time of war by Commanding Officers to show that we are civilized as a world power. If we went around shooting everyone for no reason the example the U.S. shows is that we are tyrants and no better than the insurgents we are fighting against. Somehow, these laws were put in place by the Geneva Conventions, which the U.S. is a member of located in Geneva, Switzerland. The convention makes up the laws of war and civilized fighting. Sometimes I questioned our admittance when our enemy is not a member and if one of us were ever imprisoned, we would surely be tortured or decapitated on Aljazeera. The Rules of Engagement call for an escalation of force before a final kill shot is fired:

Escalation of Force for VCP's (Vehicle Check Points)
Line 1 -> —————————- Shout, "Agaaf! Stop!"
Line 2 -> —————————- Pop flare(s)
Line 3 -> —————————- Warning shots to engine block
Line 4 -> —————————- If vehicle still doesn't stop, shoot to kill

A Sergeant from 1/23 said all this happens in a matter of about 90 seconds. You have to know what to do and when to do it at that moment in time. The ability to make quick decisions and follow orders and procedures without thinking comes into play.

I had not taken a shower in several weeks and felt nasty. The sun today turned into darkness as movies blared over newly acquired appliances and an enemy still watched us and waited for a perfect time to attack.

MARCH 12, 2005 1530-0000

I sat on my cot in the middle of all my gear that was strewn all over the deck. I didn't care about being organized or at least tried not to care. We were supposed to be going out on a patrol in a few hours and would be out until the following morning. It was rather difficult to get used to the graveyard shift with our skeleton crew driving endlessly into the long nights and early mornings that would always turn my blood cold. The freezing winds that would always start at about 0200 when the sun couldn't warm up the air before it hit you. Although going out on night patrols is more difficult, it is advantageous for us. The Muj operate mostly during daylight hours. They are what are called fair weather fighters. If there is a hint of a sand storm or light rains, the Muj won't come out and will only fight in the perfect conditions.

Earlier on in the day, some of us were tasked with rebuilding tires with run flats at motor-T. I figured it was busy work having a bunch of grunts try to put large circular pieces of metal inside the rims of tires. It was a joke.

Although it did make me feel safer about getting a flat, because if we ever did the run-flat would be there if we were in a fire fight or engagement and we would be able to run the vehicle at least another 50 miles to safety where the tire would be repaired and built up with another run-flat. This busy work kept us out of the rack and awake. I couldn't sleep worth shit during the day anyway and we were supposed to have a brief at 1530 given by none other than Lt Haunty, our Commander.

I walked to the chow hall with the rest of MAP 8 and grabbed a Coke from the fridge. The sign read, "Take one, leave one," Printed in some obscure font and hastily printed from a field computer. I looked at the warm Cokes lying next to the fridge and tossed one back in the fridge and sat down.

"Congratulations, you are about to go on your first patrol," Lt Haunty said. A lot of enthusiasm came from the sleep-deprived crowd of twenty or so.

"Our mission is to patrol starting at 1830 from our FOB to the southern most part of Route Uranium, which is a military only access road, to extract a team of scout snipers from 1/23 and bring them back to our FOB and continue patrolling from Uranium to Route Page all the way up to the 6-2 Northing which is the train station to the 7-0 Northing and back." A yawn came from somewhere near the back and someone stood up and got to the back of the chow hall trying to stay awake. Lt Haunty continued with the brief, "Our threats are known and we were ordered to stabilize any hostile activity as well as conduct normal MSR security along our routes."

Cpl Stocker, our team leader looked almost anxious to go out on patrol. Turner, our driver, however looked frustrated and having never driven a Humvee before in his life, I could understand why. Turner was going to begin his driving at night on a combat patrol with NVG's. I had no idea why they wouldn't just use licensed drivers that had experience on the roads drive, but than again that was just me thinking logically again. I was pissed off and pretty worried about our first patrol, but I guess that was to be expected.

A useless attempt to get some shuteye, some crappy chow and taking multiple Cokes from the fridge without leaving one was all I could really accomplish before the patrol. We also got word that we had to escort CNN reporters out to the city sometime in the near future and take them on a normal routine patrol as well. I already knew I would hate doing that, but I wouldn't mind getting on TV and maybe the world would see first hand the crap we had to go through. Maybe it would just be a blurb between sports and the weather or some celebrity marrying some other celebrity, but I guess that didn't really matter much.

I grabbed my flack, kevlar, my RTT radio, my NVG's, machine gun, and mounted our makeshift Humvee with little to no armor. By then it was dark and I couldn't see who was sitting with me. I knew it was someone from 1/23 slouched back trying to stay warm in his sleeping bag. His Hispanic accent didn't sound Ohioan. He had a lot of knowledge for us along our patrol. Cpl Craig was kind of like a tour guide on the vacation from hell.

Problems with COM delayed our patrol and we set out about 2200. Cpl Craig talked with us a little about what to do and what not to do when patrolling. He said:

"Don't leave your MRE trash lying around. My SSgt did that and he was killed by the Muj. They put a mine where they knew he would be going to eat chow and it blew him sky high. Also, keep your shit organized. One Marine was hit by an IED because they left trash lying all over the vehicle. A soda can lodged its way through his kevlar and into his skull because the soda can wasn't secured properly. Secure your shit Marines!"

He sounded sincere as he put on layers of warm clothing. Even though it was warm, I think from being here long enough and riding in an open vehicle exposed to the wind, he knew it would be cold.

Cpl Craig also had his own story to tell. He had been hit by a 155 mortar round rigged into an IED and lost his Sergeant, who was a driver. Cpl Craig was saved by his good friend. He said that he was out for about fifteen days because he had to have shrapnel removed from his abdomen and was bleeding internally.

"Flacks and other protection will save your life," He said. I thought pretty highly of this guy as he sat there on the wooden, non-armored seat propped up by a few MRE boxes. He stayed here even though going home was an option for him to show us how things were done and how not to get yourself killed.

Doc Baronehernandez said a short prayer before we left the wire and we all stood in a circle and prayed with him before we left the wire. After that there was nothing stopping us and nothing between the enemy and us but thin sheets of steel and the rugged environment, which they had a chance to adapt to all of their lives. We waited in darkness and patrolled in the freezing cold desert in hopes of killing someone and staying alive ourselves.

Our route changed after we picked up the sniper team. We were to go up to al-Asad Air Base and escort a convoy to Uranium and then continue on our patrol up north past the 894 Northing. The first few patrols I will probably be able to sketch a detailed map of our AO down to the cracks and craters in the roads. If there was one word to describe this patrol it would have to be cold. I had not prepared for the weather thinking it would be desert climate, but Cpl Craig was used to it and brought his sleeping bag and fleece. I used his Gore-Tex jacket and it helped a little. I was envious of him because this would be his last patrol out here. I desperately wanted to say that I was going home the next day with him, but reality soon set in and I realized I had a long way to go. This was my first patrol.

MARCH 13, 2005 0000-1300

Sand and cement seemed to blend together as I grew weary. The potholes on Uranium were atrocious and all I could think about was how much money the U.S. had for the war effort that they could have allocated to repair these roads. My M249 inclined on the turret as I caught myself dozing off a few times. I couldn't get totally in sleep mode because the breeze from the moving vehicle was freezing cold and hit me like ice the very minute I shut my eyes. That night we made two trips to al-Asad. One trip was for the convoy mission and the other was to wait for compass call while eating ourselves silly on the main side chow hall. Compass call went almost every morning at 0630 and was announced on a covered net over the PRC119 radios mounted in our Humvees. Compass call involved low flying aircraft such as F-15's that flew by periodically and blew up IED's. They tried it a few times and a few explosions were tracked right after a compass call ran shortly before. From what I have heard this helped a lot, but naturally the Muj already knew about this and could easily adapt.

We continued past the 54-55 northing, past huge four-foot craters in the road where Cpl Craig said IED's and mines had exploded which he called "IED alley." We chased the sun back to the FOB as the morning heat warmed up the air and brought feeling to my limbs. My fingers were numb with cold from holding the machine gun so that it wouldn't spin around freely on the makeshift turret which 1/23 constructed out of what looked like a hollow steel bar and a regular turret mount zip tied to the machine gun.

It felt like it would never warm up and I prayed for the time when 100-degree weather would pelt us with heat. I probably would regret thinking this. Right now, it was freezing cold and we had been like this for almost twelve hours.

When we got back, I finally was able to snuggle up into my rack around 1300 and fell asleep until well after dark. We were now on a shift and were to be ready for another patrol tomorrow night. It was a one day off, twelve hours on. I was just glad to be warm.

MARCH 14, 2005

When 1/23 left for good, I knew we would have to double our shifts and work our asses off. Our second patrol was tonight at 1830. I was not looking forward to it and I tried to get a little sleep as I always did. I guess I figured the more I slept, the less time I would actually spend in Iraq mentally and therefore, the less time I would have here in country. Those of us were not in the skeleton crew were thinking we should fill sand bags during the day when we supposed to be sleeping. MAP 8 was moving to another room aside from MAP 3, which stayed in the room we were in now. Luckily, I woke up just in time to move in on a new rack and mattress. I was also lucky enough to get a stereo and converts for the 220 to 110V outlet, which was pretty much required here to use any form of appliance. The new room was larger than our old room and it was for MAP 8 only. The thing that I admired is that Sergeant Jenkins slept right up front in the same room with us, a thing not usually done in the Marine Corps. "You are my team and we are going to be together for a long time, why wouldn't I sleep in the same room as you guys?" he said to me as he organized gear from his sea bag.

"Hey Wojtecki you got the hook up," Everyone in my platoon kept saying because it was one of only two racks that were built up with pieces of ply wood, a rarity here in Iraq especially at the FOB. I had shelves to put my books, laptop, and other gear. Soon everyone built there own with wood they found in a small lumberyard next to motor-T. Dinkelman was determined to build the best rack in the room. He created a palace surrounded by curtains and inside he had his shelves, which held his laptop and pictures from magazines. He called it "the love shack" because of his crazy photos of models cut out of Maxim magazines. LCpl Dinkelman is truly insane.

MAP 8 finished moving from MAP 3's room later this afternoon and by then we were lucky to get a few hours of sleep. We were going out all night and were probably not coming back until the afternoon of the fifteenth.

Our mission for the evening was pretty much the same as our first patrol except without the guided tour by 1/23. It felt good to go back to at least half decent living quarters, but we would soon prove that we would not be spending a lot of time in our rooms. I was falling into a routine: Get gear ready (bring cold weather gear this time), check NVG's, check COM, check my weapon for cleanliness, put on my flack and kevlar, and go.

We left the FOB around 1800 and had to extract snipers on Route Page, patrol to the 63 Northing, and drive to al-Asad to wait for compass call again. Route Page is bumpier than most roads in Ohio and would be better if we were to carpet bomb the entire route. It would probably make it a smoother ride. The interesting thing about the route that lead out to Bronze, a public road, was the unbelievably horrible smell of the sulfur springs not 800m into the watey by the bridge that ran north to south. It was a smell I would never forget and it meant that anytime we got a whiff of the sulfur springs we were almost to FOB Hit or just beginning. In this case, we had a long night ahead of us. While Crossing over Route Bronze, cars were stopping 500m in the distance to avoid an incident. They had been conditioned by the Marines before us that if you get too close you die. It seemed to be known among the Iraqis here. One Hajji truck sped up when motioned to stop in front of us. We fired a flare and he kept coming even though others around him were stopped. I fired three or four bursts of the M249 SAW onto the road just in front of his truck and he stopped immediately. They were the first rounds fired from MAP 8. Rumors got around and by the end of the night, everyone had heard I shot a bus and killed all the occupants inside with a four round burst. I told everyone it was only a truck and I fired at the ground. Cpl Stocker said I did a good job and he was right there in the driver's seat when I was firing.

The sniper extraction was a cluster fuck. Apparently, when we picked them up someone told them to pack for 24 hours and then left them out there for four days. The first thing the Sergeant said when he climbed in our high back was, "do you guys have any water?"

"Sure here you go," I said, handing him a large Mozn bottle.

"What's up my name's Ed," he said not like a typical Sergeant would give out his first name. Four vehicles sped off into the darkness on Route Page and someone could be heard quoting the movie, "*Fight Club*." We took off back to the FOB to drop off the snipers and by then I was dozing off. We bounced around, hitting each other on Route Uranium. It was like a dug up minefield. I imagined that every one of these holes had a mine in it at one point in time. It was a scary thought to have. I couldn't get to sleep. The bumps threw me around like a roller coaster.

MARCH 15, 2005 0000-2300 23 HOURS WITHOUT SLEEP

Although we stuck to the schedule closely, there are times where we had to be flexible. After all, this is a war zone and you can expect it to be routine all the time. The twelve on day off shifts were broken today and most of the night when we sat at an OP and swept for IED's along the routes in our AO. Several fresh holes were dug as if someone had been there hours earlier. For most of the 23 hours we spent on patrol being especially watchful and making sure that the holes dug were not being lined with weapons and filled back in.

We were back at the base just long enough for me to eat some good chow, better than most. It was funny because I shoved as many sodas as I could into my pockets to save for later. Every time we are at the chow hall I think I will be doing this often because there is nothing like a refreshing beverage other than water when you on patrol.

I didn't think that after 23 hours of being awake that I could sleep like a baby, but it was only about three hours after the patrol that we had to jump onto a 7-ton and be escorted to al-Asad to fall in on our remaining gear. I was so exhausted and fell asleep on the way there. One of our vehicles overheated and we stopped for a few minutes and then continued on once someone poured water into the radiator.

This supposed four-hour pickup turned into an eight-hour goat rope, which is another expression for a mess or cluster fuck. We did manage to eat chow at al-Asad, which was good, of course I put more sodas into my pockets. The weirdest thing though was running into a kid that I used to go to grade school with and was in Boy Scouts with. His name is John Kruis and he joined the Marines looking for adventure, or at least that's what he told me. John went active not too long after I went into the Reserves. I could tell that the Marine Corps had changed him because he was a lot thinner and looked like he carried himself better. He promised me we would hook up after I got back to the States. John said he was leaving in two days for home. *That bastard,* I thought. I was envious of him.

Leaving the chow hall, we saw a Hajji shop and decided to stop in. Dinkelman bought DVD's and a stuffed lion for his palace that actually growls and its eyes light up. We walked out of the Hajji shop after a few minutes and I laid down in the dirt next to my gear and waited for our new vehicles to arrive. We would be riding in these Humvees for the rest of our deployment. I was not expecting much. When they arrived, I almost cried. They had no armor and it was obvious. The vehicles looked so shitty. At this very moment, I felt that nothing could be worse other than humping clear across the AO like Kilo Company did the other night. I think that walking would actually be safer. If we ran over anything with these vehicles, we would be dead. If I looked on the bright side, I guess it would be quick and painless and I wouldn't feel anything.

The bumps were so bad on the way back that my neck started bothering me. We got back early in the morning around 0300 and at that point sleep was the only thing on my mind.

MARCH 16, 2005

There were more rumors floating around that MAP 8 was moving to Hadithah Dam where the rest of the battalion was. I hoped this was not true in one way because I had already set up all my gear and was organized, but in another way I felt that our chances of survival were greater in Hadithah because we would do less driving and would be sitting at OP's more.

MAP 8 worked on its newly acquired vehicles, applying what armor we could without using a welder, which we didn't have and putting down Kevlar blankets to absorb some of the blast and shrapnel if an IED struck the vehicle. I had an idea for my turret. We carried an old Humvee seat that was not being used and attached it to a cooler. We filled the cooler with sand and slid it up near the front of our high back so that I would have a place to sit and could keep some defilade so I wasn't such an easy target. I was impressed with what we had done to improve the vehicles. We did what we could with what we had, and what we had wasn't much. Our high back was a battlewagon. We mounted Gypsy racks on the sides so we could fit more gear into the vehicle and not be tripping over things if we were to get into a firefight. Dinkelman taped padding on the seats that we got from an old chair for those long patrols of just sitting there. These were our vehicles now.

When we were done we had about an hour until 1300 and as usual had no idea what was going on. When we had full gear on and were staged in front of the CoC, we found out that we were escorting a convoy of 7-tons to ASP Dulab for a drop-off. I had no doubt in my mind that we could finish and get back to the base, but would have to go right back out again on our normal patrol.

It was like that commuter route that people often find themselves driving to work every day. For the first few times you don't know where you are going and eventually it just becomes part of your job to drive. Except, this was all of the time and driving was our job. LCpl Turner, our driver, had a way of bitching up a storm about everything from the long drives to why the hell the Army drives at night with their lights on.

Lt Haunty rode in the first vehicle of MAP 8, which might have explained why we stopped every few minutes. We actually spotted a live mortar round set perfectly aligned with the road and passed it up completely without stopping. Later Cpl Kustra lost it, "Why the hell did we pass that up? That is totally fucked up that could have killed us!" Cpl Kustra stood next to the first vehicle.

"Our mission is to get these 7-tons to Dulab!" Our Platoon Commander angrily replied.

"Well I hope you sleep well at night knowing this is still out here." Cpl Kustra was infuriated.

We dropped off the package three or four hours later. It seemed like we just drove and drove until we couldn't drive anymore into the desert and just came upon an ASP. Don't get me wrong, this is a great place to put an ASP, but it was such a pain in the ass to get out here. *People actually lived out here on the ASP,* I thought as I took a piss into the desert. I started thinking about how you could get away with almost anything out here and no one would ever find out about it. You could only guess what we did after we dropped off the cargo. After driving for some time we traced back looking for the same IED we passed just hours before and it was never found. It was recorded as a 6-digit grid, which is accurate up to 200m, that was as close as we dared get to it.

Right when we got back to base we grabbed cold weather gear, picked up snipers, and then hauled ass to al-Asad for mid-rats (chow) at 0130 while patrolling and sweeping under wateys all the way there, which were areas underneath a road that water ran through and were hollow in the center. al-Asad was a good 40 or 50 miles from FOB Hit and it seemed like we drove that route every time we were out on patrol.

Snipers are funny guys to work with. Their job is very distinguished among Marines and in the civilian world as well. These guys will sit without moving for days on end and when they see enemy movement they have to have the conviction and strength to take another life at point blank range. They were always on a first name basis with each other and I think it brought them closer as a team. Although, by the end of the night they were not so happy to be with us because they had to sit with our MAP while we traveled all the way up to the 55 Northing on a patrol. For some reason at 0300, someone thought they caught a heat signature moving about 500m from our vehicles. The snipers kept insisting that buildings, rocks, and plants can also return heat signatures from the day and that this was what the optics picked up. We fired two flares from a 203, test fired from a 240G and cordoned off the area later to find out that the snipers were absolutely right. By then I was asleep and woke up only to be bounced around again on Uranium. I blocked traffic on Bronze while we traveled back to base somewhere around 0600 this morning.

MARCH 17, 2005 0600-2300

We were able to get back and it was a perfect time to get on the phone because of the eight-hour difference back in the States. If it was 0600 here then it was 10:00pm yesterday there. Angela was very nice to me and said she got my flowers I ordered for her. She wanted me to come home at that very moment. I wish I could have and that I could continue with my life the way it used to be. I might have taken things a little too much for granted. After our conversation, I stumbled through the dark without a flashlight to the hooch and had to stand watch for an hour from 0700 to 0800 before finally hitting the rack.

I can't help but lose track of reality thinking about my wedding day, my job, and all the happy memories that I had back home. I could fill a seven-month deployment with all the thoughts I had about my life. They say that the more you wonder off what is really real, the more you slip from reality, the harder it is to return to normal. I feel like my life right now is nothing more than a wondering journey and although I can still see the road ahead, my drifting seems to be infinite. Sometimes I wonder the more I stay in reality that my dreams may slip away. So I keep trying to hold on and take it one day at a time.

MARCH 18, 0130-

"You fucker why the hell are you making so much noise!" LCpl Stephen shouted from the MAP 3 hooch.

"Sorry, I didn't mean to wake you I just needed to get something out of my sea bag," A voice from the other room whispered.

"Oh, go walk on Bronze!" Stephen exclaimed and the rustling continued until I dozed off.

I always joke with Dan about those positive self-help tapes people listen to in their cars and before they go to sleep to raise their self-esteem. "I love myself. People like me. I will be successful," I said in a slow melodic tone as we got out of the rack in the middle of the night to go out on yet another patrol. This morning however it was the opposite, having only time to play a short game on the computer and wake up for our shift. "I hate myself!" I exclaimed, "This sucks! This is bullshit!"

We were on the road by 0230. The night went rather fast and sped off with our moving vehicles into the very early morning. In that time, we escorted a convoy of mail and laundry to the Bronze / Uranium Intersection. Several Marines lived there to observe suspicious activity in the city of Hit. It seemed like the coldest night yet. I had two blankets, a Gore-Tex, sweatshirt, a beanie-cap, and a neck-gator on, but nothing could stop the cold. Several times throughout the night, I had to observe the area while dismounts clear culverts and wateys to check for IED's and land mines. Cpl Stocker spotted two wild dogs and told me to shoot them, but I could not get a good shot on them. The wild dogs here will attack anything and are extremely vicious. Unlike the U.S., The dogs here were considered an agent of the devil and not considered a household pet. Dan fired a few rounds from his M-16 into the darkness and we moved on.

I ate almost every type of real eggs at the al-Asad chow hall. Rolling through the base felt weird now since we did more than just walk to the PX and chow hall like we did when we first got here. All the graffiti on the bathroom walls was written by people that were on base all the time and their biggest obstacle was getting to the chow hall from their hooches.

The plan today was to set up a snap VCP on Bronze / Uranium intersection just outside of the city. As we were exiting al-Asad, we loaded our weapons at the clearing barrels. Not far from the Air Base, three Arab kids approached us as they were herding sheep with their father just outside their village.

"USA Good! Bang Bang Sadaam! You good!" They shouted from the side of the road.

They were smiling at us and waving. I reached into my pack and pulled out one of the sodas that I put in my pocket from the chow hall. I gave it to the older boy. He took it and came back a minute later, "Coke?" He asked and I gave him two more sodas, "lasers?" They said and pointed to our rifles.

PFC Perry gave them a cigarette to smoke, while Sgt Jenkins and Cpl Stocker tried to get Intel from them. "Mujahadeen?" Cpl Stocker said pointing to the building in the distance.

"No, No. Sheik," The boy said.

It was either where their sheep were staying or where the high sheik was living. The boy was hard to understand and his English was limited. That's okay because our Arabic wasn't the best either and Cpl Stocker was just starting out as our translator.

Soon after our encounter with the three Arab kids, we rolled into the town of Baghdadi. Like any third world city, the place was pretty sparse. People were selling things on the streets and small shops near the Euphrates River. The people in the streets were sitting around outside and looked as if that's all they had been doing for years. They were in obvious need of employment and it scared me because these were the type of people that would do anything for money. All of us acted rather friendly to them, waving and exchanging smiles. Overall, it was a very friendly / neutral city compared to most in our AO, although there were a few frowns and cold stares. The VCP was cancelled because Kilo Company had already set one up in that spot, however I was ready to pull the trigger if one car tried to speed up and charge our convoy.

I ate some noon chow around 1245 and other Marines went to the Hajji shop to buy a hookah and pirated DVD's of movies that hadn't even been released to theaters back in the U.S. Brett bought some movies I would like to watch later. The thing about it is you have to heckle with these people or you will get ripped off. "$22.00 for 5 DVDs," Brett held the videos in his hands and was about to walk out.

"30 dolla," The Arab man said in broken English.

"23 dollars for 5 DVDs or I'm walkin' out," Brett said as he pointed to the door. The old man finally agreed with him. Brett slipped him a 50 and he got change back. We walked to the vehicles and I looked at what he got. He had to buy something every time we were here and I think it was a disorder or a complex.

MAP 8 headed back to the FOB late this afternoon. Luckily, nothing happened out of the ordinary. I knew if I said that aloud, I would Jinx us and then something really bad would happen, I just knew it would. I took a shower and stared at the moving water and the dark concrete floor as it became wet with water moving into a nearby drain. It felt good to be clean again. Mortar outgoing fire in the distance didn't bother me anymore. They still made us wear our flack and kevlar to the shower. I appreciated the fact that I wasn't in a vehicle right now because that seemed to be where I always ended up. I listened to the loud explosions of mortars as I fell asleep.

MARCH 19, 2005

A maintenance stand down was on the schedule for today. This meant taking a break from the patrols for a few hours. I slept and used the phone center for most of the day while administrative issues were schedules. There was still some debate about MAP 8 moving to Hadithah and they said they would let us know when they found out what they were doing. It sounded like the decision came from the top and was passed down to the enlisted level until it finally reached us and by then word can get very distorted.

I thought about home a lot today. I missed going to special places around town and eating in fancy restaurants. I listened to some music that made me think of being in a coffee shop arguing about politics or just something stupid. It was spring break at the college and all the students were having fun, going to Florida, or to some far away place with friends. Constantly I day dream and the more I wanted to experience the freedom that we so casually take for granted. It would be good to get my mind off home and get back behind a machine gun again.

MARCH 20, 2005 PALM SUNDAY

If there were a church somewhere in this God forsaken country, there would be a sermon and some priest somewhere would be giving a talk about Jesus and his entrance into a city which is probably very close to were we are. Palms would be given out and we would wave them in church to celebrate. Afterwards we would go home and my Mom would cook breakfast for us while my dad read the paper and drank coffee. The smell of bacon would catch my attention. I would already be out of my church cloths of course and would sit across from my dad until everything was ready. We would eat pork products and the dairy wouldn't spoil easy in the sun like it does everyday here.

We left the FOB at 1030 to escort a company of tanks just outside the city limits to provide security for them while they BZOed their main guns on selected random targets in the desert. Providing security for tanks was something I would probably never fully understand, but to my knowledge, I think that we are to provide over watch to make sure that Muj do not try to RPJ the tanks while they are firing. I was excited otherwise because for once we weren't escorting snipers somewhere or convoying more 7-tons to al-Asad. I video taped it and I think it would be nice to send home to family. We drove to just after the Bronze / Uranium intersection and then stopped to allow the tanks to site in. We must have waited there for a good hour or so while tanks got COM with the snipers in the area and the air flying overhead to make sure they were not within firing range. Just out of nowhere a .50 cal remotely fired from the tank's turret. Gunners can fire the .50 cal from the turret position using a button. This gun is BZOed to the main gun round. I am not a tanker, but from my observations and talking to these hard asses, this information is very accurate. One gunner told me about an incident where a person got to close to the tank when the main gun round was firing. The gun went off and gave the man a brain concussion. He later died in the hospital.

Their continued firing went on for three or four evolutions until the guns were sited in. The loud explosion jostled the vehicles and knocked Cpl Stocker, who was kneeling about 200m from the tank, on his ass. A large mushroom cloud made up of dirt and ash rose in the distance over the Middle Eastern sky.

It would be a good film to show my family and I would probably watch it with my dad over a few beers when I got back. The tanks rolled out to take control of Hit City, we went back to the FOB to pick up supplies, and we were then supposed to escort the gear to a checkpoint that was desperately in need of them. It was pretty boring, but it was nice to get out driving during the day for a change. MAP's that went out during the daytime usually tended to see more action thanks to our "fair weather fighter" friends. Marines have a phrase, *DOMINUS KNOX,* which is Latin for "we own the night." We are trained to fight in any climb or place, day, night, rain, or shine.

For most of the day, we spent time preparing and escorting the supplies and got back home to base late afternoon. We were to then pickup MAKO 3 snipers at the Bronze / Fleet intersection near Hit City where their hive was located.

MAP 8 pulled out of the staging area, which was where we usually parked the vehicles just before we went out so we could make sure if everything was okay with COM, weapons, and other gear so that everything was in working order when we went out.

All of a sudden, the radio lights up with traffic, "MAKO 3 is taking fire! We've got small arms fire and multiple shooters. Please send support, over!"

I don't think we have ever moved as fast as we did. Turner looked determined as he sped down the road about as fast as the Humvee could go. Tensions were high. I loaded a full 200 round drum into my SAW. We were there in less than ten minutes. The vehicles slowed down near the intersection. Rounds whizzed passed the second vehicle and over our heads. I will never forget what a round sounds like when it travels just above your head. It's like a whizzing sound sort of like a buzzing and it has its own unique sound. We all got down, this being our first live engagement. Brett ducked next to me and Cpl Stocker insisted that we need to suppress and voices yelled, "Eleven O'clock!" I spun around to the eleven and fired almost blowing out Dinkelman's eardrums. I looked straight ahead and saw a man in all black robes walking next to the intersection. This moment was so surreal to me and it seemed like slow motion. He walked casually into the intersection. I had him in my sites but when I looked for a weapon, I couldn't see one. My gut told me to fire but as long as he wasn't posing a threat, I couldn't fire. I wanted to so badly that I knew it was going to kill me. The man was visible for a few seconds and then was out of site. I heard an M203 from one of the snipers and a grenade exploded near their area. I continued suppressing the enemy and we focused on our main objective, which was extracting the snipers. "Let's hunt this mother fucker down!" one of the snipers shouted. We did a 360 and our high back made its way to the overpass overlooking the general area just above the intersection. I saw a man in a black robe that matched the description of the guy I saw earlier. My adrenaline was really flowing and my heart raced as I gripped the smooth framework of the M249 SAW. From 600m I shot at the truck, "A little high." The sergeant from MAKO 3 whispered.

"Die, mother fucker, die." The gun rattled off a five round burst.

"Come left a little," one of the snipers said.

"Die, mother fucker, die." The SAW delivered the rounds on target from a great distance and we scared the guy shitless.

Two of MAP 8's vehicles went down to the gas station to inspect the dump truck and search the nearby area for the suspected shooter. A man came out from behind the vehicle with his hands up. Three Marines then searched the building for weapons and we continued. The man turned out to be a truck driver and reported seeing a man in black robes get into a taxi and drive off.

Air was called in and with their thermal sites they searched the ground for anything that breathed or carried heat. The snipers said they saw a guy get into a white Nissan truck and drive off into the city. Marines swept the area Vietnam style for a good hour or so and left with the snipers to report to base for a debrief.

The only thing I will take from this experience is that I had a guy in my sites. Dinkelman and I joke about him haunting us in our sleep, "Why didn't you shoot me?!?" the dark figure shouts from the other side of reality.

I was shook up for the majority of the night after we RTBed. We continued on the mission after having A debrief with Lt Haunty and went out on our routine patrol. MAP 8 headed up north to search a train station. Evidently, a call was intercepted from a phone at that location talking about the firing we did hours earlier. We proceeded to search the station and found two weapons, an SKS and an AK-47.

Most of the night was spent in the vicinity of the Baghdadi area searching through the palm groves for our suspect or some clue that may lead us to why and how someone found the position at that intersection and decided to fire at MAKO 3 and take on a MAP team for a few seconds before retreating. Animals were everywhere. In farmhouses and outside trapped in wooden fences and underneath palm trees. A small camel was tied to a hay wagon and was startled by our roaring Humvees that disturbed the farming communities at this witching hour. All I could think about was how this looked like something straight out of the bible. I can see that not much has changed since the birth of Christ.

We continued up North to al-Asad after causing disruption among the citizens of Baghdadi and rounding up a few weapons that Muj could have used against us and headed up north to al-Asad. We took route Bronze straight through the middle of the city, which wasn't recommended all the time because of the frequent mortar attacks that were reported from that area and the overwhelming number of IED's that were planted. These IED's were placed in such a way that a lazy Muj camel jockey could just sit out on his front porch and press the button on us. It was definitely a lot quicker than going around the city that was for sure.

We RTBed around 0000 and I fought men in black robes in my head until I fell asleep. The occasional mortar round dropped on the FOB, but I was too tired to put my flack on.

MARCH 21, 2005

I had a dream about the man in the black man dress. He looked at me while I gazed at him through my scope. He just kept walking and I woke up twitching. As usual, there was always some big discussion or argument after about who fired the most rounds, who almost killed someone, or what we did wrong. I was sick of hearing it because it was going on all morning and it got kind of tiring after hearing it. This would be something we would be talking about for days and I just knew it. I rolled out of the rack and put my fatigues on.

The phone center had been closed for quite some time. I found out that it was because we took some KIA's and I guess it had to do with Op-Sec. It sounded like a bunch of bullshit to me. I must have told a million people about the engagement we were in just the other day and how between the three gunners we must have fired over 500 rounds. I was ready to go home already and sick of all this. We were going out again for another night patrol tonight and I was not looking forward to freezing my ass off again. I guess you could call it being home sick, but I think its more than that. It's that I don't want to lose anything. The memories of my life and college seem to become a little more distant every day. To lose my identity and who I am is a big fear of mine. I don't want to come home and people look at me like they don't know who I am anymore.

As I naturally did on any day off, I slept. I got up for a few minutes to eat some jellybeans out of my care packages and read some letters. *Some Easter this is*, I thought and I laid back down and fell asleep again.

"We have to stage in twenty minutes. Everyone get the hell out of the rack," A loud voice shouted from the doorway. It really pissed me off. It was 2230. God only knows what we would be doing. I got all my gear ready to go and loaded it onto the vehicle. I couldn't stop thinking about how we might have to move to Hadithah Dam. There was still talk of it floating around, but the last thing I wanted to do was pack all my gear up again and move to another AO. *How bad could it be?* I thought. I grabbed my blanket from my bed along with my flack, daypack, and SAW. I headed to the high back but couldn't stop this hatred for everything around me. I was becoming bitter and I noticed it. Apparently, the others in our MAP say that this is how I normally act and that they look forward to my bitching to get them through the day.

As we rolled out of the base in our vehicles, LCpl Turner, our driver, who was a COM guy detached from H&S Company and was often called "too cool" told us about the Iraqi Freedom Fighter named Blue. Blue was part of the IFF that 1/23 had trained. He must have been about 50 or 60 years old. Blue had been an inspiration to the Freedom Guards and ING as a leader and someone to set the example. He really made progress in training the troops because he brought leadership to the other Iraqis and gave us hope that the training was actually progressing. Yesterday he was picking up his son from the hospital and he was shot 23 times with an AK-47 by the Mujahadeen. *Those bastards*, I thought as Turner continued telling us about him. The man in black appeared again in my head and I knew I was going to kill him one way or another. I snapped out of it to the smell of sulfur and bright green from my NVG's straining my eyes.

Nothing really went on for two whole hours. Everyone went silent and all I could hear was the squeaking of the axels on the Humvee as we went over bump after bump.

MARCH 22, 2005 0000-2300

Some kind of rice and chicken was scooped onto my plate and I was glad to have it. I hadn't eaten in over fourteen hours, except maybe for a few jellybeans. Something about another trial for someone or other blared over MSNBC inside of the chow hall over the TV in the corner. It was hard to follow the news story because I had not been up to date on anything. From the looks of it, I was not missing much on TV. The same reports just a different person. It was OJ before and now it's someone they said Scott Peterson, but I'm not even sure what he did or why he's on trial.

It was so cold outside. I covered up with my Christmas blanket that Angela gave me before I left. I thought I would never use it because it's supposed to be hot in the desert. We hit two train stations, once in the morning and once in the afternoon. Cpl Stocker tried to communicate with six Iraqis claiming to be Iraqi Police. Apparently, they had checked out, but I didn't believe their story for a minute. Iraqi Police were so corrupt it's hard to believe anyone with a rag on their head.

We extracted the snipers that had been hiding out in an old abandoned boxcar on the railroad tracks just north of our AO. Our vehicles took off quickly after picking up the snipers and receiving a call from an Army convoy claiming that they had spotted a motorcycle on the military only Route Uranium. The three Iraqis claimed to be power line workers and invited us into their small shack of a home for tea. I sat watching through the power scope on my SAW. *God I have to get some sleep.* I gave Dan two caffeine tablets because he had taken over driving for Turner. I couldn't blame him for needing a break. We had been driving for over thirteen hours. I think I gave Dan too many pills. He flew most of the way back over every bump he could find and we returned to the base jostled around and nauseated, not to mention ready to fall asleep standing up.

I crashed as soon as we got back. The sleep was good but I woke up and I was still here with an incredible hunger. I was starving, so I wandered down to the chow hall and ate a disgusting meal consisting of some kind of chicken and Thai sauce. All it is a larger version of an MRE just made to feed a larger number of people. I checked the phone center after filling myself at the chow hall. *No sodas to steal this time, those bastards!* I was about to lose my mind and open fire at the CoC or lose myself in a book to get my mind off this place. For the sake of our battalion, they were lucky I chose the second of the two.

10

MARCH 23, 2005 HADITHAH DAM

It was a rather abnormal awakening this morning. At 0530, MAP 8 was called out for QRF. Normally, when we're on QRF, if the platoon out patrolling or some component of the line company is in trouble and needs backup then we are sent out to support them. We all knew that this time it was for no reason because that is when compass call normally takes place and all ground equipment on roadways are ordered to stay static until the call is complete. Compass call happens when F-15's fly over the AO and destroy all IED's on the roadways. Sometimes they are accurate and sometimes they're not. MAP 3 had not established COM with the CoC and we were woken up to go find them. I think Lt Haunty was giving us our farewell by sending us out one last time before we left for the shit hole, Hadithah Dam. I was rather pissed and was glad to get in bed and sleep a little more after the QRF incident. We ended up being called out and then sent back in right as we got out the front gates of the FOB, it was pointless. Sgt Jenkins came in and let everyone know the news about us, "We're not going to Hadithah tomorrow, we're going today, and we're leaving in a few hours so pack your shit." *That was great, just great.* As if things could not get worse. I've had some bad days here, but to all of a sudden to just move to another AO, it was bullshit and there was no other way to describe it right now.

We took our vehicles with us, loaded our gear on the 7-tons, and left the only place we could truly call home in this messed up country. I was told it was going to be a three-hour drive to Hadithah. Dinkelman, Dmytriw, and the rest of our team had gotten really close without even knowing it. We screwed around mostly and stopped at al-Asad for chow and one last PX call.

We packed and then we packed some more. Moving turned into an even bigger hassle than when we first got here. The place was huge and looked like the Hoover Dam almost, guarded by Azerbaijanis, a Russian unit that was supposedly trigger happy as hell and would open fire if you did not say the password, "Colorado."

"Okayyyyy…" they would reply not knowing a bit of English.

No one liked the idea of us being here at all. I spread my gear all over my cot, which I again found myself sleeping on after getting used to a mattress, and immediately began looking for the electric outlets. All outlets here were 220V as opposed to the American 110V plugs; these were larger and were two-pronged and circular. I woke up to serve fire watch about two times on our vehicles until the next morning. The idea here I guess was that the Azerbaijanis were going to steal our shit if we didn't have a post on our trucks 24/7, one of the things that I am sure would grow very old after a short time of being here.

It was good to finally talk with Angela again. The phone center was on the sixth deck, a floor up from where chapel services were held. I had to laugh because the sign read, "Services held Sunday morning in the Dam chapel."

The highly guarded Hadithah Dam provided power for cities in Western Iraq and now housed the majority of 3/25's Battalion of Marines that were hungry for blood and were anxious to pull the trigger, and now sadly included MAP 8 from Hit.

The snipers had called this place the "Death Star," FOB Hit was the Ewok planet "Endor," and the guy in charge was the "Darth Vader." That was about the funniest thing I had heard all night.

I woke up again at 0230 for watch, walked past the Russian guard post. Again, the only coming between .50 cal rounds and me was the word, "COLORADO." A guard later asked what our vehicle was doing and we explained it was cold and that we were watching it, "Okayyyyy," They replied like they always do and he marched on past with a look on his face like he had a million more paces to do before his next shift got there.

There were so many things to miss right now and as messed up as it sounded, I missed the FOB because it was a place where time went fast and people got close to one another. It was a retreat from the boot camp / Gestapo shit that they pulled on a daily basis here.

MARCH 24, 2005

We were given 24 hours in which VC's could familiarize themselves with the new AO by going out with another MAP that had already been patrolling the Hadithah Dam area since we touched down in Iraq. The rest of us worked on our vehicles by welding our own armor plates from the scrap yard onto our vehicles. Dinkelman, Truthan, and Turner decided to work on the up-armor vehicle issues in case a mine or IED attacked us. The vehicle we were riding in had no armor whatsoever and I could not understand how someone could ride around in this piece of shit with the threat level as high as it was for mines and IED's in the area. The motor-T guy told them it would take about ten hours to weld ¼ inch plates of steel onto the high back Humvee. I watched a little, but I wasn't much of a mechanic, nor did I know anything about welding or repairing cars.

Dan and I kind of did some exploring today. There are actually sub-floors that lead God knows were down below the Dam. Dan and I decided to take a trip to sub level two. We ran down really quick and found the new spot that we would go in case there were any working parties in the near future. To get anywhere else, like to the phone center or to chow, we had to climb seven flights of steps. Later on Dan and I found out that anyone caught going down into the sub levels of the Dam would be instantly shot by the Azerbaijanis patrolling down there, so that was comforting.

Time was going so slow here and I guess it made me think about how incredibly long this deployment was and of course, I thought about what I would be doing when I got back to the States. I got an email last night, which took twenty whole minutes to check because of the slow Internet connection. Dan and I explored every inch of the Dam and fooled around in the phone center and chow hall. We then decided to see what was going on down at the motor-T. The whole day was spent working on the vehicle, cutting pieces of steel and fitting them to our high back. After what they told us about the guy in 3/2 who got hit by a mine and got his leg blown off, it felt a little more safe to have armor surrounding us, even if it was from the scrap yard. It was better than nothing, but it kind of pissed me off seeing as we were supposed to have been prepared for this war and these vehicles were hardly adequate for combat operations in the hottest parts of Iraq.

I fell asleep early tonight working on my computer and just arranging and organizing my area to get my mind off the fact that I was still here. *I might not ever get used to this place.* I'm sure after a few months we would forget about our old home in Hit.

MARCH 25, 2005

At 0630 MAP 8 woke up to the COM phone that was measly wired from the NCO deck on level three to our hooch on level one. It was as if we were back in the 1920's. I'm sure I knew what they wanted. Our first patrol of Hadithah Dam was today and we were to start staging the vehicles. Unfortunately, Dinkelman, Truthan, and Turner had not quite finished with our improvements yet, so we had to walk down to the motor pool to hastily throw all our gear back on the truck and get ready to go out.

I had faith in Sgt Jenkins that MAP 8, no matter where we went we could always find action. With over 300 patrols under his belt, he would definitely lead us confidently. Most of the day we spent conducting snap VCP's on random cars. Cpl Stocker was in charge of our search team. "Enso Mensiata!" which meant, "Get out of the vehicle!" he would always scream to the occupants of several unlucky Iraqis that were stopped and searched by MAP 8. We pulled over a group of five or six vehicles at a time by pulling one Humvee out onto the road to block traffic from one way and another vehicle would block from the other side. This is known as "the box." We would always pull around so as the SAW gunner of the second vehicle high back could have a good clear shot at the driver of the suspected vehicle. Dinkelman and LCpl Back searched vehicles, Truthan searched bodies, and I manned the SAW, which was mounted ever so crudely on top of the canvas cover; the only thing standing between me and bullets or shrapnel. We didn't find much. Some fisherman who joked with us, Sunni's who had been traveling to Barwanah, a nearby city, and Hajji oil workers trying to make a flight to Beiji, Iraq for a conference of some sort. It was rather difficult to communicate because we did not have a translator with us.

Later on in the evening, we found a twenty-year-old kid that had been carrying circuit boards near a small radio tower outside one of the REI tents. REI workers were hired by the government to guard the oil pipeline running adjacent to Route Raptors. This kid was particularly odd because we found the circuits on him in a small white bag made of some kind of sheep wool. It looks like the electronic workings were from the 70's, but anyone just walking up to the kid would say he had been carrying bomb making materials. Naturally so did Sgt Jenkins and we decide to detain him, probably not because the kid was a threat, but to just to cause commotion. He had been herding sheep with his father and it was obvious that he was either mentally retarded or autistic. *What would a sheepherder be doing with circuit boards? Did the father give the son the boards to carry with him?*

Further investigation of the father's tent uncovered some drawings in chalk that were rather peculiar. Obviously, they had been drawn by the son whose name we later found out was Sahib. The drawings were of our U.S. Humvees and Marines. For me at least, it gave me a creepy feeling that something was going on. It could have just been the boy drawing for fun, but for his sake and to please Sgt Jenkins and most of the platoon who just wanted to screw around with the family, we decided to take him back to base for a while. MAP 8's encounter with Sahib would probably have been compared to extra terrestrials abducting people in the sense that we were so far ahead of this archaic culture that we must have seemed like aliens to these Iraqi's.

We brought him back to the Death Star for questioning by our HET team, who proceeded to chew his ass. That was about all that happened to the boy though and they told us to take him back to his father where we found him. By then it was quite dark and freezing cold. The air whipped off the Dam like a storm was coming. We kicked Sahib out of our crudely armored Humvee with a food ration and some water. It seemed to me like MAP 8 had found itself a new mascot.

Vehicle 4 had been having some problems so they took it in for repair while we sat up an observation post to observe route Phoenix and Raptors. It must have gotten down to right around 30 degrees that night. I was so cold and I could not go to sleep. No suspicious activity to report, other than some boats seen over the water of the large lake fishing and a few fires off in the distance, warming some cold inhabitance of the volatile desert, which we also shared with them.

MARCH 26, 2005

The Hadithah Dam was built in the late 1970s by the Soviets when they controlled the majority of Iraq. During the Gulf era, it was a fishing ground for Saddam Hussein. All of it was his and if anyone was caught fishing or walking on or around the Dam, they were instantly shot on site. After American occupation, we took control of the Dam and made it a forward operating base. From a logistical standpoint, this made sense because the Dam was a major source of power for the majority of Iraq. This we would soon find out would be a major target for insurgents and a major victory for us if we held it.

Dan and I, after returning from our patrol, went to fuel the vehicle and change a flat tire. Seeing as we were a bunch of white-collar college kids, it was definitely interesting. It took us about two hours to change the tire. We then went back to our room on the first floor. Three floors up from the ground floor felt like an exhausting eternity. It was funny that so many of the things that we really needed to get to like the chow hall, first aid, and phones were all on the upper levels five and above.

I decided to get a shower. Not expecting much, I went down and threw myself into the cold water for a while until I was somewhat clean and then dried off. I shivered all the way upstairs and then climbed into my sleeping bag.

I wanted to work on something for my fiancée's birthday and this would be the day. The phone center was closed because someone else from Kilo Company had died hitting a double stacked mine. The unarmored vehicle hit the mines, killing him instantly and sending another three Marines back to the States. *Fortunately, God was still on our side,* I thought as a drifted into a light sleep checking myself to make sure I was still alive.

MARCH 27, 2005

We are now running one day on, twelve hours off patrols. In a normal job, this would be 100 some odd hours a week.

We headed out around 0730. This time I came prepared and brought my sleeping system. My lucky rock I found out in the desert sat up on the canvas top of the Humvee. Its light colors and shimmering crystal couldn't have come from a desert as ugly and dull as this one. It was like finding a needle in a haystack. I found it on my first patrol here at the Dam. The shell casing I saved from our first engagement in Hit was in my right pocket. I considered these items lucky and now I couldn't go out on a patrol without them. They give protection against me and from the enemy. After just a few weeks out here, I started to get very superstitious.

We prayed that we would not come to harm and that we would have a good Easter. Normally I would probably get an Easter basket or some kind of candy, like the big chocolate bunnies I liked so much. I remember looking for eggs behind the couches and eating Peeps marshmallows until my brother and I were sick. Now some years later, I am on double shift patrols protecting the Iraqi people and preventing the terrorist threat from spreading.

Most of the day we spent pulling over or as we so elegantly put it, "rolling up" random cars, and searching people. Cpl Stocker seemed to be getting better at speaking Arabic and getting along with the people. There are so many diversities in this part of the country. One car we would pull over would have sheepherders and the next car could be PhD students headed towards the next big oil conference in Beiji.

We seemed to be getting good at making our presence known in the east and west villages of our AO. The kids always asked for food, water, and even for money. On this particular occasion, the town was rather deserted. I think that was because of the offensive going on right now, which was Operation River Bridge.

We stopped in the middle of the desert about mid-day, broke for chow, and BZOed our ACOG's. I shredded boxes in half with my SAW. Several others took a long time to sight in. Truthan was catching lizards. He actually caught one and thought it would be a good idea to keep it. It would be called Crazy Carl. We put it in a small empty Mozn bottle in our vehicle to bounce up and down with us all day long. It was funny that Marines always loved to screw around with animals, particularly here in the desert, because it provided hours and hours of entertainment.

I guess it was a normal thing for MAP's to set up OP's after dark for hours at a time. I remember Cpl Craig saying, "The Muj are always watching." I think if they wanted to plant mines and IED's they would just look to see if our vehicles were not parked at OP's with freezing cold sleeping Marines inside, and then plant the mines or pay some poor guy that has to decide between feeding his family with the money or starving to preserve his way of life. I guess that is just my personal take on things and how they are done around here.

MARCH 28, 2005

Twelve hours off from constantly patrolling turned into about ten. I'm sure that we would get called out on QRF, from what the other MAP's said. There was no electricity in our hooches. Dan and I joked about how we were living inside of a Dam that supplied half the power to Iraq and yet there was no power in our hooch. I dropped all my trash and headed up to a late chow and put myself on the long list for phones so I could hopefully get on before we had to leave again.

I am sure that in Hit we would be engaging some sort of enemy or be mortared at any point in time, but I guess out of all the negative things I spent countless hours complaining about, I knew I would rather be alive than dead. The Marine from Kilo Company was from the MAP that replaced us in Hit.

Sometimes I think about our vehicle hitting a mine. What would feel like? What would happen to me? I quickly wince and try to think of something else like home or Easter time and that works out pretty well for me, but no matter how much I try to push back the thought, it is always there.

MARCH 29, 2005

We were to have a 24-36 hour maintenance stand down starting when we got off the patrol last night. This would give us at least some time to fix whatever was wrong with our vehicles and gear and gather accurate accountability of everything before moving out to the next patrol. I woke up early around 0800 to be part of a safety vehicle that was required for H&S company while they fired .50 cal and MRK19's off the 7-tons at a nearby range that was marked by an old rusted Iraqi tank. We got in this morning around 0300 so I was still a little out of it. I fell asleep on my seat in the high back while Dinkelman drew "Cr8zy" on the walls with a sharpie and Truthan fired the AT-4 for his birthday present, missing the tank totally, but still giving us quite a show. The explosion shook our vehicle and kicked up sand everywhere.

The AT-4 was very loud and Truthan had to attempt to fire three times, because apparently the trigger mechanisms had malfunctioned making two of the AT-4's inoperable. About half way through the shoot, we had to call a cease-fire because some jackass hit a power line with a 203-grenade launcher round. There was always competition between H&S and 03's. We called them Segovia Commandos because they always hogged the phone center when we got back from a patrol, with the exception of a few units like MAP 7. When it all came down to it we knew that both H&S and 03's needed each other to be a fully effective fighting force.

Captain Penmettel requested our MAP be tasked with the recon of a CASEVAC sight near the city of Barwanah. "If it takes eight hours, it takes eight hours," he said. I was sure it would take even longer.

Heading south on Route Uranium we pulled off road and I braced myself for about 30 minutes while we drove off into the desert, bypassing any roads that may have covered up mines or IED's.

It must have gotten up to 90 degrees today. It was so hot. Dmytriw, Dinkelman, and Truthan humped about two clicks into town with the Captain looking for the perfect site to land a medic helicopter. If someone got hurt this was where air would land to pick them up. I took security on the gun just looking out for suspicious activity, which then turned into eating chow and eventually dozing off while Cpl Stocker looked through his power scope over the village just waiting for something big to happen. Nothing did.

About three hours later, we left. Turner caught another lizard of his own and named it Katrina. On the way back we rolled up some rock farmers that were gathering loose dirt in a rusty tractor. The man pointed to our water. He was obviously thirsty. I gave him some of my water and he sucked it down. "Just wait until he gets a hold of that MRE," I said, "He might not like us then." The horrible taste of MRE's had been a part of our life for several months now and we had gotten used to it. Dinkelman, Truthan, and Dmytriw were still exhausted from the hump into the city, cursing the Captain for dragging them all the way out there into the middle of the city to find a patch of land.

We rolled passed some kids on the way back to base. They were running for our vehicles. I felt like I was at a parade, throwing candy at them as they scurried to catch up with us.

I wanted to get on the phone when I got back to talk to Angela and tell her everything was going to be alright. I still felt bad I had to go so soon, I wish I could talk to her forever.

When we RTBed I picked up my mail that was backed up for a month or so and then went back to the hooch to hear that Sgt Carr was taking over our platoon. "This is some bullshit!" I heard everyone say. This would mean that since Sgt Jenkins was not our Sergeant and that we probably would have a boring six months ahead of us. I walked in front of everyone watching a movie to use the phone center. I was ready to call it a day. I didn't think anything more could go wrong.

MARCH 30, 2005

There were some changes in our platoon with Sgt Carr as the PL. Vehicles were changed around and things were just not right anymore. The original "high back crew" as we called it; Turner, Cpl Stocker, Dinkelman, Dmytriw, and I were split up to various vehicles. I of course stayed in the high back on the SAW.

What was good was that we had somewhat of a break between shifts, but most of it was spent cleaning up this place, mopping floors, taking out the trash, and of course phone watch. Time was slowing down for me and I think the rest of us. Days seemed to feel like weeks and we didn't care, because we were either too tired to or too un-motivated. Phone centers were shut down again because of another Marine dying from mortar attacks that had impacted several miles outside of our base.

Our reputation as Crazy 8 was getting around Camp Hadithah. A few days earlier Sgt Jenkins dismounted troops into a train station where a man was found spotlighting our vehicles. My VC, Cpl Stocker, took a shot with his ten-power scope he bought out of a U.S. Calvary Catalog. He shot out a spotlight that a suspicious Iraqi man had been holding and sent the guy screaming into the night like a little girl. What we think goes on is that these people spotlight our vehicles, then a few minutes later, relay the signal to another house and it continues down the line until the right people know we are coming and they can hide. Several of us think that is why they replaced our PL because we were being too aggressive and, "stirring up the AO" as one Marine put it. *War isn't like it used to be,* I thought to myself, *not at all.* We were stuck on checkpoints 8&9 beginning at 2000 tonight. We just sit there and watch cars go by. It was definitely not what we hoped to be doing here, especially coming from a combat area like Hit, where if you sat in an area for more than 30 minutes you would be either shot at or mortared.

I dozed off on the hard floors of the high back. We were running one person on guard at all times so we could all get a decent amount of sleep.

MARCH 31, 2005

I jumped from off the floor around 0545 when the vehicles were abruptly started and we moved our POS. I was now in the same vehicle, except Cpl

McNally was in the high back and the people I am close with like Dinkelman, Truthan, and Dmytriw all went to different vehicles. I could tell the changes were getting to everyone when we stopped to do a VCP at 0800. It was very discouraging and a lot of people were yelling at each other. Sgt Jenkins was still bitter about Sgt Carr. I would be too if they changed me to an APL and didn't tell me why. It may have been known, but it wasn't something that highers were telling us.

We rolled up a few vehicles and found nothing out of the ordinary. One family was traveling to Haqlaniyah, a town just east of here. Another two men were traveling to Baghdad by taxi.

The rest of the damn day, they had us sit on checkpoints 8&9 to watch more cars go by. We sat our Humvees right in the middle of what appeared to be a rubble pile of old Iraqi military vehicles that had been shot up by one world power or another several years earlier.

These people are very strange here, especially the truck drivers. Sometime they would get out of their vehicles and run tire drills, get back in and then drive away. We found this especially odd, thinking they may be planting mines. We searched them and found nothing.

When we sit in one place for eighteen straight hours, we never know how much goes on and how little we know about the people around us. I talked with Cpl Stocker mostly about his guns and his family at home. He is from southern Ohio and acts very southern. Cpl McNally mostly talked about his past love relationships. I told him about Angela and how we met. I was tired of eating mostly MRE's and even tired of sleeping. I knew I was bored. Lima Company was launching an offensive in Haqlaniyah to get some of the Muj to come out and fight. They would not come out when 1/23 rolled in with tanks, which is strange, *why didn't we just pull them out of their houses and eradicate them?* Finding the enemy is a little like how it was in Vietnam. It's like finding a needle in a haystack.

MAP 2 was in the area and caught a guy that used to work for the coalition. He was a sheepherder and the Muj offered him 150 USD to load up a van full of 155 rounds, .50 cal ammo, and other weapons to carry into Syria. From what I understand, they had found these weapons in underground bunkers underneath ASP Dulab, an Iraqi ammo dumpsite that was blown up intentionally just a few weeks ago by a civilian defense contractor. From what I've been told and cannot be really proven but, the civilian firm had specific instructions to blow up down to a certain depth into the ground and that was it. After they were completed, they just left, leaving the area open season for the Muj. "They have enough ammo to last a year in this AO," Sgt Williams said. I thought we may find ourselves in all out war soon, but at least we would not have to sit around and watch while the clock laughed at us. At the same time, it was like we were shooting ourselves in the foot and I'm sure we would soon see that the other eight vans out there would build IED's out of the shit they dug out of Dulab and cause a lot of death and destruction.

APRIL 01, 2005

I walked down to the CoC at 0900 to pick up three packages that came for me today. I felt like a kid again on Christmas morning. I almost dropped them walking down the six flights of steps down to my hooch and then opened them all. My brother, parents, and friends of my family all sent them to me. Also, the company I worked for before I left had also sent me a huge box of magazines, literature, and other little things I would probably need.

I spent all day organizing my stuff. My sea bags had a lot of stuff I didn't need anymore so I threw some of it out. I'm glad I had something to do and it made me so happy. I went to the phone center and wrote some thank you emails.

We were supposed to be ready to go out at 1800 to sit at another OP and the plan was the following day to actually do some patrolling. Everyone was getting very angry, including myself, with these checkpoints and we had an idea who kept sending us. Our new slogan that was probably more appropriate was, "keep MAP 8 out of the way."

I got a chance to talk to Angela before we went out again. I was glad to finally talk to her and got a chance to tell her I loved her one more time.

The new vehicle changes had been really bad for some, but it was alright in the high back. I was looking at a Time Magazine today and glanced at some of the photos of military vehicles. *If only they could see what ours looked like.* That night we pulled the same watches as we did before, which gave me four more hours of sleep and then two more hours of sleep after the one hour guard post I had on the gun. Just watching the roads and everyone sleeping, hoping one day I would wake up and it would be the last day in this hellhole.

APRIL 02, 2005

My knees were so cramped up from sleeping on the ground again. Things kicked off at 0530 when we moved our POS to somewhere on Raptors and Phoenix to an area near the city to do VCP's. A few unusual characters got out of one car in western style cloths, obviously coming from Baghdad, a city about the size of NY if not larger. We did a smart thing and brought an interpreter with us, which really lightened things up between the locals and us. I had a feeling some of them were playing stupid with us, pretending not to speak English so they would not have to tell us anything. "No, no English…" they always said.

"Have you seen Jimmy Hoffa?" Cpl Stocker would say. I cracked up laughing at them with one finger on the trigger of my SAW, just waiting for them to make a wrong move.

We then traveled to a few fishing villages with Sammy, our interpreter. He came from Baghdad and wore Marine Cammies, but was a citizen of Iraq. It was funny because he had the same attitude we had about things and we could easily joke with him.

I gave some water and food to the little kids there while they talked to the head of the household. They seemed so innocent and for a minute, I felt sorry for them having to live like they did. The place looked like something out of the National Geographic Magazine. The makeshift building had been constructed out of rocks and wood. Clothes were hanging on the line and boats traveled on the water to fish the lake that a tyrant once controlled.

The search team found ING fatigues hanging in the closet. It turned out that the guy had been coalition some time ago and for whatever reason did not stay in.

We took a run through east village near the 60 northing. Kids lined the streets waiting for us to hand out candy, footballs, and other toys. They are very persistent and after getting several things, still asked for more. There is a constant threat in the villages, so I kept an eye out for suspicious behaviors on rooftops and in alleyways. Bulldog contacted us and tasked us with reconning another area for fuel points this time. Lima Company, just a few hours earlier, launched an assault on Haqlaniyah. We listened on the radio as one Marine was killed and two were injured by an IED attack followed by an ambush. It was a horrifying experience and extremely aggravating sitting there not being able to do anything while our brothers were being killed around us. Around that time, vehicle 2 had problems with its starter and went back to the Dam to fix the problem. It was good to come back for at least an hour and relax in our hooches. Turner had just received an MP3 player in the mail filled with 10GB of rap music. Cpl Stocker and I really could not stand it in the vehicle. His headphones were so loud we could hear them from back where we were sitting. Maybe Iraq was just too quiet.

Just after the vehicle was fixed and news had hit us that Lima took casualties we rolled to the first of two grids to recon the area and provide security. The CoC originally gave us an eight-digit grid, which was supposed to have been just two, four digit grids. So we went to an area just south of Barwanah that looked like the Grand Canyon and got lost just outside of some palm groves where we would have been slaughtered, especially when the offensive was planned specifically to drive Muj out of the cities.

Going on 30 hours outside the wire, we waited for the fuel trucks and then went back to the Dam. I thought of Mexico and my vacation to Cancun before I left the whole way back.

Sgt Carr came in to our room on the first deck and told us we would be carrying gas masks from here on in, because informants had spotted nerve gas in the AO. VX nerve agent was some nasty stuff. If you inhale it your nerves go haywire and you end up going into confusions, eventually breaking your own back and killing yourself.

Crazy 8 reminded me of the book, *"Lord of the Flies"* only because we had our own organization it seemed like, and we could distinguish ourselves from other MAP's. Usually we would not wear rank and always were hostile to everyone. I think that's why so many bad things happen to us, because they are afraid we are going to get violent or out of control. Now that Sgt Carr took over, all of that seemed to have gone away. It was something that the higher ups wanted to see happen and something that I missed dearly.

Glancing at all the cards I hung up on the wall from my fiancée, friends, and family, I let another day of my life slip by.

APRIL 03, 2005

I always enjoyed a day away from the roads and the countless hours of patrolling. Major Catalano told us that the Iraqi Army supposedly was going to take some of the AO over, but out of the 1,000 members only 400 showed up for training. 600 of them deserted. Despite what the media had said to put people at home at ease, this was the way it was. It was less exiting and not as entertaining; it was the truth.

I heard from my dad that the Pope had died at 3:00pm, which was news to me and was rather shocking to say the least. Other than a few promotions, the day was rather uneventful. The Major gave us a no bullshit answer why we were moved down here to Hadithah Dam and what was going on from an Officer's perspective. I always thought the military was like a game of chess. We were moved up here to strengthen the main efforts of Hadithah, Haqlaniyah, and Barwanah. "We are in the fight," the Major said. Hit was an incredibly huge city with well over 200,000 people and couldn't possibly be stabilized with just Kilo Company. With MAP's up here, we could focus on controlling the northern parts of the AO and eventually, if the ING moved in, we could start concentrating on our efforts elsewhere.

Rumor was that by January a new constitutional government would be in place and that troops could begin withdrawing. *I'd like to see it to believe it.* I watched a movie tonight and read some of my books. Getting away for a while in my mind was something I'm sure everyone looks forward to next to getting the hell out of here.

APRIL 04, 2005

Getting in the habit of having regular maintenance days for at least twelve hours at a time wasn't hard to do at all. I tried washing my cloths today by hand in a Hajji washing machine that had a simple motor and turned clothes around without letting any water out. I had to ring them myself. Most of the knobs were broken off and I had to use a hose to fill the basin. Trying to put a months worth of dirty cloths in the small washer wasn't working out. I drug all my sopping wet cloths downstairs and began hanging them out on the balcony to dry them out in the sun.

The Dam was an odd place with its endless flights of steps and corridors that lead to unknown rooms. It looked like something that someone had abandoned years ago without regret.

Tonight we were patrolling the west side of the AO to escort some tracks and tanks into Baghdadi and provide over watch for Lima Company's assault. The line company forced its way across the town like a lynch mob. I was not in a very good mood and felt really sad and depressed. Only a month had gone by and it seemed like time had stood still.

At 1900, we loaded up the vehicles and headed to the west side. Sgt Jenkins had put himself in our high back and moved Cpl McNally somewhere else. More than anyone else in the unit, I had the ultimate respect for Sgt Jenkins because of his experience in Afghanistan and his willingness to lead by example. Here he was a Sergeant sitting right next to me, putting up with the cold like I was, and riding in this death trap on wheels with all the rest of us grunts.

We sat at a nearby intersection until about midnight. We were waiting for a convoy to escort it into Baghdadi. The village was part of our old AO in Hit.

APRIL 05, 2005

Although it was not the most exiting of missions, Major Catalano gave us a motivational speech to boost our moral, "you are in the fight," he always said. I heard a laughing voice say that while I scanned the area with thermals. The idea was to change our TTP's to make the enemy react to us. We sent out dismounts to walk quite a ways down the road and hide to see if the Muj would plant mines and IED's. Intelligence the other day picked up a tip from a local sheepherder that gave the name, time of day worked, and address of a man planting mines in the area. Our command however said they did not have time to deal with this issue and it seemed at least from my perspective that I was helpless in the matter. All of us could have hoped for some classified mission to be going on in the area to take the guy out. Although right now I was starting to think that was bullshit.

Most of the night I was in a haze until about 0400 when I woke up to the usual voice over the radio, "All crazies we're going crazy!" It took us less than an hour to get to Baghdadi. We watched from a cliff that jutted out over the city as Lima Company rolled through. It was interesting to watch things happening from above, again I felt helpless. It was like a video game or a movie. Watching rounds go into buildings and Marines cordoning off traffic. If the insurgents would not come out, I guess we would eventually find them.

Sgt Jenkins and Back fell asleep right away and I was always left to stay awake in the gun. I guess that's what I got for being a SAW gunner. My mind kept wandering and I kept thinking about my job and if I would fulfill my dreams or if I would just be an average person in an average world. *I guess that's how I got here.* I wanted to do something out of the ordinary. The rest of the day, we rolled up a few Hajjis and sat on OP's. We found 4,000 USD on one guy going to buy sheep or so he said. We saw some dogs and tried to feed them some MRE's. They just lounged around lazily in the sun and looked at us like, "What are you doing here?"

Our relief in place was caught up on South Dam Road when they found an IED not far from the Dam entrance. We ended up on checkpoints 8&9 until 0000 that night before we drove back and treated ourselves to sleep. I was so tired but I had to guard the vehicles until 0300. Although the heat from the running Humvee felt good, I just wanted to stretch my legs and stay away from anything moving for a while.

APRIL 06, 2005

I tried to relax again with what time we had left before 1800. No mail again today. I was in a neutral mood and on the edge just before depression. I don't know what the symptoms of that really are. If the signs are being overly sad for two straight weeks or if it is just something that may go away in time, I wasn't sure. It made me happy knowing that Sgt Jenkins was in our vehicle. He had bonded with us since the beginning of Crazy 8.

I got a hold of my parents today after waiting about an hour or two on the sixth deck of the Dam. It was 0300 in the morning in Ohio, but they were still happy to hear from me. My fiancée was half-asleep and she said she was waiting for my surprise. I couldn't wait to see what she thought of what I made for her. It was the only real thing that kept me going.

As always, we filed down to the vehicles at 1800 to stage them for another patrol on the east side of the AO. We had been almost everywhere and things were starting to become a little like Hit, other than the fact that we would never get used to the way things were done here at the Dam. I think it might have been easier if we had started out here, but moving all of a sudden and then trying to adapt again to being constantly screwed with mentally was always a big challenge for me.

We stood in a circle outside the Humvees while Doc Barone led us in prayer. Before we left we hugged one another and it did not matter, nor wasn't awkward because we were the only family we had right now for each other and these were the men we were fighting with.

The mission tonight was just to sit at some more OP's until morning. It sounded easy enough for me. It wasn't a very exiting mission, but thanks to the stories Sgt Jenkins told us for practically the entire night, he had made it worthwhile. He told a story about how everyone thought he was dead. His girlfriend just broke up with him and his brother told his girlfriend that he had been killed in Afghanistan. Sgt Jenkins called his family and let them know if anyone had called to tell them the same thing, so the next thing you know half of Camp Lejeune where he was stationed thought he passed. He said just recently that he ran into someone who still thought he had joined the Army of Angels at Camp Ripper right here in Iraq and how he was very exited to see him. "I'm sure it's not very funny to most of you but that's normally what kind of humor we pass around, and it gets us through no matter what people may think of us when we get home."

That night, a huge sand storm whipped through our vehicle like a hurricane, clouding all visibility and made it extremely cold. I shivered on the floor of the vehicle until I fell asleep.

APRIL 07, 2005

The light came rather late in the morning around 0800 as we began VCP's, pulling Hajjis out of their cars and little white Nissan trucks for several hours. We searched their cars for suspicious paraphernalia or ammo that had been supposedly loaded up from ASP Dulab just weeks ago. A few vans and SUV's were still on the BOLO list after the van MAP 2 pulled over was found loaded down with ammo and future IED ingredients. It was funny because Sgt Jenkins was in charge of searching people. One of many times we pulled people over he made people stand on one foot and then made them put their arms out and then put their arms down. It was a way for us to fuck with people and it was necessary because when looking for trigger men there are certain things you have to look for such as wires and things in the hands or hidden somewhere, often inside of loose clothing.

One guy we searched we asked if he knew English and he said in perfect, fluent English, "I don't speak English, I speak Arabic."

"I'll be watchin' you!" Sgt Jenkins said to him three inches from his face. Another guy pulled some guy out of the trunk of his car. The guy was actually riding in the trunk. He was paralyzed and hobbled along the ground to where we were searching people some ways away from the cars. We stayed far away from vehicles for fear that we would be blown up by parked VBIED's lined with explosives. *There are definitely some weird people here.* Sgt Jenkins asked this one kid what was up with his hair, "No English," he said.

"Oh! It's for the laaaadies isn't it?" Everyone started laughing and we let them go back to their vehicles.

We patrolled through East Village another time today. Sgt Jenkins took the SAW and I walked the rails through the village, which just meant that I would stand by the side of the vehicles to prevent anyone from climbing on them. Kids were swarming all over looking for candy and toys. Friendly faces smiled and hands waved. Cpl Stocker had a full box of candy and we handed out the whole box. We saw kids in what looked like a school and they were yelling for us. They were happy to see us there. In a way, I felt bad for the people having to live in makeshift houses and raise their kids like this, but at the same time, I appreciated my own life at home more than I ever will at this moment. I was glad to be brought up in a great country where I can fully pursue my dreams and express how I feel freely. As we rolled out of the village, a small boy was standing by the dirt road with a white burlap bag. We went over to inspect it cautiously. *It could be an IED or explosives.* "Dog, dog, mista." Just then, he pulled out the puppy from the white bag.

"Wow, he is a tricky fucker!" Cpl Stocker exclaimed.

"I bet you couldn't do that," I told him.

Cpl Stocker held out some jellybeans and a quarter. "Here! For the dog!" He shouted.

The boy looked scared, "you keep!" The dog fell out of the boys hands and Cpl Stocker picked the little dog up. Crazy 8 now had a pet dog and we named him Crazy Beans, because we bought it for some jellybeans and a quarter.

Later on in the afternoon, we did a search on another train station in the area. I was tired of hearing the same thing from these people always saying, "no Ali-Babba in Iraq!"

"Well then why are we here?" I said to Turner. Turner and I always could bitch up a storm while everyone was outside of the vehicle doing searches or raids, we were always the two stuck in the vehicle providing security.

Sgt Jenkins got along with most people in the platoon other than a few people who didn't like his aggressiveness. I felt if he ever left us to go to the sniper platoon that our platoon, would no longer be Crazy 8 or at least not what it was once before we got to Hadithah.

That afternoon we scouted positions for dismounts. We were looking for an area where we could send ground troops to stay hidden and watch the roads to fool the insurgents into thinking we had no vehicles placed on checkpoints. Sitting at another checkpoint until about midnight, our vehicle talked to our relief for a while and then headed back to the Dam. When we got back, we heard the news that mortars hit the Dam near the motor pool, injuring four Marines pretty badly. One Marine lost an arm and others were seriously wounded. For some people that stayed inside the wire, this was no surprise. It came as such as shock to us because I guess we were so far away from the Dam we couldn't hear the impacts. We were rather used to it having been in Hit and witnessing mortars every night almost. This was a reality check for us. No one had any idea what was going on.

APRIL 08, 2005

We had a serialized gear inspection this morning. Marines were scurrying to get ready, a typical morning at the Dam on a tasker day. The Operations Chief planned a schedule that was supposed to give us one day of miscellaneous tasks, a day of maintenance, 24 hours of patrolling, and then one day off which always turned out to be inspection or tasker day. With operations that threw a wrench in the whole schedule and it wasn't always followed that well.

MAP 8 was then assigned to set up VCP's on the Raptors and Phoenix intersection. I brought my books and some care packages full of food and we left shortly after the inspection for a morning of pulling Arabs out of their cars. I thought it would be an ordinary boring day until what happened when we pulled over a rusted out vehicle coming from the village. While searching the vehicle, the team found papers with a map of an intersection with the perfect position to place mines. It was printed on a scuffled old road map written in English with Arab writing all over it. We had to bring the occupants of the vehicle in. There were five males. One guy looked very young and one was very old. The rest of them were around military age. We ended up bringing them to the Dam with tape across their eyes and mouth, for extensive questioning. They smelled funny and it was rather awkward riding with them. Because of what happened at Abu-Ghraib a few months before we got here, I knew that tolerance was very low for unauthorized behavior so I sat and stared at them with a fully loaded weapon in my lap.

Vehicle 1 kept our new dog, putting him on an ISO mat in the back of the Humvee.

When we got back to base, we fed her MRE's. She was so cute. I smiled while I pet her and watched her small tail wag. She just looked at me strangely, rolling over and twitching her leg while I scratched her. It made me happy for a few minutes until I had to go back upstairs to get back to work.

My mom sent me an Easter package and some clothes and food. I was so glad to have such a great mom and dad. I wanted to tell them that right away. Tell them thank you for the care package, and give them the news about the dog that we found, but we were leaving in a few hours and by the time I waited for the phone we would have to leave.

A lot of problems were happening in the MAP and Sgt Jenkins had to talk to the Company Gunnery Sergeant about the situation. I wished for once that they would just leave us alone, let us have fun and talk about what we wanted to and do what we felt like doing. If we got things done and accomplished the mission I don't see why we needed the added stress of inspections and procedures. I was going to go crazy.

Tonight Crazy 8 was supposed to escort some detainees from the holding facility here at the Dam to the Det-Fac at al-Asad Air Base for questioning and eventually imprisonment for a long time. No word on what happened with the Hajjis we detained for the map of the landmines. I am sure though that soon we would hear about it.

I was looking forward to our mission on our day off because I wanted to go to the PX and get some things at al-Asad. The Dam did not have a PX other than the mobile shop that came around once every other week that only sold a few things. The al-Asad PX was huge and had almost anything a Marine could want; magazines, food, electronics, CD's, and video games. I ended up buying myself a coffee maker, some DVD's, and some better letter writing gear.

I watched the sun set while sitting out on the balcony adjacent to our hooch on the first floor while eating some popcorn from my care packages. Thoughts ran through my head and I felt frustrated because I wanted to get back and pursue my life. I felt stuck here and wondered how long it would be until we finally stepped on that plane to go home. I hoped to God I was going through this for a reason and that I would make it back alive.

APRIL 09, 2005 0000-2300

The starter that broke on Crazy 8's first vehicle was fixed around 0000, so we headed out to al-Asad shortly after the repairs were completed. We had to first escort the prisoners onto the 7-ton. There were nine of them in all, three of which we rolled up just the other day for the map. Apparently, two of them also had maps actually drawn on their bodies for locations to where every land mine on South Dam Road was located. Three other Marines and I escorted them out of their holding cell, which consisted of an open area with concrete slabs surrounded by thick razor wire. The prisoners smelled like they had not showered in months or forever for that matter. I grabbed one by the arm as he tried to resist and I tightened my grip. His mouth was duct-taped and goggles were placed over his eyes so he couldn't see where he was. "Get up!" I yelled not knowing any Arabic and I guided him to the 7-ton and had to drag him to where he was going. The man behind me smelled me and came way too close for comfort, "Back off!" I said as I gave him a hard nudge, almost knocking him to his bare feet.

One by one, they got up on the 7-tons until all nine of them were secured and ready for transport. Cpl Leach and Truthan were assigned to stay with them for the ride to al-Asad's Det-Fac. "If they start getting out of hand, butt stroke their ass and if you can't control them and they get out of hand, shoot them," the Sergeant ordered the two Marines. They were lucky they didn't put me up there with them. God only knows what I would have done. There was so much anger to unleash and so little time to do it. For Richardson, who died from a mine blast just outside the Dam and whose boots and rifle now sat in the phone center as a memorial, the four Marines who were injured from the mortar attack, and all the others in Lima Company who got shot at by these bastards daily, these prisoners deserved what they got.

I got back into my vehicle and dozed off for about fifteen minutes until we left. Somehow, I knew we would not be getting any sleep. It was about a two-hour ride to al-Asad. The base somehow reminded me of Neverland because every time we convoyed up there I would always fall asleep and wake up to the lights and sounds of more than 10,000 Marines and Army personnel. We arrived at the Det-Fac around 0300 and dropped off our presents to the guards. "ABU-GHRAIB!" I kept saying to them. The process began with sorting out prisoners and evidence that came with the detainees. A name was called and prisoners eventually spoke up as they sat on the ground shivering. Either they were cold or they were just scared shitless.

I watched them and sneered at them as the guards processed them and took them away one by one. By then it was 0430 after all the forms were filled out. A form had to be filled out for every piece of evidence brought with the prisoners and sworn statement had to be taken by at least two Marines that witnessed the event, plus a digital photo of the prisoner holding the evidence. That guaranteed prison time as long as we had all the above things. If something should be missing, there would be a possibility that the prisoners may have to be set free, and we would see them out there again, on the roadways, planting mines. We wanted to make sure we did the job right the first time.

I was lucky to grab a few minutes of shuteye on the hood of the Humvee before we got morning chow at the chow hall. I was looking forward to some real eggs and breakfast food. Things that we could not enjoy everyday I wanted to make sure I filled up on and took seconds. I ate until I was sick and then somehow wandered over to the phone center on base at around 0630 to call my fiancée. She was at her friend Lorie's house and we talked about her birthday coming up and the things we were going to do when I got home.

I grabbed a few more hours of broken sleep until the PX opened. I needed to pick up my coffee maker and ended up getting a CD and other stuff while I was there.

The rest of the day I was a zombie. We picked up this kid while we were there, Erickson. He had a jacked up tooth and lip, which he later told me was because he smashed it on hard ground after rushing into a position during what sounded like a pretty intense firefight that Lima Company had in Haqlaniyah. He said another guy took a lot of shrapnel after a rocket was fired at their position. "Sounds like you really got into some shit," I said to him as we talked about some of the things we did as a MAP platoon. Patrolling the roads, searching Arabs, and detaining people was not nearly as hard as the line companies humping the ground on a day-to-day basis. I would think just as stressful because of the constant threat that we could at any time die from IED or mine explosions springing up out of nowhere from the hard roads we patrol day in and day out.

On the way back to the Dam around 1400 we pulled over a car on the BOLO list and had a friendly conversation with some welders from the Ministry of Oil, Iraq's socialistic government organization that was the equivalent to our government agencies here except that the government controlled all business and commerce coming in and out of the country.

I was dying to hit the rack and get a shower, but Lima Company had taken over the showers and left them waterless and full of dirt and grime. I decided to skip the shower for tonight or this morning, which ever it was, I was exhausted. I fell asleep and had a very strange dream. I was swimming out in a lake near my house I used to go to often as a kid. Swimming and swimming, I dove under water and a figure appeared to me while I was submerged, before I could recognize it I woke up, out of breath and sweating.

After the ordeal with the detainees, we pushed right through the day. Luckily, we were able to rest a few hours at the Dam until about 1800. We then left on a patrol, out to the west side of the Euphrates River for another 24 hours. I didn't mind it because I knew we would just be sitting on checkpoints and that I could maybe get some sleep if I was lucky. Cpl Stocker started the watch in our vehicle and we took shifts for an hour at a time, giving the

Marines off four hours of sleep before they had to wake up again for another shift of watch.

Since Sgt Jenkins was now permanently kicked out of our platoon for reasons the platoon was unaware of, I had to serve three watches tonight: Once at 0000, 0300, and then again at 0500. Just try for one night setting your alarm three times and repeat that every night for a few months and you may just realize how I felt. I didn't see anything on checkpoints 8&9 the three times that I did have watch other than a few passing cars and some workers at a blacktop factory across the road. That was what was so strange about this country and its people. Blacktop factories all over, but the roads are still worse than some of the interstate highways in Ohio. Other things that were weird; people shit standing up, guys hold hands, Hajjis smile at you after they plant mines, and the class system was so screwed up to where one or two people lived in mansions outside of villages and everyone else was poor. I think Iraq needs a lot of help.

APRIL 10, 2005

It was so boring just sitting at checkpoints 8&9, but it seemed like we knew how to do it best. We relaxed in the sun like we were on a beach without water as we took shifts on the gun every four hours.

Vehicles 3 and 4 were located at checkpoint 9 and received indirect fire, most likely mortars. They spotted four MAM's running into the desert, but were distracted by some DET cord that ran more than 1400m the opposite direction. The MAM's disappeared and our command instructed us to move to the west side of the road rather than sit just 200m to the north on the other side. Honestly, it pissed a lot of people off and it wasn't the first time that calls like this came down from high above. Those things about how Marines are known for hunting down and killing the enemy have, in this case at least, proved untrue.

Following the indirect fire fiasco, we put on our flacks when we heard more IDF, but that was about all we did to stop them. Cpl Stocker was irate when we pulled over a white conversion van. All of a sudden he starts yelling at them, "All of you mother fuckers need to start talking or I'm going to start killing all of you!" We knew somehow that they spoke English, but for some reason only chose to speak Arabic, which was another weird thing about these people. I thought maybe that it had something to do with speaking the language of the infidels.

Our relief, MAP 6, was supposed to come at 2000. I ended up falling asleep and waking up well beyond the time we were supposed to be back at the Dam lying in our comfortable racks, but instead I picked a comfortable spot out on the rough sand and laid there staring into the sky. Cpl Back played his new portable Playstation his wife bought him for $400. He played that thing until the batteries wore out. Finally, waking up four hours after they were supposed to have shown up, we mounted the vehicles and sped off to the Dam.

APRIL 11, 2005 0000

I may have been mistaken for a zombie. Being assigned to vehicle watch not a half an hour after I got back wasn't exactly the end to a great day. I dozed off in the vehicle for a while Turner told me about his life. I think he made the right decision to come to the Marine Corps, but either of us probably never thought we would find ourselves here, clear across the world in a war zone. "I was on my own when I was fourteen," Turner talked on and on.

"I guess I really do take a lot for granted man," I told him holding my eyes open.

"The only real family I have is you guys," Turner said.

"Well we're here for you man, even though you are a bit ghetto," I replied.

"Shut the fuck up dude," Turner yelled as we went up to get the next watch that began at 0200.

Apparently we were on QRF, but little were we told about a classified mission that was going on in the area at the time; a raid on a bomb maker in East Village. All I knew about the men involved was that they were made up of all different branched of service: Army, Navy, Air Force, and Marines, and that they were rankless. It sounded like something of interest to me, although college was always a first priority. I am sure however that the priority list of mine was thrown out the window a few months ago.

We always teased the MAP's that started out here at the Hadithah Dam and weren't part of the Hit crew about having raids. When we first got here they hyped up a huge story about a raid on Barwanah shortly before we got there. The truth was that we thought we were somehow better then everyone here because of the engagement we had with the snipers. Our hard-nosed attitude brought us little friends, but we always had something stupid to joke about that no one else outside of MAP 8 ever understood.

I drank about three cups of coffee and read an article on PTSD in the military and apparently, twenty percent of Marines suffer from it after they return home from the war. Symptoms are emotional numbness, sleep problems, nightmares, and even flash backs. I hoped that nothing would get in the way of my life back home. I was always afraid of that. I finally couldn't take it much longer and fell asleep at 0730.

We are going out again tonight to watch East Village for suspicious activity. Intelligence from S-2 came down that said that some of the Mujahadeen in the area would be in vehicles at the edge of the city and when coalition forces were spotted they would flee to the east side and hightail it across the desert. We made it to our position and our vehicles were set in at 2000. The CO was with us in the first vehicle, he comes out from time to time, and for some reason decided to come out with us this time. We thought it might have had something to do with a confrontation about to happen, but there was no such luck. I can tell you that all of our leaders were trying a little too desperately to follow the book when doing things. I watched most of the night as lights turned on and off in the village and cars lights lit up. It seemed like no one would ever challenge us, rather just attack through mines and mortars. Most of the time the Muj were not even there, it was just someone paid off to dig the hole or someone else to plant the mine. One thing that the Muj make the mistake of doing is coming around after an explosion to see if they killed any Americans and that's when we usually have the most luck killing those bastards.

I did not get much sleep at all tonight, only a few hours. I am still depressed and feel like getting out of here is still a world away. I slept on the hard ground with a Gore-Tex draped over me to cover the sand and cold wind. If they decided to attack us, I was always ready to spring into action.

APRIL 12, 2005

As soon as the sun rose over the small village, Turner, Back, Cpl Stocker, and I raced to put our gear on before the vehicle started moving. I stumbled around trying to get my boots on, still confused and heavy eyed. Just then the radio blasted its orders over the squawk box and another day started itself. Crazy 8 went crazy and we headed back to the Dam to pick up 25 hot tray breakfasts for the platoon and a translator named Todd.

We did not stay at the Dam more than a half and hour, just loaded up the chow and the terp and headed back to our POS for vehicle checkpoints. Todd was a very likeable person. He was an Iraqi from Baghdad who was being paid to help us interpret what people are saying, so we can eventually build trust with the citizens of this new free nation. He was a businessman and always tried to get us to buy alcohol or illegal DVD's packaged even before they came out into the theaters in the U.S. I asked Todd, "How do you write this saying for me in Arabic?" I pulled out a paper and wrote down, "WARRIOR OF GOD." I wanted to know because I believe that's why I am here, as a test of faith, or at least part of the reason. God would not be disappointed with me.

We went to do some VCP's and then went into east village. Cpl Stocker brought a huge bag of candy and toys for the nagging kids that always swarmed over the vehicles and never gave up. "Bien, Bien," they would always say. I later found out they were asking me for a pen for writing. It looked like they were in school as we sat across from the other building. Cpl Stocker kicked a soccer ball to them and I sat and watched the roof tops for enemies. A very old man approached our vehicle. As usual, it was just Turner and I complaining to each other when we both noticed him at the same time. He approached our vehicle while hunched over. His gnarled extremities and warn, wrinkled face indicated he had survived three lifetimes worth of war. He had quite possibly the dirtiest teeth I had ever seen. He spoke one word and all he knew how to say was "Marines." He bowed to us as Turner gave him a smoke. By the look of his teeth and raspy voice, it looked like he had nothing to lose.

We didn't stay in the village long before we were back on the road. We headed back to the Dam for more chow. We must have done something good because we were never fed as much as we were over the past day. It may have had something to do with the CO being with us for that short time near the village. It was certainly better than those eggs we had for breakfast. We had some kind of veggie burger for dinner, they weren't McDonalds, but they weren't half-bad. I think that may have been the only time I had something good to say. Turner couldn't believe it and he had to write it down. "Are you Okay, Wojtecki?" he joked with me. I didn't pay attention; I just shoved my face full of burger and stared at the sun that filled the sky as it fell into the vast horizon.

We spent the rest of the night at OP's watching the villages for signs of trouble. It seemed like the Muj were smarter or just completely stupid. There was no sign of anything until about 2200 when we were relieved by the next MAP up for their shift of OP's. I was so tired on our way back to the Dam. It took me forever to get up those steps. I dragged my body into our hooch and racked out.

11

APRIL 13, 2005

MAP 5 took a trip to FOB Hit today so we skipped straight to a maintenance day. I rolled out of bed late as always and went down to the Porta-Johns to do my business. I watched a movie and sent emails on the Internet. There wasn't much to do other than miss everyone back home and feel sorry for myself.

Around 1600 I went on CoC watch with a few books that I brought home to study from. I was reading my book when all of a sudden Major Catalano comes in and discusses something with the Gunny. I couldn't tell what he was saying. I heard broken words over the COM sitting on the table next to me. A phone call came from Hit for the Major and I let him know. It was Lt Haunty who was informed by Major Catalano that Corporal Lindemuth was seriously injured and he didn't know if he would make it or not. He had been around the motor pool around the FOB when a mortar round struck the ground next to him sending shrapnel in his direction. His sucking chest wounds put him in serious condition and he was flown to al-Asad for surgery. The COM messages kept coming over the radio,

"Jesus God! Oh God! He's not breathing! Shit!" The Major quickly silenced the radio. Those words lingered with me and finally set in. The man that had so much to tell me, that accompanied me from the drill center, to training, and into combat, was now dead. The reality hurt and I was about to be sick. I couldn't read or do anything so I sat there. All of us dropped what we were doing, Officer or enlisted, stood together in a circle, and prayed together. I wasn't sure what to do so I sat back down with a look of fear and sadness on my face. The Major noticed me sitting there and ordered me to go back to my room.

Not long after my good friend Morgan, the guy I could always talk business with was hit just outside of Checkpoint 9 shortly after the mortar attack. He was hit with shrapnel. An IED had exploded not 50 feet from his vehicle. Luckily, he would be okay and would be better by the end of the week. Fortunately, the piece of shrapnel, the Doc said, missed his jugular vein by a few centimeters.

Something had to be done about this. I felt helpless and alone. I though about my friend and team leader Cpl Lindemuth's Fiancée was also planning to join the Marines as an Officer. I couldn't imagine how she would feel when they told her. I couldn't contain myself, but somehow I held my feelings in. There was no shoulder around to cry on, no one to comfort me. A thousand thoughts ran through my head about home, Angela, school, and work. *Could something like this soon happen to me?* I don't think any of us knew when our time was. I couldn't get over the fact that someone that I was so close to had just been taken from us.

Cpl Lindemuth was a good Marine. He served his country proudly. I believe he died so that you and I could enjoy our freedoms so that terrorists do not endanger the lives of others. I'm not sure how to describe what I felt, but it was very painful.

I went out on patrol that night with contempt in my heart and hate for this fucking country and its people. There was some regret for some time. *If we were still at FOB Hit, would Cpl Lindemuth still be alive?* I went out into the field thinking I would some how find vengeance. Sgt Carr organized two dismount teams for tonight's evolution. Osberg (the new guy) took my SAW and I stayed in the vehicle. The idea was to punch out squad-sized elements to checkpoints 8&9 so that the Muj would think that we had abandoned our post. It seemed like the Hajji's had enough ammo and were launching an offensive against us. I wanted to kill them more than anything right now, at least for my old team leader's sake.

The dismount team punched out about a click away from our position and hid themselves in an abandoned building until about 0230 the next morning. Vehicles 1 and 2 stayed about 30m apart and set up cammie netting over our vehicles. I just kept thinking how stupid this was and why we had to have a cammie net over our vehicle. *Oh my God no one will ever see us now*, I thought to myself. If one of those fuckers decided to plant an IED or mine on Raptors heading into the base we would know about it.

It was kind of a relief tonight not having any NCO's in the vehicles to scream at me and bark orders. Dmytriw had come back to our vehicle temporarily and we joked around with him for most of the night about utopian societies as well as some other weird stories. At least it was something to keep my mind off death.

APRIL 14, 2005 0000

Two people in the vehicle were supposed to be awake at all times to watch and monitor the COM. Somehow later that night only one person stayed up and the other two of us at least got three hours of broken sleep. At about 0330, Turner sprang from his mattress and started flipping out, "There's something on me!" he shouted, letting just about everyone near our position know where we were. He started padding his uniform down like it was on fire. Just then I felt something crawl on me and then scamper away. No one knew what it was. Dan started laughing historically. I thought that maybe it was some kind of mouse that got in our vehicle after someone spilled food all over the Humvee floor. The rest of the morning it felt like there were things crawling on me. I was too tired to even care. Here we were padding ourselves down in the middle of the desert with a cammie net draped over our vehicle. The enemy probably saw us and laughed.

We all woke up around 0900 to a conversation with MAP 2. They evidently hit another IED and took a casualty. I felt helpless again. These people were good friends, team leaders, and people I could talk to and trust, and they were being maimed by a cowardly enemy that blends itself into the population and hardly ever stays and fights.

APRIL 15, 2005

We were on QRF this morning, which means if they wanted us for something, they could use us. We were taking a huge amount of indirect fire in the AO, so the CO has tasked all the mortarmen with setting up our positions near the motor pool and registering into the palm groves. There were no exiting explosions to be heard because we were firing illume missions for the sake of the citizens who had nothing to do with the Muj (or so they said). I wondered how long we would be firing illumes before we broke out high explosive rounds.

I sat there and watched Dan throw rocks at beetles in our mortar position, which was just a flat area built up by some sand bags and some more cammie netting. It was as if someone in supply had ordered an over abundance of the netting, because we were told to use it for almost everything. I am surprised they didn't drape the shitters with the stuff. We waited for check fires for 40 minutes at a time, which meant just waiting while the FDC plotted grids and punched numbers into simple formulas to come up with a direction in mils for us to put on the gun before firing. Tonight they were going to fire some HE rounds at the pre-planned targets using classified counter battery radar devices, which was not very accurate but apparently is the only thing we had against the Muj and their mortars.

That night I served two vehicle watches, one at 0300 and one at 0600. I decided I was going to take a shower after I was done. It felt good not being rushed and being all alone with no one standing around me. It's amazing how much I appreciated little things; warm relaxing water on my face, the sun sets, or even a good meal. I felt like a new man. One thing I liked about living at Hadithah is that I didn't have to wear my flack and Kevlar to the shower room, I guess that's why I take more of them now, I am up to one per week compared to three per month.

APRIL 16, 2005 0000

The impact areas of the rounds we fired last night landed on the southern end of Barwanah and MAP 8 was tasked with finding where they impacted for a reference point. This meant trucking all four vehicles over the rockiest terrain I have ever seen.

We heard rounds land from the enemy while driving towards our objective, not far from Raptors and Phoenix. It was like a bright show that lit up the sky. I was nearly falling asleep and was knocked awake by the loud explosions that most certainly have a unique sound. Things sound different when they might quite possibly end your life.

Our Sergeant had us on a wild goose chase, probing through the desert. Every bump pissed me off even more and made me angry at the world. I wondered why we hadn't killed anyone yet, why we hadn't gotten vengeance for my close friend. We almost drove off a cliff a few times looking for these impact areas in an area that was quite possibly a prime ambush point for the Muj, a low point between two rocky peaks.

The palm leaves in the large grove whipped violently as an upcoming windstorm swept through. Our dismounts got out at the exact grid coordinates that Bulldog gave us and swept the area on line in pitch black with NVG's on. If I were the owner of the house that we were in the back yard of that night, I would have thought I was being invaded.

Sgt Carr promised us we would be going out to look for these legendary impacts again in the near future. The plan was to sit and watch the area where the last two IED's were placed in the exact same location to see if anyone was dumb enough to plant one again and receive a few hundred rounds from the .50 cal.

Around 0300 Vehicle 1 had been having problems with its drive shaft so it was taken back to the Dam to be looked at. Another vehicle was then traded for the broken one and brought back out to our position. We sat at the danger area until morning, which by the time we got back from playing the vehicle swap game, turned out to be only three hours.

Speeding down the east side to the Dam again to pick up the terp was a rough ride. Turner said we were only going 30MPH, but that was such a load of shit.

Chow was really good this morning. Steak, eggs, and hash browns filled my stomach and almost made my sleep deprivation non-existent. These patrols seemed to be getting longer and longer. Maybe they couldn't stop the clock, but they sure could make one day last and eternity.

Our terp's name was Ochmed and he was a Sunni Muslim from Baghdad. He accompanied us to Barwanah to look for the impacts, which became secondary to seeing who was doing the firing and to attempt to pick a fight with them by getting them to shoot at us, which was the only way (according to the rules of engagement) that we could fire back at them. Ochmed rode in the high back with us and this time we took a shorter route to what once took us four hours the previous night when we wondered around aimlessly with little to no visibility. Not to mention a bumpy ride, I sliced part of my finger on my machine gun, that being the second time I have done that this deployment.

Sweeping through the barley fields on foot looked like something directly from the Vietnam War. Some woman got mad at us for destroying her crops. In a matter of hours, we had confiscated three AK's from a guy who lied to us and said he did not have any weapons in his house before we proceeded to search it and find them. It seemed like we were enraging everyone today.

We ate chow in the mouth of a cave burrowed into the side of a cliff, which later turned out to be an impact from some kind of tank that probably had rolled through here during the first Gulf War. We went off road again after the MRE lunch and headed towards the city of Barwanah. A lot of "remember that raid on Barwanah?" jokes came up and never seemed to get old with us. We were a rowdy bunch of kids needing desperately to kill something. Our rifles almost begged to be fired. We had not fired them in so long it was getting to the point where some Marines would just tape the tops of their 16's and just never clean them, which was a sin in the Marine Corps. I hope that we could break the tape from our barrels today and get someone to shoot at us.

Vehicle 1 stopped and veered to the left side of the road. They had spotted an IED as the radio transmission came through. I saw it too, but I remembered what they said about what was obvious was probably a cover for the real IED hidden somewhere in the vicinity. The dirt behind the rubble in the round struck me as odd and I radioed it in. Stocker was crazy enough to walk up on it to inspect it. "He's gunna get himself killed," I said aloud for Turner to hear me. We both watched him pull some kind of wire from the ground and follow it back to what looked like a washer timer. That was the fastest I think I have ever seen Cpl Stocker run before. We were stuck on an IED and had to call EOD to come all the way from al-Asad to come out here and detonate it. It would take God only knows how long. Turner and I both knew we would be here for at least Three hours, so we made ourselves comfortable.

Ochmed got out of the vehicle and started talking with some of the people in the general area, who mostly worked for the Ministry of Oil and were supposed to be guarding this stretch of roadway. "You are not doing your job, you are fired! Go home!" Ochmed screamed at them in Arabic. That really made the man living in the tent mad, so he just got up and started walking towards the city. I thought it was funny and couldn't stop laughing.

We must have sat there for four or five hours waiting for EOD while Ochmed talked to us about his life in Iraq. "Baghdad," he said, "is a lot like cities in the U.S." Ochmed talked about when Hussein was in power. Uday and Kusay used to shoot people at soccer / football games for not scoring and were very twisted individuals. He said that Saddam would tell his people that the U.S. was scared of his name and that we would fall at this right hand. Our biggest problem was that the U.S. disbanded the Republican Guard, which was Iraq's main source of employment. Iraq's army was four million strong, Ochmed said, and was the main source of income for Iraqis as well. "It was America's fault," he said. A lot of the insurgency also came from foreign fighters paying these poor, jobless Iraqis to do the dirty work for them, like plant IED's. Ochmed told us he voted in the elections and said that he is very grateful to the U.S. for liberating his country.

There was a loud thud and an explosion crashed not 30 meters from our vehicle, "we are taking IDF!" a loud voice said over the radio.

"Shit!" I yelled as I scurried for my flack and kevlar just as three more rounds impacted almost in the same area near our vehicle. "Let's get the fuck out of here!" I screamed from back of the open scantly armored high back. Two more seconds and we were on the road. The IED was left behind, the mission was aborted, and we quickly RTBed.

When we got back, I got on the Internet. Just then, I had four people walk by me and tell me we were going out again in an hour to drop off the battalion surgeon at the 55 northing near al-Asad airbase. I wished it would just end right now, but it just kept getting worse. I almost lunged myself through the computer monitor as I finished writing a quick email to my fiancée. I was very tired and needed to rest, with an hour between the roadway and me.

APRIL 17, 2005

It was such a routine day today. We staged the vehicles and prepared to sit on checkpoints and watch the intersections for 24 hours. Cpl Leachman, the guy I sat on watch with at SASO training in California was switched out of vehicle 1 for Osberg and moved to our high back. Vehicle 2 moved from CP 8 to an area close to the Phoenix / South Dam intersection. We were ordered to watch it and make sure that no one stopped for any reason or else they would be littered with machine gun fire. For six or seven hours until 2200, we sat there and watched. Cpl Leachman got along well with Cpl Stocker and Back, because they were all rednecks. They had an hour conversation about hay bailing and the 4-H club when they were younger. This all seemed foreign to Turner and me. Turner was from the inner city and I was from suburbia. It was fun picking on them and they picked on us because we never hunted or lived on a farm. I wanted to move to a big city some day and start a great life there. No matter what though, we were still in this ordeal together and managed to live with each other. We were out on patrol so much we could very well call our vehicles home because we were there more than we were back at the base.

I caught myself again drifting into daydreams and thinking about being with my sweet heart that I left behind. *I really hope this gets more interesting.*

APRIL 18, 2005 0000

We were on the oddest of schedules and I'm not sure how we got to this point, where going out on patrol lasted forever and being at the Dam for only a few hours. I slept until the normal commotion woke me up around 1200. Being half-asleep, I could overhear some Marines talking about the fact that we had a class on heat casualties at 1300. It was over maintenance today. Supposedly, when in a combat zone, all bullshit was supposed to stop, but it didn't seem like that here, seeing as every time I blinked I was on some type of watch or working party. I guess I was just exhausted from all the extra duty that MAP 8 was pulling when we were not out on patrol.

I ran into Cpl Ickes in the phone center who talked about Cpl Lindemuth's memorial service. We all were to attend and it would be like a roll call, except when they called Cpl Lindemuth's name, no one would answer and then a single bayonet of Lindemuth's rifle would be placed upright into some sandbags to remember him. His kevlar would be placed on top of the butt stock and his dog tags draped over the top. My fiancée and the people back home also got word of his death and they were pretty worried. I told her to be strong and not to worry about me, that I would be fine and come home safe to her.

Word got around base that they were putting a permanent PX on the seventh deck, so I went to check it out for myself. It was on the Azerbaijani side of the Dam where the Russians lived and worked. We had our side and they had theirs. It was amazing though how every time chow was served I always saw more of them gathered in line waiting to choke themselves on some of our great food. A few odds and ends were there for sale at the PX and shoved up in the little room next to the showers. Several Marines bought tons of food as if they had starved and somehow got to eat for the very first time. It was nice to have around and I guess everyone wasn't as lucky as I was to receive care packages every other day in the mail.

At 1300, Doc had prepared a heat casualty class for all of us, as very soon it would be getting in the 100's during the daytime. They say that our only mechanism against heat stroke is when our body sweats moisture. If we do not drink enough water we may find ourselves unconscious and even in a coma. Of course, there is the infamous "Silver Bullet," which is a rectal thermometer that measures the body's core temperature in the event of a heat case. No one wanted to get it up the butt with the Silver Bullet, so we all drank plenty of water.

About half way through the class, a loud "BOOM!" shook the Dam followed by another loud boom. "All mortarmen man their tubes!" the CO exclaimed. We all ran down to our positions next to the motor pool and were ready to fire in two minutes. Our enemy was getting closer and the mortaring seemed quite frequent now more than ever. The two rounds landed a little left of the Dam. The grid was not very accurate so there was an immediate stand down and we were placed on QRF until further notice.

I brushed off the fact that the threat was still real and at any time, we could be hit with an attack. I was still pretty weary and decided to take another nap until chow.

Something told me I should run up and get chow, but instead of eating it on the seventh deck like I always do day in and day out, I decided to take it downstairs with me and eat it. That probably saved my life because as I was eating chow in the room, two more very loud explosions shook the Dam. This time the impacts were right in the middle of the seventh deck balcony, "Oh thank you God, I'm still alive!"

Second platoon was in charge of the mortar tubes. We fired six HE rounds this time, all hitting on target and supposedly destroying a hidden sunk in base plate for an enemy mortar system somewhere in the palm groves across the Euphrates. Everyone from all the decks on the base were on their balconies cheering, "Yea! Get those fuckers, OORAHH!" and then back to silence. Wind picked up and it seemed like our lives had never been threatened. It kind of reminded me of Hit.

Tonight we were tasked with manning checkpoints 8&9. I was one of the dismounts this time with the SAW. We were to punch out in an abandoned building and hide out, just waiting for someone to stop and plant a mine or do something stupid and then we would take care of business. We arrived at our drop-off point somewhere around 2330 and were set in. It was just Cpl Stocker, Cpl Leachman, and me.

APRIL 19, 2005 0000

Everything seemed surreal as I got out of the Humvee. It was like that one movie when the main character finally finds out that the movie is actually really happening. We were told to keep silent, which is very difficult to do with packs, gear, and rifle on. We ran a two on two off shift between the COM guy Perry, The VC Cpl Stocker, and our new hillbilly friend Cpl Leachman.

In the broken down building glass was shattered everywhere and trash was lying all around. We sat and watched the desert out of one of the broken out windows with our thermal sights as things around us moved and never acknowledged that we existed. A coyote scrapped around for food. Ants ran up my pant legs and all over my body. I thought I was going to be sick. All of a sudden, I heard seven loud booms off in the distance and lights flashing in the sky from the explosions. We found out over the radio that they all had impacted the Dam. It echoed across the desolate landscape and broke the silence that we sought so hard to preserve.

My dreams kept getting even more bizarre with each two-hour period that I would try to fall asleep on the concrete floor. For the entire day, we observed inside the abandoned building. Some kid's toys were scattered about, writing was drawn on the wall in Arabic letters, and the broken out windows were the only things inside. I saw a car stop for a few seconds on the side of the road and I was ready to pull the trigger. It was obvious they were up to no good. Just then, the car sped away before I could fire off a single kill shot. It wouldn't be the first time I had someone in my sights. I was told to hold off on pulling the trigger. Cpl Stocker got on the radio with Crazy 1 actual (our Patrol leader) to instruct him to pull over the car we just came close to blowing away and see what they were up to.

More silence for eight more hours. I ate an MRE and stared out at South Dam Road as the sand kicked up from the heavy winds and a storm brewed outside. MAP 6 stopped right in front of our POS around 2000 and killed our only chance of catching anyone doing wrong. They had some vehicle problems, didn't know we were there, and just stopped to call for backup.

One guy in the second gun pointed his machine gun in my direction and at that point, I thought I was going to piss myself. "Make sure you let MAP 6 know we are out here!" Cpl Stocker yelled at PFC Perry to radio in the transmission.

Fifteen minutes later, we were on our way back to the Dam. I felt so dirty from laying in filth and broken glass, not to mention a few ants were still crawling on me. Dirt and sand had blown up into my face during the sandstorm and got into my hair. I was covered in it. I had to get a shower right away.

After a cold shower, I sat on the balcony at 0300 looking out at the stars and wondered where my life was. It felt so good to actually fall asleep for more than two hours.

APRIL 20, 2005 QRF

I did not want to get up this morning. It was 0900. MAP 8 was on QRF today, which meant most of the mortarmen were to be down at the pits filling sand bags to fortify our positions. The Sergeants were laying in the guns using the celestial sight method, which uses the direction from the stars to sight in the guns. The reason they had to use this method was because a lay by compass method would not work because of the high voltage power lines over head and the extreme amounts of metal and iron from the Dam screwed up the compass readings.

I must have filled 30 or 40 sandbags today. The hot sun crept up from across the Euphrates and baked the sand outside of the wire where we were digging. I hated dust and absolutely detested senseless manual labor. While we were working, I heard some talk and rumors that our reactivation was not going to be until 2008. I was going to be out of the Corps by then and it made my digging just a little bit easier knowing that. Who knows, it was just a rumor, but I hoped to God that this time the rumor was true, not that we were getting activated again, but that it wasn't going to happen for another two years after we got back from this paradise. It seemed funny that this was already a topic of discussion and we had not even finished our first tour here.

Dan was helping Morgan and me with sand bags. It is more difficult than it sounds because one person has to fill sand while the other holds the bag and ties the string on the burlap bag so the sand won't spill out. I think Dan and I screwed it up a few times by filling the bags inside out, which at that point they had to be refilled the correct way. It was just weird digging and talking about our last years' returns on our stock funds. Two trucks filled sandbags three times and we stacked them neck high until it was almost ridiculous to have a mortar position with this many sand bags. Dan and I eventually found a way to sneak off to our room to avoid any more of this frivolous work. I bet Dan ten bucks we would be tearing down the pits in less than two weeks, and so far, Dan was making me a very rich man with these repeated bets.

I needed sleep, but there was a movie on and I couldn't stop myself from watching it. A few hours went by and I ate some of the things out of my care packages and drifted slowly off.

I pulled my sleeping bag from my head, as the QRF phone in our room began to ring with its loud obnoxious beeping that would drive a normal person up a wall. This could mean two things: Gunny needed you to run and get someone for him, or we were being called out on QRF. It turned out to be that MAP 6 was taking heavy fire and needed backup. Crazy 8 was up again.

We ran to our Humvees. I quickly grabbed my AP brush and began hastily cleaning my M249. Within seconds, we were up and running. Speeding across the Dam, we headed to the west side towards Hadithah. On the way there, we must have passed seven or eight AAV's headed towards the city to support the engagement. Passing checkpoints 8&9 where we sat countless numbers of times before we turned onto Haqlaniyah Road. MAP 6 was caught up in small arms and RPG fire for close to an hour before the call came in for backup. We slowed down on Haqlaniyah Road to a slow crawl and everything went into slow motion. Two guys on a rooftop in white robes and one in orange robes appeared out of nowhere and then ducked behind a wall. An explosion from next to vehicle 1 shook the ground around us. It wasn't even twenty feet in front of us. Rocks and shrapnel whipped everywhere around us. I could here them whipping through the air over my head. It was like a movie playing. An IED had exploded in front of us. I couldn't think or could hardly breathe because the explosion had kicked up so much dust. "Holy Shit!" I managed to get out as I ducked behind the canvas top of the Humvee. "Is everyone ok?" I shouted. There were no words to describe what I felt like, but I was glad I could still feel my legs and arms. The IED was buried deep into the rock pile next to us so the rocks absorbed most of the explosion and shrapnel. The two fuckers on the top of the roof were nowhere to be found. I reached my SAW around and aimed it at the building where the men were and started opening fire. I was still a little shook up from the blast, but I was ready to empty an entire box of ammo into the village ahead of us. Ever since we left FOB Hit, I had been saving up rounds and now had over 3,000 that rested underneath the seats of the scantly clad high back. Dan and Back had their M-16's and fired as well. All of a sudden I heard the sound of the Mod Dues / .50 cal open fire on the building. I continued firing for what seemed like an eternity until my barrel turned hot. Cobra helicopters flew overhead. They saw what we were shooting at and opened fire with their 25mm three-barrel mini-guns. If anyone was in that building, they were most certainly dead. I brushed off the empty links and machine gun shells off the top of the high back and continued firing. God must have been with us at this very moment. I reached down and felt the St. Michael metal that hung around my neck.

We sat in the high back holding our position in anticipation of another engagement. My heart was racing a mile a minute. 40 minutes went by, then an hour. An RPG fired from a nearby white building and we watched as MAP 6's TOW vehicle backed up from the building and prepared to fire. The blast from the TOW blew a huge hold in the side of the house, killing everything inside. The air Officer in the first vehicle got out and started rambling over the radio to the F-15's at al-Asad. He began walking them on to the building in front of us still suspected to have the triggermen that set off the IED just a few feet from us. They were planning to drop a JDAM on the building. All the while, we had been sitting here in our vehicles watching and observing to see if the man in orange would show his face and come out from the now demolished building. We may have killed him with the TOW missile, but no one knew and we were not so quick to assume. I saw flashes of orange and the figure disappeared behind a group of women and children. He knew what he was doing. Air was now cancelled due to the winds and not having positive identification on the target.

That night we sat and blocked egress routes on Haqlaniyah road out of the city. No one would get in or out as long as we were there. Our six-day operation had been kicked off early.

12

APRIL 21-23, 2005 OPERATION RIVER FLUSH

MAP 8's objective was to support Lima Company as they pushed through Haqlaniyah and eventually up into Hadithah. As a MAP, we were ordered to help cordon off the city and then push forward into the city with our heavy weapons as support.

So far, we have been sitting on the outer edge of the city listening to gunfire and constant explosions that won't let up. A company of tanks rolled in last night at about 0300 and they supported the line companies by showing force. We ran two and a half hour on three hour off watches to look for insurgents that attempted to flee from the battle. Since the operation kicked off early, plans were rather unorganized and the word was we would now be staying out here for somewhere around ten to twelve days.

Some people had compared the tactics used in this operation as those similar to Fallujah, the house-to-house fighting and clearing were similar to those of Charlie Company 1/23 that we relieved just a few months ago. Just a day earlier, Aljazeera reported the "Besieged Marines" were accompanied by the ING and that the insurgents had executed thirteen of the Iraqi National Guard in the city. This news caused riots to break out in the city of Hadithah and surrounding areas. Fox News supposedly was going to be there and a Lieutenant Colonel retired reporter was going to report on the operation, although I think that the hostile environment we were in prevented him from doing so.

Dan, Perry, Cpl Leachman, Cpl Back, and I sat in the back of the high back in 120 degree smoldering heat on the edge of the city. A prayer call sounded five times a day. "Allaaaaaaaa Achbar!" or "God is great!" the man shouts over the crude speaker in Arabic. Women hang out their laundry as tanks and Lima Company sweep into the city.

3/25 had to pull back on the 22nd because it was a Muslim holiday, Muhammad's birthday. We were prevented from acting at full force for political and media reasons. Because we acted so early, the insurgency had moved further north and the Major operations involving the line companies pulled out of the city. Another classified mission went on that night to hit some of the higher valued targets based off top-secret intelligence from the CIA. We were all anxious to get some action or at least move into the city with our Humvee into the city and kill some people. We were called Crazy 8 for a reason.

I ended up falling asleep under the Humvee for a few hours. It was the only place we had shade and it was rather cool. The arid weather is hot in direct sunlight and can send you into heat stroke in no time. The heat was getting really bad and it was messing with my head. It as good to get some sleep to make up for last night, but things all became too real when we linked up with Tinian to re-supply. As we drove our vehicle down Haqlaniyah Road, three people running inside the K-3 oil refinery fired an RPG directly at us and then scattered. It may have missed us by a few feet if that. It was another close call with death. I wondered how many more chances we had to live.

The one thing that the operation taught me was that the insurgent threat was real, that they were a bunch of cowards and had taken advantage of people's freedom for long enough. It was good that we got to show our presence and it felt good to shoot something.

Gunny P rode with us the morning of the 23rd to get breakfast at al-Asad. As usual, Dan complained about almost everything and how the operation was compromised. It was good to be alive though. That was something he couldn't argue about with me.

Mid afternoon came around and we returned to base marking the end of the operation. I got on the phone and talked to Angela who was really sad and hadn't talked to me in a while. I told her not to worry and I would be coming home in just a few short months. She said she wrote a letter to the President about my deployment and how they should send us all home. She told me about what was going on at home and how North Korea had plans for a nuclear program, which was scary. Somehow, I knew everything would be okay and I held onto the dreams I had about coming home to her. I always imagine Angela standing on the runway and me get off the plane and run to her. She grabs me in her arms and we kiss. Everything is perfect, we get married, and live happily ever after.

Our day off was shortened to about twelve hours. We were going back out to the west side to relieve one of the MAP's that had been sitting out on checkpoints during the whole operation.

Today I hung up the cards from people at home sent me and posters of my future job over my cot where I only spent maybe eight hours out of the week sleeping.

If you have ever been somewhere for an extended period of time somehow you take a picture in your mind of what life was like back home and it stays still for you, but can become faded. In some way, I hoped that the picture I still had of my life stayed the same and for once in my life, I could enjoy happiness. I cried today for the first time. It was good to know that my feelings were still there and that I had not become lifeless and numb.

APRIL 24, 2005 MEMORIAL

A dust storm kicked up desert into the open high back, as I stayed awake on watch. It was impossible to see anything past the road or even past my arm if I held it out in front of me. Iraq now seemed more desolate than it had ever been.

MAP 7 rolled up to relieve us from Checkpoint 9. We were going to attend Cpl Lindemuth's funeral ceremony. Our vehicles rushed through the dust storm, passing traffic on the left side of the road. We arrived on the tenth deck of the Dam to form up right behind the sniper platoon and we were told to do what we were told and follow the commands of the First Sergeant once the ceremony began.

Everything still seemed like a movie. The First Sergeant said a few words up at the podium and the Chaplin read a short prayer. One of Cpl Lindemuth's best friends told us about how he always used to make us laugh with his ridiculous aviator sunglasses. I remembered him always making me laugh when I was in his platoon. His call sign was "ICEMAN" and he always joked with us about hillbillies and white trash people. He could always motivate me no matter how hard the task.

I stood up on the tenth deck in front of the battalion to say a prayer for Cpl Michael Lindemuth in front of his boots, Kevlar, dog tags, and rifle, a symbol to memorialize the fallen. I felt helpless. I took off my kevlar, pulled out the shell from my first firefight in Hit when he was still with us and laid it next to the lifeless memorial. Tears poured from my eyes.

I tried to be tough as I made my way to the edge of the Dam and watched the waves crash up against the concrete walls. *Why did this have to happen?* I knew God had a purpose for everything but wondered why Mike had to die. He was walking around the motor pool next to where MAP 8 used to stay, like we always used to do when we were there with him.

I thought about all the things he told me that I wrote down. He had already served a tour of Iraq, but he knew he had a purpose in this war and voluntarily came to support us. Cpl Lindemuth was a friend, comrade, team leader, and part of our unit of Weapons Company 3/25.

Final Farewell to Cpl Michael
B. Lindimuth
Rest In Peace 1978-2005
"you will always Be In our
hearts, Semper Fidelis"

We spent a few minutes in reflection and then headed back to checkpoints 8&9. 3/2 was at the Dam along with Kilo Company and with Iraqi Freedom Guard from FOB Hit. They were getting ready to finish what we started on April 26, although I believe they are going to cordon off Hadithah and rush into Barwanah, since the insurgents knew we would try to strike again in Haqlaniyah. I had no doubt we would probably be supporting that operation. We waited patiently for nothing on CP 8&9. I listened to country music and watched the dirt fly up across the desert. I think everyone is anxious to "get some" and kill the enemy, although no matter how many we killed we could make up for the death of a Marine. Killing a few Insurgents would be a good start.

APRIL 25, 2005

It was unbelievable suddenly having this much time off during a major operation. I sat on watch listening to other MAP's roll out of the Dam headed for the city. Word had come down today that they had taken more mass casualties in Hit today and that eleven Marines were seriously injured. It seemed like something thought to be a secondary objective by higher command could have produced so much death. My friend was gone and there was no bringing him back.

I slept in, thinking that the more I slept, the less I would have to actually be here. We were still in the fight but were now sitting on the sidelines. We received more news from Hit. Word was that Conjemi, one of the machine gunners in our old original second platoon got his first kill. He had used ROE's. The guy's last words before they blew him away with the .50 cal were, "I just have chickens, just chickens." Other kills came from Lima Company, who just this past week killed 45 insurgents. Since the insurgency was running thin these were great numbers.

I called Angela today. She is so great and I could have not asked for anyone better. Other Marines worried that they would be coming home to Ex-Wives and broken up girlfriends that once made them happy, but I was fully confident that my fiancée would never leave me and I trusted her. She said she missed me and she was sending me another care package. I love her care packages. The food here really sucks most of the time and it's great to get some real food once in a while.

Temperatures reached 120 degrees today. We mostly just cleaned up our areas in our rooms. Our permanent homes were in our vehicles and it seemed pointless to make an area spotless that we were never really using. We were stuck to our vehicles, like instruments, controlled by steel and iron. We were killers when they wanted us to be.

Later that night I woke up sweating. A feeling of terror came over me and I didn't know why. I got a drink of water and fell back to sleep praying for a way out of this awful place.

Earlier that day I was sitting on the balcony and I almost got knocked on my ass by three incoming mortar rounds. I immediately jumped from the cheap lawn chair I was sitting in and ran to the mortar tubes. We fired four HE rounds at the grid we got from the CBR. I overheard the radio saying that the AZ's had spotted three MAM's running from the position of the grid. The discussion in the head shed up stairs, as it as sometimes called, was that the radar was inaccurate and ineffective. For the rest of the night we were on a five-minute strip alert, which meant we had to be ready to go on the vehicles within five minutes of a call up. We never heard about the three Muj Mortarmen that just seemed to have disappeared.

APRIL 26, 2005

Major operations for Operation River Flush were to kick off this morning at 0400. Gunny P called me on watch over the QRF phone, waking a few people up and startling a few others, just to make sure I was awake. The military phone was crudely connected to a long wire running down from the sixth deck up stairwells and in hallways. A conference last night ended in a decision that was being made to totally break down the mortar positions and not use them against the enemy. I guess people higher than me had better places for fighting back, or at least I would hope so. The good thing was that Dan owed me ten bucks.

Changes were also being made in our MAP. Evidently, they were pulling me off the SAW and making me a driver. Although I had never drove a Humvee in my life, not a whole lot could happen inside the safety of the fourth up armored vehicle. I know it will feel weird at first to be safe from every little threat I once was exposed to in the high back. I supposed I didn't really mind the change of pace, despite my lack of experience driving as opposed to over four years of being a SAW gunner. I had so many complaints, but I guess it was better not to fight it and just to get screwed all the time. We had gotten used to it.

Although a million things had gone wrong, I had not lost sight of my life as I knew it. I thought today that a lot of things would change when I got home; events, people, and places. It was like a time machine that broke, dropping us off in this hellhole. All the time I spent away from the world was going on and being lived by others, but when I got back that time would be gone for me and everyone would be living their lives as normal. When I got back home reality would hit hard and maybe it would even be interesting once I got used to it.

APRIL 27, 2005 0000

We left for the west side of the AO around 0000. Cpl Leach joined our vehicle until Dan got off chow hall duty. Dan seemed disgruntled about doing his time in the chow hall, but he always managed to sneak something good back for us. Cpl Leach and I talked about college. He is a mechanical engineering student at Ohio State and we both agreed that we couldn't wait to get back to the college life.

Today a major offensive on high value targets kicked off today. Weapons caches were found and whole batches of bomb making materials, mines, and IED's were found and destroyed. MAP 6 was on tasker today as we patrolled near CP 8&9 and were running detainee missions all day long, similar to the one we did to al-Asad's Det-Fac not long ago.

As Crazy 8 traveled up and down Uranium with its four Humvee caravan for what seemed like the entire day, we also ran snap VCP's looking for weapons and suspicious ordinance. Gunny P was with us so everything had to be done precisely. Our boots had to be bloused and our sleeves had to be rolled down. The weather was not as bad as the 80MPH windstorms and lightening that went on last night.

We rolled by one car that wouldn't slow down and the lead vehicles littered the tires with .50 cal rounds. Later we turned around and gave him a paper he could take to our mechanics to get it fixed free of charge.

It was not a very exiting day. I hated being here when so many things were going on. I was hoping we would get into some action, but until 2045, we stayed static on OP's, patrolled the MSR's to find IED's, and provided support for the Marines in Haqlaniyah.

Another thing that 3/2 had done while they were visiting the Dam was watch some of the Dam workers and observe some very suspicious behavior. They noticed that some of the Dam workers were raising and lowering the water levels to the Dam to signal the Muj when major operations were going on. When water levels were, up we were still back at the Dam and when water levels were down we always seemed to be out on operations. Things were taking place right under our noses. They would also purposely move heavy equipment in front of our convoys so we couldn't get out. They questioned all 3-400 of the Dam workers to find out who was up to no good.

I had watch again in the middle of the night and fell asleep around 0400. I felt alone and cold. Nights around here in the desert always make me feel uneasy.

VOLUME 2

"As I walk through the valley of the shadow of death, I shall fear no evil."

———◆———

APRIL 28, 2005

I woke up early this morning to hopefully contact my loved ones and send some pictures of our last few days out here in the field home for my dad to put on a CD. I had no doubt in my mind why I was here, those people in powerful positions I prayed would send us to war for the right reasons and for the sake of my friend and team leader Corporal Lindemuth, we would do our jobs, accomplish our missions, and come home.

The month seemed to drag on slowly as it eventually reached its end. Major operations were still going on and several times through out the day we could hear controlled blasts of exploded weapons caches and enemy buildings just outside of Haqlaniyah. I told myself that this would be a good day to relax despite all that was going on. Our platoon had been on a cycle of QRF, west side of the Dam, and then back to QRF again.

I wrote a few letters today to some close friends and brothers. One thing I found myself writing repeatedly was that a few minutes of excitement was always followed by extended periods of boredom. The movies that I watched before I left about intense fighting all the time seemed to be just a snapshot of the events that happened every so often and the parts not worthy for movies or television I was now experiencing first hand.

A few Marines sat around and smoked a Hookah on our porch while others watched movies on small portable DVD players and even played poker. I closed my eyes several times today and imagined myself on the beach in the Caribbean with my Fiancée reading her magazine and little kids splashing in the waves.

I walked down the dark hallway of the Dam and up the narrow stairwell to the seventh deck for chow. "Same old shit, different day," I would hear Marines say after a few months here in country. I chewed down on some kind of chunky rib meat, vegetables, and an MRE lemon cup cake for desert. There were no more Sodas / Pops in the chow hall and rumors went around that they just stopped serving them so that the newly opened PX could make money off us.

I took a short nap hoping it would never end, but woke up to shouting voices and the announcement that we were staging our vehicles in twenty minutes and waiting for MAP 5 to get here. We waited until nearly midnight to leave. Cpl Leach and I were discussing something or other in depth. It didn't matter what, as long as we could pass the time. This time it was rock and metal of the early eighties and nineties. There's always that anticipation that we would get some action every time we went out on a patrol. That feeling in my stomach would never go away, the feeling that this would be the last time for us being alive. At the expense of our lives, we would still look forward to making this deployment worthwhile, that we could finally do what we were trained to do as Marines.

APRIL 29, 2005

I tried to think as far back as I could remember and aside from the memories of the high chair and being two, I thought of some other early memories that stuck out in my mind. I visited my brother when I was about five years old in his apartment in Dayton, Ohio. I found a jar of change in his kitchen and he filled up a red container full of pennies just for me. I thought I was rich from that day on and I was so happy that my brother gave them to me. Several other memories came to mind, like when my brother would take Rudy and me to a soda fountain in Mantua, which we started calling the "Candy Shop." Chris used to always take us everywhere in his Black Fiero. The funny part about it is he still owns the car today fifteen years later.

I snapped out of my day dreaming on checkpoints 8&9 on a ridge overlooking route Bronze. I slept most of the morning away while we all took shifts on watch in our vehicle. I heard loud explosions late into the night. I was used to hearing them and really paid no attention.

It was another hot day that felt like 100 degrees. Brett said it was about 85, but I think he argued for the sake of arguing just to kill time. We must have sat there in the blasting heat for six or seven hours until we heard over the radio that a car was spotted fleeing the city and we were ordered to peruse it. It was so useless even starting our engines, because by the time we got there it was long gone. I don't think we were going to be chasing anything in the piece of shit we were driving.

I was fed up with everything in the Marine Corps, this war, everything. We could not do our jobs as Marines, which was to kill. Sometimes, I think we're here for someone's sick amusement.

We pulled over a few cars and found nothing as always. Bulldog rogered over the radio and ordered us to a permanent VCP at 2200, surprising us by throwing in an added bonus of an extra two days in the field without preparation. I always thought that there was a reason for everything, but really, there is no rhyme to any of this. It's when they feel like doing something; they just do it without thinking about how it will affect the grunts on the ground. There was no deep dark conspiracy theory behind anything. It was just a giant cluster fuck.

I fell asleep behind some HESCO barriers and cammie netting. I was sleeping in the dirt with the dogs and filth and I didn't care anymore. I pulled out the little stuffed frog my fiancée gave me. "Carry me in your pocket so that when you're lonely you will always remember you're my prince charming."

I would say that at this very moment I began feeling lonely, hateful, and bitter towards everyone. I hated everything, except for life, because I could never take that for granted again.

APRIL 30, 2005

Crazy 8 relieved another MAP from its permanent VCP for 24 more hours. The monotony that I despised hit hard today. I sat in the gunner's chair listening to MP3's, watching cars being searched and people being questioned as they went to work or carried on their sorry lives outside of the city. I felt like a cop or a police officer.

We took two-hour shifts on the guns between vehicles two and three. While one vehicle's Marines slept underneath the dirty HESCO barriers I slept in the night prior, the other team poked and prodded Arabs for information and searched cars. I had never been more bored in my entire life. My mind started wondering again into daydreams and fantasies. Thoughts were about school, about my brothers, and about my fiancée. I hated being here knowing that I could be learning something in college and walking across the deck on graduation right now would be the greatest day of my life. I used to walk around campus thinking how nice everything was and how thankful I was to be there. I was especially thankful that my dad had taken a job as a professor at the University and I could go to school as much as I wanted at no charge.

Getting into the shade of the barriers was nice. Our APL, who can be quite negative at times, mentioned the word extension. I could not even comprehend staying in this country for longer than seven God damn months, although I think some people who had unfortunate and sorrowful lives back home embraced staying here longer than necessary. I was fed up with the hostility within our platoon and I think that if we just communicated more we could be more effective.

As the hours rolled on by on what seemed to be such as surprise of a mission, I became more and more delirious. Towards the end of a most uneventful day, explosions were heard off in the distance from Haqlaniyah. One Marine was up to no good with his fetish of taking small objects like lighters, cigarettes, and even diabetic syringes. I just laughed at him, because I found it completely hilarious and it was the only thing keeping us entertained.

Dan was back in the rear serving chow and I thought about him. I was rather envious of him because he got his nights off and it seemed like he was accomplishing more than we were out in the field.

We heard over the Battalion net that 25 VBIED's were headed into Iraq from Syria. I wondered how they got all of this information without getting any details. It didn't make sense, but then again I'm not sure much did around here. Now having this information, or as they liked to call it, "intelligence," we knew we were in a very bad position at this VCP, especially if even one of these suspected VBIED's were to head towards our vehicles. I felt vulnerable and helpless. Plans came down that we were to be staying here static for another 24 hours and I lost it. The rest of the night, I spent bitching about everything, venting to everyone around me in the back of the high back.

MAY 01, 2005

I woke up to the sound of engineers tearing down HESCO barriers on the far side of the VCP. Quickly, I moved my gear out from under the barricades and back into the high back. It seemed like the leaders in our MAP were becoming rather hostile towards us. Maybe it was because we had not expected to be out here for this long. "Get the fuck over here and clean this shit up Wojtecki!" The Sergeant did not look like he was awake yet. It was only 0630.

Once the barriers had been knocked down, it was as if the VCP never existed, although we were still supposed to hold our position here. There is always a breaking point for human beings where they just get fed up with everything. I think I had reached it yesterday and it seemed like I didn't even care anymore. I wanted to get the hell out of here and sitting around was just a waste of my time.

We pulled over a few cars at random and a few ING personnel and police were searched. I did not quite understand why they were not doing their job if they claimed to be police. I was confused on what happened after February of 2004 that disbanded their forces, but I assumed corruption or the fact that Muj would be hired as cops and then use it as a position of power to get what they wanted from the people.

Boredom comes to new heights when you have absolutely nothing to do except talk about religion, finance, and politics. I think we argued about all three of them today. I took another nap until about 2000 until we were relieved by another MAP, but we were not going back to the Dam. Major operations had succeeded in Haqlaniyah and Marines from Lima had been holding the city for over four days. Our command decided it was time for the second phase, which was to invade and flush Hadithah of all of its insurgents. This meant they needed a stabilized force that was ready to react to anything. We heard about more casualties and it became unreal after the eighteenth person was injured in this operation.

Our mission tonight came down from Bulldog ten minutes before we were to RTB. An Amtrak flipped over on Route Uranium and we had to provide security for it while the casualties were ground MEDEVACed to al-Asad.

When we got there, they were still pulling it out from a large crevasse not far from the side of the road. I don't know how it got stuck. We must have sat there for eight hours or so until sometime the next morning.

MAY 02, 2005

Strange dreams invaded my head as I slept aside the right side of the high back. All of which I could not remember very well. I wanted to stay asleep for as long as I could. I slept until 1400 and got up because of the wind blowing sand violently in my direction and making it impossible to lay there for any longer. I did not lay there because I was tired, but because there was nothing else to do and when I was asleep, I could be anywhere I wanted. The rare pitter-patter of raindrops and the huge sand storm almost blew my sleeping bag away. I checked to make sure I was still on checkpoint 9. *Oh yes, I was.*

The other MAP's were in Haqlaniyah, Hadithah, or back at the Dam working on the next level of a video game or the next DVD of a television series. Somehow, I knew God was punishing me by sending me here, but I think our leaders were punishing us by sending us on bullshit missions. It sucks and I hate it more and more every single day.

MAY 03, 2005

A mixture of rain and dust covered my sleeping bag. It was a rude awakening. I didn't realize I had slept through half the day and it was 1430 already. I think that maybe it was the sound of the radio transmissions constantly being relayed between vehicles three and four about strange vehicles that were stopped near checkpoint 9. The Bullshit from vehicle 4 always came over to Vehicle 3 about the weather and wondering how we were all doing, "well I'm doing miserable how about you?" they would often say. I shook my bag off, stood up, and faced the hot Iraq sun. I think everyone was ready to just get back to the Dam and get some R&R. I just wanted a shower and a phone call.

We linked up with MAP 7 at the Bronze / Uranium intersection. They were supposed to relieve us so we could RTB. I sat there wired out of my mind. "They need us to sweep for mines on Hadithah road," Cpl Stocker shouted back to our vehicle from the lengthy discussion with our platoon Sergeant. After a long meeting amongst the vehicle commanders and the patrol leader at vehicle 1, we traveled some 2,000 meters to a road that looked like it never had been traveled on before. As we went over every bump in the road, the dust covered the truck and settled on the four bodies in the back of the high back. We were covered in the light, fluffy moon dust. It would have been impossible to spot a mine in the powder we now were treading through as four vehicles maneuvered their way down Hadithah Road. A mere footprint made in this dust would have tracked up enough dust to cover every piece of gear I was wearing. Cpl Stocker handed me the GPS and told me to let him know when we got to the 79 easting. It was incredible that the satellites would even pick up a signal on this part of the planet.

Shortly before we hit the hardball and returned to base, we stopped and shot our guns at what looked like a box and then turned out to be a fuel can on the side of the road. We couldn't be too careful, if that was an IED and we just went roaring passed it. I'm sure we would all be in a world of hurt.

I dropped my gear on my rack and went up to the NCO hooch where the 81's click just sat there with their blouses off trying to look like hard asses. "Is everyone here?" the Sergeant mumbled and then proceeded to tell us that because of our insubordination that we could not call our families. I was about to lose it and have a shit fit right there in that small room on the third deck. All I could do was just stand there in disbelief, not thinking this could be happening.

I think that people become Marines for three reasons: 1) because they are curious for adventure and would like to do something to show their loyalty for their country, 2) they were picked on in school and joining makes them feel superior to others, or 3) their life at home sucks so bad that they have to come here to pull their rank and make others feel insignificant. From a reservist's point of view this is, I believe, an accurate observation only because we all have other jobs and lives back home that we go back to. I believe that there are a lot of three's in this platoon. This was a war for God's sake, not boot camp. It was bad enough we had to deal with being away from our families and our friends dying, but the constant fuck-fuck mental games were pissing a lot of people off.

After the little, "pow-wow" on the third deck, I headed down to the vehicles with one of the three care packages I got and sat there and waited for someone to relieve me. I was almost crying as I opened the packages. I did not even remember what the people I loved so much looked like back home, but could feel them in my heart. If only they knew what I was going through. No one knew and no one was here to talk to me. Keeping the anger and frustration built up inside, I watched the lightening crash over the Euphrates River in the rear view mirror of the Humvee. I think I had reached a new low point. After an hour and a half of staying on post and not being relieved, I went back upstairs and opened my care packages. I began feeling better as I read letters from my family and ate some of the food that the Adopt a Platoon people had sent me. A guy from Kentucky, John Neuhous, who had a nice family and a wife sent me packages every so often. *It was very nice of people who don't even know me to send me care packages*, I thought as I ate some snack food.

A warrant officer, one of my brother's friends, wrote me about the Vietnam War and what life was like in the Marine Corps in those days. It sounded like not much had changed. The CWO went on to say that the support for the war was still high back in the States, unlike the conditions during the Vietnam War that he returned to years ago. I smiled a little as I organized my things.

At about 0400, I rushed to the phone and talked to my fiancée. I needed to let her know that we were going to be leaving for a long time on a dangerous operation in al-Qui'm. I told her that I didn't know what to expect and that we would be back in roughly two weeks. I hoped that we would do something interesting, but I was still afraid in the back of my mind. Such uncertainty of whether or not I would return from this operation alive scared me.

In the mean time, operations continued in Hadithah and Haqlaniyah with 3/2 and ING support. I fell asleep for a few hours and it was good to be back at the Dam even if it was for a day. Although the more we were back at the Dam, the more that we had to play stupid mental games that I grew tired of very quickly.

13

MAY 04 – MAY 16, 2005 OPERATION MADITORE - AL-QUI'M, IRAQ

We received a brief at 1800 today for an operation taking place in al-Qui'm. MAP 8 linked up with MAP 6 out in front of the Dam just outside of the stairwell. To sum up the brief, our mission was to link up with a large Army bridge company at al-Asad and escort them up to al-Qui'm where they would build a bridge across the Euphrates near the city of Ubaydi, fifteen miles south of the Syrian boarder. This area was always a hot spot, because of insurgent camps training foreign Syrian fighters and even Iraqi terrorists and then deploying them a short fifteen miles away to small lawless towns over the border.

It took us about three hours to get to al-Asad from Hadithah due to a very harsh sand storm. I finally managed to get a 240G on top of our scantly clad high back. I test fired it on a black pile of rocks about three clicks outside of camp Hadithah. In a way, I was glad to have the powerful machine gun that could easily rip apart a human in seconds, but I knew there was a reason for switching out the weapons. We were about to get into some hostile territory and this would be a weapon that would keep us alive if I needed to use it.

The sand storm went on for hours, forming what looked like a huge wall of sand in the sky. It grew dark and soon enough we were driving in the middle of it.

Before I left, I told my fiancée goodbye and told her to tell my parents I would be gone for quite a while on a major operation that was classified at the time. I hoped to God that I would make it back to talk to them myself.

We arrived at al-Asad and claimed a spot inside a small tent number nine near the chow hall. At al-Asad, you were in a good place the closer you were to the chow hall. They had great food from pizza to hamburgers served fresh daily. I knew that every chance I got I was going to be in the chow hall, because we never knew when we would ever eat a good meal again. We would probably go months without seeing good food. The chow at the Dam didn't even compare to the cuisine here at the KBR chow hall.

I had to take a leak so I stopped off at the head. The Porto-Johns lined the outer edge of the camp and looked strategically placed as though to avoid a most unpleasant fate in the event of a mortar attack. The KBR signs were hung up to mark when the facility was last attended to. I used to have a swaying opinion of the controversial contracting firm, but realized they were the only company large enough to handle these kinds of projects and God knows I didn't want the government to handle their work. KBR does a great job with chow and we felt like kings every time we ate in a KBR chow hall.

We didn't do much at al-Asad, other than wait for the Army's bridge company to link up with us. I racked out in the large tent, wall-to-wall with 60 other Marines. The tent smelled arid and musty. I felt cramped, but I sucked it up and passed out on the olive drab cot next to the other members of Crazy 8.

⟫◆⟪

I woke up to the sound of pounding boots against the cheap wooden floors and yelling Marines bitching about the PX and chow. As we walked out of the tent, Leach started cracking up as he imitated the other Marines. "Hey lets go get CHOWWW, BOOOM, BOOM!" he would say as he stomped on the ground with his huge combat boots. I hurried up and shoveled down some food while watching some television about some of the current events happening in America. As LCpl Leach and I walked out of the chow hall, we saw what looked like to be MAP 3 from FOB Hit, our old brothers. It was! I ran to LCpl Knox and nearly knocked him over. We talked about things that had happened, about the chicken guy that got his head blown off and other recent events. We avoided talking about Cpl Lindemuth's death. It pissed me off and it was depressing. "How is my favorite Jew?" I asked Knox jokingly. Knox just laughed and we talked for quite a while before leaving for the motor pool, where our platoon was meeting the bridge company. I think we were here to make some last minute adjustments, like getting a scissor mount for the 240 and other various maintenance issues that would hopefully improve our odds of surviving. After our adjustments were made, we were to link up with the Army and take Route-10 all the way to al-Qui'm, about eight hours from here.

Our truck quickly changed out the tripod mount that I had been using for a scissor mount for the machine gun. It was better than the tripod because it allowed me turn the gun horizontally, 360 degrees in each direction. Shooting to the left and right hand side of the vehicle quickly is very important so that the driver does not have to turn every time I want to take a shot and can keep his focus on driving in one direction.

We left shortly after twenty or more large vehicles, including MAP 6, Crazy 8, and the one and only Bridge Company arrived at our POS. Captain Macintyre was in charge of us and decided that it would not be such a wise idea to just plow through Route-10 straight into al-Qui'm with twenty vehicles. We decided to travel three hours to an ammo supply point called "Wolf." This was a desolate looking place, Captain Macintyre described as, "Something straight out of a Mad-Max movie."

Our vehicles stopped inside the base and everyone ate a quick lunch. Captain Macintyre talked to us about his plan to leave ASP Wolf the following morning and then head into al-Qui'm to secure the bridge for Lima Company and Tanks to egress through.

Most of the mental games and meaningless working parties were left back at Camp Hadithah, although there were a few things that were always done to screw with us, especially if we had down time. For instance, when I left the 240 inside the tent after cleaning it and NCO's cleverly made up a game called, "carry the machine gun and A-bag all the way to the chow hall and back." That was fucking stupid and a ridiculous thing for me to do.

I don't think anyone or anything would ever follow us out here to this desolate place. The Marines who lived here looked restless and except for the mail that came every few months, I don't think they had seen anyone outside of their platoons since they were shipped here.

The night was long and uneventful. Three vehicles were supposed to leave for the bridge sight at 0600 to sweep Route-10 for mines before the bridge company and the rest of the MAP left. I woke up for watch at 0400 feeling delirious as always and it felt like I was living in a movie and that someone out there was watching me. I remembered where I was and the average person on foot would have to survive some pretty harsh conditions to make it out here. I think that's why it was a perfect place to put an ammo supply point. The hour of watch passed by fast and I laid down on the single mattress inside the tent in the cold and fell asleep.

After several dreams, I woke up late and looked around to see the same uneventful place I fell asleep to. It was so quiet, only the sound of Army trucks, the squeal of their breaks, and the yelling of the drivers littered the air with sound.

In times of great boredom, a million different things can run through a person's head. I thought about what my life would be like once I returned home. This hadn't been the first time I thought about it. It was reoccurring and it scared me at times. If I would live in a nice house, if I could make it through college, and what would it be like to live with another person for the rest of my life. I knew my fiancée and I would have fun and would try to work together to accomplish anything. I tried to get my mind off home by reading a few books. It was obvious we were going to be here for a while doing absolutely nothing. I just hope we would not play any more stupid games.

There was a chow hall nearby that served tray rats and remnants of al-Asad's supply convoys like Power Bars and sodas. A few of us went down to the building later that evening, partly out of boredom, but also because we hadn't had a good meal in three or four days now. The building looked like something out of a western movie. The buildings were covered in dust with writing in crude paint and Arabic signs, as well as a few orders that higher-ranking Marines were tired of repeating printed out in Microsoft Word on the back of some scrap paper. "TAKE ONE, PUT ONE BACK!" or "POLICE YOUR AREA!" some of the signs read.

I ate my meal and then walked back to the tents on a very dusty road that made me look dirty and covered with sand. Leach and Perry talked about how leadership should be in the Marine Corps and of course, the daily bitches and complaints that were heard almost every minute of the day that kept us going in this place.

If time ever came closer to standing still it would have stopped. In training environments, it took the bridge company only two hours to set up the bridge across a body of water. How it took ten days to escort them, set the bridge up, and get back was beyond me. I guess I would find out what we would be doing in about a day or so when we left this rut of an ASP.

Official operations would kick off the night of the sixth and from what I understood the Army was in charge of the bridges, not the Marine Corps. They wanted a speedy exit in ten days or less, so the planning was altered slightly from when we started out at al-Asad.

Cpl Stocker came into the tent while I was reading one of the books I brought with me and showed us a map of the al-Qui'm area. The city we would be traveling through was only a stone throw away from Syria. The night of the seventh, Bridge Company and MAP 6 and 8 stepped off from here towards our objective. Vehicle 2 was to punch up to Bronze and provide security for the convoy as it came through the city, then link up with the last vehicles 3 and 4, and head to the bridge site. It takes about two hours to construct the bridge and eight more days to provide over-watch for the entire operation as the line companies moved across the bridge and raided the nearby cities north of the Euphrates.

From what I hear, we were going to be almost guaranteed action, but I was not very optimistic about that. I think other Marines were getting so bored that they would rather be engaged in a firefight or some type of shoot out than to sit around on our asses and get screwed with by the Sergeants and Staff NCO's.

We waited around again today for the advanced party to sweep part of the roads before we stepped off with the larger, main body of the convoy. Boredom set in again and my mind raced with thoughts. The order-of-march was going to be the second vehicle high back and then the first vehicle always blacked out ahead of the bridge company and on the lookout for suspicious activity. Our vehicle thought this was a ridiculous idea, because of our lack of armor and exposure of the open, canvas topped vehicle. Even the VC, Cpl Stocker thought it was a stupid idea. If the order went through and the high back was hit directly on by a mine or some type of explosive device, the vehicle would be totally destroyed, and everyone would either die or lose legs or arms. I think we made a good point and our Sergeant changed us to vehicle number 25 after bringing up the fact that we would be letting the least up armored and vulnerable vehicle lead the entire convoy.

Leach and I walked to chow and bitched about everything. I talked about me being anxious to get home and he agreed with me. We found the time to count how many days were left and wondered what America was like. I missed my Fiancée. I hadn't talked to her since I snuck a call before we left for this operation. It would be almost the end of May when we returned to the Dam. Nine more hours to zero hour and we would be either absolutely bored or extremely exhausted from combat.

Most of the Marines from our MAP were attending a six-hour class today on demolitions and how to blow up mines, should we encounter any while driving. While they were in class, I continued reading my book and quietly drifted off into hours of sleep in the hot and musty tent that our platoon spent days in sleeping and playing video games. The hot sun baked the desert outside like an oven, and made the water we were drinking in the vehicles turn warm.

We left at 2000 for the staging area on the other end of the ASP. Two reporters, one from the Chicago Tribune and the other from the Washington Post accompanied the Army. We were there to provide security for their vehicles and make sure the bridge site was constructed successfully without interruption from enemy forces.

We stood around for about an hour or so, looking at the Army's 15-20 vehicles and playing loud metal music from our MP3 players. We huddled into a circle and the female Lieutenant in charge of the Army bridge company gave a brief. "These Marines are here to protect you, so make sure you follow what they say. Don't go wondering off on your own like a drunken ass, because the Marines will shoot anything that moves."

We formed up now as vehicle fifteen and headed out the gates of ASP Wolf. "Someone ran into the razor wire," Vehicle 3 roared over the radio. One of the trucks hadn't even reached the gate and it ran into something. The bridge company made the impression that they had never been on a convoy in a hostile area before.

It was a very long drive to the bridge site. It was 2000 and we had not quite made it there yet, driving through the town of little Beirut, a small populated area of a few thousand, about the size of East Village in our AO. This area had been nicknamed "the mine strike capital of Iraq" by 3/2, who occupied and guarded this area surrounding al-Qui'm. Route Tin was a very bumpy and worn down road. Heading into Little Beirut, we found out why they called it the mine strike capital. Huge craters made from mine blasts that were not yet filled in made it difficult to maneuver through the town.

As soon as the trucks got into the town, we marked the intersection with a chem-light. To the right was Route Gold, which we turned onto from Tin. The cluster fuck began when we traveled a short way up the road and the bridge company attempted to follow our lead. "What do you mean one of the vehicles turned down the wrong road?!" The platoon Sergeant screamed over the PRC. They had taken the wrong route even though it was not difficult to follow a huge 30-vehicle convoy heading down the MSR and turn where the American made chem-light glowed shortly off in the distance. Our vehicle punched up to take the place of Vehicle 3 and we stopped for a good three hours to wait for Vehicles 1 and 4 to round up the last truck that went down the wrong path. It was like herding sheep, I thought while I sat by the gun watching for suspicious vehicles.

The next thing that came over the radio was hilarious. One of the vehicles had rolled over going 5 MPH while following Vehicle 1. We waited in our position for what seemed like forever. All of a sudden, three vehicles popped up over the hill and started shooting at us. Machine gun fire lit up the night sky and it was directed at us. I fell back into the corner of the high back. "Pop a red star cluster!" Someone shouted from the cab of the high back. The flare could be seen for miles. Helicopters flew overhead and spotlighted us to make sure no one was dead. I almost pissed myself and Leach was laying on me as he avoided live rounds by a few inches. Vehicle 2 had been mowed down by its own people. They pulled up in their up-armored vehicles and Cpl Stocker almost ripped them a new one. "What the hell were you doing?" A voice from the dark shouted, "We were just following our ROE's, we saw shooting so we shot back." I think all of us were ready to jump out and start kicking the shit out of some people, but I think we were still shook up from almost losing our lives. We found out later that it was a platoon that was part of 3/2's MAP. They were driving on a routine patrol and were not looking out for friendlies. I thought about what a bunch of careless assholes they were and how we should have reported them to the commander. When I thought we were going to get some action, I did not expect it to be from a 240G American machine gun. We were advised to move over the hill so we wouldn't get shot at again and we sat there until sunrise. At that point, we were right next to Ubaydi, a large metropolitan community about the size of a small American city. The bridge company sat there with no COM, a downed vehicle, and people who didn't know their asses from a hole in the ground costing us time and risking our lives.

A vehicle pulled up to from the rear of the convoy. It was the female Lieutenant from Bridge Company that drove up here to report an RPG fired at one of the bridge vehicles. "Go back to your post ma'm, we're not supposed to move yet," Cpl Stocker said to her. We sat there for another two hours and then took one of the side streets to block, while the convoy finally headed to the site near Ubaydi. It was 0700. I was tired, disgusted, shook up, and just plain angry. By 1000, we moved outside the city and went static in a blocking position to guard the bridge while it was being constructed. Targets of opportunity had been acquired inside of Ubaydi and Kilo Company thought it might be a good idea to take the city. Bombs dropped all around us from close air support and fixed wing. Thick, black smoke billowed out of the buildings in the city. It lingered there for hours as tanks and AAV's rolled in. All we could do was watch in amazement and hope that some crazy Arabic driver would come traveling down the road we were on so we could shoot it up.

We sat at our POS for days on end. The flies got really bad and came at our vehicle like we were food. I slept outside on the ground and woke up shortly after 1000 to the sounds of a flare and a vehicle turning around. We fired a few warning shots and the car turned around and made its way back down the road in the opposite direction.

It was now our fifth day out here and it felt like everyday seemed to creep by. It was like they did not matter anymore and I had lost track of time. We were running out of food and water and hoped there would be someone by soon to re-supply us.

I started watch for an hour and Cpl Stocker was up. I sat there reading what was left of my books and tried to stay clean with baby wipes and hand sanitizer. Nothing worked against the flies that would land on our hands, face, and any area of exposed skin. A few cars came down the road and turned around. Then one car, a white Chevy kept coming. We fired a flare to get it to stop. It kept coming, slowly creeping to about the 200-meter mark, which was our disabling line, according to ROE's. I could hear the 240 open up and litter the engine block. The car kept coming and the 240 littered the windshield with bullets. Both machine guns from Vehicles 1 and 2 opened up after letting the vehicle creep to about 100m of our vehicles. The car came to a stop and a guy got out and fell to the deck. I stayed on the gun and three others went to investigate. The rounds completely tore up the inside of the vehicle and fatally wounded the passenger, who was missing part of his head and pieces of his fingers that were scattered all over the road. Two other occupants in the back seat were shot up pretty bad and would have to be life-flighted. From what I was told, it was a pretty gruesome sight and other Marines advised me not to go up there if I did not have to. Cpl Stocker looked pretty shook up and the other three that went up to the sight looked like they were going to puke. Dickason told the passengers they were going to be okay and the interpreter was there to translate. MEDEVAC was going to escort them to Camp Anaconda by 7-ton. Doc Barone took care of the wounded and patched them up. The 240 had done some damage, but we were told over and over again that we did the right thing, that they had come too close to our vehicle and with the current threat of VBIED's, that was all we could have done was follow our ROE's. We heard all kinds of horror stories about Marines getting blown up because cars would get to close to their vehicles and they would be loaded down with explosives. Some Marines think that giving a 200m disabling line may be too close for comfort.

The body bag sat there next to the shot up vehicle as onlookers from other units rolled by. "God-damn!" we could hear them say as we sat under the self-made canopy, constructed out of cammie netting and some tent poles to keep the sun off us.

We finally got a temporary re-supply around 1900. Water was the best part and everyone guzzled it down by the large bottle. For some reason killing didn't really matter next to getting some food and water and didn't bother me that much. Maybe because I had not seen it up close, or just because compared to Marines that are shot at by these people every day, this was not as traumatic. I thought about the injured passengers later that day and hoped they would be alright at the hospital. It must have been pretty scary for them. I thought about if that was someone I knew and something happened to them, how concerned I would be. I tried to get it out of my mind, but it kept playing back repeatedly.

Later that night, explosions rained over Ubaydi on key targets such as houses belonging to IED makers, bomb engineers, and tribal Sunni leaders that were members of terrorist organizations like the Mujahadeen or al-

Qaeda. 200 to 500 men from an Arabic tribe were also fighting Iraqis from another tribe. They were left alone to kill each other off and hopes were that both sides, who hated us, would not try to strike against us. We had taken quite a few casualties since the operation began. Plans were to obliterate targets with tanks and aircraft fire after insurgents used anti-aircraft rounds on us just the previous day. Throughout the day, thick clouds of smoke rose into the sky and loud booms could be heard in the distance. The sun baked down on us while the lifeless body stared at us from his vehicle.

It felt like we would be here indefinitely and we were bored again. There was only so much to talk about. It was now our sixth day here. I wanted to talk to someone at home and thought about how great it would be to get off that plane and step foot onto United States soil. I wondered what everyone was doing back home, *had they forgot about me? Were they carrying on their normal lives? Were they having fun, laughing, crying, working, eating normal food, or shopping?* I did not want to lose sight of my old life.

The Dam reported that eleven Marines were hurt and three killed. The report was passed down to us from the Battalion net. They did not say how it happened, but I assumed it was by mortar fire. Leaders that normally stayed in the CoC, like the First Sergeant and other Officers, were doing foot patrols through the cities just outside the Dam. They formed a platoon and called it "Team America" after a popular movie that recently came out on DVD. Crazy 8 had a way of escaping death. I hope that we would not lose faith or the luck we had so far would not run out.

The bridge that took two hours took about half a day to construct under hostile conditions. Marines could finally cross and attack targets and enemy training camps to the north.

Anaconda, a construction engineer platoon, set up razor wire across the road and stop signs indicating that if vehicles didn't stop, we would shoot, to prevent people from traveling past the trigger lines. If someone were to try and get around the barriers, we would consider this an act of hostility and follow our ROE's accordingly. To prevent VBIED's from running our position and killing our Marines, this was a necessary precaution. A few trucks turned onto the restricted road and dropped their cargo trying to hastily turn around. As the sun came up over the road that headed east into Ubaydi, flies buzzed all over our vehicle and us. We were sitting not far from a huge trash dump, the site where the city threw away all of its waste. Trash was strewn out onto the desert for miles. The sun baked it and the smell of trash lingered in the air. It was horrible.

At about 1100, Cpl Leach went on watch and I attempted to get some sleep. I was able to get eight hours, but it was broken between four-hour periods for watch. Broken sleep fills my mind with negative thinking and weird dreams that I forget once I wake up.

A black sedan turned down onto our road. It kept moving slowly. We fired a white flare, indicating that our intent was to warn the vehicle that this position blocked the road and it would have to find another way around. By that time the car crept passed our 200m trigger line, warning shots were fired next to the vehicle, and then into the engine block at 150m. All of a sudden, a man got out of the car and raised his hands. He looked scared shitless, but the car still kept on rolling. He must have forgotten to put it in park, because it picked up speed and ran past the 100m fatal trigger line. Cpl Leach opened up with the 240 and the SAW opened up soon after, aiming for the windshield. The car stopped somewhere around 80m to the right of our POS and caught on fire, which was excessively close by far. The terp ran up to the kneeling man, his hands still raised and told him to come over to us. Cpl Stocker dismounted our vehicle and went over to talk to the man, who was quite distraught and out of breath. The man told Cpl Stocker there were still two people in the vehicle and started wailing in agony. "Why didn't you stop?!" he asked the man. Two of his family members were inside the vehicle, which was now engulfed in flames and was soon to explode. A few Marines from Vehicle 1 rushed to the burning vehicle to rescue the occupants who were un-conscience and woke up burning alive. One of them managed to get outside the vehicle before it exploded.

The chubby, scruffy looking man sat not far from our vehicle and sobbed, "My family!" he kept wailing. Evidently, there also was someone else in the vehicle and we were not able to pull them out. The terp kept yelling at the scruffy looking man in Arabic. Something about why he didn't stop. Apparently, he thought the vehicle that was there with the bullet holes in it was pulling into a VCP to be searched. I guess he didn't notice the body bag next to it and the stop signs hoisted up on the HESCO barriers in Arabic indicating that IF YOU PASSED THE LINE WE WOULD SHOOT YOU. I couldn't believe that for one second and it was so stupid for him to abandon his family by jumping out of the vehicle and to leave them to burst in flames. The man's face would probably be burned into my mind for life. Although I know we did our job, I would still have trouble living with death, but it was better then dragging my buddies out of a vehicle because this moron decided to crash his car into our roadblock.

Later that day they fortified the position even more, putting higher barriers up and more signs indicating certain death if you crossed a certain point. At the same time, they buried the body of the man, who had to stay out on the desert for 72 hours because of Muslim traditions before it was buried. Anaconda dug a shallow grave for the man on the side of the road. The skeleton and charred remains of the passenger inside of the burned vehicle were put into an MRE box and buried. I was rather stunned for most of the day. The thing that bothered me the most was driving up on the burned vehicle and seeing the skeletal remains of a person inside.

Shortly after the ordeal, the man was told that the member of his family that was alive was life flighted to a hospital and the officer on deck took down his name and told him that we would take care of everything and would compensate him for the car. Vehicles 1 and 2 then moved from their POS and traded with 3 and 4, which was on a QRF observing activity just outside of Ubaydi. Brett was in Vehicle 3 and had to respond to the situation at MAP 6's POS, where they too had shot up a vehicle. Brett said he had a person in his arms and saved his life by giving him CPR. His flack looked bloody and he looked exhausted. In a way I was glad we were trading off to get our mind off things. It was rather traumatic, but as the SSgt said, "We did the right thing and although our job really sucks at these times, someone has got to do it."

We moved further into the city closer to the bridge sight where we were to stand a QRF post, observing suspicious activity in the city. The morning of the eighth day, we sat and protected the bridge company from anyone that might fire an RPG at one of the 27 vehicles.

Earlier that morning, we spotted one MAM digging something next to the old bombed out gas station, but could not get positive ID. FAC came down to our vehicle to try to get better eyes on with their laser range finders and all the necessary equipment to call in an air strike. According to the Captain, we were making sure that area was secure before the line companies would sweep through, house-to-house, similar to tactics used in Fallujah or Ramadi. 3/2 had already taken eleven casualties and the commander got so pissed he took a company of tanks through and almost leveled the entire city.

The geographic makeup of the cities was new. There was an old Ubaydi and a new Ubaydi. Both of the cities were governed by different tribes and both of them hated each other. The thing they had in common was their extreme dislike for coalition forces.

We came close to witnessing a TYPE 1 air strike, which was made up of large bombs from F-15's. Crazies 3 and 4 had a front row seat to the bombings the other day when hellfire missiles rained down on a gas station where IED's were being made.

It was another hot day which we could not escape, other than to drape our cammie netting over the side of the vehicle, which helped a little on a day that got to be somewhere in upwards of 120 degrees by noon. The heat made me feel very lazy and I did not feel like getting up to do much of anything. Think about how long you have sat in one place for a period of time and then imagine sitting in the same position for weeks on end. I couldn't motivate myself to do much other than eat and scout out some digital picture opportunities to add to my computer collection. I became very good at sitting and moving the gun on watch, in which I did scans of the area with it's thermal sights that had night vision capabilities and could also pick up heat signatures of living things. Most of the time the scope, called a PAS13, just picked up the heat signatures that a rock gave off, from the sun beating down on it that day.

We chatted with some of the Army folks about the area. We talked to them about how this sucked and what they found over the past few days. Sgt 1st Class Potymouth was a real character. His New-York accent and chubby looking demeanor were amusing, and it was a perfect example of someone who was salty, and been in the military for years. The impression that I got from him was that he inspired his troops, excited them, and they would probably do anything for him because of his attitude. I guess when you are a leader you have to think about those kinds of things.

The rest of the day drained me of energy and thinking of the past few days didn't help much either. We were told we were returning to the Dam in another 72 hours, but I was used to being told something and then ten minutes later being told something different. I was sick of being out here and for that matter, sick of everything all together. Turner's ghetto fads and way of talking was entertaining, we passed the time by getting into arguments about music, and what kind was better. We told wild stories from back home and Cpl Leach and I got so bored we started working algebra and math problems on scrap pieces of paper. We were officially bored again.

That night I kept waking up to the sound of explosions and had some very strange dreams. I dreamt I was on a checkpoint and we were searching vehicles. A man ran at me and I told him to stop, but he did not listen and I blew his head off with my rifle. Then somehow, I was at an intersection and traveled to a swamp where the Sgt Major lived and he made me do all sorts of crazy stuff, even though I kept telling him there were weapons at the checkpoint. I walked endlessly down hallways of a building that had white rooms and then woke up gasping for air and went on another watch to break another eight hours of sleep in half.

For the next several days, we watched explosions hit buildings and Hajjis carry things back and forth between houses and drive away in white Chevy Suburbans. We all knew what they were doing, but no one could do anything about it unless we had Positive ID. They had to have weapons on them or intend to harm us before we could do anything back to them. 3/2 and Lima company had assaulted through their main objectives, which were Curbasa and five other cities to the south of Ubaydi, just seven clicks from the Syrian border.

We had talked in Vehicle 2 about our families in the military. We told stories about our relatives in the military and I told them about my uncles being in Vietnam and my dad being in the Air Force. By then, half the day had passed.

This operation, from several sources, was grueling and quite exhausting for the line companies who had to push through hundreds of houses on foot and over seven cities in the surrounding areas. Sgt Ohair, whom I later talked to while staying at al-Qui'm for a few days, told us he was there through it all, while we sat at the southern blocking position. He said it was not fun at all. "I'm tired of killing, I'm tired of smelling the blood, I'm tired of good Marines dyin', I'm just tired." They had pushed through the objectives at full force and that when they came to Ubaydi. It was a blood fest. He said he killed ten insurgents by himself and told us about entering a house where apparently the Muj had made it so well fortified, that there was even an anti-aircraft gun they managed to bring in and plant under the floor boards. He said they came in stacked on the wall. One by one, they went into the house, and one by one, they were mowed down by anti-aircraft rounds shot point blank from no more than 20m away. Rounds that the Muj took from some caches mortally wounded the Marines. One Sergeant got hit right through the top of the mouth and the anti-aircraft round hit him so hard his kevlar fell off as he fell to the ground and he was killed instantly. Sgt Ohair quickly shot the man who ran upstairs after shooting the Marine and wounded him. They all exited the house and lobbed grenades into it. They called in air and dropped two 500lb bombs, which both missed. Tanks shot up the fortified city and they pulled out two hours later. Although Ubaydi was not included in their five objectives, reports from interrupted cell phone conversations confirmed that Zarkowi, a known terrorist leader, was in the city and was wounded.

Reporters from CNN, The Washington Post, and the Chicago Tribune paraded around the battlefield trying to get shots of insurgents and Marines fighting and dying. Sgt Ohair called them "Vultures" following him around to get a big story and getting video of his Marines being killed. It made me sick just hearing about it.

Later on in al-Qui'm we saw Operation Matador on the news in one of the chow halls. The report was for about a minute or two and then they switched subjects to some missing girl on some island somewhere. I could see the level of importance this had to the news in the U.S. Someone will eventually find out the real story in detail, rather than a two-minute blip on the bottom of the television screen.

They reported there was heavy fighting near the Syrian border and that we had killed over 128 insurgents. It was still nice to be acknowledged, even for a brief moment. I could just think what Angela and my family must be going through watching this on the news. I hoped that they were not worrying to much about me. I had not been able to talk to them in over a week and felt sick to my stomach.

Lima Company sustained 29% casualties in the operation. They lost seven Marines and an entire platoon was wounded by the heavy fighting. They even talked about pulling India Company from al-Asad, who were not directly involved in fighting and were there as a combat replacement company. The Army reported a great success for the bridge construction. We pulled out during the early morning, 28 vehicles pulled into the desert towards our staging area. al-Qui'm was about a two hour drive from Ubaydi if we traveled at 30 MPH looking for mines. The plan was to stage there and escort the convoy to al-Asad when the word was given by higher command.

I was so upset because of all of the deaths that had happened. As if that wasn't bad enough, Marines from MAP 7 went out on a QRF patrol while we were gone. They were looking for the enemy point of origin that caused the mortar attacks on the Dam just days after we left. Their first vehicle was hit by a VBIED killing four Marines instantly and injuring three more. It was a massacre.

I missed everything about my life and desperately wanted to get the hell out of this God-awful place. I kept thinking of how this war would affect me long after I was home. I would give anything to return the same as I was. People would like me and laugh with me again. I tried to cry before I fell asleep, but all I could feel was emptiness and how I was alone here. I stared at the open sky and the stars while I said a short prayer to God.

The next day we ate chow at al-Qui'm. I had hash browns, omelets, eggs, and bacon, all of which I could hardly eat. Being so used to high energy, disgusting MRE's I was not used to such a treat. The coffee was good and something inside of me told me everything was somehow going to be okay. I'm not sure how that was true, there were a lot of Marines dead and I couldn't help thinking that I could have been one of them and how easy it would be for me to die out there. There were always doubts, which are perfectly human that led me to believe that I was unwanted, that there was no home, and that here was where I was going to be indefinitely. I realized that love was the only thing keeping me going and remembering home. Love was something that couldn't be broken, no matter how much death I saw or how close to death we might come. I couldn't wait to get back to the Dam and use the phone, get a shower, get my mail, and get some kind of sign that I was actually a human being. After being in the field for as long as we have been, I'm sure the showers would be packed. I would enjoy waiting for them.

Captain Macintyre announced at 0900 this morning that we would be here for another day until we could leave for the Dam. I wanted to get back as soon as possible. I wasn't really looking forward to all of the games we had to play when we got back though. When we got back to the Dam, there was always something stupid we had to do before we could shower, shit, or use the Internet. I hated that part and I was just sick of everything. It seemed like ages ago that we were back at the Dam running regular MSR security patrols and sitting on checkpoints 8&9.

———◆———

Flies buzzed around me as I took my morning nap and watched time slip through the cracks. It was good to rest at al-Qui'm for another day. Their facilities were far better than ours were at the Dam. KBR had provided them with flushable toilets, four star chow halls, and even a huge PX. I caught a glimpse of the CNN reports as I woofed down pizza and burgers. Making my way back to our Humvees, I was stopped by another Marine from my platoon and told there was a memorial service for those Marines that died recently. A few others from Crazy 8 and I made our way up to a parade deck near the chow hall on what looked like an old worn down railroad depot. Four Marines from 3/25 died in an AAV when a mine exploded near the hull of the vehicle, killing them instantly and wounding several others.

Later, I heard one of the engineers talking about how the insurgents created the explosion. It was made with two mines and two metal contacts, one positive and one negative. When the AAV made contact with the pressure plate in the middle of the road it moved and touched the two ends together, thereby detonating a mine on the side of the road as well as a mine in the very middle of the road. I felt so much hate and discontent for the insurgents and felt sad for the fallen as I stood at attention for the ceremony and listened to the Marines up front talk about how they knew the fallen and how much fun they used to have together when they were alive. I didn't know the Marines personally, but still felt deep remorse for them and their families. These were our brothers and they were dead.

Taps echoed throughout the base. Several other Marines who knew them well held back their tears. The ceremony was very reverend and organized. As I paid my respects to the dead, hundreds of Marines filed off into an alleyway and were grouped together to talk. Joking, crying, swearing, and bitching about how things were fucked up beyond belief.

I stayed awake late into the night thinking as I always did and fell asleep to the Army, who had a never ending spades card game going and could be heard all over the staging area.

We woke up early to the last official day of the operation. I wasn't used to being wide awake at 0600, it was really cold out so I couldn't fall back asleep if I tried. VC's and the PL were briefed on escorting the bridge company along with parts of Lima back to al-Asad. Just that morning "War Pigs" the Weapons MAP from 3/2 found five double stacked mines on the road that we drove down today with more than 30 vehicles. War Pigs filled in holes on the road that could possibly be used to plant more mines and IED's.

The ride back was a grueling experience due to the heat wave. It must have been the hottest it has gotten here since we first arrived. Thermometers we brought from home did not even read past 125. I drank about four or five bottles of water and had to piss every few minutes in the empty bottles as the road jostled the high back around and I lost my balance. Leach and Dickason started laughing historically while I tried to hold my balance and urinate in the empty Mozn bottle. I started pouring salt packets in the water so I would retain more water and it seemed to help a little. I was exhausted from the heat and couldn't wait to get a nice cold shower. I had not had one in two weeks and had dirt and grime everywhere on my body.

MAY 17, 2005

We came back to the Dam earlier that morning, walked up a dark hallway, and entered our room to a different layout. It looked like someone had remodeled the place. The two weeks that we were on Operation Matador, Cpl Ickes and Back built wooden bunks and tables for our platoon. I quickly went over to my rack to arrange my gear, which had been haphazardly thrown into boxes. It bothered me that it wasn't organized and in place. The shelves and racks built out of wood were a real moral booster and made this place a little bit more like home.

I sat on my new wooden rack and opened my mail for the first time in two weeks. It didn't really matter because the average package took roughly two weeks to get to Iraq, and letters took about a week or so, although I still had one or two letters. Before I got to my second letter, the company had plans to send us out on another mission. We were to have a brief at 1630 about what we were going to be doing, as well as filling us in on what happened in our own AO while we were away.

It felt good to take a shower and make a phone call home. My fiancée had been in the ER for a few days and I was so worried about her. My parents were worried about me and everyone heard about the operation that played over every news network. Reports mentioned 3/25's efforts to stabilize the insurgency several times and I felt like I was part of something. It felt good to feel proud of being part of a unit that was on TV. These were little things that I think would eventually pull me through being at war.

It was good to hear that my mom had a good Mother's Day. My dad was feeling a little bit better with his radiation treatments and mom said that he has gained some of his weight back. I asked him how they could have possibly fit all those candles on his birthday cake this year and he just laughed.

All the Corporals from Crazy 8 had to report to the NCO hooch to see what would be in store for us during the next few days. We were leaving first thing tomorrow for a foot patrol through the palm groves. We would be transported by AAV's through Haqlaniyah and dropped near a large area of palm groves where the POO and the cause of these frequent mortar attacks on the Dam had been reportedly coming from. Just this morning three more mortar rounds had impacted inside the Hadithah Dam and hit our fuel supply sending flames and thick black smoke high into the air that could be seen for miles. Imagine waking up to large explosions and look outside of the balcony of our room to see the Dam burning. I felt helpless and wished I could have done something. We would be doing something tomorrow when we hunted down these sons of bitches. We were traveling on foot.

Our platoon Sergeant did not know much about the mission at hand, but said that the First Sergeant would fill us in later that day. Meanwhile, around 1630, we were ordered to report to the CoC where Major Catalano would be meeting with just Crazy 8. Dan, Brett, and I showed up there early at 1600. Major Catalano casually talked to us about his gun collection and how he went shooting with his brother. He went on to say how his brother always had to be perfect when he shot. If one piece of equipment was even a millimeter off, it would alter the trajectory of the round and his brother would lose his accuracy. Major Catalano told us about his Brother Mike's experience with the gopher-shooting club that they both attended locally. He told us a funny story about how Mike entered a contest to see who could shoot the largest gopher and how Mike captured one, fed it junk food for a year, and then proceeded to kill it and turn it in to claim his prize. The Major went on to say that the judges eventually found out he had cheated, because they opened the stomach of the giant prized gopher to find pieces of bread and maple syrup that Mike had been feeding it. The story made us all laugh and loosened us up a bit from the grueling routine of patrols that were always accompanied by ridged by the books discipline.

Major Catalano was a very likeable Officer and had earned the respect and morale of his Marines by always knowing how to motivate us and by swearing up a storm. "Fuck this and Fuck that" he would always throw the "F" bomb into everything. One Marine actually counted how many "Fucks" he said in one speech and stopped counting at over 100. Major Catalano is a good leader, because he knows how to identify with his Marines and can always be a person that we could talk to like a normal person if we had concerns or problems.

Everyone from Crazy 8 finally piled into the CoC and Major Catalano began his explanation of the events that happened. He told us about MAP 7 and how they had taken small arms fire and how a VBIED with enough explosives to level a city block came crashing into the lead vehicle, killing four Marines and wounding three.

Several other MAP's had hit Mines including MAP 4, our brothers from Hit, hit a double stacked Italian anti-tank mine that injured several Marines I knew personally, including LCpl Pratt.

It seemed like we were in the CoC for the entire evening. The CO talked about the disbanding of MAP 9 for reasons that were unmentionable.

The CO looked around and asked if we had any questions that he would answer them at that time. There were quite a few and it looked like we weren't getting out of there for a few more hours. Someone asked a question about combat replacements and if we were going to be receiving any. They were told that several Marines from India Company and brand new, boot SOI graduates might be taking over to fill MAP 7.

Other questions like how we may be doing away with some of the drill centers back in Akron and Cleveland and how we might have to report to Columbus instead. I had no idea why they would do that, but I'm sure it was a funding issue.

A question about 7-tons replacing high backs came up and a Marine that was serving radio watch from MAP 7, Cpl Stan Mayer, was there and said that if it were not for the 7-ton, he believed that he would not be alive right now. I agreed with him that something had to be done about riding around in high backs. It was a tragedy waiting to happen. Ever since we were first put in the un-up armored high backs that were basically death traps on wheels and exposed us to shrapnel, offering little to no protection against an attack.

The CO joked about the LCpl network and how Lance Corporals always mysteriously know everything before he is even briefed on it. Lance Corporals had ears in every room and seemed to know everything before it was brought down from higher. A Lance Corporeal was always there when an important meeting went on, happened to be sitting on radio watch when the important subjects were discussed, and always happened to be around the corner when important things came up.

As soon as we were dismissed, Crazy 8 raced to chow, which was only being served for another five minutes.

Later that night, the First Sergeant and Captain Penmettel briefed us on what sounded like a day long mission policing through the palm groves just south of River Road, though he said it could very well easily turn into a several day event. We were to report on the ground floor tomorrow at 0430 to walk down to the tracks and ride to an area where counter battery radar had logged the grid of an enemy POO. We then would get on line and sweep 500m, get back in the AAV's, and be done in time for afternoon chow. If we took fire, we would have tanks and F-15's supporting us while we fired and maneuvered through the palm groves until the threat was eliminated. Cpl Johnson from my old team in 29 Palms, California was in our squad, number one and first out of the AAV.

The night was short and there wasn't a lot of time for sleep. I prepped my gear and ammo for tomorrow morning and fell asleep on my new wooden rack, on the bottom bunk.

MAY 18, 2005 0430

Feeling groggy as hell, I picked up my heavy flack, daypack, water, and ammo. I put on my boots and then went down to the ground floor of the Dam where others were waiting. First squad second fire team was huddled over by the Porta-Johns and the Captain decided to go over the plan of attack:

If we take fire we will all assault through the objective. We are going to be doing some detective work out there so make sure you are observant and looking around for enemy mortar positions. When the track opens, we will be getting out second position after first squad first fire team. Haul ass to the palm groves and stand by until I give the word to move.

The Captain had us get in fire team order. I traded out my saw for an M-16, because our squad already had one and Cpl Kustra in first fire team did not. I was not used to doing this 0311 ground pounder stuff and it felt weird to be outside of our Humvee.

I lay down on the cement with others and watched a bearded man in a white polo shirt and dress pants. He was a reporter from the Chicago Tribune and was going to accompany us. The man looked very perplexed and nervous as he took quick shots with his camera. Later the CO came up to him and told him to turn the flash off and explained to him that it could be seen for miles, and would alert the enemy of our position. He quickly adjusted himself and his camera. It was odd to see someone from the civilian world in a combat zone with us. I'm not sure what he was looking for, if he wanted a look in us, an emotion, or some major tragic event to happen that he would be first to get on film.

The line of Marines stretched across the Dam as it became light outside. We loaded up onto the AAV's and traveled to the west side where we would carry out the mission.

We jerked around in the tracks for several miles, squished into an enclosed space, once again proving that the Marine Corps could always fit a lot of Marines into a little area. The door suddenly swung open on the death trap, which days earlier had housed the four Marines that were blown apart by the ingeniously crafted double stacked mine, ripping it's hull apart. We all filed out quickly into the palm groves like something out of a SWAT movie. I could almost hear the Hendrix playing as we got on line Vietnam style to patrol more than 500m of palm groves. We were looking for signs of the enemy, but I wished I could find a way home, at least inside of my mind, to get me away from this place.

We tromped over fields of crops within the palm groves battling the insane humidity, which was really bad inside of the palm groves and felt like a sauna. Small bugs swarmed around me, flying into my mouth, nose, and eyes. Sweat rolled down my forehead as I attempted to keep on line with the rest of the squad and kept my eyes open for evidence of enemy activity. I found a small paper, probably written by some Iraqi organization, but I did not know what it said. I guessed it was some kind of recruiting poster for the Iraqi army, but the words were in Arabic and I could not read them. I quickly shoved the paper in my pocket and kept on walking.

We were only out there for about two hours and we found two enemy mortar positions. Sandbags were laid out and 120mm mortar round ammo boxes were scattered about as if someone had been here just recently, fired, and then took off leaving a fresh set of tire tracks.

Just then, we saw a large group of Marines from Lima Co. in the streets. I remembered them being known as "light 'um up Lima" and did not want to test them on their nick name, so I followed the Captain's orders, "Point your rifles at the sky," he whispered to us and we hastily pulled back to the tracks. We walked on the road for about a minute or two. I was scared shitless because I was walking point, but I kept going until I reached the AAV. We got back to the Dam just in time for chow.

I hope the reporter got his story, *although a story is not interesting until someone is killed.*

We finished off another half of a maintenance day. Marines were scurrying around the hooch trying to make things look organized and clean. I tried to fall asleep several times, but was always woken up to do a particular task. God, I love the Marine Corps.

MAY 19 – MAY 20, 2005 R&R

Around 1000 this morning, our truck drove up to the tenth deck of the Dam to install a new frequency jamming device for our vehicle. I figured if we had little to no armor, maybe we could take a gamble and run through a minefield hoping the device would work. I had a lot to complain about and my dark humor kept everyone in my vehicle entertained. I was pretty tired and snapped at everyone, especially Turner who was really getting on my nerves and kept up the usual routine of speeding up the Humvee and then slowing down fast to the point where my neck felt like it was going to snap.

After our task was complete on the tenth deck that we were so rudely snatched out of bed for, and Cpl Back's chores were done, which he pulled out of the air, we had a few minutes to relax. Cpl Back was leaving for al-Asad soon due to some kind of back injury and it was probably just his way of saying good-bye to us.

I lounged around on my bed sheets and mattress, both a commodity around here and something that every Marine wanted. Brett and I had the first sets of bed sheets that we bought from the PX or sent to us from home. We always had little contests to see who could be the cleanest and most organized. I think I was just not satisfied that someone was neater than I was. Cleaning took my mind off things too and helped me get through stressful times.

We watched some show later that day Brett had on DVD about the drama that happened in Orange County, California not far from where we trained. In "The OC" Brian always got Melissa, Randy was always dealing with business, and Seth always had something smart to say. It was like normal life or close to it and I think that's why all of us liked it. Plus, I think it was a little bit amusing that a bunch of grunts were sitting around watching prime-time soaps that college girls normally watch. It made me laugh and I had a lot of fun watching it with the guys. The thing that pissed us off was that they always had the littlest things to bitch about, like who was sleeping with whom. *It must be nice to have nothing to worry about.* "Okay now lets never tell our girlfriends back home that we have been watching this shit!" Cpl Leach would always say.

I waited at the phone center for about two hours to talk to Angela. She still loved me and it was always a relief to hear her voice. We talked about her friend's new love, Bill, who is in the Air Force and always talked bad about the Marines. Bill told her that Marines were trained to be easily agitated and jealous all the time. He also said that reservists are not real Marines and I thought if I ever saw this guy, I would show him some of the anger we were trained to have. Just a day earlier, I sent my fiancée a surprise. A message in the bottle that read:

My dearest love, know that everyday I fight, I fight for you and I will be home soon.

Love,
Matthew Wojtecki, USMC

I hoped she liked it, and I figured that I owed her a surprise after all the care packages she sent me. Resting for two days made me happy, but I assumed it was given for a reason, in preparation for a future operation in Hadithah or Haqlaniyah.

The thing about war as I probably thought about before is that after maybe fifteen minutes to an hour of action, there may be days even weeks of boredom. For the next several days, however, boredom was well deserved for MAP 8.

MAP 6 came in from the field today because one of their vehicles hit an IED and they needed to borrow one of ours. No one was hurt in the explosion, but I'm sure a lot of people were shook up.

Rumors from the Lance-Corporal underground circulated that someone had a video conference with their parents and the First Sergeant told them that 3/1 would be here in mid August, not September. I hoped to God that this was true. I missed everything so much back home. I looked at some cruise brochures that Angela sent me and I hope we would go on a vacation when I got back. I started daydreaming about the cool, gentle waves of the clear ocean, the soothing sound of the waves and the smooth sand. For just a brief moment, I was on the beach relaxing in the sun, leaving my cares behind me.

Tonight we were going out to cover the ever-popular checkpoints 8&9 that we always ended up being on at 2000. I was not looking forward to it. I hope that we would fall into a normal routine and that the clock would speed up. Right now things were dragging on as we hoped for June to roll around.

They said we would be flying via C130 back to the U.S., but this was another rumor. I didn't care if I flew back in the crappiest aircraft in the world as long as I could get out of this God forsaken country as soon as possible.

Thinking about home got me thinking about my family and how much they mean to me. My four Brothers have been my good friends for my whole life and I'm sure they are concerned about me right now. My Brother Tim, who is a Colonel, said he might actually fly to Iraq to see me. That would be very nice. Chris is busy working on a new circuit for cell phones and enjoys a lot of adventure and outdoors. Pat plays the guitar, but wants to get into psychology, Rudy is working on a degree and has been more places in the world that I know of. Sometimes I think that Rudy and I are in competition to see where we could go in the world, although I would rather have skipped Iraq. I thought about my brothers as we loaded up our gear and brought it out to the vehicles. I always remembered smelling up the basement with cigar smoke every time my brothers and I were in the same room together.

I already missed sitting on my ass doing nothing, although I'm sure we would be doing plenty of that at checkpoints 8&9. I wish they could keep us at the Dam or since we are at checkpoint 8&9 all the time if we could just set up camp there for the entire time. I thought about it and started laughing to myself as I got behind the gun of the second vehicle.

The night at the checkpoint was hot, humid, and uncomfortable. Our fire watches started and I was woken up every four hours to take my turn at observing the area, until about 1100 when I was told to put my blouse, flack, and kevlar on. One big thing they make us do is require us to keep our blouses on, even though we had spent half the deployment taking them off at every checkpoint. Putting our blouses on would not save us from enemy mortar or rocket fire and wouldn't stop a bullet. It was one way of keeping us in check to make sure we were not becoming complacent because "COMPLACENCY KILLS" a saying that was incorporated into every long-winded speech, printed out onto cheap paper signs in Times New Roman font, and written on walls with map pens and El-Marko's for all to see.

MAY 21, 2005

Sitting underneath the dwindling shade of the old ING checkpoint, we sat around and rotated through the watch schedule while cars whizzed by. Something about indirect fire came over the PRC. I put my flack and kevlar on and enjoyed what was left of the shade. The sun would soon be overhead and we would be stuck out here to fry.

The buildings around here looked shot up and rubble was laying everywhere. It looked like the remains of a country that had tried to help itself at one point in time and had failed to a faceless enemy. The vulnerability of the people after living under a dictatorship rule for so long is so great that it is a wonder how the country has managed to stabilize itself. Without our help, I am not sure that it would have been possible. I look up every so often when writing to glance at the occasional white Nissan truck going by or to grab for a drink of warm nasty water.

I had to remind myself that the reason we sat on these checkpoints was to make our presence known in the AO and also to watch the MSR's to make sure no one decided to plant mines or IED's along the roads. By sitting on checkpoint 8&9 we made it more difficult for the Muj just by sitting here. I hated them because they would not even show their face and when they knew we were in the area, they were fearful of us. They would either run away or blend in to the population. Threatening weaker people in small lawless towns was their last resort against us.

At about 2000, we were relieved by MAP 6. I got up off the ground covered in tiny ants, which I didn't realize were all over the ground, carrying scraps of food that we had thrown out. I brushed off my flack and mounted the vehicle so that we could RTB. It wasn't a bad 24 hours, but complaining about everything killed time.

As soon as our boots touched the Dam floors, we were stuck on a strip alert for about two or three hours. This meant that we had to be ready to move out within five minutes of getting a call from the CoC. Being called on a strip alert meant that shit hit the fan and we were being called out to support Marines under fire. As usual, Turner and I ended up having to refuel our vehicle after everyone else got to relax and the NCO's went up to their hooches and the CoC to get further word on what our next assignment would be. It was just a typical 24 hours for Crazy 8. I was still trying to fall into the routine of Checkpoint 8&9, tasker, maintenance, QRF, and then back to checkpoints again.

I fell asleep that night and for a brief moment, it felt like I was sleeping in my bed at home, until the sounds of an argument about who was supposed to be on fire watch next woke me up around 0300. I drifted off sometime after that and counted one more day closer to home.

MAY 22, 2005

Tonight we were going out on patrols for 24 to 48 hours. The plan was to do VCP's as well as find a bridge sight in the middle of Barwanah for a couple of hours after evening chow. We did not get much of a warning as to when we were leaving, but I prepared for the worst and was already ready to go out.

The heat was so unbearable today. It was 119 degrees in the sun with nearly no wind except for a few gusts of hot breeze every few minutes that made me want to puke and gave me a splinting headache. A FAC from the CoC went with us to recon an LZ sight for the upcoming operation. As if we had not done enough operations and enough people hadn't already died, in a few days another operation in Haqlaniyah was going to kick off. We were only out for about three hours to recon the area, but in that time we almost took fire from several buildings in the city. On coming traffic were close to being fired on for not pulling over. The humidity in the palm groves was sickening.

When we went into Barwanah, it was like a scene from right out of the bible. Everyone was living as if no one had come along and gave them the news 7,000 years ago that we had advanced in technology and innovation. The people here gawked at us outside their houses as if we were aliens from another planet. I'm not sure how some Iraqi households actually managed to have satellite TV.

Drudging over bumpy roads while looking out for mines and IED's, we sped back to the Dam just in time for chow. The thought of eating this crap was disturbing to say the least and I'm not sure how I forced myself to eat it.

When we got back, we were told we were going out again in a few hours. Somehow, this did not come as a surprise.

For the past few days, the rumors have been floating around about an early ticket home around mid-August. This place was starting to get to me, though I think starting is an understatement. I tried to use the phone today as much as I could. The lines were long and so many people were crammed into the small room waiting to use the four phones that were limited to 30 minutes each.

For the remainder of the evening, we staged the vehicles outside of the main entrance to the Dam and eventually headed to the east side of the AO where we sat static just outside the city until first light. Kalouf, one of the combat engineers had just been attached to us from Lima Company. I worked with him before in Hit and he is a cool guy. I would always joke with him about if he ever ran up behind one of the vehicles that we would mistake him for an Iraqi and shoot him. Kalouf is originally from southern California, but his nationality is from somewhere in the Middle East. "Don't even say I am related to these fuckers Wojtecki!" He would always say to me when I made fun of him.

For most of the night, we talked about how nice it was not to be with Lima Co. marching through the cities on foot. He described his eleven-hour track ride from hell while traveling to al-Qui'm from Hadithah. We talked about the CNN reporters being kicked out of our AO for writing derogatory and inaccurate columns about our Marines. Most of us here thought that the media was making us look evil, showing angles of footage that made us appear like "ravenous blood fiends that would kill anything for sport."

I slept out in the dirt again and watched the bright moon light up the city, reassuring us that we were still human and alive. Somewhere out there in that city, a few people had an appreciation for the Marines that protected them.

MAY 23, 2005

Not wanting to wake up, I sluggishly shoved my sleeping bag into the gypsy rack of our Humvee and prepared myself for a full day of VCP's. I felt like a cop that was sworn to serve and protect. This country had not yet established its government and there were no police, so you could get away with just about anything. Iraq was like the Wild West.

We drove up and down the crude roadways, pulling over cars at random and searching the occupants for signs of suspicion, hoping to find some evidence of the Muj so we could break this streak of boredom that seemed to last forever. We found one guy that had a weapon on him without a permit, which we confiscated and later found another man claiming to be the sheik of Barwanah. At that point in time the man had $10,000 in U.S. currency on him. We hadn't taken a prisoner since the guy who drew a map of mine locations on his chest. I was stuck having to load this asshole into the high back and keep a close watch on him. I also tried to look out for mines and IED's on the roads while we drove back to the Dam to drop our friend off at the Det-Fac. The vehicle bounced the detainees around like rag dolls as they tried to remain motionless.

It took us three hours to process the prisoners. Paperwork had to be completed for every piece of evidence we had against them and pictures had to be taken with the cash. Inventory of the personal items had to be taken, but I think that despite all the hassle, the Marines of Crazy 8 appreciated being back at the Dam for at least a little bit to cool off in the shade and relax for a while.

A special feeling came over me while handling the $10,000. I wish that I could have that much at one time and I wished that I could just keep it right now for myself. Each bill had to be serialized and checked for counterfeiting. HET teams did something with the money, but they wouldn't tell us what. God knows that we were way underpaid as it was and it would have been nice to collect a $10,000 paycheck this month. It would have most likely come back on us, but I still joked around with Kalouf, "That's a lot of money, and this is a big desert. It would be a shame if this guy got lost without his money or a car." Kalouf was a guy who believed in karma and what you did in life came back on you. After all, we lived through these past few months, I was starting to believe in it too.

We did the right thing in the end and continued our patrolling towards Barwanah. Who knows, maybe we could arrest another car full of Arabs, making two trips to the Dam in one day.

I must have sweat a million gallons of water as we drove back and forth, sometimes going off road, BZOing our rifles in the middle of the desert, and then sitting at OP's later on that evening. Turner kept raving about his hip-hop music and Kalouf loved talking to him about it.

A huge sand storm blew through the open desert like a violent storm. I could not see two feet in front of me. Sand is very dense when it enters the air and it is a great conductor of electricity. You can almost feel the static in the air as it conducts when it moves in the air, also causing massive lightening storms that light up the sky. As we walked around the vehicle to explore, the storm attracted something very peculiar, a camel spider. The five-inch long creature followed Kalouf around for a few minutes and then began to charge at him, making a hissing sound. Kalouf, being the crazy Marine that he is, walked over to the angry arachnid and stepped on it! Spider guts went flying in all directions and I took some pictures of it. I told Turner this would be the last time I ever slept on the ground again.

We managed to make our way back to the Dam and I opened a few more care packages that were waiting for me on my rack. I was surprised when I opened Angela's package. She spent the last few months working on a notebook full of letters from family, friends, and co-workers. It made me so happy to read some of the letters that thanked me for defending our country and co-workers like John Adams, who wanted to honor me by including me in his talks at business conferences. John said that what I am doing is more difficult than anything in the business world is and if I could get through this, I could get through anything in life.

I went to bed feeling happy. So many people remembered me and I felt even more anxious to come home to my life. Kids at Copley Middle School in Akron wrote me letters and I felt that no matter what happened that I could overcome any obstacle. I would have to say that without my fiancée and family back home that this would be a long war for me.

MAY 24, 2005

At 1300, the Gunny ordered us to take out two Marines from 3/2 to give them an idea of how we did VCP's and what our tactics were like. It was the worst patrol ever. The heat was unbearable and everyone in Crazy 8 just wanted to get some rest. So we left for the west side and drove up and down the roadways trying to find some suspicious vehicles to stop and search. One car, while we were driving on Route Bronze came to a complete stop in the middle of the road. Everyone from our vehicle was screaming, "What the fuck!" we should not have let the guy block us like that and I wondered what was going on when we did not fire off kill shots, but instead rolled right passed the halted vehicle. MAP 7 lost four guys because of a SVBIED and I just thought we might have learned something from them. I think it had something to do with the guys in 3/2. We didn't want to make a bad impression killing people on our guided tour.

We continued on following the sun for a while and then turned north on Bronze. At that point I had no idea what we were doing and decided to just go through the motions. I think the patrol left a bad taste in all of our mouths. I wasn't looking forward to the up and coming operation near Hit and I prayed everyday that I would make it out of here alive and in one piece.

Cpl Leach always had a way of stating the obvious and was one of the few NCO's I knew that I could talk to and that wasn't full of himself. He and I talked for several hours about how things needed to change. We went to chow to eat right what was served right on schedule every Tuesday. The spaghetti was not too bad and was better than MRE's, but then again anything would be better than MRE's.

Later that evening I tried to fall asleep. It seemed like time had slowed down to a crawl and we were never getting anywhere no matter how far we went through this deployment. *We were never getting out of here,* I thought as I tossed and turned. It scared me and sent me into a panic. I found myself getting up several times and walking around aimlessly. I tried to think of other things until I dozed off depressed and wondering why this was happening to me.

MAY 25, 2005

Operations in Hadithah had been going on for about three days now. Things started not to make sense and everything around me was worth bitching about. I'm not sure if it was because I was getting salty or if it was our command's decision to confuse us. Sometimes things looked different from the bottom of the ladder and on the ground than they did in the conference room and on paper.

Since the operation started, we had been on a QRF and doing tasks for the company, like doing reconnaissance of areas for fuel farms, VCP's, and bringing detainees with us so we could escort them to al-Asad.

As we traveled to the west side of our AO, we pulled on to Hadithah Road and the dust kicked up, covering us in a fine powder of desert. Our Humvee and all of our gear were covered in dust. The day could not get any worse. The two detainees brought from the Dam in the back of a 7-ton were Mujahadeen and we had to escort them to al-Asad from the firm base in the city. One had watched his brother get hit in the eye with a SASR round that blew off half of his head and he just stood there as if nothing was going on. The other prisoner was found with bomb making materials on him. Kalouf seemed to like prisoners and we always made sure that they would not become hostile and try to escape. It made me angry that they would try to fight us and then when they were in front of us they acted like a bunch of cowards and would start crying because their flex cuffs were too tight. Kalouf tied the blind fold around the detainee's head and he kept saying, "Water mista, waaaata!" We gave them some water to drink and I couldn't help thinking about how these people had attempted to kill our brothers. I stayed alert as we sat at the firm base in the middle of Hadithah to see what the hell we were supposed to do with these guys. I watched some AAV's drive around the schoolyard, it seemed so funny to be parked in a basketball court and watch tanks roll around on patrol.

Suddenly, a loud explosion came from behind the school. We didn't know what was going on, I didn't want to be sitting here right now and I thought we were being mortared. I kept an eye out on the city and saw the usual on lookers that stopped and stared at us being injured. Those mother fuckers didn't even run, they just stopped and stared at us! We found out a few minutes later that the AAV had hit a mine out back behind the school where the kids would have recess. Four people walked passed me with a stretcher that held the driver, who broke his ankle, but was going to be okay. The people that were just standing around watching everything happened bothered me more than anything. Normal people would run if they heard a loud explosion. *Who would be sick enough to plant landmines in a schoolyard?*

As we sat in our Humvees in the middle of the basketball court, we heard shots being fired. Someone told us that snipers were shooting at a guy with a black bag and a white piece of paper that had stopped at a bridge and planted something from out of the bag he was holding. They ordered us to escort the snipers to where the kill sight was near the bridge to see if they could find a body or if anything was planted there. We moved slowly to about 500m down the road and stopped. Vehicle 1 halted right where the guy had planted something, "back up!" Cpl Stocker screamed over the radio. We stopped, got on line, and spread out on foot to look for this son of a bitch. After a few minutes of searching, one sniper found a piece of an Italian anti-tank mine and some shock-tube just lying in the pipe by the bridge. No sight of the guy anywhere. We went back to the firm base, dropped the snipers off, and then RTBed with the other prisoners they had captured earlier that day.

We soon found out when we got back that we had to escort another AAV company back to Hadithah again to the firm base we were just hours ago.

On the way back, the EOD vehicle that was with us received reports that the AZ's had waxed a guy trying to plant an IED, which we found out later to be false and was only just a refrigerator laying in the spot where we checked for a body.

Now everyone in Crazy 8 was getting very agitated as we sped back down Route Bronze and then the dusty off road path called "Texas" into the heart of the city. We were accompanied by AAV's or rather we were escorting them, that way if we hit a mine we would be the ones to take a hit and not the large expensive AAV. We parked in the schoolyard again and our platoon Sergeant went in the CoC to see what was going on.

By this time, it was well after 2200 and everyone in our vehicle complained about everything without taking a breath. We could not believe the meaningless tasks we were doing and what a cluster fuck this mission really was.

We spent the night at the firm base in Hadithah listening to Mortars and bombs explode all around us. Cpl Leach and I talked about how stupid being here was and how we should be in college right now. Our company's casualties and deaths now totaled over 200, which is 20% of the total deaths in Iraq right at this moment. We were proud of the support people gave us back home and I talked about my brother's friend, the Warrant Officer that was in Vietnam who came home to people spitting on him and calling him a "baby killer." It was nice to hear that people appreciated us. It was the politicians that sat behind their desks and moved us like puppets or like a game of chess into the insurgency.

I fell asleep next to some old school desks in what looked like an auditorium. I could almost picture little kids putting on a play for their parents on stage. I remembered when I was in second grade and I was a knight who made stone soup to give the king. The floor was hard and uncomfortable, but I was tired so it didn't matter. I slept with my SAW close to me and prayed I would wake up to see morning.

MAY 26, 2005

I always look forward to the end of the day. The sunset sinks into the Iraqi desert and the thought that I was that much closer to getting home was a feeling that put me at ease. The beginning of today was not ordinary by any means.

We were doing VCP's on Route Grizzlies and escorting personnel and prisoners back and forth to the CoC. I woke up in one piece at 0600 and surprisingly was not blown apart by IDF that had been going off like the fourth of July during the night.

We went back to the Dam and started our normal watch on the vehicles, until we had to go back out on patrol three hours later. We had a ridiculous number of Iraqis tell us they were fishermen or policemen with no ID's. One guy was being a smart ass and acting weird, so we arrested him. He also had three dots tattooed on his hands, which no one knew what it meant. We roughed him up, asking him, "Wen Mujahadeen?" or "Are you Mujahadeen?" He kept saying that he was not in the terrorist group and looked scared. He reeked of fish and it was obvious that he was a fisherman. We let him go and sent him on his way with a bottle of water.

It was usually crazy in the high back, because the MP's had their dogs with them and one of the requirements was that they had to ride in a vehicle with air conditioning. So they kicked Doc Barone and Dmytriw out of the first vehicle, put the dogs in their place, and threw them into the high back with us. It was funny the way Dan complained, but he seemed to be happy to be back to the high back with us even if it was for a little while. I felt like I was in grade school. When we talked too much or got along too well together, the teacher would move us to a different spot in the room.

Dmytriw, Kalouf, Leach, and I were all in the back of the high back together. We had several things in common, we were all stuck up college kids and we could not stop talking about when we were going home. No one understood what we were talking about when we mentioned parking fines on campus or cramming for final exams.

The rest of the day flew by quickly, aside from the driving up and down the dusty roads at least five times and the heat, which now approached 110 degrees. We were still in disbelief that we were staying at the Dam that night. It was too good to be true. When we got back, Cpl Back said that the Gunny had found Brett's secret project to run Internet cable from all the way up to the fourth deck to his little room he called the "Jack Shack" that he built for himself out of MRE boxes and cardboard from care packages. Fortunately, the Gunny didn't punish all of us, but I couldn't stop and wonder how Brett planned out the whole thing. He would have to get up early in the morning, and run a cable all the way down the long hallway, up the stairwells, and up four flights of steps. Sometimes when you really wanted something bad enough, it didn't matter what you had to do to get it.

15

OPERATION DESERT RAT / CASHCE SWEEP - PATROLS IN SW HIT AO MAY 27-JUNE 08, 2005

The op order started out like any other, changing three times twice every five minutes. At first, we were leaving tonight and then all of a sudden they told us we were tasked with a mission in Hadithah or a working party to clean up trash outside or set up racks for Kilo Company in the hallway of the first deck. The order came down and was explained to Crazy 8. A mission that involved 50 Marines including snipers and two MAP teams, MAP 3 and 8, two 7-tons with 800 gallons of fuel and two pallets of water would head into uncharted, un-patrolled territory, for the sole purpose of finding and disposing of enemy ordinance. The operation was going to take place in an area to the far east nicknamed "The Balsac." I had a heart attack when I heard the name of the area on the map, but it was for obvious reasons. The 50 square mile area resembled the shape of, well you know.

Captain Haunty (recently promoted) was in charge of the mission and planned on taking about seven days, give or take a few. We didn't know what we would find up in that area, but if we took contact, we were expected to assault through and destroy the enemy. The nearest MEDEVAC sight was a half an hour away at al-Asad and air was on station at all times, although COM would be an issue since we were so far away from the CoC and if something bad happened we would probably be in a world of hurt.

The night of the brief, I was using the phone and all of a sudden, Osberg came into the phone center, "We are leaving right now," He said trying to catch his breath. Sweat dripped off his face from running up six flights of steps. I ran down to the vehicles and we left for Hadithah, where we would receive further word on what to do from higher command. For the past few days, we had been running tasks for the Hadithah operation and still were waiting to receive further word on leaving for Hit. Every time we received word, it always changed on us. Three hours prior to departure, MAP 2 hit a mine near Hadithah. It had been formed into the cement and it was just a matter of time before it exploded in the middle of the road. Some might say that it was fate or by some miracle that when we traveled that route several times over the past few days that it did not explode. PFC Dawson is eighteen years old and has a wife and kid back home. I always remember him as the kid that talked with a hillbilly accent. Dawson was hurt pretty badly and fractured his pelvis. He had internal bleeding in his upper chest area and was MEDEVACed to al-Asad soon after we left for Operation Desert Rat.

When we arrived at the Hadithah firm base where we had spent the night a few days ago, the First Sergeant said we would be escorting a prisoner that had been wounded while planting mines near the hospital. We were to take him to al-Asad along with a Gunny that injured his hand in a mine strike today.

Three armed Marines escorted the prisoner outside to our vehicles from the BAS. He was blindfolded and had flex cuffs on. We sat him on the floor of the high back and he wouldn't stop wailing like a little girl. I personally was not in the mood for all this bullshit, because we were back at the Dam relaxing and preparing for the operation and had been called out to pick up this asshole. Everyone was fed up and you could tell. The man kept wailing and we kept telling him to shut up. In every language, everyone in the world understands yelling. I personally did not feel any remorse for the prisoner who was now draped over himself on the ground. He was exactly a spitting example of the people we were fighting for. Plant mines and then when we shoot you in the leg and capture you, you whine like a little girl. He was the kind of guy that would drop a few mortars into his mortar tube and then go sit down to dinner with his family a few minutes later. He made me sick. I just hoped that he would die on the way there so we could turn around and end this nightmare of a day.

It took us seven hours to get to al-Asad, drop this knucklehead off at the Det-Fac, and get back to the Dam. We were so tired and as we pulled out of the air base, the sun rose as we drove on and on forever back to the Dam. By that time it was already 0800 when we got there and I just wanted to pass out. We were told to stand by to leave at 1500. I slept the entire day and word changed again while I was asleep. It was pushed up again by another day and that was a relief for Crazy 8.

Kilo 3/2 was staying at the Dam and cots lined the hallways on the first deck all the way up to the fourth. The stench of 1,000's of Marines in one enclosed space was unbearable. I quickly dove into our room where Crazy 8 was playing video games and watching movies. Several Marines also had a poker game going on our new poker table. Dickason wore a ridiculous pair of sunglasses to hide his poker face as a pile of money sat in the middle of the table.

It was no surprise that the time we had to leave was now pushed to 0230 and then 0430 that morning. We left not knowing any specifics on exactly what we were doing and if anything else had changed from when we were first briefed. I got up in the gun with my cup of coffee and shortly after 0430 took off to the east side, past where MAP 2 hit the mine.

We headed towards the railroad off in the distance and we were to find a way to cross. This would put us on the eastern most end of the AO and halfway to the Balsac. It was rather difficult to cross. The railroad was surrounded by razor wire and sharp rocks that took several attempts to traverse. We traveled with two 7-tons, two high backs, and eight Humvees. It was our turn to drive over the large obstacle, and as usual Turner decided to floor it. We got at least a foot of air driving over the railroad ties and landed on the other side. There was nothing but open desert as far as we could see, until we reached a primitive road. It looked like it had only been traveled on a few times, but when we approached it, a thick dust cloud behind a large bus kicked up. We flared it a few times and it stopped along with a white vehicle that was driving close behind the large bus. God only knows what they were doing. I kept a crucifix by me and it blew in the wind as we drove up to their POS, with our interpreter, Cpl Stocker.

It was good to visit with MAP 3. I had not seen Knox since that time at al-Asad when we suddenly ran into each other. We had no idea what was going on half the time, but things seemed to speed up while we were in the field and on large operations that lasted a week or two. The thing I think that aggravated everyone was getting back to the Dam and then having to go back out an hour later. I told Knox how excited I was that when we got done with this op it would be June. His vehicle was parked next to our crappy high back and we talked for a few minutes until the bus came to a stop and two MAM's got out with their hands up.

Cpl Stocker shouted something at them in Arabic and two Marines searched the vehicles. They found an AK-47 and an Iraqi pistol. We were instructed to confiscate pistols, because we were told that during the Sadaam era they had only one purpose, they were used for executions. Stocker wanted to keep the pistol with the picture of Sadaam on the handle inscribed in gold. I told him it was just a matter of getting it out of Iraq. That was the problem.

The man in the pickup had a license on him in which the card read that he received from a "Captain David XXXX." The card was a license to transport rockets. Evidently, this guy didn't know Sadaam was out of power because he thought he was still working for the Republican Guard.

For whatever reason we just took the guy's ID and then let him go. We probably figured that running him back to the Dam would be time consuming and we didn't want to set off the operation that was already on schedule. We pushed forward for hours over bumps and rocks in the rough desert. We bounced around in the back of the high back until we took a security halt and refueled our vehicles. We had emptied an entire gas tank driving as far as we drove and we were not there yet. It was mid-afternoon and MAP 3 went off into the palm groves to the east and did their own thing while Crazy 8 pushed west. We approached a large rock face and below there was a large patch of farmland in a valley. This was a true oasis, because there was absolutely nothing out here other than sand and this 50 square mile patch of grass and farmland.

We drove down a narrow road leading us into this area and then immediately stopped a bunch of Iraqis standing around by their house. It looked like they were putting something into the ground, which we later found out was a water pipe for irrigation. Twenty people filed out of the house with their hands in the air. We questioned them, and a terp from MAP 3 told the Iraqis that we were looking for suspicious activity in the area. One of the people in the crowd stuck out when I looked at them. The man was only about three feet tall. He walked around in front of us and then sat down. A bunch of kids were laughing and whispering to him. Then he smiled, did a handstand for us, and then sat back down. Everyone was laughing and cheering him on.

We didn't find anything in the house and we continued doing VCP's that day until we came to the 95 easting and sat on an OP for the night. Kilo had been here for a few days before us and found a large number of weapons caches buried in an Iraqi's back yard. That moved the operation's length it would take to complete from seven days to right around ten to seventeen days. This was because Kilo Co. had to sweep the 50 miles on foot with engineers, searching every part of the desert for ordinance.

I woke up to a car beeping its horn on the road leading into a small village. We stopped and searched it to find nothing. Crazy 8 did what it did best and OPed for a day or two until Gunny decided we should do something more constructive.

The night before our vehicle started in a deep discussion of religion to pass the time and this went on for 24 hours. We argued and debated and everyone seemed to be getting into it, particularly LCpl Dickason, who I think, played the devil's advocate just for the sake of arguing a point. If it wasn't about politics, religion, or building his muscles it was about getting out of Iraq. "My body's a temple!" he would always tell us. We only had a few months left and the clock wasn't stopping now.

The following day we swept the palm groves. It was hot already and it was only 0730. We questioned a few people in nearby houses and searched around the general area. Kalouf had a metal detector and had a feeling to check by some nearby trees. He picked up a signal from a metallic object, which when we searched more thoroughly, found 50 artillery, anti-tank, anti-aircraft, and armor-piercing rounds just buried in the ground. It took us most of the day to dig all of them up, but the first thing we did was send a party of Marines to question the guy who's backyard this was. His farmhouse was one of the larger ones in this area. They told us that a guy came by and buried them in his yard and then told him if he told anyone, he would hunt down his family and execute them. They took a Humvee over to his house to arrest him. He must have been frightened because he told us where the guy who buried the ordinance was. HET showed up and asked him to show us where he was. They took two Humvees to look for the guy and found him near the edge of the desert oasis hiding out. HET brought him back to the cache site and interrogated him where we received intelligence that revealed the names of houses in the area that were secret locations for Baath party members. The prisoner also had pictures of the Muj that met there at the houses.

In the mean time, when I was not helping carry rounds and watching out on the gun, I went down to the Euphrates river to a nice spot in the shade under a grape vine. Brett and Dan had already found the undisclosed spot. I talked to them for a while and propped my head up with some palm leaves. I took some pictures of the ancient structures on the edge of the river. They must have been old bridges or locks for ships to get up and down the river. The ruins were probably several thousand years old. Brett and I talked about how I was getting married soon. I told him I couldn't believe I found such a great girl and it was kind of a miracle how it happened to me.

We guarded prisoners in a small area of palm groves just outside the farmer's wheat field, while combat photographers and Marines took pictures of one of the largest weapons caches found on this operation. One prisoner looked bad and he was whining and slouching over from the heat. For those that were found to know specific Intel, they were told to show us where certain cache sites were on a map or face punishment. The mere mention of Abu-Ghraib prison made them shake with fear. One of the prisoners was flown to al-Asad where he was being processed and incarcerated.

When it started to get dark, we had to move the cache to a sight more secure so it could be blown up and destroyed. The best idea we could come up with was making about twenty trips back and forth from the cache sight to a remote area where we could detonate the rounds with more than fifteen pounds of C-4.

The next morning we woke up and Kalouf began positioning the C-4 between every other round in a long row of fifty large artillery and mortar rounds. Each charge had to have a string of detonation cord that would connect every stick of C-4 and to make the controlled explosion even larger and make sure that it all went off at the same time. In 45 minutes, it was ready to be blown up. I just wanted to blow the cache so we could get on with the operation. Vehicles 1, 3, and 4 left us alone and went to warn the locals of the explosion that was about to happen once we lit the end of the det-cord attached to the C-4. The det-cord had to be timed so a small end of it was cut from the spool and we timed how long it would take for an inch of it to burn to the end. It took about five minutes, so that meant if we set it to blow there would be about twenty minutes until detonation. We monitored the radio and heard a transmission to blow the charges and then turn right to get in position. We quickly gathered up our gear and got in the high back. We had twenty minutes to get about 800m or more away from the site and watch the controlled blast. We sped away as fast as we could and then sat there in confusion. "Why did you not hold off?" a voice came over the radio. Leach and our Humvee heard that we were supposed to set the charges to blow, so it was a little late now. A minute was remaining and everyone watched. All of a sudden, A huge mushroom cloud covered the ridgeline and sent smoke and shrapnel sky high. After the explosion, vehicle 1 came over to the sight and the platoon Sergeant started yelling at us, "Who the hell told you to blow the cache?"

"You did Sergeant," Leach said and he stomped off to his vehicle as others looked at the huge twenty-foot crater that the explosion left in the ground. There was no noticeable evidence that a cache was even here. We stayed on the other side of the mountain were Kilo was and the NCO's got in their little circle and started talking.

Later on the platoon Sergeant handed Leach a piece of shrapnel that came from the explosion and said, "This came one inch from a Kilo Marine's head, hold onto it and I don't want to see you without it."

We also were reprimanded for someone in Crazy 8 slashing the tires of a motorcycle outside of an Iraqi farmer's house. The owner of the bike was paid twenty dollars by the Muj to mortar us. Their exact words were that Kaybar 8 was being "too mean to the people around here." We were ordered to turn in all of our AK's we were holding in our vehicle for safekeeping and told to OP the area for the rest of the time. I felt like a little kid again that just got grounded.

On our way to the OP sight, the transmission on our vehicle went out completely. We all were thinking that if the transmission had given out any earlier, we would have to run for our lives to get more than a mile away from the explosion. God was on our side that morning even though everything seemed to go wrong.

———◆———

It was now the fifth day of us living out here. It seems like every few feet that Kilo sweeps through, they find another cache of enemy weapons. I heard explosions long into the night. Caches and doors of houses were blown apart and the search continued long after we slept. We sat static next to a building used to store grain. It wasn't a surprise that every few hours of sitting on the OP, we were screwed with by the Gunny, the platoon Sergeant, or the Officers there. It even went as far as in the morning us having to clean up our own shit from inside of an empty building because we were told after the fact not to go in there and do the hajji squat. It was getting ridiculous. The longer we got into the deployment, the more stupid the decisions were being made and the more we were screwed with. I guess that was expected of the military and MAP 8 had gotten more than used to it. Like one of the leaders talking to a Gunny after he had just lost he majority of his platoon, the only thing he could say was, "how do you like the chow?" Gunny went off on him, "That's all you can say to me and my best friends just died?!" or when a sniper in one of the MAKO teams was pulled off the gun a second before he made a kill shot to tie his boot lace. I would hope these were just incredibly stupid rumors, but even if they weren't, it still was stupid decisions that were realistic to us and during wartime, they were expected I guess, especially from Marines who only showed up one weekend per month and then were suddenly thrown into an active duty status.

The bulk of the maintenance was done today from our position. Three vehicles from MAP 3 were down and our vehicle was still down. Our high back was like the used car that you bought and couldn't seem to get rid of. Like any day of OPing, we sat around and continued arguing about whatever came to our minds.

It is the fifth night of the OP. The high back is still being towed behind the seven ton and was totally flat-lined. There wasn't much to occupy our minds so I began to get delirious especially in the scalding heat. I felt sorry for Kilo who had already taken seven or eight heat cases and had already walked over 30 clicks since the beginning of the operation. Temperatures rose into the hundreds with little to no wind to cool us off.

Apparently, the weapons cache we found was very large and actually drew attention to the Commandant of the Marine Corps and President Bush, or at least that's what they told us. Although there was no way to watch TV to find out what was going on, they told us that it drew media attention as well.

The 7-ton pulled up to a position where we would be staying the night. Kilo Company and the freedom guards camped next to us and I could see the fatigue on their faces. The freedom guard, in their old Gulf War desert cammies, relaxed out on a small hill next to us. We were still stuck to the 7-ton and plans were within the next day to get an up-armored high back to replace this one. Regulations that obviously were not being followed did not allow Humvees outside the wire at al-Asad airbase unless they were up-armored. It was quite a relief for us and for our well being and it always made me think of the Soldier who refused to go on that mission in southern Iraq because he and his troops were not properly equipped with up- armored vehicles. The Soldier asked Rumsfeld why we did not have this equipment in which he replied, "You don't go to war with what you want, you go to war with what you have." That saying was the butt of a lot of jokes for us in the back of this high back piece of shit. We always thought that although it was dark humor and only we could laugh at it, still it was funny as hell that we were still driving around in this thing even though it wasn't even running and were being towed around for miles.

As I was laying out my sleeping bag for the night, we saw darkness on the horizon. A wave of blackness was closing in on us. Within ten minutes we were surrounded by darkness and it was like a wall of sand and wind just hit us. Violent winds blew most of our gear away that wasn't tied down and blinded us from seeing anything at all. I curled up inside my sleeping bag as the storm blew by us for the next four hours with no visibility and only the clean air that was inside of my sleeping bag to breath. Dan was right next to me and started violently thrashing around so hard that he hit me a few times while inside of his sleeping bag. We started wrestling in the middle of the worst violent sandstorms in the history of Crazy 8 until we were exhausted. After a few minutes, I attempted to feel around for my gas mask, which was still inside the vehicle. It was so dark. I had my hands out in front of me and when I finally got my gas mask, I noticed that my sleeping system had blown completely away! I spent the night that night sleeping on sand with my trusty gas mask on praying for morning to come.

The line companies, Kilo and India seemed to work better at night and when it was cooler for obvious reasons, but we were not finding as much after a few more caches were found and so time moved a lot faster for Crazy 8. We would probably be out of here in a few days and had to strip our broken high back of all our gear and equipment for its pickup.

This was India Company's first operation. Most of them sat at al-Asad on reserve for the other two companies (Kilo and Lima). They stopped for breaks every so often and everything looked suspicious to them, kind of like how we were when we went out on our first patrol. Some of them voluntarily wanted to come because they hated sitting around on the second wire of al-Asad's parameter and I would guess they were probably bored out of their minds. I couldn't imagine how the clock must have laughed at them. India and other new SOI boots filled in for the wounded and KIA Marines in both the line platoons and even MAP's. al-Asad was rumored to be putting in a Pizza Hut, Burger King, and a swimming pool. It was quite clear that we were living in shittier conditions than most of the other Marines in Iraq and you would have to be crazy or stupid to enjoy this. I wanted to do my time and get out of here as soon as possible.

⟫·◆·⟪

It is now June 07 and we have been in the field for quite a while. Our vehicle is still down and we moved up to the point of advance at the 55 easting, which is as far as we could push and so far found more caches including some RPG's and rockets. We spent some time with the freedom guards, who are quite the characters. They invited us into an empty house and we watched Arabic TV. Iraqi cable TV is free to everyone and the airwaves are filled with mostly music channels showing Iraqi Muslim culture. They offered me sunflower seeds and tea while we sat down on foam pads in this building made of cinder blocks and hard cement floors. "Five minutes American, five minutes Arabic!" one of the freedom guards said to the room packed full of Marines and Iraqis as he controlled the remote. There was a Colonel here from the old Iraqi Air Force. He spoke English very well and translated for us to most of the Freedom Guard. That was fun while it lasted until someone came in and told us to go to report to our vehicles and set up VCP's.

The following day they extracted us from the 76 Easting in a CH53. I loved those helicopters because they were known for their speed and agility. The President flies in one, although his is probably much more accommodating. We were temporarily riding with India Company back to al-Asad. I was just glad to get out of there and thanked God that our vehicle broke or we would be staying back with Kaybar 3 and Crazy 8 for four more days of the operation.

We loaded the bird shortly after 0900. Our truck was in the second stick with the Freedom Guard and parts of India Company and was actually flown out of the field with harnesses all the way to the air base. The high-pitched sound of the rotors whined loudly. I tried to shut my eyes as it bounced through the turbulence and unloaded it's cargo less than an hour later.

Shortly after we landed, a Sergeant that Cpl Kalouf knew from Lima offered us the use of his can, a small air-conditioned room about half the size of a trailer, which most Marines lived in if they were based at al-Asad. He was very nice and walked to chow with us. KBR had added some new things to the chow hall like a new room for hand sanitation. The food was excellent as always. We sat there while listening to the liberal media reporters ask on their TV segments like, "Why are we in this war?" I shoveled down cheeseburgers while I listened to the incessant whining of the reporters go on and on. Some of the things I liked better here were grilled cheese, Coke, non-alcoholic beer, and real cole slaw. The chow hall was packed with Marines that never left the wire and their clean cammies and fresh haircuts offset our field infantry looks that came from being out in the field for more than ten days. We chatted with the Sergeant about what was screwed up with our MAP and what happened during the operation.

I walked back to the Sergeant's can and dozed off in front of the A/C for three hours or so before we left with Major Blancher. Cpl Stocker had overheard the meeting the Major was in and heard that a few hundred ING were coming to Hadithah Dam to be trained with our MAP's.

There was some concern for the possibility that most of the ING would be Muj. Something had to be done to insure that the Dam was not compromised and so far, I had not heard anything other than keeping them outside the wire in circus tents near the river.

The bumpy ride back on the seven ton was uncomfortable, but better than riding in our piece of shit high back. We all had hoped of getting a new vehicle, one that would work all the time and would have greater survivability. We got back to the Dam that looked like it was abandoned. Everyone was either on a major operation or out manning the checkpoints. We saw workers from KBR that looked like they had been there for a while working on the plumbing and electricity. The Dam looked more fortified as well. HESCO barriers protected the tracks and the motor pool from future mortar attacks.

In operation New Market, we accomplished a lot. We collected weapons caches, which could have potentially hurt us in the future in the form of IED's. We at least prevented the threat of insurgency temporarily from that area so that people could live free and peaceful lives and we gained more experience for future operations. I was exhausted and felt like I could sleep for days.

16

JUNE 09, 2005

I can barely find the words and the strength to put the next few days down on paper. The words I write, no matter how well I write them, will not do justice or give me or any of the other Marines that witnessed these events peace of mind.

It started when we were sitting back at the Dam thinking we would be enjoying a few days of R&R, but the next thing we knew we were to go out with MAP 2 as dismounts in support of a mission. It seemed simple on paper as all of us gathered around maps of Hadithah, Haqlaniyah, and Bonidari. I sat by Cpl Kalouf and Keeling while we discussed with Sgt Williams what the plan was. To block insurgents from fleeing south while tanks rolled through the city to show a presence to the people. Everyone knew that the mission was a bit screwed up and it didn't feel right. Everyone I spoke to sounded hesitant about going out and we just had a bad feeling. We gathered our gear from our rooms and loaded up the vehicles. There were two dismount teams. One was in the high back and included Cpl Leach, Cpl Stocker, Rodriguez, Cpl Kalouf, and me. The other included five other Marines. Kalouf and I BSed in the back of the high back about what we thought we would be doing when the rest of MAP 8 got back and about how we had a running joke about 7-tons and how they still made us ride around in the high back no matter where we went. The funny thing about high backs and really vulnerable vehicles is whenever a higher ranking Officer or enlisted Marine joins our patrol, he always refuses to ride in the high back, but yet it's okay for us to ride in here all the time.

As we drove west of River Road, just off South Dam, we passed the point where we usually go off road and just then, we heard an explosion. We all got up and looked for the blast as we all saw the huge cloud of smoke billowing up from the Abrams Tank not 700m in front of us. I was worried that the

Marines inside were hurt until I saw the two tankers and the tank commander running from the crash sight. Shavez and a guy that I knew only by the inscription written on his helmet as, "Stormin' Norman" (Whom I now know as LCpl Birch) ran towards our high back. We helped them up into the high back and they were both relieved to be alive. Stromin' Norman smiled and told us about how he was a reservist from Idaho. Kalouf knew Shavez from prior operations with the line companies and he told him they should go to BAS after we got back just to get checked out. Kalouf knew other Marines who had concussions and were feeling alright after they survived crashes and then experience severe problems later. "Did you leave your MP3 player in there?" Kalouf asked.

"Oh shit, yea we did and a game boy too!" Norman exclaimed.

"Maybe we can take up a collection back at the Dam for you, we are just glad you're alright," Kalouf said as he lounged in the back of the high back now packed full of Marines. The tank commander expressed great concern for his Marines and was glad that his crew was alright and made it out of the explosion.

Cpl Kalouf kept saying, "This is the K3 district, everyone always gets hit here." Everyone agreed with him. We backed off the crash sight to Route Texas, a road that was normally taken off road for operations in Hadithah. As the situation was assessed from what just happened, the most powerful tank in the U.S. just was blown apart by an IED, the decision was made for us to dismount the high back and clear buildings from what looked like a cement factory where cinder blocks were made. The two tankers, Seymour the gunner, Cpl Squires the VC, and Keeling the driver all stayed back in the high back.

The two teams rallied around the vehicle 1 and split up to clear the warehouses on the eastern end of River road. The two large buildings were opened and pretty much abandoned from what we saw at a distance. It looked like work had not been done there in quite a while, but one building was locked in which we had to break into it. Cpl Stocker smashed the front door down and glass flew everywhere. The *four* of us went in MOUT style, stacked on the door and proceeded to clear all the rooms. The lights were off and the power was out so visibility was a problem. The place looked like a regular warehouse that could often be seen back in the States, there was a floor room where the work was done and offices that we searched individually room by room, where management conducted business. I found myself leafing through rulebooks and ledgers as well as other miscellaneous items in the offices. Each of the rooms was locked and there were about ten rooms in the building not counting the storeroom. I kept looking for a souvenir to take with me. We got to a room near the outer most edge of the building and Cpl Stocker rummaged through desk drawers and found some expended 7.62mm rounds lying out on the conference table. The cheap looking boardroom looked like something out of the early eighties and reeked of a foundry. While searching around we found some miscellaneous electronics on top of an old knobbed TV. It looked like a base station to set off an IED and we weren't sure if it was to the TV or radio. When we made our exit, we took anything that looked remotely suspicious.

As we were walking outside, we heard a large explosion. We didn't know what it was and thought it might have been more rounds cooking off inside the exploded tank, which was still burning in flames.

We quickly exited the building and I watched as everyone was running toward the road. I didn't know what was going on and all of a sudden, I heard someone say, "THE HIGH BACK HAS BEEN HIT!" I walked around aimlessly and I stumbled towards the vehicle. My stomach felt weird and I was going to vomit. I was in a daze. I kept an eye on the detainees we had captured as the situation was being assessed. I started yelling obscenities at the detainees, "WHY THE FUCK DIDN'T YOU DO SOMETHING?!? DIDN'T YOU KNOW WHO DID THIS? WHAT THE FUCK?!?" All I can remember is those detainees and their blank stares they gave me and me thinking how I wanted to kick the shit out of them. I sat down on a rock next to the black powder we found in one of the warehouses and the electronics we ripped out of the boardroom. I didn't know what to do and just sat there while everything seemed to go in slow motion. There was no security to the east of us towards Hadithah so I punched out a little ways with my SAW and kept watch until the others got back. Sgt Williams came back around 2000 and got us all together. "I'm not going to bullshit you: Three Marines were just killed in the high back: Squires, Keeling, and Seymour. The two tankers are being MEDEVACed via helicopter."

I heard the rotors overhead moving, like something out of Vietnam and sound moved slower as I tried to take in all that just happened to us. The Humvee I had just dismounted had been blown to shreds and nothing was left of the vehicle.

Later that night we rested by vehicle 1 and I could hear the radio transmissions that replayed like a broken record inside of my head. "We have just done a crash analysis on the vehicle, there is nothing left to salvage from the vehicle, nothing is left of it… There are remains all over and scattered about…"

At that point, I zoned out and blocked everything out, while others were affected by it too, and for good reason. "Can they not have some respect?" some Marines said. I was at a loss for words and kept a close watch on the detainees while I tried to block out the voice on the radio.

We were able to take fourteen detainees and HET was doing a good job of interrogating them. He talked to the women that were there about what their husbands could have possibly been responsible for and finally got some answers. We then moved our position across the road closer to one of the line companies that were using a large mansion for their firm base. Before we stepped off, we made the detainees carry the black powder bags, which were pretty heavy, to Lima's position so that they could watch them while we provided security for both crash sites, preventing people from looting things and the enemy from viewing the damage that they had caused. By then it was 0000.

JUNE 10, 2005 0000

I did not get much sleep this morning and kept thinking about what just happened. It was still all so surreal to me. I woke up about midway through the night to the sound of the tank that was on post shooting its coaxial at something in the darkness near the crash site. The radio transmission crackled some faint words and I heard them say they were shooting the dogs that were trying to come close to the crash site. I was going to be sick. *Do they have to do that?* I asked myself silently as the guns kept firing off tracer rounds at the creatures of the night.

On South Dam, two dump trucks refused to move and just sat their waiting for us to let them by. Highers kept saying not to shoot them, but just let them sit there. They were there all morning until they finally turned around. If it was Crazy 8 up there we probably would have shot at them by now and someone would end up in the hospital, but ROE's had to be followed and everything had to be done according to procedure. *Who the hell would just sit there for hours waiting for us to move unless they were Muj?*

During the early morning, some other Hajjis tried to stop at the tank and loot things like weapons and other items found. We observed the two men drive up and shot 25 rounds of MRK19 grenades at them and they finally decided to leave, or remain permanently there. These people obviously had no decency or respect for the dead. I was just thinking how long the night was and how I just wanted to get back to the Dam and even back home. I didn't want to be here any longer. Doc gave me two Tylenols and I tried to lay down for a while until my watch started at 0400. I got up and had watch on the MRK for about two hours until first light when I was relieved.

We heard that the two tankers, Shavez and Norman died on the way to al-Asad and Doc tried to resuscitate Shavez three times before he died.

I ate some of an MRE for lunch and some of us decided to check out the Iraqi mansion that Lima had been living in for the past few days. The nearby mansion belonged to an old Iraqi Republican Guardsman and we walked down to visit it. Walking past lavender fields, the smell was so refreshing and reminded me of the fresh fragrances of springtime. The rest of the Marines went down to take a final inventory and assessment of what was left of the high back.

We walked up the slowly sloping steps of the large mansion. A vineyard grew next to the marble pillars that led up to the door. Everything was amazing inside. Marines from Lima were lounging around in luxurious chairs and couches in a room full of priceless paintings and a chandelier made of crystals and gold. There were so many rooms. You could get lost in the house. We explored and it got my mind off things for a while. While walking around I saw some china and I took some for myself as well as an engraved cup coaster that was inscribed in gold Arabic lettering, "Be patient and God will bless you," I later found out it said from one of the terps. I thought I could take them home to my family and Angela. I kept thinking how much they would like that. It looked like everyone had taken most of the valuables inside, but there were still some things left. Among the more impressive things were an outdoor pool, a Jacuzzi, and an elephant sculpture from Africa. A large hookah sat in the living room that the freedom guards and the terp said that Sadaam Hussein had smoked out of. They said he used to come to the house to party. The guy was killed and his daughter now owns this place, but has a much bigger house in the green zone in Baghdad.

So we left with some loot and went back to our vehicle and waited for our ride back to the Dam and for EOD to finish their reports on both crashes. Kalouf had a gold robe from the mansion and a Christian Dior necktie, which he wore around with his uniform. It made me laugh so hard. *What a comedian.* Kalouf and I, at least I would like to think, were pretty good friends and he was a good guy and someone I could talk to who had experienced death before at al-Qui'm, when his best friend was shot and killed.

As we drove away from our POS with MAP 6, we passed the crash site and I was horrified. The IED that contained ten 120mm mortar rounds and a shit load of explosives packed into an oxygen tank left nothing of the vehicle except for the front axel and the tire. I closed my eyes and tried to sleep until we were dropped off at the front steps of the Dam and greeted by the CO, the Captain, the First Sergeant, and Cpl Ickes. They told us to stay strong and focused and they were sorry for the loss of their Marines. All I wanted to do was lay down for a while. I was sickened, horrified, and exhausted.

A half an hour later after they had cleared MAP 2's room of all the Fallen Angel's personal effects, we were told to see the Chaplain on the third deck. All of MAP 2 was there and the combat engineers and those in Crazy 8 that had come out with MAP 2 including myself. We were supposed to talk about some of the good things we remembered about the Marines that died.

Seymour was remembered as the country type and always used to dip all the time. Some people had said he was the only guy that would dip in the shower.

Keeling was remembered as someone that you could talk to and I always saw him at the student center at Kent State University. He graduated from college before he came here and was going to the in the FBI.

Squires was a guy I had always been a familiar face at the drill center. When I was there, I always saw him joking around or smoking with Trexler, his best friend.

The grieving was broken up by some laughter. We finished talking and then the evening was spent in our rooms watching movies and trying to sleep. Turner came up to me afterwards and tears were in his eyes, "I thought that was you in there man, you scared me. Don't ever do that again."

JUNE 11, 2005

The next morning Sgt Pace came in our room at about 0830 and woke everyone up for morning cleanup. I was not in the mood for it and tried to sleep as much as possible. We were also supposed to talk to a psychologist about what happened at 1000 with the rest of MAP 2 and those who were attached to witness the events of that horrifying twenty-four hours. The doctor came in and sat down in a circle with everyone. The idea was the same as with the Chaplin, except we were to go around the room and describe where we were and what happened that night. Several people had seen more then us, the bodies at the crash site, the blood, and fragments of metal strewn all over the asphalt in the high back that we climbed out of not ten minutes earlier. They agreed not to talk about the details for the sake of everyone.

The shrink was not that great at helping us out. It was as if he was there just to hear about the graphic parts and to just mark off in his book that we were okay and that we could keep on going out and risking our lives. Everyone went around the room and told their side of the story and then it came to be my turn. I told everyone how I felt and what I was feeling the night of the accident, describing it the best that I could for an event that was too hard to even think about. Whenever I close my eyes I can hear the radio transmissions play back, "total catastrophic kill, there is no salvageable piece of the high back." The two tankers, Chavez and Stormin' Norman were smiling at me and waved to us as we dismounted the high back and I was standing there after the explosion, the world moving on around me and me just standing there trying to understand why. A sudden feeling of hate for all these people in this country came over me. I wanted to get revenge on the people that did this and take out my anger. Others felt the same way. We also told the shrink about the issue of high backs verses the 7-tons and the survivability rates. I didn't think the guy helped any of us much. I could not imagine what Trexler, Squires' best friend, was feeling at that moment.

I listened to music and slept most of the day. Knowing we had to go out the following day to the east side to sweep for mines. I guess they didn't give anyone a break for a little while, "mission accomplishment" as they always say in the Corps.

The First Sergeant came into our hooch to talk with us and was someone that I confided in as a leader. "Remember that image in your mind and never forget it, because war is not a glamorous job."

"Only the dead will see the end of war."
-Plato

17

JUNE 12, 2005 2000

We waited until dark to go out to the east side near East and West Village on the intersection of Phoenix and Raptors, where MAP 2 was hit a few weeks earlier by a mind buried and hidden under a layer of pavement. Kalouf was going to sweep the area with his metal detector to make sure the area was secure of mines and IED's. It was difficult to stay awake on the gun while dismounts and Cpl Kalouf swept the road and fifteen feet on either side of the shoulder. I tried to stop thinking about the incident that happened just days earlier. I was glad that we finally were able to get a 7-ton and kept thinking that maybe if MAP 2 had one that it could have made a difference between everyone dying and Marines still being alive. Still I felt safer now and didn't have any problems doing my job. Lloyd was our new driver from an artillery company in Mississippi that had been utilized as motor T. All of those lean fighting artillerymen were now trained to be drivers. He was a soft-spoken Marine, maybe that's because it was his first day on the job, but he would eventually get to know everyone and I think everything would be okay. I still missed Turner's bitching though. He was sent to be the radio guy for MAP 9 down in Hit. As much as Turner and I had our differences, I missed him being around and the little arguments we would always get into about the dumbest things. The night of the accident, Turner thought that I had still been in the high back and took it hard. It really showed me how someone could care about you when you are on the verge of never seeing them again. The attachment we had among all the members of Crazy 8 would never change. We have an indescribable bond among brothers.

The 7-ton was very nice and had it's luxuries as well as little things that need to be fixed. We swept for mines until 0300. I didn't even know what road we were on anymore. We finally turned to OP's for the remainder of the morning until we began doing VCP's shortly around 0800. We made a stop back at the Dam to pick up the terp and the sniffing dog named, "Star" that had to ride in the A/C vehicle.

JUNE 13, 2005

Doing VCP's is very frustrating because it was like picking a needle out of a haystack. We took a few detainees, but for a gunner it was just a matter of sitting in the vehicle and watching the road, although a few interesting things came out of the checkpoint we set up. A guy in a suit got out of a van and claimed to be a financial planner. Everyone in my vehicle gave me a hard time about it, "Hey Wojo he's a financial planner just like you!" We also spotted a caravan of five black vehicles driving about 1,000m out that completely avoided our VCP. One of the vehicles had a gun mounted on it and shot at us from over 1,000m away. We fired on it with both of our .50 cals and both of them jammed up. They looked like they were in a hurry and later on found out that Zarkowi was spotted in our general area and those were his escorts. I wondered what they were doing all the way out here in East and West village.

We searched an abandoned white vehicle and then pulled up on an REI tent with two hajjis inside. They came out and smiled at us. I yelled, "What are you smiling about?" loudly in English and I knew he could hear me. My anger for these people and my close call with death came out in a fit of rage. Luckily, I was able to control myself long enough for the Sergeant to search the tents and for us to get the hell out of there before I did something I might regret. "Next time a bomb goes off and kills Marines we are coming for you!" Kalouf yelled at the men as we drove away.

Crazy 8 RTBed at 1600. Our vehicle worked on getting the 7-ton ready and organized for the next mission. Kalouf, Leach, Dickason, and I put kevlar blankets down and arranged our gear. We were supposed to go out at 2300 to insert the snipers. We also switched out the 240 for the .50 cal, probably having something to do with the malfunctioning that day, I thought, but went about my business of having only an hour before we were to leave again and attempted to get at least one hour of sleep.

We inserted the sniper team in a town outside of Hadithah called Bonidari not too far from where the high back crash site was. For now, life was not worth living when I only existed and was not able to have the ability to think or make decisions that don't involve death and dying.

Dismounts did dummy drops to make the enemy think we were dropping off at that point. We did this three times before we inserted the MAKO team, finally dropped them off, and then left them. The drop only took about three hours, but by then it was 0350 and we were told we had to go out yet again at 0600 to pick up Major White and Major Gardner, our new Commanding Officer from al-Asad. Lack of sleep did not help my awareness at that moment.

JUNE 14, 2005 0630

We hurried to our vehicles and it was a quiet ride all the way to the air base. Everyone appeared to be sleeping except our new driver Lloyd and me. It was about a two-hour ride that lasted forever. The rumors of there being a Burger King at al-Asad were true. It seemed as unreal as this deployment, a fast food restaurant in the middle of the Iraqi desert. I hadn't seen fast food since January and I woofed down a whopper and fries while I thought of everyone that enjoyed this everyday. At that point, it became clear to me that there were obvious differences between admin and field Marines. We were different and it was as if we were placed in the shittiest area in Iraq, I was certain of it. I appreciated anything at this point, even a greasy hamburger.

I stopped at the PX to buy a fathers day card and went back to the vehicles to pick up the two Officers. Our platoon Sergeant called a briefing, once again making things worse for us, and took morale down to zero. "Everyone that did not wear covers to this formation will have to carry their kevlar's around, and you Wojtecki have to carry the 240 everywhere you go because I said to carry it with you on the bird." I knew for a fact he had not said that nor did I hear him say that, but at that point I didn't even care.

Our APL was on a power trip and liked to throw his weight around. No one would say it, but we all were starting to be fed up with all the orders that the APL gave us because most of them were frivolous. I sulked and pretty much just sat on the gun without talking on the way back. When we got back to the Dam, we worked on our 7-ton at the motor-T again while we bitched about everything. If we were treated just like humans, I could guarantee that we would perform better out on the roads. The war was supposed to be out there, not inside the Dam and within our platoon.

After we turned in the vehicle, I laid down and was unaware that I even fell asleep. I woke up and it was 2200. I fell back asleep and tried to think positive, thinking about home and my fiancée's smile.

JUNE 15, 2005

Our command ordered us to get rid of Beans that we rescued from East Village, our sole source of motivation that everyone at home and at the Dam talked about. Someone even said, "If I find that dog here again I will shoot it." Any happiness I had was thrown out the window. I made it a point when I went to Segovia to tell everyone I talked to about Crazy 8's dog, Crazy Beans to get everyone to support keeping our dog.

Today was our maintenance day and our PL came down to talk to us, apologized, and listened to what we had to say. There was so much frustration and it was good to talk about it. Today I had officially been in for four years and had two more years to go. As much as the Marine Corps had shaped my life and turned me around from a punk kid to a leader and a businessman, I wanted to know what it felt like to live a normal life, although at this point I was just happy to be living.

JUNE 16, 2005

Today was an official, on the books day off. I woke up and looked at my watch and it was almost 1100. I stumbled around for a bit and then heated up some oatmeal, even though I hated oatmeal, in our small microwave by the TV. Everyday I woke up I was farther away from the first day and closer to the next. Some shrinks probably recommend that we have some time to ourselves because of the stress that we have undergone in the passed few weeks of going out on patrol constantly. There were some psychological effects coming from working every single day since we got here. Whether we liked it or not everything was affecting us one way or another. Some Marines have different ways of dealing with it and most choose not to talk about it at all.

I told my fiancée about the command's decision to get rid of our Crazy Beans. I was growing quite attached to having Beans around all the time. She was a great morale booster for the entire battalion and one way or another Crazy 8 was going to put her on a convoy to Kuwait and back to the States. The greatest story ever told was of Beans and how we rescued her from certain death out of a burlap sack, traded her for a quarter and some jellybeans, and brought her into our platoon. Now they wanted to get rid of her.

I watched the movie, *"Equilibrium"* about a government existing without feelings and how a dark and corrupt ruler takes over, declaring himself the great father.

A few hours before we were to go out on patrol again I found out I was now the new driver of the first vehicle. I had never driven a Humvee before in my life and honestly, I was somewhat nervous about it. *What if I hit a mine?* I kept thinking of my body exploding inside of the vehicle and my body parts scattering everywhere while the rest of me painfully awaited death. Horrifying thoughts and feelings were playing in the background of my consciousness as I put my hands on the wheel.

The first victor had been down for repairs, so we had to drive around in a non-armored piece of shit. The doors were scattered with AK rounds and the trunk would not close. I joked around with Dan and Brett. "It seems like I am always stuck in a vulnerable position, oddly enough." First, I was the gunner of the un-armored high back and now that we have switched to the more sturdy 7-ton that could hit a mine and only blow a wheel off, and now I'm stuck in a non-unarmored Humvee driving in the lead. This would be something that would have to wait to be told to family until I was safe at home.

Sgt Carr was known for screaming at his drivers so I tried to drive as good as possible. Gurgol said that I drove pretty well, but I still had no idea what I was doing. As we popped up over a hill, a white car kept coming towards us. Gurgol fired the 240 and the car was filled full of holes and stopped on the side of the road. We stopped the Humvee and sent dismounts to the vehicle. Two people were shot and sustained massive head injuries. We had to ground MEDEVAC them back to the Dam and they were life flighted to al-Asad. One person puked in the 7-ton, luckily I was not back there with them, but later on they found out that it was pieces of the Iraqi's brain matter. All I could think about was, better them than us, and the Chaplain kept reassuring us that we did our jobs and we would be fine. Although I wanted to blame myself for being a first time Humvee driver and I tried to think what I could have done to prevent this from happening, but I couldn't think of anything.

After all of the excitement we went back to our favorite spots at Checkpoints 8&9 and stayed there for the night. I woke up at 0230 and felt an intense burning all over my body sort of like something was shocking me. "What the fuck?!?" I screamed in confusion as I swatted my body. LCpl Perry shined a light on me. There were ants all over me! I stripped down to my boxers and got in the Humvee trying to shake off the remaining army of red ants that were trying to devour me. I could hear Crazy Beans whimpering from inside the vehicle as she rolled in the dirt. The ants were attacking her too. I spent the entire night in the Humvee.

JUNE 17, 2005

For most of the day today, we sat in the first vehicle. Sgt Carr, Perry, Gurgol, and I watched the raid that was going on in Hadithah. Hilo's flew over and the tank company sped down River Road where the IED's went off a few days earlier. Over the past few hours, I got to know the people in this vehicle pretty well. Perry was only nineteen years old; he had just graduated from high school and was our COM guy from H&S Company. Gurgol was a bit older and is a journeyman for the company he works for. He was a working guy who always had something interesting to say about politics or drinking. Sgt Carr was a cop who was big into order and organization. I absolutely hated driving this vehicle, but in a way, it reminded me of driving back home and for I second I thought I was behind the wheel of my car. The smooth sound of the tires against the pavement of U.S. roads and the roar of the engines made my daydream that much more real.

It was a relief to come back to the Dam. Sitting at checkpoints 8&9 was not the most interesting thing in the world, but every time I came back inside the wire with all my fingers and toes, every time I came back alive it was a good day.

That evening, a reporter from the Akron Beacon Journal e-mailed Major White and wanted all the guys from the Akron area to write a few short words for an article he was doing for Independence Day. The first question was, "how would the fourth of July be different for you now that you were in Iraq?" To which I wrote:

When I was at home I used to watch the fireworks and I thought of all the men and women who gave the ultimate sacrifice to protect our country. Now this year I found myself being part of the very service members I thought of when watching those colorful explosions in the sky. We are fighting a war on foreign soil to peruse the happiness that a lot of us, including myself, have taken for granted. I hoped that when my family, friends, and fiancée celebrated the fourth of July this year that they would think of me while they watched the fireworks like we always used to do together.

The second question the reporter asked was to, "What personal experience that happened to us in Iraq illustrated being a true American?" I quickly wrote on the back of the e-mail print out:

Bravery illustrates being a true American. Like those firefighters and police on September 11, 2001 who saved lives, pulling victims from the rubble. Bravery is doing what is right even though you are scared and would rather not do it. You are willing to give you life so that others can have freedom. Every time we go out on patrol not knowing if we will come back alive, to me, this was illustrating what being a true

American in Iraq meant.

I looked around me and the Marines I lived with, slept with, talked and argued with, were true Americans too.

At home there were a few that did not support what we were doing, but I fight for them as well so that they are free to express their opinion, no matter if I agreed with it or not.

I got a few packages today from my brother. I opened them and then attempted to take a shower. I went downstairs and tried to turn on the water. "Damn!" I shouted loudly. A few drops came out of the low-pressure nozzle.

I walked slowly back upstairs, shrugging off the mosquitoes that organized an ambush on me as I made the journey to the seventh deck showers. Soon after midnight, I made it back to a quiet room, felt my way into the dark room and into my rack for the night.

JUNE 18, 2005

The other bad part about being a driver was that I had also inherited all the responsibilities of fueling the vehicle, getting chow and water, and staging a half an hour before everyone else. Our armored vehicle was supposedly fixed and the Blue Force Tracker was installed and waiting up on the tenth deck. I had to drive it down to the first deck and organize it just how Sgt Carr wanted it. I was out of bed at 0830, three hours before anyone from Crazy 8 woke up.

Motor-T was supposed to have fixed the starter problem, but when we prepped for the patrol and I turned the switch to fire up the ignition, nothing but sputtering came from the engine. We had to get a jump from vehicle 3. It reminded me of the time I took Angela to the movies and my radiator exploded. We had to drive it to the nearest station and get it repaired and I could remember Angela getting so mad at me for that. I was clueless about fixing cars, let alone Humvees. I am not "automotively inclined" as Gurgol would say.

We were out of the gate by 1545 to run observation posts near Raptors and Phoenix. We had a new schedule that probably was brought about by the change of command. We go to the east side, west side, maintenance, a day off, QRF, and then start the whole cycle over again. Who knows how long this would go on until the next big operation.

I drove over pavement and rough patches, which I tried to avoid, knowing that there could be mines. Then I thought about driving at home and how it would never be the same for me again. I would probably freak out when I saw potholes on the roads at home.

Just then, Sgt Carr starts screaming, "Stop, Stop, STOP!! Something's burning!" I stopped in the middle of a farmer's field and we ripped the passenger's seat off to uncover a fire coming from the battery. "Fucking motor-T!" Sgt Carr yelled as he put out the electrical fire and inspected his ass to make sure that he was not on fire. "Well I guess we are staying here for the night." We would most likely not be doing anything but OPing tomorrow until we could get the vehicle fixed. I sat there while we listened to the sounds of the late fifties illuminating from Sgt Carr's mini-disk player. Dean Martin, Frank Sinatra, and The Planters were all in the Humvee with us tonight.

We discussed our common interests like how the majority of the people in this vehicle think that you can't spell "CRAP" without "RAP." Perry had a debate with Sgt Carr about why the VC's didn't have watch and how he had to serve it three times the other day. Sgt Carr gave an explanation of the chain of command and how it's a privilege that those with higher rank had, and how he didn't necessarily agree with Corporals not doing anything it's just that they made up for it with constant meetings in the CoC and long hours discussing plans for future operations. "There is to be a separation between the lower ranks and NCO's as leaders," he went on to say. I thought, *if I told that to half the people downstairs who had no idea what was going on half the time, there would probably be less discontent for our leaders.*

I set out a new Mosquito pop up tent tonight around 2200 hoping that the ants or some huge crawling camel spiders would not be able to crawl in and bite the hell out of me like a few nights ago. I stared up at my crucifix that blew in the constant wind causing it to rock back and forth. It was somewhat soothing. My eyes began growing weary and I let God rock me to sleep.

JUNE 19, 2005

The farmers I observed at 0630 on watch reminded me of the country back home in southern Ohio. It was interesting to see them set up the irrigation ditches and till the dry sandy soil to plant crops, without any site of rain for what seemed like years. The women took care of the house and the kids while these men went out everyday in hopes that they would turn what was once barren desert into fertile farmland. It was almost as hopeless as trying to turn the water in front of me into an iced cold beer, it just seemed like it would never happen. We were parked in the middle of such a field and I looked through my ACOG hoping I would see someone doing something wrong so I could pull the trigger of this 240 and end the extreme boredom that I was experiencing right now.

The AZ's later on in the day spotted two suspicious men digging in the palm groves. We went to check it out and it turned out to be just farmers trying to till the soil. We turned back out near the future spot for the Iraqi army camp near the Dam and went back to our original position. We were to stay there until our 24 hours were up and then rotate back to QRF at the Dam. I read a comic book and part of another novel that I borrowed from the Richardson Memorial Library on the seventh deck by the chow hall. I took turns with Perry and Gurgol on the gun until we were relieved by Kaybar 7 shortly after 1630. I drove the best I could back to the Dam. So far, I assumed I was doing a good job because no one had screamed at me yet. It was a lot of work being the first vehicle driver. It seemed like I spent most of my time at the motor pool fixing problems, fueling up, or getting chow and water for the next patrol. That's what I did most of the evening and it didn't leave much time for anything else other than to tidy up my area and fall asleep. Tomorrow we had to get up early to patrol Uranium. A lot of activity was going on down there and an IED had exploded near the train station.

JUNE 20, 2005 0600

I was nervous about driving on Route Uranium. The road had been known for its excessive mine and IED strikes. It was only wide enough for small vehicles and it was difficult to stay on what was left of the pavement. Shortly after OIF II, officials had cleared the road specifically for military vehicle use only, which made it an easy target for the Muj. We left the Dam shortly after 0700 and headed for Uranium. We were ordered to patrol and sweep all the way to al-Asad road near al-Asad Airbase.

Traveling up Uranium, which Sgt Carr called "Uranus" we spotted several mine strikes that blew half of the road apart. One in particular was part of an oxygen tank that terrorists had been using to blow up tanks. You could imagine how nervous I must have felt driving on this road, especially since it had only been my third day driving. "Under no circumstances will you drive off this road!" Sgt Carr made clear to me. Snipers / MAKO 4 were in the area to stop any activities or anyone from planting mines or IED's while our patrols were in progress. Surprisingly the day went by fast and we decided to stop at al-Asad to fix more of our vehicle problems. It pissed me off because we always seemed to get the shittiest equipment to do our job with that broke down frequently and was not dependable by any means. Not to preach politics, but an army with good equipment has better odds of succeeding than one with shitty equipment that breaks down all the time.

It took the Mecs two hours and a case of non-alcoholic Coors light beer to fix our steering problem. We sat there in the motor-T at al-Asad, some of us sleeping, others eating chow that vehicles 3 and 4 brought us from the chow hall while we waited. I took a test drive with one of the Mecs and he started laughing when he saw what the vehicle did once you got up to a certain speed. It shakes violently and feels like the wheels are going to fall off. They fixed the problem and we were in route back to the Dam via Uranium again. I felt confident, but still kept my leg tucked underneath me. My crucifix was still hanging from the sun visor.

Although the shaking problem was fixed, it was like when I used to ride roller coasters all day long and afterwards I could still feel myself on the ride. That is how I felt most of the way back. Perry joked with me, "What's the matter Wojo, you look shook up."

"Hah hah Perry, very funny!" I went inside the Dam after using the Porta-John and organized my trash for the next day.

Our schedule had now taken us to a maintenance day that started at 1630 today and mostly involved fixing our vehicles, cleaning weapons, and cleaning our room. I took a shower while all the nonsense went on downstairs and then talked to my fiancée. I then found myself outside on our balcony looking out at the sky. The moon and the stars sure looked different in this part of the world. All the stupid things I had to do, every patrol at that moment seemed minute. A letter from my dad read, "*I am so proud of my son and we have such a great family.*" Feeling rather depressed, I laid another night in this horrible country to rest.

18

JUNE 21, 2005 DAY OFF

I felt like I was a kid again. I had to finish all my chores before I could do what I wanted. Plus, highers had conveniently arranged a working party to clear the sandbags we had filled up more than a month ago and pile them near where the Iraqi workers always washed their cars. The soapy water always flooded the streets and became stagnant next to the showering facilities. *So much for the stress free day off that the shrinks wanted to give us.* Luckily, I received some care packages in the mail. I think that everyone at home giving us support were heroes to us here in Iraq. Packages always kept my spirits high and let me know that I was not forgotten. I piled some food on my bed, some DVD's, and a coffee mug my brother sent me. I also reached into one of my packages and pulled out some toy squirt guns. I gave one to Dan and one to Steve. "Take that!" I shot him in the face and ran onto the porch. I opened up the door and Steve squirted me square in the chest. Dan smiled and ducked behind the racks as I sprang up and shot Gurgol just missing Steve. He was cleaning the .50 cal, "You fags!" Gurgol shouted. The fight ended and I was victorious. I went to chow with Dan upstairs. It was spaghetti, which seemed to be cooked most often and was probably very easy to make. It was also the best tasting. Dan and I would only go to chow when we knew there was either spaghetti or chicken. It always reminded me of how my mom used to cook for me and how good everything used to taste. I wish that I could go back and show her how grateful I was. Being a teenager and very rebellious, I never realized how good I had it and was often not satisfied with anything. My mom put up with my yelling and fighting for most of my life and yet she always thought of the good things that happened between us during our childhood. Somehow, when I got home I wanted to show her how thankful I was. In many ways, being away from home for longer than I have ever been before and not knowing whether I would live to see tomorrow really made me think about a lot of things. "You ready?" Dan looked at me and then we walked downstairs together. I had to check on our vehicle again so I walked down to motor-T and Dan continued playing "the bike game" for Playstation. I got down there and they told me they would call me when I was ready. Frankly, I was tired of walking over there, but needed the exercise. It only took about twenty minutes and I went upstairs to use the Internet on the sixth deck where there was a memorial that always depressed me. Every time I looked at the kevlar, boots, and M-16, there seemed to be more dog tags than the last time I looked at it. Pictures were hanging up to commemorate and remember the fallen. It was unfortunate for those Marines who were so young to have their lives taken from them. It was the kind of thing that really affected me and kept me up at night thinking.

I checked my email. John Adams, a co-worker of mine, wrote me a note letting me know how his talks went in St. Louis, Chicago, and LA. Not too long ago I sent him a picture to use at the office and then a picture of me in fatigues. The point of his talks was the fear of rejection and how my situation really puts things in perspective. "You have to have the courage to get in front of people or else your practice will fail." I could see him telling attentive audiences around the U.S. John said that watching the nightly news was a lot different for him now that he knew someone that was over there. I wrote John a short reply and then hopped on the phone to talk to my fiancée, which I had been quite worried about and missed. We only had 30 minutes to talk, which didn't seem like much. It was unbelievable that I used to talk to her on my cell phone for hours.

The new DVD's I got were good. My brother and Fiancée always knew what I wanted. Everyone else was playing poker tonight and the minimum to get in was $20. Dickason was a serious poker player and always played with sunglasses on. Sgt Carr and a few other NCO's were there from the third deck. It always seemed like they came down from a different world to visit our room. I didn't pay much attention to the game and my movies too me away from here long into the night. I passed out to the credits of a movie that my brother and I used to watch.

19

JUNE 22, 2005

Our vehicle was finally done being repaired and I went to pick it up around 1000. It reminded me of some of the problems I used to have with my first car. I drove back to the motor pool and then went up to my room to go back to sleep. The subtle end to yesterday was no surprise and it only came around once every seven days if we were lucky. I made some coffee and read some magazines at our table. Talk around the Lance Corporal network was that we would be moving rooms because of India Company coming in. It was rather unfortunate for Crazy 8, but talk about moving had been going on for quite a while.

Another package came for me today. The manager at a well know financial firm in Akron wrote to me about three employees from the Company that were killed in the World Trade Center on September 11, 2001. He wrote that there is a memorial up for them in the office and there isn't a day that goes by that he does not think about them. The manager wrote that he appreciated the service we give to our country and looks forward to meeting me when I get back to the States. I put the letter face up on my rack and left for 8&9, beginning another week's rotation. The manager's letter gave me a lot to think about as Crazy 8 rolled out the west side gate and waved to the AZ's. We were on our way to relieve MAP 2, who had been on 8&9 for 24 hours, keeping the checkpoints constantly manned and maintaining MSR security. I was getting the feel for driving, although being vehicle 1's driver was absolutely the worst place to be. It was nice to change things up a bit, having been a gunner for four months.

Vehicle 1 sat on top of a hill overlooking 8 and Route Bronze running into Hadithah and Haqlaniyah to the east. I remembered my encounter with the ants several nights earlier and thought it might be best if I slept on the hood of the Humvee tonight. About an hour later, a convoy of eleven vehicles sped past, "It's ISF!" I said loudly from the gun. It was part of the Iraqi security forces who road in white Nissan pickups and AK-74 machine guns that looked like they had been salvaged. America, during the first Gulf War started a vehicle for oil program in which they would give us oil in exchange for food and trucks that were identical, and were seen driving around almost everywhere in Iraq. The Iraqi's waved to us. I thought it's about time those sons of bitches got here to defend their own country. The numbers looked slim, considering the Iraqi government started with over 1,000 ISF and were now down to less than 400 when they found out they were going to the worst area of Iraq, the Sunni Triangle. Not long after the convoy pulled into the Dam, three mortar rounds impacted near the motor pool. We assumed the Muj were aiming at the ISF, trying to scare them into retreating. Luckily, no one had been hurt during the attack and who knows how the ISF would react. *If I were the Muj, I would join the ISF and then attack the Dam,* I thought while standing in the turret watching over barren roads.

We took two-hour shifts on watch and while one person was on watch everyone else read books, slept, or played video games. We listened to music that made the time go by fast, especially the more patriotic of country tunes that I listened to with my Fiancée before being deployed. Several more convoys went by tonight, hopefully more mail and supplies.

JUNE 23, 2005

Kaybar 7, our relief, ended up being two hours late because of a mission they had with India Company. When we got back to the Dam, we would be on QRF, prepared to load up and react to any emergencies that may happen. Visibility was almost zero after a violent sand storm kicked up dust for miles and disabled the possibility of air and MEDEVAC birds. The conditions expected to worsen for the next 24 to 48 hours. India Company was back from Operation Spear near al-Qui'm so the facilities were overcrowded. There was a three-hour wait for phones and computers, even a wait to use the heads. A half and hour after we RTBed, The Lieutenant Colonel called all of Crazy 8 down to the first deck to basically thank us for what we were doing thus far. "If it wasn't for you Marines the MSR's would be free reign for the terrorists and the entire OIF III would fail because you keep the MSR's open and free for us and the citizens of Iraq to drive on." The LTC also discussed Operation Spear and said that 50 insurgents along with some high value targets were destroyed with minimal U.S. KIA's making it a huge success. He touched on the operation in Hit, which would take an entire division to occupy along with members of the Army and ISF forces to successfully occupy a city of 180,000 people. "We don't want them knowing exactly when we are going to do it, but they have knowledge of it simply because it's the last city on our check list," He said. A short five minutes of Q&A revealed that the LTC knew when we were going home, but would not tell us, again for the sake of Op-Sec and for the unit that would be RIPing. "A lot of violence broke out during our RIP and the best thing we can do is to give the unit replacing us a fighting chance of succeed at their mission."

I was exhausted and wanted to eventually use the phone tonight, but the wait was so long. It was 1230 before the place cleared out and I had to go on watch. Cpl Back told me that the cutting scores had been released for picking up the next rank to Corporal and I was close. Being promoted would give me a raise, which was about all I really cared about at that point. I did not want my friends to think of me any different so I promised myself that I would not totally change and separate myself from them.

Several Marines stayed up and watched the *"OC."* Soon after walking back from the vehicles in my sandals and t-shirt, I put another "X" on my colander and hit the rack.

JUNE 24, 2005

This morning the only thing I could think about was how much I missed having a coffee served to me at the coffee shop, an espresso that wakes me up and makes the rest of my day manageable. I hurriedly put my boots on and slammed the door to my room going down for yet another watch post. You are probably wondering why we do this and the answer I got was so that no one could steal anything from our vehicles or as it is so bluntly put, "Rat fucked."

I finally got a chance to use the phone and soon after I did, we had to out again on another mission. I wasn't really feeling up to going out and reducing an IED right where the high back exploded. We were headed towards Route Grizzly's near the town of Bonidari, the worst place to go in our AO. I had just gotten off the phone with Angela, who was feeling pretty sad, "you missed so much with me, my birthday, going to Florida, and just being with you," she said as I tried not to cry. It made me sad and for a moment didn't feel like being here anymore. In fact, I don't remember when I ever felt like being here.

I nervously grabbed the wheel of vehicle 1 and we left the gate with two tanks, EOD, snipers, and Crazy 8. It took us less than three hours to reduce the IED and the suspected mine. One thing I did notice today is that once an event really traumatizes me, I start acting suspicious of everything. The rosary still hung from my visor. I felt that removing it would be bad for us and would mean death. I lost it later that day and spent a half an hour looking for it before I gave up. I'm going to die, I convinced myself as I sat in the drivers seat. "Oh, I guess we're fucked!" I screamed and threw everything out of the Humvee looking for it. When we later returned I felt relieved that nothing happened to me. EOD had their robot out looking at the IED. Soon after, the IED was blown in place not 200m from our position. The explosion rocked the vehicle, shook the windows, and scared the living shit out of me. "Jesus!" I said. The dust still kicked up in a storm that seemed like it would never end. For a while, I had to stop and could not follow the tank in front of me.

On the way to the IED site, Vehicle 4 was being followed by a red Crown four-door sedan with two MAM's that would not stop when we flared them. Soon after, five .50 cal shots from Ross' third vehicle gun ripped through the glove box and steering column sending the two Hajjis to Allah. It was later found out that that they possessed anti-coalition propaganda and fake ID cards. BOLO was a list of vehicles that intelligence reported being suspicious, and the Red Crown had been on it. No matter how many we killed, it could not bring back my friends that died. In addition to lighting up the vehicle, we also detained three MAM's observing us from an abandoned building, which we also brought in for questioning. I would say that in a matter of three hours that we did a good job and I was a relived to come back inside the wire intact. There was about a half an hour where we were permitted to eat chow, but had to be out at the vehicles. I did not know why we were not attending the ceremony for the fallen. Maybe it was too difficult for some people to handle or had possibly been rescheduled for another time. Either way I wanted to pay my respects and say goodbye to some of the Marines that I knew personally. The tenth deck was always a place to reflect. Its view of the Euphrates and the lake out to the east were very relaxing.

We punched out to the east side. Our new tip was that at least three ISF and one interpreter would be rolling with us. No one knew what to expect from them. Some of them fought side by side with Marines in Fallujah so maybe there was some hope for them, although rumor was that they were not that incredibly bright. Some of them even shot each other up because they could not handle their weapons properly. They were one step closer to us getting out of their country and them taking over for themselves.

Here I am again punched out on an OP facing Route Phoenix / Raptors intersection and the small farming villages that we observe time and time over again. The wind still gusts and the sand is aggravating me. My lungs can only handle so much as I sit in the driver's seat and write this. The sun shines through the layers of light brown mist and dries everything it touches. Sgt Carr is sitting to the right of me, Gurgol is up in the gun reading some kind of Better Sex brochure he got in the mail, and Perry is reading one of the six lengthy fantasy novels that we call "fairy tail books." I start to daydream and drift farther away from this place. I hope that I will wake up one day and it will all be gone.

20

JUNE 25 – JULY 11, 2005 OPERATION SPEAR - HIT, IRAQ.

We conducted VCP's for most of the morning. It was rare to see so much traffic on Route Raptors and the road is usually calm. I was part of the search team that searched personnel once they exited their vehicles and walked more than 100m to our Position. For the most part, people were friendly and we worked along side the ISF, who surprisingly did a great job of searching vehicles and personnel. They knew the language so you could see that people were more receptive to them.

We searched every car that came down Raptors. It wasn't unusual that we would search eight or nine vehicles at one time. A few interesting people stopped and claimed to be cell phone businessmen and possessed large amounts of foreign money from Syria, China, Europe, and Jordan. They seemed rather suspicious so we detained them. A Russian looking guy, another white guy who looked "metro-sexual" wearing an expensive wrist watch and all Armani clothing, and two other Iraqis that were riding with them came aboard the 7-ton with eyes taped and hands zip tied behind their backs. Their GMC Jimmy was loaded full of money. The ISF took sodas from the cooler. I also came across a sizable amount of U.S. currency. We were all searched as well to make sure that we had no cash on us and to protect ourselves in case those bastards reported anything stolen. There was probably about 1,600 dollars in U.S. cash here. Overall, it was a fun experience. I had never searched people before, although I was very hesitant to touch any of them for fear I could catch some kind of man eating bacteria or some kind of mutant disease that would put an end to me long after my contract of enlistment was up. I had always been the guy up in the gun just sitting there waiting to shoot someone, but this time I was padding people down and checking IDs.

Another guy we searched looked very familiar and it seemed like we were always running into him everywhere we went. We saw him near Barwanah asking for water and sure enough here he was again. That fucking ridiculous smile and bright full head of red hair gleamed in the sunlight. It was as if he was making a mockery of our system. I had my picture taken next to him as everyone around me started laughing hysterically.

Later that day, we brought back our catch of detainees and stood by our vehicles for an hour or so to get word about another mission. Ever since the Hit operation officially started, we had been going non-stop, although we were not the tip of the spear in this operation, we were supporting from the Dam as the line companies searched more than 100,000 houses in the city of Hit along side the ISF. Anything else that highers could dream up for us to do, we did that too.

They left only four MAP's at the Dam so now it was like we were working overtime. When we got back to the Dam, I was stuck guarding the detainees for a few hours in the blazing 100-degree sun. We were on a split section; vehicles 1 and 2 were back at the Dam, while vehicles 3 and 4 were out on patrol. Until they got back here to meet up with us, we could not go back out again. Of coarse, almost everyone was upstairs sleeping or playing video games while I had to stay down here with Perry and guard these lowlifes. I was able to get chow and talk with Perry about how much life sucked among other things. Ross, the gunner that lit up those two guys the other day with the .50 cal had two confirmed kills and we talked to him about that too.

For the next 24 hours straight, we would be running back and forth on Uranium to al-Asad to drop off ISF, then we would come back, pick up Officers for the Hit operation and return them to al-Asad again. You could imagine how drained I was. With the amount of mileage that we racked up on the odometers over that last 24 hours, we could have traveled from Ohio to Florida almost twice. It was kind of like a road-trip, except the roads were mined and we took four rounds of IDF driving down Bronze. I slept on the hood for two hours from 0400 to 0600 that morning and then we left for the second time somewhere around 1630 when everyone was done getting fat and happy at chow and the PX.

We stopped briefly back at the Dam to prep our gear and then went straight back out to relieve MAP 6 on 8&9. MAP 6 wrapped up a few guys from Syria and one of them stupidly tried to run away so they shot him in the back. On the way back, we tried chasing down six black vehicles in a perfectly aligned formation. They sped off before we could catch them. I always wondered why if we knew that the vehicles were a big deal why we did not call in air on them. Probably for reasons that are highly classified, or because this is a cluster fuck as always and we do things that don't make sense.

I needed sleep so bad and I was trying to fight it off by taking some caffeine pills that I found under the Humvee seat. We could officially get a good night's sleep although it would be a broken sleep. *What did I care? Every night I have ever spent here has been broken into four-hour chunks,* I thought as I rolled over in the sand.

21

When we RTBed it wasn't more than six hours later that we were back out on patrol on the east side. ISF and a few other Kaybar units officially kicked off the Hit operation by opening fire at a white vehicle outside of the city. They killed the four MAM's inside and soon after, people came running out of their homes to fight with their AK-47's and other small arms including RPG's. The Marines quickly called for backup, but the cobra helicopters that arrived did not equip themselves with type 2 capabilities, which are mainly tomahawk missiles. They called in two F-15's that were in route to al-Asad. They made about nine strafe runs through the city, mowing down dozens of enemy insurgents until they finally stopped fighting. Later after the dust settled, the line company Marines of 3/25 assessed the situation and found huge arms caches including four mortar tubes, anti-aircraft rounds, and RPG's. Crazy 8 was on QRF at that time and had just RTBed. Not a half-an-hour later, I was sitting at the vehicles while Marines from Crazy 8 went up to S-1 to fill out some paperwork on the eighth deck, something about emergency contact sheets. I stood around on guard looking out over the lake when all of a sudden a huge indescribable explosion about 50m away from me almost knocked me over. Soon after two more large explosions, "BOOM! BOOM! BOOM!" the sound of the delayed fuses cracked against the Dam and into the water, stirring up the bottom and sending water raining down for a few hundred meters. "Holy Shit!" I screamed as I ran into the concrete enforced hallway to take cover. There turned out to be six in all. I could smell the exploded rounds. It was a strong pungent smell, sort of like sulfur. That had been the closest I have ever been to a mortar attack and I was lucky to be alive. Having my arms was a bonus too. My legs shook with nervousness as I walked upstairs to the room. I was exhausted.

Sgt Carr brought along a backgammon board for us to pass the time while on OP's. We were out on the east side for a few days, mostly just observing the local farmers in the surrounding villages, doing VCP's, and watching Sgt

Carr learn how to play backgammon with Gurgol while we waited to relive MAP 6 on the west side. They were on about their seventh game when the call came over the radio for us to escort EOD to an IED sight that MAP 6 found on Uranium. They had been doing a patrol on Uranium when their vehicle hit an IED with no significant damage, but they discovered another IED further on down the road.

I was not really up to rolling down Uranium today. We were relaxed and I don't think anyone felt up to it. Sgt Carr and Gurgol finished their last game and we headed out to the road to meet EOD on the tenth deck, where we would escort them to the IED sight.

I still kept my leg tucked under me as I drove down South Dam road to Bronze, a heavily trafficked public road, and then left on Uranium. Five vehicles followed us. As I turned onto Uranium, my heart dropped in my chest, a normal feeling I expected when turning onto this road. Sgt Carr was doing something on the Blue Force Tracker and smoking his Turkish Gold's, Perry was monitoring the radios, Gurgol was ready to pull the trigger up in the turret, and my hands were gripped tightly around the steering wheel. I was driving like an old lady.

⋯⬦⬦⬦⋯

As we came up to Train Station Village, there was a bend in the road. I turned as the road narrowed and a large explosion enveloped our vehicle. Time stood still as parts from the engine flew everywhere. All I could see was dust and all I could hear was a loud ringing. *AM I ALIVE?* I asked myself. *Yes, I have to be.* I was in shock because my mind was working but my body wasn't. I didn't know what was going on and drew a blank. "Shit!" I yelled as soon as I finally realized what just happened, which seemed like a good five minutes later. Gurgol was yelling, "I'm hit!" I tried to help him. He was bleeding pretty badly. There was a lot of dust in the vehicle that soon cleared enough to where I could see Gurgol laying in the vehicle in pain. He had shrapnel in his legs from what I could see. I quickly tried to comfort him and asked Sgt Carr if he was alright. He looked fucked up too. Perry and I were pretty much okay with minor ear injuries and some pain in our muscles. I was not thinking about pain or myself at that point. My adrenaline kicked in and I was only worried about getting Gurgol and Sgt Carr to safety. I had watched a lot of movies where the vehicle catches fire and blows up, so I was worried about that and wanted to get Gurgol and Sgt Carr out as soon as possible. It came down to doing what I could to help Sgt Carr and Gurgol. Doc Barone came over from the third vehicle to help assess injuries. We loaded Gurgol up on a stretcher and Gurgol's blood was all over my hands. We cut his pant legs and wrapped the wounds with gauze as he screamed with pain. "You're going to be fine Gurgol!" I said. Sgt Carr wanted me to get a picture of the vehicle for him. I was so delirious and out of it, I started taking pictures of him. "No! Not me you idiot, the vehicle!" I tried taking pictures of the vehicle, but my hands would not stop shaking. The front of the vehicle was completely gone. Pieces of twisted metal and shrapnel were everywhere and I thanked God for being alive. I immediately started throwing stuff out of the vehicle: NVG's, 240G, rifles, packs, and Sgt Carr's maps. I found Sgt Carr's backgammon board that he was playing just hours earlier and pulled it from the wreckage. I was so shook up, my head was spinning and a high-pitched whistling sound in my head would not go away. I went over to see Sgt Carr. He looked up at me. Blood was on his face and tried to talk with his neck brace on, "Is everyone alright? Your not bullshitting me, Gurgol will be okay right?"

"Yes Sergeant, everyone is fine and you're going to be okay," I told Sgt Carr. Perry and I helped load the stretchers into the 7-ton and we were taken to the MEDEVAC LZ sight where we were life-flighted to al-Asad. Sgt Carr was acting a little crazy, "watch for secondaries!" he kept moaning repeatedly as we waited to load the bird. I just hoped everything would be okay with him.

As the bird landed, Cpl Stocker and I carried Sgt Carr and helped him onto the helicopter. He hugged me and it made me feel a little better. It all happened so fast. The IED had exploded on us and we had survived, we were on the bird to al-Asad where we would receive medical care. This kept running through my head while I listened to the sound of the rotors. Gurgol had massive injuries to his legs and was rushed to the ER. Sgt Carr had a problem with his foot, elbow, and hearing.

We arrived at the hospital and were taken to an examination room where our vitals were taken and we were checked for signs of trauma. I kept asking if the others were okay and the nurse said they would be okay. I could still hear the ringing as I lay down and stared into the florescent lights. I could smell the cleaning agents they used to wipe down the tables with. It was a very strong smell and was overpowering. Perry and I checked out with hearing loss and some other injuries. The blast that went through me felt like someone had just kicked my ass. A voice from the other room called my name, "Sgt Carr would like to see you before you go," the nurse said as she walked me down to patient room two where he was lying. He looked pretty banged up, but still had his bearing and we talked about the vehicle and how we would probably get replaced with a shittier, less armored vehicle and how we would be riding in what he liked to call "the hot seat." Gurgol was flown to Balad, Iraq, where surgeons would take out the pieces of shrapnel from his legs and he would probably end up rotating back to the States. Sgt Carr would be staying here for a few days and Perry and I would stay for a couple days here at RAS to rest and recover before going back to work again. A convoy would be here in three days to pick up the AZ's who arrived about the same time we did. The AZ's suffered an intense mortar attack on the Dam that hit the seventh deck and the motor pool, injuring ten members of their army.

The naval officer on deck drove us by bus to our birthing area just outside the RAS where we would be staying for the next couple of days. The comfortable seats and soft music reminded me of the simple things I took for granted at home and it was as if I was back there for just a minute. A doctor escorted us to the tents and helped us call out families via a satellite phone. He also got us blankets for the night. It was 1400 back in the States and about 2130 here. I left a message for my parents and called my fiancée, "I just want to let you know that I am okay. I'll be fine," I said and she asked if something happened, which I didn't feel I should lie to her so I told here what happened to us. It was very upsetting to hear her crying at work and I probably shouldn't have called, but I needed to talk to her to make sure that she did not hear from someone else that I was hurt. She had to call off the rest of work because she took it pretty hard.

That night I thought about Angela and started to cry. Why did our life have to be interrupted? I felt like it was all my fault and I hoped she would still have fun on her vacation to Florida. She was leaving soon.

There were a number of people who were staying in the tents at the RAS. An Army Sergeant from 1st Bradley Battalion had completed a year tour in Ramadi and just came from a tour in Korea last year. We talked with him about our unit, how the Army fights in Brigades, and how the Marines are only a Corps. He seemed like a good guy. He hobbled around with crutches because he broke his leg somewhere, probably evacuating his tank. Several injured Iraqi Freedom Guards that were injured in Operation Spear. My friend, the Iraqi Colonel, was here that I watched TV with during the cache sweep a few weeks ago. I'm not sure why he was here. Maybe he was rotating out to civilian life.

Perry slept on the top bunk and I slept on the bottom. I was so exhausted I passed out after the recent horrific event had joined with other horrific events inside my mind like the sounds of the explosion, the engine not shutting off, and the blood. For three days, LCpl Perry, Sgt Carr, and I were kept at the RAS for observation until we were booked on a flight back to Hadithah on a CH53. New cipher fills for the radios at the Dam were given to Perry to drop off. For most of the time at al-Asad I could not go to sleep without thinking of the explosions and maybe I thought I could have prevented it if I would have gone slower or been more observant. Perry and I got back to the Dam around 0200 and checked in at the CoC. The Gunny on deck said he was proud of the way we handled ourselves out there and the Officers gave us a look like they were happy to see us alive.

When MAP 2 went out to patrol Uranium the following evening they spotted two MAM's in an old Crown Victoria driving on Uranium so they shot a few .50 cal rounds into the vehicle, killing both occupants. They searched the car and found a propane tank and four to five artillery rounds in the trunk. These most likely were used to make more IED's to plant on

Uranium similar to what hit our first vehicle. MAP 2 put the vehicle in neutral and let it roll into the desert where they shot it with a TOW missile sending flames miles into the sky.

As Operation Spear progressed into its second week, insurgents moved south towards the Dam. MAP rotations were 72 on and 24 off, although most of the time we usually got called out to cover checkpoints 8&9. Reports came from several sources saying there were more than 60 insurgents by the water tower in Haqlaniyah the night we went out, armored with RPK's and AK's. Our forces were running thin due to the operation so I assumed if we were engaged we would have to assault through until nearly our entire platoon was obliterated.

Crazy 8 must have patrolled Uranium seven or eight times within a three-day period. While Perry and I recovered back at the Dam, they spotted the body of the guy that supposedly set up the IED that blew up our vehicle. Later that day they saw him again and his upper torso was ripped to shreds by hyenas. I hope that the horrific display would heed as a warning to oncoming terrorists or Iraqis with a death wish that valued money over love for their country.

EOD reported that the IED we ran over only contained one 155mm round and was triggered by two saw blades that made contact by a pressure plate over the road. I was fearful of even thinking about what an improvised explosive device containing more than one mortar round or even an oxygen tank would do to our vehicle. After the explosion, I remained the first vehicle driver when released from light duty just a day ago. I cringed going over every bump and piece of debris in the road.

My parents and fiancée were hysterical when a Naval Officer called my house and read my medical form from the incident verbatim. Angela was in tears when I called her and it made me sad too. I just wish I could go home right now and this would all be over.

Over the past few days, I had been thinking about what I would do when I got home with my life. Over Independence Day, we did not get a day off or anything other than a piece of red, white, and blue cake at chow. It was very disappointing, but the word that I was being promoted to Corporal was the best news I had heard yet. Let's hope that it was more believable than the rumor that the USO was going to come to the Dam for the fourth to put on a big show.

On our QRF, we ended up going out five or six times. It was something to be expected while major operations were going on. Officers predicted that Operation Spear would be drawn out until the end of July. Resources at the Dam were spread thin and we were being worked "day on stay on."

Brett flipped out yesterday and is not taking things very well. I came and saw him in his room and he slammed his rifle down on the deck, "I don't think I can take this much longer Matt," he said. I tried to cheer him up, but he sat there sulking and when it was time to go out, he let out a murderous scream and threw up his arms. He stayed back at the Dam while the rest of us went out on the east side to run patrols and provide security for EOD while they disarmed another IED on Phoenix. Brett's mood, I think, was shared by all of Crazy 8. It was just that others had a different way of showing it. We had no time off and we were being run thin. It was 24 on zero off and it was fucking with everyone mentally, especially all that happened to us the passed few days.

Last night it grew very cold and the wind cut across the desert like ice. I sat up in the turret of Vehicle 1 and stuck my head out into the darkness. I stared across the landscape at east and west village. It was 0300. My hearing was still bothering me and I felt groggy. A piercing high pitched sound was driving me crazy and I think I was the only one to hear it. I don't know if I could keep this up much longer and for a minute I felt like Brett, like taking my rifle and throwing into the blackness. I just kept thinking about my fiancée, who was probably in Florida right now, how she would always say, "you're my hero, Matthew!" That feeling of happiness faded into the coldness of the wind that would never stop and the desert that went on forever.

After the Officers at the Dam had several meetings and smoked several packs of cigarettes under the cammie netting of the CoC, they agreed on a set schedule for the four MAP's that remained behind at Hadithah Dam. We were divided into AO's for four days at a time. We would go to the east side for four days until 10 July and then go back for QRF for 24 hours, after which we would rotate back to our AO for another four days until the operation was complete and we were back to full force. I would have almost preferred being in Hit being shot at by Muj than to drive myself crazy with this schedule.

Meanwhile the objective in Hit was to secure a permanent FOB in the middle of the city. The strength of the operation was backed up by a brigade (1,000 soldiers) of Army troops that moved in from the south from Ramadi to link up with Lima Company and the rest of the Marines in 3/25. Word was that after Operation Spear that they would take Hadithah again and set up a permanent FOB there too, but that was just rumor.

Our relief was due to arrive the beginning of September, but for the sake of Op-Sec, the exact date was not given. It was exciting to think about while we forced ourselves out of the rack every morning.

The insurgents blocked the north end of the city of Hit with IED's that were laced with PE4, oxygen tanks, and mines. They managed to stage a full scale assault, but our efforts moved in from the south, unexpectedly and proved to be a flawless move with minimal casualties and no deaths.

Meanwhile, Crazy 8 sat on the east side, our AO for four days. It was nerve racking to say the least. I could see the boredom and the stares that came from Crazy 8's faces as we trudged on day in and day out. Cpl Maple and his dog Star stayed with us for a few days to do VCP's and search the roads for suspected IED's. Military dogs proved to be rather effective in combat operations. Cpl Maple was an active duty Marine who had been to Okinawa and Saudi Arabia with his dog. Star is a very well trained dog and does only what he is told to do.

Mid-afternoon came and we took a break for an MRE chow. I slept for an hour or so and woke up to the sound of the other vehicles starting their engines. We sped off and back onto Phoenix where we would search for more IED's. A few miles down the road, we spotted something suspicious. I stopped the Humvee. Cpl Maple and Star got out and found an IED containing three artillery rounds just outside of east village.

Driving still was not working out for me. Every turn we went around, every bump we went over, I kept envisioning explosions that sent me into these little fits of anxiety that would not leave me alone. The incident also affected the way I slept. During the night, I always woke up in the early hours of the morning to complete silence. I have never experienced complete silence before. It was not like back home where I could hear cars or trucks that downshifted when going up a steep incline. No, this was different. It was complete and utter silence. Now all I can hear is a high pitched sound coming from my right ear and the night before I could hear explosions before I dozed off and had strange dreams of tanks invading my house and war invading my life at home. As I lay down and looked up at the stars, I prayed:

God, thank you for giving me a great life, thank you for everything you have given me, but why do my friends have to die around me? Is it a test of faith? Please give me the strength to carry out my mission and let me return home to the life I had, that I loved. Amen.

<hr />

Since we were now in charge of a permanent AO on the east side, Sgt Carr and our APL wanted our MAP to start using more aggressive tactics, such as the use of claymores underneath overpasses and spike strips hidden near military access roads. Our QRF day set most of us temporarily at ease. Taking a short break before we had to punch back out to the east side was a good thing. My promotion was today and it gave me a little bit more confidence in my abilities. The extra pay was not bad either.

Just recently, the Congress denounced the lawsuit and accusations by fellow military that being ordered to receive the Anthrax vaccine was unlawful. It was now optional to get the vaccine and we had an hour class pertaining to information on the deadly illness and its vaccine. We were required by our parent command, 2nd MAR DIV. We now had a choice on weather or not to receive the vaccine, which was one of six inoculations to prevent the onset of pulmonary Anthrax inhaled through the air. Ironically, several Marines had started receiving the vaccine when it was still mandatory and so it would make sense to just finish it rather than just receiving half the dosage. Right now, we were told that there were supposedly seven countries that have the virus and could use it against the U.S. in weapons grade form.

The short QRF day came to a close shortly after 1700 to punch out to the east side for three more days. The night before, we were on the brink of being called out to extract the snipers after they acquired a target on River Road near where the two explosions happened and by the concrete factory. Supposedly, the CoC has a map passed down from some Hajji that told exactly where the mines and IED's were, but would still send us out on the road blind. It seemed absolutely ridiculous and the reason was that they could not validate the accuracy of the document.

Things seemed to be getting worse here. The morale is very low and sometimes despair sets in, the feeling you get right after fallen hope and right before insanity. When I was on the phone was the only time where I truly felt happy. The fear of coming back and being ignorant and unfamiliar to the life I had before was something I felt daily.

Plans for the east side for our rotation seemed to make going out a little more meaningful, but all together boring as hell. It just seemed that after the explosion that nothing to me seemed interesting and driving the first vehicle still is not one of my favorite things to do.

Operation Spear ended on 11 July when permanent FOB's were set up and the line companies had finished sweeping the large city of Hit along with the Army and several other supporting units. Trying to provide a first hand account of the events is difficult because Crazy 8 held the eastern AO. The definition of living somewhere is if you spend the majority of your time at that place or the place where you resided. Crazy 8 no longer lived at the Dam, we lived in the field, and the east side was our new home.

We have been receiving a lot of our information from radio transmissions. Just recently, we heard that two Kilo Marines died at the FOB from mortar fire in Hit making the total number wounded or killed in our company out of 1,000 more than 20%. Combat replacements were scheduled to come from India Company and surprisingly the drill center in Akron, which must have been weird. I felt sorry for the poor son of a bitch who got a call at home, "We are running low on bodies over here in Iraq and we need to you to come here and stay for three months until we rotate back to the States." Supposedly, they said this would be the last major operation our company would execute. Crazy 8 could see a light at the end of the tunnel.

On the east side we continued being aggressive and sending a message to the locals that we were a force not to be reckoned with. Today we ran a humanitarian through east and west villages with an interpreter and happened to talk to some of the elders there. We were told that there had been no city council or any form of government in place at all. People just walked around doing as they pleased. Not long ago, they said the Mujahadeen had killed them all. *How could these insurgents justify their existence proclaiming Allah and then destroy any hope its country had of making progress?* We slowly drove through the village as kids came out of their houses, gave us thumbs up, and took as many stuffed animals and sweets from us as they could. Some kids even fought each other for the stuff and obviously had no intention of sharing. One kid in a green shirt and sweat pants walked away with ten stuffed animals in his shirt and came up to me asking if he could have the light off my flack jacket. We also passed out two hundred pamphlets with numbers for an anonymous tip line that people could call if they had any information about the Muj. I could see why they were hesitant to take it because if the Muj found them with it they would most likely be beheaded or shot in the streets in front of their kids.

Later that day we made another run through the fishing villages near the Dam to show our presence. I expected to see the disciples themselves fishing out of the river and living in these small shacks. Dismounts talked to the people living in the small huts next to the Euphrates and gave some food and water to the women and children before heading back the way they came from. I was pretty exhausted and rather fed up with driving and very annoyed at our APL who seemed like he did not have any hobbies or life outside the Marine Corps and got off on doing this shit. Then the most hilarious thing happened when we pulled over a four door Nissan pickup. We told them to get out of the vehicle and 21 people proceeded to exit the truck! It was like one of those contests back in the 70's to see who could fit the most people in a phone booth or a VW beetle. It almost reminded me of that day at Wilson where they shoved us in the back of a high back for twelve hours. These guys had even beaten the Marine Corps at cramming people into vehicles. It was so hilarious, especially just seeing them driving out in the middle of nowhere.

The night was long and I woke up three or four times during the night. It was bad enough that I had to wake up once a day to this country. About 0100 a vehicle with its headlights off drove past Crazy 2 (vehicle 2) and they were getting ready to shoot a Javelin Missile at it until they lost sight of it. By then I was fast asleep and looked forward to waking up in two hours to start this all over again.

JULY 12, 2005

Today it was so hot I could hardly breathe. The wind was like a blow drier that blew against my face and dried out my eyes to the point where I couldn't see. We were supposed to be relieved today by another MAP, but due to the low visibility everyone stayed where they were because of grounded MEDEVAC's. The Muj were always watching, they told us, so developing a routine of sweeping the same roads the same way everyday should have been avoided, but that was exactly what we did. A transmission came in while I was monitoring the battalion net about a tribe of local Haqlaniyahens who were going up against the insurgents last night. *Finally, they realize they need to stand up for themselves.* I wrote some letters to make sure everyone at home remembered me while occasionally napping and taking turns with Perry and Ross on watch every two hours. Some of the people I wrote to did not exactly support what we were doing over here, but I respected their opinions and knew what I was fighting for was the freedom to express those opinions even when writing those letters.

In London the other day, I heard from reading several magazines that terrorists had attacked a subway station killing several hundred people. This problem of terrorism worldwide had still existed. It was unbelievable. I hope that the U.K. will realize that the threat was real.

JULY 13, 2005

I tried to make the most out of our "day off" by waiting in the usual three-hour line to use the phones and then trying to fit everything I wanted to do into a six-hour period including sleep. I found out my dad had been in the hospital for the past few days. His blood counts were low and they said he might need kidney dialysis. I felt worried and depressed, but at the same time angry that I had been dealt a bad hand of cards. My mom did not want me to worry and my brother said she always remained positive even in the most traumatic times, especially after the IED blast I had experienced a few days ago.

I spent most of the night out on our balcony thinking about my life and feeling bad. I said some prayers and went to bed.

The threat that the Dam would be overrun was surprisingly still a reality and highers confirmed this from anonymous sources that more than 300 insurgents were going to try to overrun the Dam. Road blocks were put out in front of us that we almost flipped the 7-ton trying to get around on our way to observation posts on the east side. The First Sergeant informed us earlier in the day that MAP 7 had been hit by an IED south of Route Uranium and someone got shrapnel in their legs, but he said they would be okay.

I received the article about me printed in the Akron Beacon Journal on July 4th today. Several Akron Marines got a chance to write about their experiences here and it was a great opportunity to send a message to everyone back home. My smiling face was put between Sgt Bee's article and the Inspector / Instructor's. I started to think about how true my article was after everything we have been through so far, being brave was defiantly an important part of being an American in Iraq.

I prepped myself for another four days in the field and hoped that soon the schedule would change. Lieutenant Colonel Catalano talked to us. He was up here from the Hit AO and mostly talked to us about EOF and how it is necessary with all the VBIED threats now even if that meant using a disabling strategy. Any way to make the vehicle stop was appropriate as long as we followed the ROE's. More importantly ten or even twenty Iraqis lives were not worth injuring or killing one Marine.

We were going out on Routine Patrols yet again. By the time we got back it would almost be August and for a second I could almost feel the cool fall air of Ohio on my face.

23

JULY 14, 2005 0000

A radio transmission coming from Bulldog advising us of a "no shit" planned attack by insurgents on the Dam from outside intelligence blared over the squawk box while I was on watch. MAP 8 is back on the east side for another rotation of VCP's and OP's. Ross, at 0200 shot a car traveling 1,600m away from us with its lights off. It ended up traveling at a high rate of speed over the dunes to the southeast. Perry is always fucking around trying to fix the COM or eating some type of candy. Sometimes he reminds me of a twelve year old kid. Our APL, who is filling in for Sgt Carr while he went to get his hearing operation in Balad is writing in his maps and planning what to do. Highers wanted us to do VCP's all day, but earlier in the morning, they called in and advised us to stay static because of the visibility. My back had been hurting me and sharp pains always hit me out of nowhere like I had been shot. My hearing seemed to be doing better, but I was curious to see what my eardrum looked like after the explosion. Sgt Carr was supposed to come out with us the next rotation after he recovered from the surgery. His right eardrum was half gone and every time I talked to him he would say, "What?" We always joked with him. I'm just glad we are all alive even if we are still in country.

A newspaper from home reported that the support for the war was at an all time low. 64% of the America says we should pull out immediately according to a recent CNN poll. 1,744 soldiers and Marines have died since the war was officially over. I disagreed with pulling out. It's such an asinine idea from a majority that has not even set foot in a combat zone or does not even know what it's like over here. The insurgents expect it to happen and if we fight our battles here in the offensive then we can avoid fighting in the defensive on the home front. The thing that really pisses me off is the politicians in Washington that talk a lot and don't deliver results, like the equipment we are supposed to be getting. Being paid almost nothing over here is bullshit too.

When it all comes down to it, these explosions are real, Marines dying all around us, driving down roads that are laced with IED's and mines, that's real. When it all comes down to it, the politicians, the media, and the masses don't have a clue. We are living proof of that.

JULY 15, 2005

I feel so helpless right now. I am mentally exhausted and everything inside of me screams and cries for help. A huge weight is on top of me, pushing me down slowly. I am in a prison of expectations that never come and dreams that are just within arms reach, but I never seem to get there. I am scared. Scared of getting back to a changed world that doesn't want me and rejects everything I do. There is not one minute I don't worry about my fiancée and how she might look at me when I get home and see a man who has witnessed death and been run ragged by war. I worry about my dad's health, how he promised me a cold glass of beer and those words, "you make me proud son." I am on the verge of tears every time I take a breath and fear that soon I will not be able to take much more of this. Sometimes I daydream that I am getting off the plane and maybe the world being the same, but me being different.

As reality sets in, I find myself at another infamous vehicle checkpoint that Crazy 8 is known for doing. One man that struck me to be interesting and rather suspicious was driving a white van. His ID read that he was a reporter for Aljazeera and was headed for Hadithah to visit his uncle. The reason for suspicion is that Aljazeera was a network that was corrupt and reported on terrorist events, portraying them as the protagonists in this war and us as the infidels. During an earlier OP several months ago, we were told to detain such members because they were responsible for video taping several beheadings of Haqlaniyahen elders and ING by the Mujahadeen. We ended up letting him go since there was no evidence of footage or camera equipment on his person.

That afternoon we searched forty some cars and 147 MAM's. I was dropped off from the first vehicle to the 7-ton to assist searching vehicles. Brett was there in the 7-ton with Shoto, a dark green Marine from Mississippi that had been attached to us from the 3/25 artillery company. Brett always made me happy because he reminded me of when we went to *The Boot* and would always hang out and talk. He would always wear the most expensive clothes and I don't think I ever saw him in the same outfit twice.

Searching vehicles with Brett and Shoto was an experience. After the occupants had been searched, we would run up the vehicles and search the hood, trunk, glove compartment, and the interior for anything suspicious. If I only stopped and thought how dangerous it was to run up on a vehicle that we knew nothing about and could have been packed with explosives. One vehicle I searched even had a flat bed full of oxygen tanks and some electric saw blades similar to the ones found when we hit the IED on Uranium. Seeing them gave me chills and visions of explosions rushed into my mind. It turns out the guy was a merchant and sold the tanks and miscellaneous items for profit in the Hadithah / Barwanah area. If it were up to me, I would have emptied the truck of its contents and sent him on his way.

As stressful as searching vehicles was, I was still relieved to get out of the first vehicle. I always feel helpless behind the wheel and if something happened all I would be able to do is sit there. We searched about forty more vehicles today and told them the usual; that they are responsible for their roads now that we have liberated them, and the next time we find an IED, we are going to arrest everyone in the general area. By the time we set into our OP's, the sun had set over the Hadithah Dam and the light glistened off the lake towards the small towns to the west. Tracks, AAV's, and dismounts from Lima Company were planning a raid in town. One house in particular belonged to a HVT that was supposedly a Colonel in the old Iraqi army. This man was being paid by the Muj to mortar us. Cherry 87, which was the station for air, was called in and F-15's whizzed by our heads as they flew to the west side of the river where the Colonel lived just outside of town. Just then, we saw a large explosion that severed the sunlight and sent smoke high into the air like a small mushroom cloud of a nuclear explosion. An IED had just been hit on River Road going into the city. The area was still a problem for AAV's and the line companies who traveled in and out of the FOB area. No one was hurt in the explosion and the raiding party advanced on into the city towards their objective while Cobra helicopters equipped with missiles flew by us. The raid was conducted at dusk as the sun fell out of the sky and another day fell over the horizon. Eventually tanks and AAV's surrounded the house and destroyed everything inside including the mortar tube sitting in the courtyard of the Colonel's property with a blue tarp draped over top of it.

Knowing I would have to get up in another three hours for watch just added to the feeling that I did not want to be out here any longer. The Dam threat was still going on so I constantly scanned the area for cars and potential armies of terrorists that were supposed to be marching toward the Dam. I didn't see the Muj army or its mortars, only a barren desert and dogs that were like nomads traveling in packs and wanting to devour food of any sort.

JULY 16, 2005

Our spirits were higher today because we were supposed to be relieved so that we could take a shower, call home, and get good night's sleep. Our morning began at 0630 when a crypto rollover had taken place and my antics of driving over a bump in which we must have got two feet of air with the Humvee, had somehow screwed up the radios. We RTBed and Perry filled the radios while we sat around and tried not to doze off. We were supposed to do VCP's on Phoenix until we were relieved at 1400. Our APL did everything by the book from constantly checking to see if our weapons were in condition four, to sweeping the Raptors/ Phoenix intersection every time we traveled down that road. Frankly, everyone was getting pissed off because it was bad enough that we had to be here in Iraq and it seemed like this guy got off on making our lives a living hell and as stressful as possible. Doing a sweep down Phoenix towards Barwanah filled our morning with excitement in a sick and twisted way. We spotted an IED just behind a huge sand dune next to the road. A thin pointed wire ran from the base station that was neatly hidden in the dirt, to a South African 155mm round buried near the road. The APL and I dismounted the vehicle to go check it out and stood about 50-100m from it looking at the instrument of death with our ACOG's and a spotting scope. "Well, it looks like there's an antenna right there, a base station, and a washer timer sitting right there." The APL looked through the scope, "Oh shit it is!" as we ran like hell about 300m away from where it was. Perry radioed EOD to come explode the ordinance. Meanwhile as the first vehicle dealt with the IED, I was still stuck in the high back with Cpl Maple and Osberg, who was the gunner of the 240. Osberg looked through his bino's and saw a man on top of a roof. "Hey Wojo do you see that?" He pointed to the roof and I looked into the binos. "Holy Shit!" I screamed, "He's got an RPG!" We radioed into our APL who told us to hold our fire for some reason and then Cpl Leachman put the newly up armored high back in reverse until we got about 500m from the rooftop where the crazy Muj Rocketeer was still standing, now reaching for something below him.

It took three hours for EOD to set the charges and blow up the IED. By then, Kaybar 5 who came out to escort EOD to the site was long gone to the Dam and were probably already in their rooms playing video games. We were to stay out near the 96 easting because of the threat to the Dam, until our relief came, which was already an hour late. It seemed like the hectic schedule would be going on forever until we left, because two MAP's just packed up their trucks and left for Hit. After Operation Spear and the creation of four new FOB's inside the city of Hit, Hadithah became the secondary objective and spear was to be the last major operation that we would have before our relief in place, hopefully within the next two months.

Shortly after 1500, a transmission came over the radio that we were supposed to go directly to Checkpoints 8&9 from our POS, but was then changed when our 7-ton broke down and had to be repaired. By that time, we had been waiting at the Dam for the vehicle to be fixed and MAP 5 was not far from the Dam after having picked up several key Officers at al-Asad airbase, home of Burger King, Pizza Hut, and the swimming pool. Fighting positions were constructed on top of the motor pool and the east gate was blocked with HESCO barriers, all in preparation for what officials had reported as a threat to the Dam. Our vehicles now had to be parked on the tenth deck and staged.

Shortly after we entered the gate, a huge explosion startled me. Evidently, reports said that in the city there were large flares being fired off and looked like they had been firing rockets at us. We sat inside the vehicles for a good ten minutes trying to spot a point of origin from the top of the Dam, but there was no sign. Hastily, I gathered up my gear and headed down ten flights of stairs to mail, food, video games, and hopefully a night off.

JULY 17, 2005

After talking to my dad last night, I felt a little better, but was not extremely thrilled about going out again in another four hours. Sgt Carr would be back with us in the fist vehicle, which was a good thing because our APL was driving everyone up a wall. For an hour today at noon the Navy medical staff gathered everyone up in the chow hall where they passed out informational pamphlets about the optional Anthrax shot and administered it to those that wanted to get it. No one that I saw wanted it from our MAP. So I guess until they ordered us to get it, most Marines would not.

Our mission for the next three days seemed to be a little more aggressive than before with raids and searches that were planned inside of East and West Village. Tonight we searched a water tower hoping to find some trace of weapons or at least something. Several Marines including Brett and Perry climbed to the top of the tower near Phoenix to find nothing except that the ladder had been baking for several hours in the hundred degree sun and left their hands blistered and burned.

Cars were also spotted entering and exiting a few buildings about a click north of where we did our VCP's so we searched them and they checked out okay. With Sgt Carr back, driving seemed to be a little more interesting and I was actually motivated to do better. I guess when you are involved in something as life threatening as we were you tend to be closer with the people in your vehicle.

This afternoon as we set in for the night, I was thinking of how scared I was to go back to my life now. I've never really thought about it that way until we had just a few short weeks left. I was afraid I would come home to people that will not understand me and thought what I fought for was a mistake. It made me angry to think of it, but I knew when I got home I could count on the people that were close to me to support me. The men that fought beside me would always be there and would understand no matter what.

24

JULY 18, 2005 SEARCH OF WEST VILLAGE

The plan of attack this morning was to search the southern most block of West Village where the RPG was spotted, next to the Mosque. We were to go in and cordon off one city block. The dismounts would search every building while drivers and gunners stayed in the vehicles to provide security. We were also going to keep to our word and arrest five people near where we found the IED and send them to prison, or at least give them a day or two worth of trouble before releasing them.

We drove off road towards the village over mounds of dirt, piles of trash, and fields that hopelessly would not survive the desert sun, to the first road entering West Village. Dismounts exited the vehicles and we moved into positions for security. Kids raced out of their houses thinking we were there to pass out candy as we rolled on by and they ran to try and catch up. The fist house we found a bag of AK-47 clips and tracer rounds along with six or seven AK's. Neil, our terp, was there to question the guy who apparently didn't want to tell us anything, so we zip- tied him and wrapped him up to take back with us. Sheep flocked passed our vehicle as two women carried burlap bags full of crops to their houses. Children played soccer / football around us as the search of one block of West Village took place. We ended up searching two blocks of buildings and rolled up five MAM's in the area that were acting suspicious and were in possession of weapons. One of them included a sixteen year old that tried to run from us down a nearby alleyway. Two kids looked at us from nearby houses as I sat there in the driver's seat waiting for the search to be done and talked to Ross as he did about ten scans of the area. I grabbed a pen that had run out of ink and threw it to the kids standing on the porch. They smiled, waved to us, and then went back to their house. I have never seen a kid get that exited about an inkless pen before.

About 45 minutes later, we exited the village with five prisoners, hundreds of AK rounds, seven AK's, and a German mouser rifle. "And a partridge in a pear tree," I shouted to Ross as we sped off. We drove down Phoenix and then RTBed to fill out some paperwork for the prisoners and to refit and refuel. *It would be less paperwork if we killed them.* We rolled up to the tenth deck, an AZ woke up and opened the gate for us, and we sped on through. As we drove through the gate, Ross spotted a boat not 75m from the Dam walls. We radioed Triton North, which is a company of swift boats equipped with mini-guns. It turns out that the guy had been spotted near the Dam before, so they towed him all the way out into the middle of the lake and left him there. They also proceeded to tell the rest of the villagers that they couldn't come close to the Dam or they would be shot on sight.

Two of our vehicles had problems and had to go back to the motor pool for repairs. We waited up on the tenth deck for them and I watched the wave's crash onto the shoreline. I could see everything up here, although there was not much to see other than sand and the Euphrates. Even the most horrible place on earth could have its beautiful scenery.

Crazy 8A (vehicles 1 and 2) drove out of the NW gate to go to static OP's for the night while 8B (vehicles 3 and 4) were repaired. We drove for about five minutes, found a spot overlooking the Dam and nearly everyone fell asleep for about six hours until dark.

JULY 19, 2005 SEARCH OF EAST VILLAGE

The morning came quickly. I watched the sunrise up over the Dam from 0400 to 0600. Crazy 8's plan of the day was to pick up six Iraqi security personnel and take them to East Village to search the NW block of East Village. There had been some issues with ISF killing people and beating them for no reason. Partly because of their emotions from their friends getting killed in Fallujah had something to do with it. The ISF are a great asset to us because they know the language, know how to read people, and can tell whether they could be Muj. They also have ways of getting information out of people in ways we could not.

The raid was similar to that of West Village just a day prior. We targeted known areas such as a house on the north end of the village where three brothers who were arms dealers in the area lived. ISF quickly searched through houses and came out with three AK's with Chinese bayonets and a pair of soviet binoculars, which are illegal to use for observing coalition positions, and three bags of black powder used for making IED's. The binoculars were Russian with communist logos printed on them and perfectly focused for 600m where we were sitting at an OP.

Today we arrested the two owners of the suspicious house and then went back to the Dam to process them. We were in the village for three and a half hours. Kids were still running up to us thinking we had candy and I threw some more pens at them. Somehow they thought that pens were called "biens." Entering a swarm full of kids that kept shouting, "Bien, bien," was so annoying. We bought three liters of RC Hajji Pop and traded some sunglasses and some American magazines for some food that a local vender was selling out of his shed. I guess we could have just taken them, but we kept a sense of friendliness about us that we were here to help them and keep them safe.

Later that evening I got a chance to talk to the ISF. They sat around smoking their Pines, which was a cigarette that Hajjis loved and were imported from Korea. They were talking Arabic amongst each other and listening to music on a cell phone that they stole from some guy in the village. One guy with a blue bandana on told me about the battles and fierce fighting they experienced in Fallujah, although his English was not very good so I could only just nod and smile. He caught a round in part of his face. It was rather obvious and I couldn't help but stare at it. They offered me soda that tasted like a red 7-Up ginger ale. It was cold and he insisted that I drink, "again, again!" he said repeatedly and kept motioning me to drink with his hands. They seemed to be close to one another, that bond between fighters that someone who was not familiar with couldn't understand. While visiting with them it seemed like there was some hope for their country if there were more soldiers that were willing to fight like they were.

I began thinking again about home and thought about why we were fighting. How no one would understand why we fought for their freedom and how America could think this war was a mistake. I could never imagine thinking that way after losing some of my friends and being so close to death. It made me mad that so many people could not see the value in securing a country full of terrorists that have already hurt American once. *How many more times are we going to wait around as our country is attacked by these savages?* I guess it's just one of those things that people with blinders on can't see. Although my desire to go home had not changed, my fear of the world was overwhelmingly strong and it was disturbing.

We spent the night in a tight 360 near the village. Plans were to go in and do more searching tomorrow at first light. I guess we were going to try to catch people off guard. Meanwhile back at the Dam, we heard reports that a rocket had been launched and slammed into the first deck where the NCO's stayed. The large object slammed through the window throwing shrapnel out into the hallway. Sgt McNally was staying back at the Dam in that room and he said it scared the shit out of him. "It was unreal and absolutely unbelievable," he said, "I can't believe this is happening."

JULY 20, 2005

I watched the sunrise over East Village. Revile sounded at 0700 and we mounted up, heading towards East Village before most Iraqis woke up to search three more houses suspected to be insurgents'. Driving down a crude road into the village, we observed a memorial for a Sheik that died not too long ago. The mud brick buildings looked thousands of years old and a woman and child carried bricks to another building in front of where our vehicle was parked. The kid looked so cute helping her mother with the bricks as Marines searched the houses to the left of our vehicle. The ISF were still with us and although we didn't have much luck in our search of East Village this morning, we also drove up to some REI tents and arrested a guy who was on duty right near where the IED was planted. The scruffy looking Iraqi man broke down crying and told us everything. Sgt Abas, the leader of the ISF said, "Your way [of talking / reasoning with people] may work in America, but it doesn't work here in Iraq." We found that out from experience of trying to talk to these people nicely. These people usually gaff us off and are accustomed to just giving us that shit eating grin and lying to us about everything that goes on.

When Sgt Carr was with us, I seemed to be more motivated. Something had happened after the explosion that had affected all of us. We talked as we sat at OP's at the 84 easting while the 7-ton and the fourth vehicle took the detainees back to the Dam. We were supposed to be relieved by Kaybar 6 again to go on QRF to end our exhausting rotation and start us all over again at the beginning for three more days. I tried to fit all my phone calls, laundry, and showers all into 23 hours. Most of the time here at the Dam, we ended up staying up the whole time without sleeping. My fiancée was at work when I called, so I stayed up until 2am to talk to her. She was mad that I was not allowed to call her. I love her very much and I was sorry and felt bad about only being able to call her every three days. She had already planned some of our wedding and talked to me about it. "Well, only two months and I will be home soon," I reassured her as they called my name to get off the phones. I was tired so I went to bed around 0300, which was pretty early for me. *It was going to be a long exciting day tomorrow that would never end.* The only way out is through.

JULY 21, 2005

MAP 6 was surprisingly on time for our relief. We took bets on when they would arrive and couldn't believe they were back at the Dam around

1500. We did what you would call an express refit refuel in which I followed SO (short for Steve Obrst) reaching speeds of up to 60MPH inside the Dam straight to the fuel pumps and back to the tenth deck in less than ten minutes. Staging on the tenth deck, I thought was pointless now. The threat to the Dam predicted was over.

This morning we woke up to someone saying there is a class up in the CoC at 1030. *What a surprise on our day off.* The CO is making us go to an EOF class. During the meeting we talked mostly about the rules of engagement and what to do when you feel threatened and how to properly escalate force. They posted statistics during the PowerPoint presentation showing the number of civilian and enemy KIA's since our deployment began. Major Gardner also acquired an Excel spreadsheet of what he called "the wheel of pain." It was a pie chart showing our time left in Iraq and it read, "At this moment we have 5,857,357 seconds left in Iraq or 2.01 months." The pie chart made me happy because the bigger part was time we already spent over here and the small splinter was the time we had left.

Soon after 2000, we had to punch out to pick up the snipers and extract MAKO 8 that had already been out there for 48 hours. Driving at night was a pain in the ass. I could hear Ross, "left Wojo, right Wojo," he would say to me. I could not see very well. Bumps were rough heading off towards Barwanah. Through NVG's, I could not see much and the depth perception was horrible. We could drive off a cliff and it would look like a puddle of water or a pothole. We ended up almost dropping off a 50ft cliff until Ross noticed what we were doing, "Wojo Reverse!" It took us about an hour and a half to get to the extract point marked by an IR strobe light. Tanks had been out taking our place on OP's as the investigation continued. They were able to escort us onto Route Phoenix and then back to the Dam to drop off MAKO 7 only to punch back out and sit on OP's until tomorrow. It was the first time I had slept on the ground in a while and the bugs were out to get me. I was too tired to care.

JULY 22, 2005

We spent the night in the field and RTBed around 0800 when tanks relieved us. For most of the day until about 1600 we waited in our rooms until one-by-one, all of us were called up to the CoC. I fell asleep for a few hours and although the Segovia was closed, I was still happy to be back at the Dam, it didn't matter what it was for.

The new vehicle watch was in two-hour shifts and was a walking post because apparently not everyone wants to stay awake while on post. The SOG and COG rotated out to surprise the watches and catch people sleeping. Although we were not back for that long, we had to punch out and pick up snipers. Anything over a few days of picking up and dropping off in the same period from the same place was considered a routine, but then again what do I know. Apparently, MAKO 8 had taken a detainee. The man had been out talking to someone in black with body armor on and an AK near the Hamsters / Phoenix intersection. The terrain was the same as last nights getting over there. It was absolutely horrible. Mountainous ruts, tilled earth, and cliffs threw us around the inside of the vehicle like rag dolls.

When we reached our destination, picked up the snipers and the detainee, and then punched back out to our OP's on Raptors, I was ready to die. I pulled out my sleeping bag and fell asleep right away.

JULY 23, 2005

Since the Gunny was with us in the first vehicle, he suggested that we look for the POO from where the mortar rounds that hit the Dam almost daily were coming from. Soft dusty roads off to the south led us to some rough, rocky terrain with the occasional 100ft drop. Ross would yell, "Stop, turn around, and go left." We were just yesterday talking about how this exact spot on the map was worse then when we inserted the MAKO team the other day and here we are. The terrain was rocky like the surface of Mars, not to mention it was hot as hell outside.

After putting the vehicle in low lock, which means the wheels move slower to get over rockier terrain, we made it to a house and stopped about 400m away in a farmer's field. I still thought these people were wasting their time plowing the desert earth because nothing fertile would ever come out of it unless we decided to blow up the Dam and let water flow everywhere.

Ross, while attempting to fire his pen flare, accidentally shot it directly into our vehicle. It burned for a second or two behind Perry's seat while the Gunny was sitting there. I could imagine he was pretty pissed about the whole thing, but he was pretty calm and collected as if it happened all the time. We put the flare out with as much water as we could find. Once we were ready, we headed towards the house. The thing that I didn't particularly like about driving was that I felt so helpless and was not able to do searches when everyone else got to. *It's like the road trip from hell that never ends,* I thought as they ran inside and searched the house.

Dismounts from Crazy 8 spoke to the people and pretty much got the same response as everyone in this God forsaken country, "No Ali-Babba in Iraq, Shwaya. Shwaya." This meant there are no bad guys in Iraq, and that I knew was just bullshit.

We were up in this area once before after a mortar attack and we saw a silhouette of a man running as he talked on a cell phone, which is why this house was particularly suspicious, as well as the fact that the counter battery radar always gave a grid for that very same spot every time. A day ago, three rounds landed in the water not far from our room. Ross was yelling, "Get in the hallway and get down!" for fear that we might get another rocket flying through our room and land somewhere between the TV and the refrigerator.

As we headed towards Route Raptors, we looked for OP spots by a dirt road that headed into the desert and looked like a good route for the Muj mortarmen to egress through. Crazy 8 continued through the rough terrain and took a road to the right of a huge mountain. As we veered off to the right, some soft brown earth fell beneath us and I buried the tires completely into a sinkhole. We were stuck. "Good job, Wojo!" Perry's annoying voice shouted from the back seat.

The 7-ton came around and eventually pulled us out, but not before everyone gave me shit about getting stuck. "It wasn't even my call to turn this way!" I yelled. It was actually kind of funny and I laughed and took pictures of our piece of shit Humvee that was now about to be pulled out of a large sinkhole. We got out after several attempts and this time we veered to the left and went off to find a spit to sit until our relief came.

I think we are on the roads more than anyone else is. In Hit, we were labeled as a secondary objective. Crazy 8 was moved up here specifically because of the major operations going on and the extra manpower they needed. Now that three new FOB's were set up in Hit after Operation Spear and they were to be permanent, they needed the manpower down south and our AO simply fell by the wayside as being secondary.

While we waited for our relief and the Gunny and I discussed my career and how I was an intern and in college for finance, we saw a man heading toward us with a white flag in his hands. Our APL notified us over the radio and said that they told people in the fishing villages if they had any information for us at all, they should approach us with a white flag. Cpl Stocker got out of the 7-ton and approached the man on foot. I thought about suicide vests and bomb jackets laced with explosives as he talked to him and a couple minutes later there came a voice over the radio, "The guy walked all this way just to come over here for water and food." He didn't have any information for us. I was beginning to wonder if we were on a relief effort or if we were actually here to do what Marines do, kill. We gave him water and sent him on his way.

Somewhere I read in the newspaper, *"Stars and Stripes"* that the Iraqi interim government was setting up a constitution and soon a government would be established. Many people feel that as soon as we pull out of here that this country will go to hell. I didn't know what to think, but what I do know is that we were leaving here in less than five million seconds and the whole country could collapse on itself if it wanted to.

Last night, the Gunny talked to Perry and said they were trying to get Perry, Gurgol, Sgt Carr, and I the Purple Heart, although I fell into daydreams. My special girl was smiling as I stepped off the plane and into her arms. I was almost there.

JULY 24, 2005 0745

"Hey guys we gotta be out to the trucks in fifteen minutes," I heard a voice come from the darkness as I rubbed my eyes and rolled out of bed. *Damn it,* my body ached all over from constantly jerking around in the Humvee for almost two days straight. We had just picked up a new guy, PFC Harris that just graduated from SOI and was sent straight to Iraq. I couldn't imagine being sent here right from my schooling, especially the reason why Harris was here. We were short on bodies.

We fucked around with PFC Harris last night. "The guy whose seat you are filling is no longer with us anymore," we joked. More of that dark Marine Corps humor that no one would understand but us. Doc Barone cornered him out in the hallway, "put yourself at ease when you talk to me!" Doc screamed at him while trying to hold back a smile. Harris pretty much kept to himself, but I'm sure he would fit into our MAP once he got to know everyone. A few Marines had been up late last night drinking some kind of concoction of 151 and Gatorade. You could tell who had participated, because they all looked like shit that morning.

Once we got out to our OP's which we were supposed to stay on until 2300 tomorrow, Sgt Carr told us he might have to have surgery to get his hearing fixed because the Doc told him that his eardrum had not healed since the explosion. We joked around with him and told him we would make a stuffed Sgt Carr to put in the front seat. The reality that no one looked forward to was that the APL would assume command of Crazy 8 permanently and make our lives a living hell. I told him I could not drive anymore if that happened. Sometimes I wondered if we had been grounded to OP's because we were being too aggressive again.

Children of East and West Village near Hadithah Dam (photo taken by Cpl Tucci)

An Italian anti-tank mine found in the road near Raptors /
Phoenix intersection (photo taken by Sgt Williams)

Sadaam Hussein's money – now worth less than the paper it's printed on

*Insurgent's attempted to plant this South African 120mm mortar
round outside of our checkpoint (photo taken by LCpl Ross)*

Fallen Heroes Ceremony at the IX center in Cleveland, Ohio for fallen members of the Armed Forces, particularly 3rd Battalion 25th Marines based out of Brookpark, Ohio

(photo taken by Cpl Ickes)

Gunny Sergeant P. rests up against a wall spray-painted with the words, "Let Freedom Ring" near the hospital in Hadithah, Iraq. (photo taken by Cpl Ickes)

LAV's prepare for one of Iraq's infamous sandstorms during Operation New Market

One out of the thousands of weapons 3/25 located and destroyed
during Operation Cache Sweep / Desert Rat. Cpl Alexander Kalouf
demonstrates proper usage of an enemy RPG launcher.

Supply drops during Operation Cache Sweep / Desert Rat

Random searches through the villages South of Hit City, Iraq

Village markers. Legend has it that Shepard's use them to locate villages and property boundary lines, but no one really knew for sure.

One of Salaam's concrete factories that used to supply to the major cities fifteen miles south of the Syrian boarder near al-Qui'm, Iraq.

A Javelin Missile "Lindemuth Special" drawn by Cpl Back

"Crazy 8" at ASP Wolf near al-Qui'm, Iraq

Scorpion found near my sleeping bag in Barwanah, Iraq

*LCpl Perry demonstrates how insurgent's built and used this position
to detonate more then fifteen IED's found in Barwanah, Iraq*

*F-15's shooting at insurgents in the nearby bushes
not far from our position in Barwanah*

*An Iraqi market, now "Closed" shortly after Crazy 8 moves
into position near the palm groves in Barwanah*

One of many Minuets in Iraq that sound prayer call more then five times a day

Tiger 3-A holds it's position on the ridge line during an assault on Barwanah

(from left to right) Cpl Kustra, Oliver North, USMC (Ret) and
Cpl Leachman during Operation Matador, al-Qui'm

Road markers in Iraq

LCpl Richard Turner (photo taken by LCpl Dmytriw)

Starbucks at the Kuwaiti Airport "Ali-Asalem" in Kuwait City, Kuwait

Arab Airways

*An Amphibious Assault Vehicle or AAV during an assault on
one of many lawless river towns near Hadithah Dam*

Iraqi Police armband confiscated in East Village

The ISF questions two Iraqi prisoners in Arabic

LCpl Dickason passes out stuffed animals and candy to the children of West Village

*Cpl Wojtecki (myself) holding a Chinese AK-47 with bayonet
that we confiscated from villagers near Hit City*

*(from left to right) two members of the AZ army, LCpl
Ross, Cpl Wojtecki, and LCpl Dinkelman*

*A Sadaam Hussein Republican Guard recruiting
poster found during a raid of West Village*

Our Humvee after an IED exploded on Route Uranium: Sgt Carr, LCpl Perry,
Cpl Gurgol, and Cpl Wojtecki (myself) were all in the Humvee when it exploded

Cpl Travis Stocker holding $10,000 in U.S. cash found on an suspected Iraqi terrorist

Random vehicle searches conducted on Iraqis outside of Hadithah

(from left to right) LCpl Truthan, LCpl Dinkelman, Cpl Wojtecki
(myself), Cpl Leach, Cpl Kalouf, and LCpl Turner

Crazy 8's weapons cache found in a small village south of Hit City

(from left to right) LCpl Perry, Cpl Kustra (back), LCpl Truthan, LCpl Osberg (back), LCpl Turner, Cpl Leach, LCpl Dmytriw, and Cpl Wojtecki (myself)

Hadithah Dam

Doc Barone (left) plays chess with Cpl Johnson (right) (photo by LCpl Dmytriw)

A "Camel Spider"

The Akron Beacon Journal's article on LCpl Montgomery's funeral. Pictured is LCpl Montgomery's brother in dress blues comforting LCpl Montgomery's wife Pam. (lower right) LCpl Montgomery's son with his dress blues on

*Our dog Crazy Beans, who MAP 8 bought for 25 cents and some
Jellybeans outside of East Village (photo taken by Sgt Kustra)*

*The memorial for fifteen fallen Marines killed in the AAV
explosion and the snipers who were killed just days earlier*

Posters like these litter the streets in small villages in Iraq. This one talks about preventing progress by planting IED's and urges Iraqis to stop the planting of IED's and mines.

Tanks guard a school house taken over as a firm base during one of the many operations in Hadithah

Third platoon's hooch / ice-box / tin can we stayed in during training operations at Camp Wilson in California. Quiet possibly the "worst place on earth" (photo taken by LCpl Dmytriw)

LCpl Knox (left) and Cpl Lindemuth (right)

Cpl Wojtecki (myself) stands behind a large hole in the condemned houses of an Iraqi training village during SASO school near MARCH Air Force Base

Photo of a Psy-Ops vehicle from a covered SAW position in training operations – 29 Palms, California

Crazy 3 parked in the middle of a farmer's field outside
of Hadithah (photo taken by Sgt Kustra)

(back) Cpl Timothy Gurgol, LCpl Steven Perry, LCpl Jonathan Truthan, LCpl Jason Ross, LCpl Brett Dinkelman, Cpl Stephen Obrst, Cpl Travis Stocker, Cpl Michael Back Jr., Cpl Matthew Wojtecki, Cpl Anthony Kustra, (front) LCpl Daniel Dmytriw, Cpl Jason Leachman, Sgt Thomas McNally, Sgt David Carr, Sgt Robert Jenkins, Sgt Corey Overmyer, HM3 Yoel Baronehernandez, LCpl Richard Turner, LCpl John Dickason, and Cpl David Leach

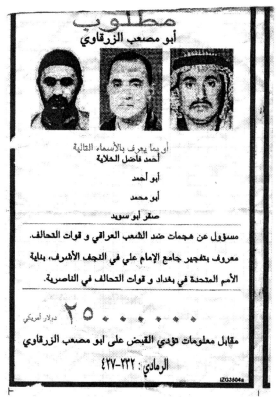

A Zarkowi wanted poster

VOLUME 3

"That which we persist in doing becomes easier-not that the nature of the task has changed, but our ability to do has increased."

—Ralph Waldo Emerson

25

JULY 24, 2005

We have been patrolling the roads less and less. Observation posts are Crazy 8's new home. Long days of sleeping, fire watch, and reading books cover to cover in a day's time. Sgt Carr always talks about his time on the force as a police officer near Warren, Ohio. He told me that at work, sometimes big cases and drug busts are just "avoided" to make the area look good and crime low. It was a silly way to decrease the statistics at the company level. There was a lot of time to think about these things. What were we doing here? Why are we just sitting here? Why aren't we killing something and causing havoc around the little towns of Hadithah and Barwanah? When I wasn't reading, talking, or on watch, I was writing.

The long and endless road, Route Bronze, cut a large mountain in half outside of the city. Our vehicle one parked itself on top of the sharp cliff that looked over the barren desert landscape and we all relaxed for another day of observation posts. We had cold pop and non-alcoholic beer so it was almost like a summer vacation, except it felt like we were in hell it was so hot and the wind blew sand constantly in our direction. We even went as far today as to try to work on our tans. All four of us lined up on cots and baked our pasty white skin that had been covered up for months by long sleeved blouses in the hot July sun.

About mid afternoon, everyone fell asleep except for the watch, which we ran every two hours. If I would have known we would have periods of this much boredom simply to show a presence, I would have valued some of our MAP's more intense moments. Firefights, explosions, mortars, and rockets were some of the more exiting times Crazy 8 had. I'm happy to be sitting here being able to think about them. There are still a lot of things I wish would have never happened such as MAP 2's high back exploding and surviving an IED blast. I'm just glad to be alive.

JULY 25, 2005

We continued the OPing until later in the afternoon until the schedule was juggled around and we were sent to 8&9 on the west side. We would then go to extract MAKO 6 snipers from the rough terrain about two miles west of the oil pipeline. We had traveled that area a few days earlier when we scouted out OP positions in search of the Muj mortarmen who kept lobbing rounds at the Dam almost every day after prayer call.

After OPing all day, we stepped off for the extraction around 2100 when we were just about as close to dark as we could get. The setting sun made visibility rather difficult. MAKO 7 waited outside of the tenth deck. A few guys were sitting on their packs cleaning their sniper rifles. Others were "smokin' and jokin'" and probably bitching about how they had to go out for another three days without a decent meal or a cigarette. They were supposed to blow a satchel charge near the Raptors / Phoenix intersection and then Crazy 8 was supposed to drive them out to where MAKO 6 currently was and swap teams.

When we got to the intersection we "flipped the bitch," which meant that we did a complete 360 on the road and were supposed to haul ass because we only had a minute until detonation. MAKO 7 had already planted the charges near the road so as soon as they got in, I hit the gas, and we broke off the road headed towards the 49 easting. As my NVG's slipped down over my eyes, I don't think the thought that I hated driving ever exited my mind. By the time we got to the extraction site I was ready to scream. Two Marines were telling me to go and one was telling me to stop, we almost got the Humvee stuck twice, and we had to find creative ways around drop-offs, ruts, and cliffs. It was about the most annoying as the guy on an airline flight that always complains about the service and the worst thing he has to worry about is the vintage of the wine they are serving. *Ma'm this Latté is warm. Can I speak to your supervisor?* I heard a voice in my mind say while I took an imaginary flight out of Iraq to God knows where, but surely not where I was at this very moment. Perry was getting as annoying as a twelve year old kid sitting in the back seat commenting on my driving. I was ready to smash his head in with a rock. The MAKO team found our position north of the pipeline and we extracted them more than three hours after we started our engines on the tenth deck.

The ride back was a bit easier following our tracks to route Raptors. We RTBed shortly after 0300 and our day off began. I decided to go up to the phone center and catch up on the events happening at home. The key volunteers, usually wives, girlfriends, and mothers of the Marines serving over here held a family day at the drill center. They had food and a fun Hawaiian theme in which they wore Hula skirts and flowers. I could only guess that they all wondered what we were doing at that very moment. Sgt Carr's wife talked to my fiancée and Gurgol's Mom was there too. She said that Gurgol was home and his dad went over to his house a couple days ago and said he was lying on the couch next to a case of beer and an assortment of pain medication. Sitting on the table was a clear glass jar with two bloody pieces of shrapnel the doctors pulled out of his leg. They said he was having some problems with his foot and it would take a few months of physical therapy to recover. "He might have to walk with a cane the rest of his life," his mom told my fiancée. Although there was no doubt he was in pain, he was probably glad to be home.

When I called, Angela was looking after her little sister. She was part of the Big Brothers and Big Sisters of America program and was mentoring a little girl once a week after school. "What are you doing? Sounds like your busy making a list of things to do, is Angela there?" the little voice traveled over 5,000 miles to where I was and then two seconds later I heard a faint, "yes, one minute." She sounded very adorable. Angela is so good with little kids. I think it was something I would have to work on more.

By the time I finished using the phone it was after 0600. Still feeling rather depressed, I pulled the covers over my head and hid from this place for a few more hours until sunrise.

JULY 26, 2005

Brett was ready to get out of this place more than anyone I knew of in Crazy 8. He stole boxes from the chow hall to ship some of his gear home. His area looked virtually bare. I woke up and he was mopping the floor, trying to somehow make this place like home. He is one of those people that have to have everything clean and organized. I wish the rest of the platoon would share in his compulsions.

The schedule, I think, had pretty much been ironed out in-lieu of a small operation called "Saber" that took place in the K3 oil refinery in Haqlaniyah. Reports were that several insurgents possessed rocket launchers and were going to attack the school where the Americans were. Over the past few days, we had been mortared several times at checkpoints and my guess is they probably originated from that area. Battalion requested crater analysis, a procedure where we were to stand behind the impacts and take a direction reading from the tails left in the ground. The tails were literally burn marks on either side of the mortar fins that indicate where the mortar came from. In taking theses readings, they would compute a point of origin, although the distance was usually just estimation, so we usually ended up patrolling in the general area of about a three-mile radius looking for that point.

For 24 hours, we would be on a tasker operation on the east side to show a presence and extract the snipers if necessary. Harris the "New Kid," who we just called "Kid," would be riding with vehicle 1. I think we scared the shit out of him at times, but I think he eventually caught on and knew we were just playing with him. When Harris asked Sgt Carr where he was to stage his gear he said, "Just set it right there in that empty seat where we get hit the most often."

We left the Dam at 2100 after a most unnecessary serialized gear inspection. I wasn't going to complain that much because it was another good indicator that we are going home soon. We stayed static at 8&9, but were tasked in support of Operation Saber, if need be we would be ready at a moments' notice. Perry was pretty much the Kid's mentor and showed him the radios and how the fire watch worked.

That night, reports blared over the radio every few seconds. At some point, they took fire in the city and were mortared over 30 times in a matter of a few hours. The lone Muj rocketman was still at large. A cell phone connection was intercepted in which an insurgent requested more ammo delivered for his rocket launcher. I just sat there next to the tire of the Humvee just trying to picture this guy with his homemade rocket launcher out of some cheap piping and a coat hanger for a trigger trying to get more ammo. It was so comical and seemed so desperate. Somewhere along the line, we would find him and kill him. I jokingly told Sgt Carr that I thought that might have been the very last insurgent and after we killed him, we could go home.

NSTR, or nothing significant to report, was what the APL always whispered to me after he would get off his watch. There absolutely was NSTR tonight on my watch, other than a crypto change over and the two hyenas fighting back and forth trying to mortally wound the other. Killing was in the air, but we probably wouldn't be doing any tonight.

JULY 27, 2005

I woke up to the heat burning at my feet. The sun crept up my legs and slowly reached the lower part of my body before I finally decided to get out of my sleeping bag. It felt like another very hot day on checkpoint 8. Sgt Carr is playing his video games on the PSP his wife sent him, Perry is still reading his, *"Wheel of Time"* fairy tale books, Ross is drawing pictures of trucks in his writing tablet, and the Kid is on fire watch. I got up and sat down in the driver's seat, wipe the sleep off my eyes, and grabbed some piss warm water from the back of the Humvee.

I am still half-asleep as I start writing this. The wind blows hot air across the desert and the sand whips around in small cyclones. There wasn't much to do today. Our orders were to occupy 8&9 after 24 hours of a QRF or tasker mission. I just guessed that we were grounded from being to mean to the locals and for making statistics for the regiment go up. I couldn't stop thinking about going home in less than two months and all the things I planned on doing. I think I will be more sure of myself and confident about what I want to do with myself for the rest of my life. Of course, nothing really seems clear out here. My mind wonders and I catch myself being caught up in strange daydreams and fantasies.

The thing about the desert is that it is very quiet at times. Perry always had a way of annoying us the way he gulps his water down and smacks his lips while eating. A few times, I was ready to turn around and punch him because he kept drinking his water every few seconds and it was driving me up a wall.

Sgt Carr's wife bought him a disposable DVD camcorder in which he could shoot about twenty minutes worth of video and then he would just mail it back for his wife to develop and put on CD. He put on a fake interview and asked us questions while filming, "We are in an over watch position" he said sarcastically and I said, "This is for Gurgol. Bet you wish you were here, man." I went back to reading the second book out of the three that I brought out here to read. The DVD video would be something that Sgt Carr would probably put in a shoebox of memorabilia: (2) ID tags, (15) pictures, miscellaneous, (3) currency, Iraqi Dinar, (2) bullets, 7.62mm. He would probably always remember inventorying his shit and would add (2) DVD's, Iraq between money and bullets. *Those are the kind of things you cherish when you grow old.* That shoebox will eventually make its way out of the closet and into your grandson's arms.

It seemed weird to think about what I would do when I got home. Although that's really all that I have been thinking about the whole time I have been here. It just seemed weird to come home and to be called a war veteran.

Today I finished a couple self-help books, took a few pictures of a tank convoy that headed down the road near our checkpoint, and tried to make my farmer's tan not so obvious for a certain someone back home. For a second when I poured water all over myself I felt like I had just finished swimming in the Pacific Ocean. I imagined I was on the beach and laughed to myself as the sun beat down on us.

A cyclic burst of sounding sort of like an MG42 anti-tank gun or an RPK ripped through the desert over Hadithah. The squawk box exploded with traffic and transmissions could be heard related to where it came from. It reminded me I was still in a war zone and not in that dazed tropical fantasy I had tried to desperately make real for myself a few minutes ago. Soon, the witching hour between dark and light came and we were to be relieved in a few hours as the rotation was going. Kaybar 5 had been caught up in wrapping up a Dam worker who they had suspected of stealing addresses off boxes, but it turned out that he was only searching for boxes to put fish in. I bet everyone ten bucks that's exactly what he was doing before they even said it over the radio. These people were so predictable. Kaybar 5 also called out EOD for suspected IED's near Raptors and Phoenix that was laid in a tank track. After the controlled detonation, MAP 5 refit their vehicles and punched out to relieve us on checkpoints 8&9. We were turning onto South Dam Road to RTB at that time. Driving at night was still somewhat difficult when lunar visibility was high and looking through my NVG's was like looking at the static of a TV.

We got back around 2300 and not a half an hour later, Sgt Carr passed the word that we would have to get up and move out again at 0430 in support of some operation, it was hard to keep track of them there were so many. I was happy I got to talk to Angela again and she talked more about our wedding, which was more than two years away, but I could tell she was excited and happy. I am so lucky to have a girl like Angela. "You're my hero," she said as I wished her a goodnight. She seemed so close to me, but was so far away. I just wanted to feel her touch.

I walked the seven flights of steps back to our room. The lights were already off and everyone was asleep except for Dickason, who always stayed up late staring at the wall and eating popcorn.

JULY 28, 2005 0430

Our APL woke us up a half an hour before we had to get up. I'm not a morning person, especially at 0430. We were moving out this morning to support Lima Co. by setting up blocking positions on Bronze near checkpoint 8. Nothing would get passed our blocking position set up 100m from where the Humvees sat just waiting for someone to cross our trigger line. I must have dozed off an hour or so before we moved out to escort Tinian 2, a line company element that consisted of five high backs, ten Marines per Humvee, and the Iraqi army along with Gunny Delgado's Marines. Gunnery Sgt Delgado was a legend from what we heard about him. He cared for the morale of his Marines and knew how to motivate them. Sometimes from some of the reports we would hear about over the radio, I think he would do anything; even risk his own life for his Marines.

Our platoon's Operations Chief was riding with us today and explained what we would be doing, which I could tell pissed Sgt Carr off, because it was his patrol and he always seemed very possessive about running things in his platoon. We were to escort Tinian to a shithole town called Hushfah, which they currently had troops in contact and need support. We headed north down Bronze to the 33 Northing and headed off road near where Tinian 2 was located. We were supposed to pick up two routine WIA's and ground MEDEVAC them back to the Dam along with five wounded Iraqis. Earlier in the day, the battle started when Tinian 1 Marines were doing cordon knocks on key houses in the town. Locals were saying that five Syrians came into the city and set up defensive positions and told the people if they helped the Americans that they would be killed. First Squad kicked open doors and searched everything inside. I was not there with them, but from what I was told, one of the Marines was searching around in the back yard when a bull charged him and he suffered a mild concussion. It was almost comical in a dark Marine humor sort of way, but he suffered major injuries and had to be air MEDEVACed. Tinian 1 continued searching houses. LCpl Lyons kicked in a door and an insurgent was waiting behind it. The Syrian shot Lyons multiple times in the face. He was MEDEVACed and soon after they touched down at the RAS, he died.

The Syrians were aggressive fighters and came over the Iraqi border highly trained. They grabbed grenades off the fallen angels along with their M-16's and used them against the remaining elements of Tinian 1 and the ISF. One Marine rushed inside a bathroom and was shot several times. They fired RPG's from a house in the NW corner that resulted in multiple injuries and conclusion wounds from Syrians throwing the grenades down the hallways that they snagged from the flack vests of the fallen. A FAC called in a six-line air request for a 500lb JDAM to be dropped on the house, which turned out to be a dud and did not explode. If it had exploded, it would have taken out the entire village. EOD had to wait 27 hours for the batteries in the bomb to run out before they would even touch it.

I felt so sorry for Lyons. We met while I was in the hospital shortly after our Humvee accident on Uranium. He was a short skinny kid and didn't look much older than nineteen. He talked to me about his wife and how he was going to have a baby. It pissed me off that he only had less than two months to go and he would be home with his wife. He was there to get something done with his teeth and although I was high on painkillers for the most the time I was at al-Asad. I remember him playing on his laptop and how intelligent he was. I just wanted to kill every one of these motherfuckers. Although I had only heard it over the Battalion net, I think that Lima Co. should be acknowledged for their bravery and I give them more respect than any other unit.

We still managed to walk away from this mess with two detainees. One was an old man that told the Marines, "No there are no bad guys in this village, of coarse not! Shwaya, no Ali-Babba!" The other prisoner was a Syrian who was one of the five to ten foreign fighters shooting at the Marines. They threw him up into the 7-ton and Crazy 8 had to take him back to the Dam for investigation. They would most likely go to Abu-Ghraib and they would probably be more of a hassle alive than if we just shot them right now. Crazy 8 would not give these assholes the pleasure of martyring themselves. We managed to shove sixteen people in the back of the seven ton for us to escort back to the Dam.

I had been driving for about four hours now and just wanted to go to sleep. I felt like shit, especially after what just happened to Lima and to someone I just met a few weeks ago. It seemed like one minute we were pulling people out of a hot zone, and the next minute I was in my room passed out. I felt like I could sleep forever, and believe me I wanted to. Before you know it we were back out on checkpoints 8&9, I was reading my book where I left off and everything picked up where it was before. *Another couple of dog tags to add to the M16 in the Segovia room,* I thought sadly as the day finally ended. This was one of those things that I was sure would haunt me and cause me to have nightmares. I don't think I could ever forget it no matter how hard I tried.

26

JULY 29, 2005

We were to be relieved again at 2100 to follow the normal rotation that had somehow worked itself out to be 24 on 24 off with a sniper insertion usually taking place routinely right after we were relieved. It was expected and sure enough, Bulldog north called us on TAC 2 and ordered us to come up to the tenth deck after we were relieved to pick up MAKO 8. It seemed that aside from making phone calls and checking email back at the Dam, checkpoint 8 was more of a haven to us. It was a place where we could listen to music, lounge around, and talk with the people we were close to without being involved with working parties, vehicle maintenance, and early reviles. We could sleep in as long as we wanted and it was great, but the focus was still about leaving the place as soon as humanly possible.

It was time to insert MAKO 8 and Ross and I navigated about 30 clicks over the same rough terrain we had been over three times already over the passed week. We were able to reach our objective in less than 40 minutes there and an hour back. I guess it's because we had trouble that way so damn much that we kind of got the feel for how to orient ourselves. MAKO 3/2 just as we left checkpoint 8, had been hived in the general direction of the train station and Uranium. They were setting in dummy IED's with C4 hoping that the explosion would attract on looking insurgents trying to assess the damage and salvage anything from the wreckage. At that point, the MAKO team would put them out of their misery with usually one or two rounds from a SASR or some type of 7.62mm sniper rifle.

I talked to Angela this evening until early in the morning. She had just gotten back from having eye surgery and said she had to wear these funny goggles, which made me laugh so hard. I wished I could have been there to see that. She was happy today and it made me happy.

JULY 30, 2005

I did the normal cleanup and routine maintenance on the vehicles this morning. We also found most of our gear that was salvaged during the explosion and had to check them into supply. Our gas masks and canisters were turned in, preparing to go home in under 40 days. I organized some of my stuff and put some souvenirs into packages to ship home. Brett had mailed his full sized Sadaam poster home the other day and I was going to mail home most of the stuff I took from the mansion on River Road. Cole was in the room with Dmytriw playing that stupid video game. He had absolutely gone crazy, showing everyone the three bags of pills he was on and pressing me for financial advice for him and his new baby. He just found out about it a few weeks ago, he didn't even know his girlfriend was pregnant until after he was deployed. Cole was a funny guy, and he's been through a lot with MAP 2. My friend Montgomery came into the room, I hadn't seen him in a while because he is always hanging out with the snipers. "When are we going to get down to the yacht club and get some more beer tickets?" I asked him, "Hey, when we get back we'll have to go down there one night with ya." He mostly told us stories about some of the terrorists that they killed. One guy got out of a white car and started digging in the road. They shot one round at him, which penetrated through his chest and he kept on moving so they lit him up with the SAW and then at the same time, two rounds impacted his head from the other two snipers, penetrating his skull, and forcing his eyes out of his sockets. They said it wasn't a pretty sight when they went up to the car and they guy was laying a few hundred meters away from his car in a pool of sand soaked blood, because he ran away even though he had been shot several times. They guessed he was hyped up on some kind of drugs along with the normal adrenaline rush that came from running for your life.

Classified organizations were doing a raid in Barwanah where a suspected schoolhouse had been littered with booby traps. They wouldn't even go in because of the reports so they sent in none other than Lima Co. to do the dirty work. The company did what I would have done and questioned the order. "If they won't send in a national asset then why should we go in?" They had the brilliant idea of sending in a dog with a video camera strapped to it. The dog came within 20m from four mortar rounds. FAC decided they would drop two 500lb bombs on the school. "I guess the kids from Barwanah won't be going to school for while," Sgt Carr said as we sat at the checkpoint, which we would be getting familiar with over the next few weeks. That was fine with me. I would rather be bored off my ass then dead. The radio warned us four minutes before the bombs went off. The bomb was on target and actually exploded this time too.

We were questioning some of the intelligence we got, but these were a lot of Iraqis that actually do want to help us out. One guy from Hadithah was sitting out near the front gate. He witnessed two of his brothers being executed by insurgents and when they got to him, they cut his arm and his leg off and told him if he didn't stop helping us they would be back for the other two. That man now usually sits just outside our gate as we come in from patrols. He lives with the AZ's and always reminds me every time we go out, their loyalty to us and how not everyone in the U.S. would sacrifice their legs and arms for what they believe in.

We went to sleep early tonight because we were planning on wrapping up some people tomorrow morning if they were driving a white BMW or a blue Kia van. The BMW was spotted by informants claiming they saw insurgents shoving an MIA from the Army into the trunk just two days ago. He had been reported missing for a year. The blue Kia was reported to be full of suicide bombers headed to Baghdad. We were to stop these cars, be on the look out for them, and do what was necessary to apprehend or kill them.

27

JULY 31 – AUGUST 11, 2005 OPERATION QUICK STRIKE - BARWANA, IRAQ

"Grab your gear and get on the trucks we've got five KIAS!" was the last thing I heard this afternoon before all hell broke lose. We moved out as fast as we could to the east side toward where we dropped off the snipers / MAKO 7. They had taken contact. One second they had COM with them and the next just silence over the airwaves. MAKO 8 humped three clicks to their position and we drove 30 clicks, over the usual rough terrain route we took during the night. This time we made it there in twenty minutes. On the way there, my heart was pounding out of my chest. Sgt Carr yelled over the engine, "Expect contact and casualties!" as we continued moving over stones and rough terrain of the east side of the Euphrates and up a huge surface that jutted out by River Road.

MAKO 7 found them on top of the hill, blood scattered across the rough sand, and the bodies of five fallen Marines lay faced down shot up by small arms fire and then shot in the back of the head. The fifth sniper in the MAKO team, Sgt Boskovitch, was shoved into a truck and taken away by insurgents. His dog tags were found at the site. I just talked to Montgomery and Deyarmin the night before. It hit me as I sat in the driver's seat staring out over the open desert. Tire tracks led to Route Hamsters and a bloody blouse marked with Boskovitch's nametapes. Nine bullet holes were in it and were among the only remains at the scene. Apparently, Sgt Bosko had been dragged into a car or truck and taken away. *This is so horrible,* I couldn't even believe this was happening, especially only 40 days away from getting the fuck out of here. *How could someone have done this?*

So the search began for MIA Boskovitch as we were ordered further east to conduct VCP's of enemy vehicles moving south out of the village. 3/2 was dropped from cobra helicopters just north of east village and two squads of

Marines from al-Qui'm were sent to conduct VCP's on Raptors and Phoenix. One guy was overly rude in describing his experiences in OIF I. He had that condescending tone towards reservists as if our blood didn't spill the same as active duty blood. It reminded me of my of a guy who always bragged about war and how he was such a bad ass. Well there is nothing to brag about and as much as I just wanted to forget this and go home we owed it to five snipers to avenge their deaths, and we would.

At 2300, we were ordered by LTC Catalano to RTB and stand by for an OP order. Officers gathered in the CoC to discuss the push of Lima Co. coordinating with 3/2 and the ISF. Crazy 8 fit into the operation by being the first into Barwanah with an escort of tanks to provide a southeastern blocking position while Lima Co. leveled everything from South to North. I laid in bed for about an hour wondering if when we went out tonight, if I would ever come back alive or in one piece. We just got word that sometime this morning Kaybar 9 got hit with an SVBIED and Sgt Graham was killed. Turner, who had been in my vehicle for the first three months of this deployment in Hadithah with Crazy 8, was severely injured. He lost an eye and injured his legs bad. It was a shame for Turner who just wanted to make something for himself, now suddenly within a few seconds he was fighting for his life. Before we left I talked to Ross, who was taking the sniper massacre pretty bad. Deyarmin was his best friend and roommate for many years now and he was distraught. What was really screwed up was that just a day ago I was talking to Montgomery about how we used to go to his parent's yacht club and get beer tickets. "When are we gunna do that again?" I remembered asking him. I think that it will affect me the most when I see his parents and brother.

28

Soon after 0300, we pulled out of the Dam, escorted by two tanks, headed right into Barwanah. Earlier today, Kaybar 6 secured the Barwanah Bridge, a huge structure that stretched across a large canyon off to the north of the city. The search was soon over for Sgt Boskovitch when they found him lying near a fish market and it appeared as if though he had been dumped off the bridge.

Kaybar 6 soon took IDF from an area near River Road. A white van had been spotted by air fleeing the scene with a mortar tube. A well deserved fate for the Muj mortar team as it drove down River Road and thought it was home free. The van stopped for a minute, just long enough for F15's to drop a 500lb bomb.

From a nearby house near the river, Kaybar 5 was also taking fire. AK's and RPG's whizzed by as they loaded up a TOW round and shot it directly into the house, leaving no trace of the structure or the people inside.

It was one of the darkest nights that I have seen here while in Iraq. Tanks sped up ahead of us leaving dust trails in the darkness and an infrared strobe that lit up my NVG's. I followed the tanks almost blindly and it seemed like forever as we traveled down Raptors, lights off and NVG's on, then turning onto Phoenix. We passed through our temporary AO on the east side all the way past where the terp, Todd fired those REI workers for not spotting the IED, and pushing right into the now silent sleeping city. I could feel that we were in harm's way, not even 100m from the nearest house, watching for RPG's as we pulled into our blocking position. Originally, we were going to sit down by Route Nuggets, which lead around into a valley and extremely low ground, perfect for an ambush. Tanks agreed that a spot on higher ground would be better at least for the night. I pulled in and followed the tanks close to a nearby hill. We uncomfortably slept with our flacks and kevlars on just waiting for nothing, wondering not *if*, but *when* we would take contact. My legs cramped up from sleeping behind the wheel with the windows up, it was impossible to sleep, so I just sat there and stared at the hundreds of houses with thousands of sleeping Iraqis not even 200m from our Humvee.

I woke up this morning around 0640 to a large explosion and then what sounded like machine gun rounds cooking off. "God Damn It! It's an AAV!" The explosions continued about a few hundred meters away, directly in front of us. We listened to the radio traffic and could not believe it. The track traveling down the same road we did last night exploded and flipped completely over, killing the entire first squad of Lima Co. The commander on the scene was distraught and said several times over the net, "Make sure if you see anyone on rooftops they need to go." It took about fourteen hours to clean up all the remains of the fallen heading into Barwanah that morning. Gear, parts, and shrapnel scattered everywhere. It was horrible and by far the most tragic experience I have ever been through. It will haunt me forever.

Later that afternoon, we saw the crash site for ourselves as we were ordered to screen down Phoenix for Kaybar 10 as they went back to the Dam. Sgt Carr stepped out onto the road to sweep for us and spotted two wires under a culvert. *This was so fucking stupid.* Fifteen Marines just got blown up and they want us to screen down Phoenix for them. EOD was called on scene to assess the situation. "This would take some time," one of the Officers said over the radio as we watched the Marines carry the body bags to the helicopters and then take off. Soon after, Schnooks arrived to load up the remains of the fallen angels and take them back to al-Asad. Tinian still was able to push into the city, but at the same time forces also moved into Hadithah, Haqlaniyah, and Bonidari, which should have been done a long time ago to prevent insurgents from simply skipping town every time the Marines rolled in to take over another town.

EOD set it's robot out to plant a charge of C4 on the IED sight and reduced it. God had to be on our side when we ran over one IED that would have completely obliterated our vehicle and then almost ran over a second coming out of the city.

Tinian called over the radio along with LAV's and told us to return to our original POS to block the SE corner of Barwanah. Kaybar 10 decided to RTB with another escort, Gun smoke, and we were left to block the city at an OP which time was not an issue. *You can't stop the clock, but they can make the time we have left a living hell.*

I woke up on day three to more explosions. Tinian reported gunshots. This morning there were a lot of controlled explosions from more than five IED's reduced along Phoenix to keep me awake.

Later on in the afternoon, Sgt Carr radioed battalion concerning the visibility of Phoenix / Nuggets intersection from our POS. One vehicle could see part of it, but our orders stated that we had to cover the intersection effectively. Across the west side of the road were some dirt mounds and nearby houses next to the palm groves near the Euphrates River. Across the river, there was high ground and the K3 oil complex with perfect view of Hadithah and Haqlaniyah. From our position that we held the tip of the spear with Tiger 6-A, we moved to the west side of the road, only after moving a few feet and finding two more IED's. It was a wonder we were not blown up on our entrance into this shithole city. Vehicles 3 and 4 moved right up on the intersection into an over watch position on a small ridge near the palm groves. Our POS, in order to effectively cover vehicles 3 and 4, we would have to be on top of the small hill next to some urban terrain that all made us uncomfortable and uneasy to begin with about moving from our old position.

I drove Crazy 1 to the top of the ridge next to the houses and Ross helped out and cleared the small shack. Behind it were two sets of wires that they followed to a switch and power source by some built up rocks. As Perry and Ross followed the wires and I parked the vehicle, a shot echoed loudly and dirt flew up right next to us. Someone did not want us to ruin his position. A sniper shot suddenly landed about two feet from Ross' head! They quickly got inside the Humvee and rolled up the windows. It was either sit in a hot vehicle, which the temperature had to be above 100 with flacks on, or be shot by the Raghead sniper outside. We radioed battalion and reported the shot that could have sent either one of us home in a box. After a few minutes of authorizations, they decided to push two tanks down to us to show some force.

When Tiger 3-B arrived and pulled up right next to us, the engines whined and tracks cracked large rocks around us, we were so relieved and grateful to them. As far as I was concerned, they saved our lives that day. The tank stopped and a large man got out, "Hey what's going on what do we got here?!" We proceeded to tell him about the Muj sniper and the several MAM's headed towards us under the cover of the palm groves.

Gunny Laden sat upright just outside of the large tank and I could tell he wanted to get some action. He had been up for the last 48 hours and was keeping awake with Red Bull he bought at the PX. I respected him, because I could tell he would do anything for his Marines.

3/25 and 3/2 pushed across the west side of the river, driving insurgents out into the open. Tankers sights had infrared and thermal capabilities and could see across the river into the K3. No more than fifteen minutes of scanning and Tiger 3-B spotted six MAM's digging on the road and two with AK's. It was ridiculous how long it took us to get an authorization over the battalion net. The first mistake we made was calling it in. It had to be cleared with the regiment because the oil refinery was within shooting distance and

God forbid we would destroy that. The thing that fucked the guys on the other end of the radio up was the fact that the maps were topographical and they couldn't see what we were seeing in front of us, a large cliff that jutted out near the Euphrates, blocking the K3. After nearly a half an hour of giving grid coordinates several times over again, we were able to engage with COAX, which is the gun on top and BZOed with the main gun. It was a 240 without the butt stock and a metal plate attached to an electrical system that increased the rate of fire. As far as we knew, because of darkness we didn't know whether Tiger actually hit what they were looking at, but defiantly scared the hell out of them. Gunny Laden was grinning from ear to ear. I felt safe sleeping between two tanks that night, but still kept alert just in case.

I jumped up from my position in the dirt to the sound of machine gun fire from across the river. 3/2 had been engaged for about a half an hour and some how I had slept through it. It was 0600. I could hear the faint sound of the Gunny inside his tank, "This is bullshit! Man we don't get some and they get all of the action."

I was on watch for an hour and then started reading my murder mystery book, a weird psycho thriller about a deranged author who kills brides and grooms. Perry got up in the turret and just when he did, tanks spotted six MAM's in additions to the two I saw while I was on watch that were all armed with AK's and RPG's. One MAM had a black bag with what looked like a mortar tube similar what battalion described over the Intel reports. They were walking along the riverbank and then out across a hill into a defiladed area where they could not be seen by us. Quickly, we rushed to get authorization, which seemed so stupid for being in combat, *you should be able to engage the moment you see someone with a weapon.* It took us more then two hours to get clearance to shoot across the river with .50 cal or below. I knew if we didn't engage soon we would be taking mortar rounds from them and Marines would die. Right at that instant, we were cleared hot. Gunny Laden and Tiger 3-B lit up the targets with .50 cal and 7.62mm COAX. Perry, Dan in vehicle 3, and Osberg in 4 joined us with the 240G and .50s. The man casually walking along side the riverbank started running franticly and fell down the incline into the river. We could see him trying to swim. "I can see him flailing his arms around," Gunny said between bursts of the 240. I could see the guy through the bino's trying to swim away as gunny traversed rounds right up into his chest. A warm body sank behind the small island jutting out from the middle of the Euphrates. Perry let about three boxes go into the river and the other three MAM's tried to find cover, but it was useless. Firing more than 1,000 rounds, three of which were from Cain's .50 Cal, which he thought he had fired off all the rounds. "What do we do if we catch them robbing the river bank?" he said, being a smart ass as usual. We lit up the mortar position, but could not give an accurate BDA. Soon after fixed and rotary wing were on station we called in an air strike on the whole area where insurgents were trying to flee to the nearby town just adjacent to Haqlaniyah. First F-15's swooped down from 7,000 feet to shoot a type 2. Machine guns and rockets in the area were unleashed to make sure the objective had been destroyed. About twenty minutes later, they flew another mission, and I was up in the turret marking the grassy area along the river with tracer rounds. I thought I saw someone moving in the bushes so I shot a few bursts on target. Whatever was back there was still there, but not alive. Three more large bursts of large caliber heavy machine guns lit up the west bank and destroyed everything that breathed. Needless to say, we did not see any more enemies cross that way into the nearby village. Later that afternoon 3/2 sent a recon down to that area and they spotted more then nine dead bodies, one of which lay face down in the river. "That's for the snipers," I told Ross and he smiled.

29

The sun moved over to the west side of the river as we followed wires from the IED trigger spot to an area underneath the road. It was patched up with tar and a faint outline of a South African 155mm round could be seen. Off to the left side of the road there was another 155mm round daisy chained to the first one we spotted. A huge IED that we drove over many times that would have left no trace of our vehicle was still frozen in tar, just waiting for someone to roll over it another time. EOD came to our POS to assess the situation, followed the wires to the IED, and blew both IED's in place with C4 charges that caused huge explosions behind us and scared the hell out of me. At the second it exploded, I flashed back to when I was inside our vehicle on Uranium. The controlled explosion shook our vehicle and sent Ross flying up against the front of the turret. Now that both IED's had been blown, the LTC wanted to move us up into an already cleared sector with LAV's to cover an intersection near a soccer field. Tiger 3-B stayed behind. We let them know that we really appreciated them being there for us. Gunny Laden had a smile on his face from having killed some Muj and wanted to stay with us, but had orders to move with Kaybar 6 to the Barwanah bridge where they had increased traffic.

Intel and Tinian 4 passed over the net that there was another school in Barwanah, one that we did not blow the hell out of with a 500lb bomb that contained anti-coalition propaganda and papers describing the execution of snipers. We knew we were doing our jobs to destroy anyone sick enough to do what they did to snipers, but nothing could bring back my friend. We manned our position at a trash dump just north of the crash site to watch the already cleared intersection.

Until early morning all I could hear was the sound of controlled explosions as 3/25 Lima advanced into the city, blowing open doors and destroying enemy weapons. I woke up this morning and I could tell Barwanah was different. People were outside their houses, children were playing and laughing, and an area that once had been terrorized and was now free. I kept thinking when I got home how it would feel to run down the street or in the park, go shopping, or go to a restaurant. How good we have it in America and how easy it is for someone to compromise that freedom with a roadside bomb, a landmine, or an IED.

Last night the sky lit up with 60mm illume rounds. Bashio 3/2 claimed its battle space just across the river and said the rounds were a disruption method for insurgents. Several elements of Kaybar 6 were planning to ambush some insurgents and the illumes gave away their position. That really pissed their patrol leader off. A house near the limit of advance had been known to have three brothers who had planted the IED's that killed fifteen people. We watched with thermals and telescopic lenses as they moved into the house and arrested the brothers. One of them tried throwing his flack jacket into the trees to hide it from elements of Tinian 4, Lima Company's fourth squad. They also tested positive for gun residue.

So far, Crazy 8 has been out here for eight days since we rushed out to uncover the remains of the fallen snipers. MAP 10 re-supplied us with more ice (which some Marines needed more than others), water, and chow. This allowed us to get through another three days before re-supplying again. Each of us was up to four chows a day, two of which were probably thrown away because they were shit, and four or five water bottles of Mozn. I was tired of sitting here, tired of missing everyone back home, but I knew when we got back we would only have about three weeks and our time here is short. Harris the "New Kid" asked me if the feeling of home ever went away, in which I told him that I was still feeling it and we were about to go home. I could only feel myself growing emotionally numb and unable to remember what it was like to laugh, have fun, relax, and be free to feel again. Brett had my video camera and recorded a message to his folks. At the time, he thought we weren't going to make it out of here alive. "Somehow if you find this tape, I just want to say that I love you Mom and Dad." I think at one point we got really bored with sitting around so Obrst made a poem of our MAP, about the different personalities we all seemed to have in Crazy 8. I think it went something like:

Sgt Carr has no fear,
But what will he do when he can't hear
Our APL hides behind a burm and all he can do
Is stutter and say A-firm
Sir Perry of North Olmsted with his lance and
Wojo trying to teach everyone finance
There's Shoto who can't drive at night and
Eore saying, get to the fucking right!

The sun killed another day as I sat up in the turret and watched the cloudless sky. I observed several children playing next to us who had cleaned up all of our trash and rounds earlier when we moved our position temporarily to the trash dump to watch the intersection. A little girl with a dress on was swinging on a swing set with a little baby. I saw them playing and I did not feel anything, just something resembling sadness and a warm sensation. The IED trigger spot where the son of a bitch who made this would kneel down and wait until someone came down the road to flip the switch was not 100m from where the children played. I couldn't imagine living this way.

A large sand storm knocked out power to the surrounding cities next to us and made it nearly impossible to sleep with the wind gusting, sand covering us, and the darkness that made me extremely paranoid of what was going on around me. I couldn't see a thing in front of me.

We were supposedly leaving tomorrow and moving out with Tinian, but that was still based on the movement that was covered at night. Lima made a habit of searching at night. It was easier, and much cooler on the Marines who had to hump several miles in hot weather if done during the day. Later that night, Bulldog-Actual (the Commanding Officer) had confirmed our retrograde back to the Dam, but the ridiculous part was that Crazy 8 was leading the Tinian element back to Raptors and Phoenix. I guess this would have been expected since we led the assault coming in. I was extremely fearful after I saw what happened to the track and the horrifying sight of the remains and I did not want to be responsible for driving over an IED after we had already lived through the last explosion.

Around 0300 this morning a very strange report came over the Battalion net about LAV's and their return trip to the Dam. As they approached the east side gate near an AZ guard post, they heard and observed shots fired at them. As they approached further, they called Bulldog and asked, "Are there any friendly forces in the area and is someone shooting at us?" They replied, "No, there are no friendlies." LAV's shot a flare and saw it was coming from an AZ guard post. "The AZ's are shooting at us!" Bulldog finally figured this out and asked the AZ's if they fired. They said, "Well we might have fired." *The Russian terp translated wrong,* I thought, while I listened to the transmission in the turret while everyone slept. The commander of LAV's / Mustang was not happy and didn't care of this bunch of AZ's had just arrived a week ago or not. At the time it didn't seem funny, because Perry had just woke me up for watch and I'm always a zombie when I first get up, especially after coming out of some strange dream, which I forgot when I woke up. I took a piss behind the triggerman building and the stones the Muj had used to aim in on the road with and then hopped up in the turret to man my post for an hour before going back to sleep for another four hours, or at least until machine gun fire or mortars woke me up.

Earlier today, Cpl Stocker got really bored, like all of us were, and decided to create something. Using an empty aircraft round, a ravioli can, and a straw, he designed the SITFU award, or "Suck It the Fuck Up" award. I had a feeling that tomorrow I would be in the running for the SITFU, not wanting to be the first vehicle to drive down Phoenix. I rather liked being alive.

There was some hold-up this morning. At 0600, TIC and MEDEVAC air was down temporarily due to the visibility, but soon after 0630, they were on station and we made our way to Tinnian's POS to escort them back and screen for IED's and mines. I love the word, "screen" because it basically means, "to filter out" so we would get the first chance at hitting something. We waited for about ten minutes and Tinian instructed us to go ahead of them. They would be down the road as soon as we got about 500m ahead of them. About a click down the road, we spotted a hole that we spray painted about a month ago and it had been filled in and packed with dirt. I just drove over it, but the wheels did not touch it. We called EOD to come up and take a look at it and it turned out that there were two Italian anti-tank mines shoved in the hole and buried. We were about a foot away from getting blown sky high. After EOD set charges to the two mines they pulled out of the hole with a Kaybar, we continued CAUTIOUSLY down Phoenix, observing every bump in the road for IED's and mines. My guess was the Muj thought we might have had plans to pull out of Barwanah at night, because the hold would have been nearly impossible to spot the markings through NVG's. Tinian elements soon followed us as we approached the more familiar sights of East and West village and the Raptors and Phoenix intersection. Sgt Carr, the Kid, and the radio guy Perry went out and swept the intersection. I was still tired from this morning and as soon as I laid my head against the bulletproof glass, I saw Perry running. He was screaming to me, "Back the fuck up!" He got in the vehicle and told me that they found another mine shoved in the cracks in the middle of the road. As we cordoned off the site, we heard that MAP 2 had found another IED on Raptors just up the road from where we were.

EOD was constantly keeping busy, that was for sure. They finally reduced the second mine we found on Raptors. It was a plastic mine attached to a SA 155mm round. I was relieved that we were still alive and my hands ached from gripping the steering wheel too hard. I couldn't wait to get back to the Dam. Although we all knew how things worked in the Marine Corps. As soon as we got close to something good that you wanted there is always something to do first. In this case, it was probably waiting three hours until our weapons were cleaned, our vehicles were fueled, and some other shit they would make up on the fly was completed as well. Today was one of those special days where we got to watch everyone RTB as we OPed Raptors and Phoenix for at least another 24 hours or so. I was happy to be alive, but I was sure that my family and fiancée would be quite worried, especially if they put what happened these last few days on the news. Well, I'm sorry nothing good happened to us, and a lot of Marines died, so yea, I figured they would be putting it on the news. Who are we kidding? I wanted to make a video like Brett did and mail it to Angela so she knew what I was going through and that she could see that I was alive. I was anxious to talk on the phone to my dad to see if he was okay too. I have nightmares about getting a Red Cross message about my dad over the radio. There were so many things I wanted to do with my dad when I got back. I wondered when I would get to see the day when I could feel Angela in my arms.

When we got back to the Dam that night, almost everyone found out what was happening back in the States and everyone knew back home. Secretary of State Donald Rumsfeld said the reason the track was blown up by an IED was because, "The insurgents are getting desperate." News of the sniper massacre was also all over the headlines and CNN had a field day with it. President Bush referred to 3/25 as, "Reservists in the hottest part of Iraq." Neither the media nor anyone back home would have any idea what we just experienced over the past few days.

The Captain came into our room and talked about the reason we pulled out early was because a certain classified organization had identified some high value targets in Hadithah and would engage in approximately five days. The reason we pulled out was to lure the insurgents in so that we could destroy them. It got me wondering if somehow it had been planned to weaken the Hadithah AO to do just that, to make the Muj think this was a haven. It really angered me to think of it that way. I'm sure I was just not thinking clearly. I'm sure no one in their right mind would ever think it would turn out as horribly as it did. I was glad to find out when talking to my fiancée that there was so much support for the families of the fallen. They even had a memorial ceremony at the IX Center in Cleveland, which over 10,000 people attended. Angela said I was her hero and it made me smile. She said she missed me and thought I might be dead or injured, but I said, "I'm still here and I'll be coming home in a few weeks." I never thought I would say coming home and weeks in the same sentence.

Over the course of the operation, over 23 dog tags were hung up in the Segovia memorial, the names of college kids, fathers, and husbands. They were all the heroes of 3/25 and will never be forgotten. 3/25 has the most casualties and KIA's of any Iraqi Freedom operation, which unfortunately put us on the map as a battalion. I think that if there were ever an operation that showed me what war was like, this operation would rank the highest. The good news was that several hundred insurgents were killed and approximately nine or more of which were claimed by Crazy 8. After a day or so off, we went back to the normal one day on one day off checkpoint 8&9 routine, which I was almost glad to see, although it was good to break away from the routine for a while.

Every time I closed my eyes I pictured myself getting off the place to a crowd of people and coming home as a hero. Although, I know I will feel the pain when I get home and see those people missing in places which they normally were; Montgomery at the yacht club, Squires always smoking and joking with Trexler, and Keeling talking to me at the Kent State student center about what he wanted to do when he graduated. All I can think about at this point is getting back to my life that will most definitely never be the same.

30

AUGUST 12, 2005

Crazy 8 spent most of the day at checkpoint 8 resting up from the operation. There was not a lot of room for sleep. I woke up to explosions throughout the night. I woke up around noon and then going back to the Dam at 1300 made it a lot easier for me to handle. An upcoming operation in Hadithah was supposed to be going on in a few days. Our map would most likely be on a QRF and rotate between MAP 5 and MAP 2, probably on checkpoints or VCP's.

That night we spotted a car with its lights off, but we lost it in the desert before we were able to engage it with a missile. Sgt Carr's ear surgery was supposed to happen soon and he said it would be a few days until he knew. His eardrum was half gone from the IED explosion and was not healing properly. My ear felt like it was healed, but I could still hear a constant high pitched noise that was annoying as hell and wouldn't go away.

As we all sat around reading, relaxing, or playing video games on checkpoint 8, there had been an accident on Bronze. A van ran into a telephone pole near checkpoint 9. Crazy 3 and 4 were at the scene and controlled traffic. In Hadithah, predator drone planes spotted an SVBIED because of its odd heat signature and placement on the side of the road. Just before we were relieved by Kaybar 5, it was blown up by a tank round which we could hear almost two clicks away.

Tonight I got on the Internet at the computer center and saw the most horrible thing in my life. I was mostly pissed off and discussed. Some sick fuck had decided to post live video footage of the sniper ambush, how it happened, the people being shot and then all you could see was a pair of dog tags being ripped off and a guy being shoved into a vehicle. You couldn't make out faces in the video, but I knew who each of them were. I emailed the webmaster of the sight and told them to remove the video. I don't know what S-4 planned to do about controlling the spread of the video, but there was a war going on in cyberspace as well as out here. I wanted to puke and I'm not sure what I was doing, I just stared at the screen and then went back downstairs to sleep.

Viewing the video just made me hate everyone in Iraq even more. Finding IED trigger spots in people's backyards, seeing all the shit in Barwanah, and asking the Iraqi people why, only to hear, "I don't know." There were always smiles and shit eating grins all the way up until they blow the hell out of your vehicle and leave your platoon dead.

AUGUST 13, 2005

A few people that had attended the memorial at the IX center said there were protesters there. What could they be protesting? They held signs like, "God bless IED's." I swore to myself if I ever saw someone who was part of that small crowd of ten or so people out of 10,000, I would hardly be able to contain myself.

The General was going to be here today so we spent the morning cleaning up and preparing. Everything had to be polished, decks had to be swabbed, heads clean, and hair cut. I saw him land in his escort of helicopters. He had lunch with the VC's, was more than 30 minutes late, and then gave them the usual speech. "I'm sorry for your losses. You guys are doing a good job. Keep it up." He also mentioned that troop strength would be increasing due to the sole fact that the ISF would be taking over.

Our dog "Beans" was something of a major celebrity. I guess he was featured on a lot of the national news networks. The president of militarymascots.org worked to draw the donations of the 3,000 dollars it would take to ship the dog home to the States. The puppy we bought for some jellybeans and a quarter. The dog had been an uplifting source of morale for the troops in the wake of the most horrible events that had happened and all the death we saw around us.

I can't really describe what I am feeling at this moment. A sense of anticipation most of all, knowing in a few weeks I would be taking walks with my dad in the yard and watching movies close to my fiancée.

Sgt Carr left for his surgery today and our APL assumed command for the time being until he returned from his operation. We continued our rotations to checkpoints 8&9. I could almost feel what it was going to be like to leave Iraq, but nothing could even compare to when I sat down in the plush seat of that military aircraft.

We filled out souvenir forms for the items we were going to take home. The Battalion Commander had to approve of anything we took with us that we didn't land here with six months ago. I had still kept the things

I took from the mansion in Haqlaniyah. I also saved an Iraqi bayonet that we snagged from some mentally challenged farmer in the Balsac near the city of Hit. There was to be a search of our gear and computer equipment as well, or at least that's what they scared us into thinking so that we wouldn't bring anything home that the Marine Corps deemed inappropriate or certain members of our platoon's chain of command. I honestly didn't care what they searched as long as I could throw my shit on a plane and get out of this hellhole.

AUGUST 14, 2005

Shortly after noon, we were relieved at CP 8 by Kaybar 5. Nothing exiting really happened and I used most of the time to sleep. I get more sleep on CP 8 then I do back at the Dam. I kept to myself and was not really in a talking sort of mood. I was just sick of being around people and just wanted to be alone for once in my life. Perry tried to talk to me and he immediately noticed how I was feeling when I chewed his ass for no reason. The thought of not having to eat, sleep, shit, and live with these people was a comforting realization. In another way however, they are closest friends that I have ever had, they wouldn't stab me in the back, and I could trust them with my life. We had grown close over the last ten months.

I went to start the vehicle and the engine made a faint rumbling sound and then died. The radios beeped at us as I turned off the power again. This was right after Vehicle 2 had radioed in to us and said that their vehicle was dead. It was so amazing how we were this far into the war and we had not gotten the funding to get new vehicles or parts. Just the vehicles alone, the shape they were in was ridiculous. *What if there was an ambush or we were being mortared and our vehicles just die all of a sudden?* It scared the shit out of me but I didn't care anymore.

When we got back to the Dam, we were immediately put on a fifteen minute strip alert. Kaybar 6, tanks, and AAV's were assembled as a task force to investigate the sniper executions. They went down to where it happened and tried to pull a story together based off what little evidence they knew. *Why don't they just watch the video that some Muj asshole posted on the Internet.* Crazy 8 had to be ready to go out to assist the task force within fifteen minutes. The QRF lasted about two to three hours and then we were free to do whatever it is that we did here at the Dam with what little free time we had. Of course, since Sgt Carr was gone, our APL decided that it was a good time to have a gear inspection of serialized gear. If any gear was missing, it had to be written down in a missing gear statement. My gear list changed slightly from the other night when we did this the first time and included a few things that were destroyed in the two explosions I was involved in, with MAP 2 and with Crazy 8.

The phone center was packed with Marines. Navy Sea Bee's were talking construction as I sat in the uncontrollably hot room. I sat and talked to Obrst for a while. His wife and my fiancée had become friends since we had been in country. I was finally able to use the phone after three hours. No one ever stops and wonders what it would be like to sit in the exact spot and stare at the wall for three hours waiting for a phone. I'm sure you wouldn't want to either.

Angela was enjoying a Saturday afternoon off work. I missed her so much. She and I would go to Wal-Mart sometimes just to have fun and even get a pretzel or an Icee and make fun of the rednecks and weirdoes who always walked into that place. The red Icees are always the best. She had been on her way to the store and she was talking to me on her cell phone in the car. We laughed a little together and I closed my eyes and imagined I was in the car with her. I would always ride in her car and somehow always get her to sing to me. Sooner than never, my half an hour was up and I headed back down to the first deck like clockwork to fall asleep.

AUGUST 15, 2005

It was payday today. One of only four more paychecks we would receive until we got back to the States. I got up early this morning at 0800 and woke up Dan. We were going to breakfast and then eventually after the ceremony to honor the 23 Marines that died both in Charof, the sniper incident in Barwanah, MAP 9's VBIED, and the catastrophic AAV explosion that we sat about 500m from. Dan and I finished our horrible breakfast together and headed up to the tenth deck. We were called to attention and the names of the fallen were called as one person each with a dog tag placed it on the pistol grip of the weighted down M16 that was now stuck into sandbags. The wind blew the kevlar from side to side, as it always does and never stops. When they got to Brian Montgomery, my heart sank into my chest and I held back the tears as I stood at attention in the formation. This had been my fifth ceremony. I never knew how to act at these things and never for once thought I would be going to one for someone I knew so closely.

I stood and listened to the eulogies being read, coming from those men who knew the fallen warriors so well. One Sergeant from STAX said, "You can have your opinions about us being here whether we should or shouldn't, but these men did their jobs and accomplished their mission, which is to kill insurgents, and they did a very good job."

The time came to pay our final respects and I preceded through the long line, knelt down in front of the Kevlar, 16, and dangling tags and said a prayer:

God, these were good men that died. These Brave men with families and great lives. Please help me to cope with the loss of my friends, to help me be strong, and carry out your will. That this test of faith will soon be over and these men will be remembered and honored always as heroes. Please watch over them in heaven. Amen.

I saluted to the kevlar that a Marine once sweated his ass off in the blazing sun, and a 16 that shot straight and hit what it was aiming for. I walked away following Dmytriw to the first deck to stage our vehicles and go back to where we belonged, the field.

31

AUGUST 16, 2005

The overwhelming frustration and expectations of going home made time go by sluggishly. At this point, our death rate is so high it was probably better for us to remain inactive. Ross looked bored as our gunner since Gurgol wasn't here and was probably curling up at home to a six-pack, cheesy daytime soaps, and a bottle of painkillers bigger than a Coke can.

I woke up to Perry passing a message to Bulldog over the radio. The AZ's spotted several MAM's just outside the power station digging out on the road. Ross had bets that it would just be some sheepherders and we didn't know what kind of drugs the AZ's were smoking, but always made the stupidest calls that would more often than not be nothing at all. This is a call coming from the same AZ's that shot at LAV's when last time I checked Iraqis were not in possession of LAV's. So we left CP 8 open to the enemy while we searched for the suspicious diggers. For several weeks now, I observed busloads of Dam workers riding back and forth between the power station and the Dam. Supposedly the Dam employs more than 400 workers, making it one of the western Iraqi's greatest source of legitimate jobs (at least that I knew of.) Some of them were probably working double shifts, working at the Dam during the day and planting mines at night.

The results of the patrol were as expected. We pulled over a group of Dam workers and questioned them, getting the same answers we always do. The two sheepherders nonchalantly strolled through a small patch of green grass near the power lines. Ross won some money today after making such an obvious bet, if he would have been serious. We drove back to CP 8 and waited about an hour for Kaybar 5 to show up. We swept for mines and IED's on our way back to the checkpoint for fear that while we were checking out the AZ's reported sighting that Muj had planted something where we used to be sitting.

I hope that this wasn't something that we made a habit of, leaving our post to investigate activity. It would be easy for the Muj to organize an ambush.

Although being at the Dam made time go by slower, it still allowed me to relax and of course communicate with the real world back home. In recent news, rumor said that they were going to change the name of the, "Global War on Terrorism" to a more politically correct term, "The Global Struggle Against Extremism." The point was to try and take war out of the picture. The things that politicians think of while on the golf coarse or at the office. What a great idea, to tell the armed forces who fight for freedom that what we are doing is not a war it's a struggle. It really pissed me off, even though it was probably some untrue rumor that circulated around the Dam like wildfire. About as true as the one about how we were leaving the first of August. Rumors flew around the Dam faster than ever and half of them were not true. *I couldn't imagine that ever happening,* I convinced myself as I poured a cheap bag of ramin noodles into some water.

Back home a new series made it to FX called, *"Over There,"* a reality TV show about a group of soldiers fighting in southern Iraq near Baghdad. It is the only show historically to portray the events of the Iraq war in real-time. Angela has been watching it religiously since it started a few weeks ago.

I made another phone call home and would call home any chance I got. There were only four phones for the Battalion so my chance to make a call was always limited to a half an hour. Lately, I have been telling myself that I have to feel things at appropriate times. Otherwise, I just feel emptiness. *We have been here a long time,* I thought to myself as I flew down the steps to the hooch. My fiancée was already planning the wedding and her wedding dress, "No, I can't tell you what it looks like its bad luck!" I pictured our wedding day. Her green eyes looked at me as I fell asleep.

AUGUST 17, 2005

This morning we had to escort the Battalion Commander and Sgt Major and it was a nerve wrenching experience especially for the driver. I had to make sure to go the exact speed the Sgt Major wanted and do everything right or else face getting my ass chewed by our APL later on. Both the Sgt Major and BC had to meet at al-Asad with the regiment. At CP 9 near Phoenix / Bronze intersection we witnessed an IED explode on Kaybar 5. At the time there was not a whole lot to tell whether or not it was mortar rounds or whether someone had planted an IED. Their first vehicle took some shrapnel and was punctured two times in the windshield. Luckily, no one was hurt.

This evening was spent clearing a four click grid square to find the suspected trigger man with help of Revenge 1-1, which was a section of

Cobra helicopters. We ended up clearing the grid square, finding nothing other than some trash, a lean-to where a bum had stayed, and a few wires. I couldn't sleep until about 0300. I was thinking too much about home, about college, romance, and the usual things in life. There is still a ringing in my ears, which bothers me and has now gotten to the point where it's affecting my sleep. It was another uneventful nonsensical day in the Marine Corps. I kept thinking about that show, *"Over There"* and I thought of us as being on the show except the cameras weren't there and I was watching myself. It's like the past few days have been really dragging. It's always like that when we get to the middle of the month because we are always anticipating the next month. Like Sgt McNally's logic for when we are going home, "Well you can't count August because we are already in it and you can't count September because we are going home in September so…" *So technically, we should be leaving here any minute,* I thought to myself as I shut my eyes. I had just carried on a conversation with myself. I was going crazy.

I tossed and turned until about an hour before my watch as the hot wind blew over me and the moon slowly set.

32

AUGUST 18, 2005

This afternoon we came back from CP 9 and got word that another General would be coming to the Dam, General O'Dell. We had no idea what he would say to us. Crazy 8 and other Kaybar units met outside of the chow hall in a shaded area. Ice and cups were put out for us, which was a real treat. It was one of the hottest days on record, probably in the 120's. "Attention on deck!" a voice screamed from the corner of the patio. "Relax, stay comfortable." I watched the older man walk toward us. His grayish hair gave me the impression that he had been through a lot. I kept looking at his three stars and it was a little bit unreal that he would come all the way out to this shit hole to see us.

General O'Dell began by letting us know we only had a few weeks left and then went on to describe the funerals of Deyarmin and Montgomery:

The motorcade to the funeral home was almost unreal. 10,000 people gathered in the streets waving flags and paying their respects to these heroes. Vietnam vets could be heard driving their motorcycles and leading the procession. At the funeral, heartfelt speeches were given. Montgomery's brother spoke about why we are here in Iraq, and said it better than any politician or higher up. I just want to let you know that these are the people that are waiting for you when you return home.

I had to keep myself from sobbing when he mentioned Montgomery. He was a short and slender man who carried himself very well. It made me feel better. He told us we had been through a lot and wanted to reassure us of what would be ahead. "Don't get lax because the Muj know you're doing a relief in place and I've seen it time and time again where they stick it to you one last time before you leave."

After answering a few questions, everyone stood up at attention and saluted while the General said his final words and stepped off into the crowd of brass. I eventually made my way downstairs and ran into him. I got to shake his hand and he let me know we were doing a good job. Dan didn't think Generals existed because he never saw or met one. "Hey Dan do you think they exist now?" I asked him as we exited seventh deck.

I went down the seven flights of steps to grab my mail to send out. I had absolutely everything ready to mail home including souvenirs. The problem was that getting it to the seventh deck was a bitch. An Officer helped me carry one of the large boxes packed full of gear. We waited in line behind a large trailer for what seemed like over eight hours. First, they searched our boxes and then gave us customs forms to fill out while we waited in a second line. It was such a relief to get things taken care of and sent home. I went back down to my bed. My shelves were bare and everything was packed, it was motivating.

My dad was not doing well and I knew it, because he stayed in bed a lot and my mom doesn't want to worry me. I just for once think that God would make things right for me. It was more than I could take. Something had pushed me to the edge. I was neither her nor there, afraid of the world and hating this place. I was quite possibly even in hell.

AUGUST 19, 2005

I woke up this morning and went with Doc Barone to go straighten out the medical record mess and hearing problems with BAS. Apparently, all they have on file for me is a mild case of dehydration, which was not true. I remember that day when time stopped for an instant and the next thing you know I was staggering around in the dirt trying to carry everyone to safety. The Chief and Captain in the BAS said they were working on it and followed up with my hearing problem. "I think you may have some permanent damage," he said referring to some diagnosis that people usually get after being in explosions.

"I hear a ringing in my ear and it's hard to sleep at night because it's a constant ringing," I told the Chief. When I got to al-Asad along with psychological tests that we were required to get to make sure we wouldn't unload a full clip on innocent people, they were to give me a thorough hearing test to further diagnose the problem. When we got to CP 8, we were notified about six MAM's that were just recently captured on the Tinian OP in the city. They had no idea about the time of arrest, but later after further investigation, they found that these men were involved directly in the sniper ambush and may have been the MAM's that killed them. We had a conversation in our truck about it. Ross was infuriated. His best friend that he lived with was dead and he said if he had to escort the prisoners they wouldn't make it to the Detention Facility alive. I shared in his feelings that he had. Montgomery was my good friend and the people responsible were sub-human and did not deserve to be alive. I told Ross that leaving them alive would deprive them more because killing them would lead to martyrdom and exoneration in this terrorist community.

The moon had never been so full and bright this evening and it practically lit up the entire desert with its glow, almost like the sun. The moonlight here was like the sunlight back in Ohio. But for some reason it grew very cold about the time I went to settle down in my bag before watch. It was probably because we had been so used to 100+ degree weather that if it dropped just 20 degrees to 80 we would freeze our asses off. I crawled inside my sleeping bag as the never-ending wind blew up dust.

AUGUST 20, 2005

I would be content with myself if from now until we left we followed the same routine, because unlike other parts of service when shit starts to happen, Marines start to die. It was simply unbelievable how many Marines left this world in only a matter of months and I could only imagine how this would affect me when trying to go back to work or school as if nothing happened. My faith grows stronger in God even as we are about to leave country. My only request every night and hour of the day is that I come home alive and in one piece. I know that he keeps us safe because we are the only platoon that has not lost someone yet. I try not to mention that fact because I'm afraid if I say anything or even write it down that something bad will happen. These will be words that will be written well after I am home.

Colonel Urquhart, our Company Commander, copied the evening news special on a DVD and we watched it after we returned to the Dam. I couldn't believe so many people were there, it was unreal. The speakers were mostly politicians, who in some respects said some good things, but I didn't know who to believe or who to think was just using the ceremony to get votes. I liked the veterans who gathered there and as I watched the crowd from our beat up TV. I could almost see my family and fiancée in the crowd waving to me. Everyone gathered around the TV for that hour until a left wing reporter on channel five was saying, "I was a reporter in Vietnam so I'm not used to this kind of support." The crazy assholes that were around in the Vietnam era protesting in the streets were now speaking there minds on TV as reporters and politicians. I have news for them; their cheesy experiences have nothing to do with what we are going through and they could not possibly even begin to understand.

Tinian was conducting a raid beginning at 0130 in Barwanah along with top-secret CIA operations giving them plausible intelligence on high valued targets. Although most of the time the information was accurate, at times our platoon questioned its validity. We were on fifteen minute strip alert from 0130 to some time around 0400 and if Lima got into the shit we would be called out with tanks to pull them out. I think I was getting rather paranoid as I went to the head looking out cautiously across every corner and out every window.

Cpl Bauer brought a thumb drive of interesting pictures in for me to swap with him. He got most of them from the snipers who had been known for their taking some pretty gruesome photographs.

The pictures were pretty graphic, outside of Hushfah an insurgent with an RPG lay dead with his weapon just outside of a doorway. Photos of jaws blown off, two MAM's in a car were blown away. Guts were everywhere. The guy that most likely blew us up with the IED on Uranium was found mangled and eaten by dogs and hyenas. It left his upper torso severed from the rest of his body. I'll never forget the look of a dead man. That blank stair of someone that isn't anymore. *So this is what happens when you fuck with the Marines.* It appeared as if though our reputation as Marines has in fact preceded us.

I felt sad tonight as I crawled into bed. The mosquitoes were inside and I had to put bug spray on before I racked out. I was thinking about Angela and my family and hoping everything would be alright. I stared up at the top bunk and into the darkness blankly. Like the cold stare of a dead man.

AUGUST 21, 2005

Most of my time at CP 8 was spent sleeping or reading because I had spent most of my time awake at the Dam the night before. I usually make a habit of staying up as much as I can well we are back so that I can use the phone, eat real food (not MRE's), and play on my computer, then sleep all day at CP 8.

Our APL would always get on my nerves because he would never stop talking and when he talked, it was always about the Marine Corps 100% or making fun of other Marines. I pretty much kept to myself and hoped that he would stop talking. He had a fucked up notion that I was the best driver because I didn't have to be told where to go, but despite his compliments, I still hated being in "the hot seat" as it was referred to, because I was in the most vulnerable position for mines and IED's.

A report came down to all Kaybar units from an operative who believed that an enemy unit was observing our position in order to effectively employ surface to air missiles. They didn't say how or when they just said you are being watched. How scary is that? I was paranoid that night and made sure to look out for this enemy "unit." I believe that Intel was as good as the threat to the Dam fiasco back in early July and just as valid as some of the rumors that float around the Dam.

Tinian 4 Lima Co. was occupying most of CP 8 on South Dam with AAV's. They hoped to kill and disrupt the enemy. Our POS was then slightly changed, because Tinian had been running VCP's and taking up the whole area where we usually slept / sat. We found a spot in a trash dump overlooking a watey on Route Bronze. It wasn't a bad spot, but the flies were horrible.

At night, I imagined what the rain would feel like. The smell of the humidity just before a storm and the crash of thunder are unforgettable. In fewer than six patrols, we would be on our deactivation at al-Asad and soon enough, back in the States. I think that is how I am able to go on and endure the monotony, the scenery, and the hot rainless weather that I will never miss.

AUGUST 22, 2005

Our APL passed out the list of things we absolutely have to have in our ILBE packs for the RIP. Half of it was already packed in my sea bag, but we had to have two sea bags packed for al-Asad before 3/1 got here. We would then give up the rooms to them and we would sleep in the hallway, which was fine with me. I spent about an hour packing before the mail came to the seventh deck and, of course, we all had to walk up and carry the entire company's mail, a ritual that was done every time the trucks dropped off mail from al-Asad.

They finished my personal action request while we were gone concerning my Purple Heart and apparently I was MEDEVACed to al-Asad, put on pain killers and bed rest for five days all for a case of dehydration, or at least that's what my medical records say. I am not going to make a big deal about a Purple Heart because there are a lot of Marines out there who lost legs and arms and I most certainly think that they deserve it more than I do for a hearing problem. It's just for the fact that the inaccuracy of record keeping in the military was absolutely unreal.

I unloaded mail from the truck and made about five trips up and down the stairs until our mail was delivered to the first deck. A real live example of taking the stairs would be to walk all the steps in Chicago's Sears Tower with boxes in your hands and that's about how many times we have walked up and down the steps over the past few months. *Well, why don't they just drop off the packages on the first deck?* I always ask myself, *but that would be too simple,* the voice inside me would reply. Sitting in the trucks for the majority of the time and not getting exercise was the downside of the mobile assault platoon so I didn't mind getting some exercise.

The last day to send packages home was the fifteenth, so I got a package from just about everyone I knew. I remember when I first got here I thought that getting mail was like Christmas morning. I opened a package from my parents and pulled out an article in the local paper about Montgomery. The picture on the front showed his brother hugging Brian's wife Pam and his son about three years old was dressed in a miniature dress blue uniform. It was unbearable to look at him without feeling remorse and pain. I remembered all the times we spent together on a gun team together. We would talk about computers and he would always tell us stories about his old National Guard unit that he used to be in. His absence would severely affect me once we returned to drilling one weekend a month. Montgomery's funeral was something that would be remembered. It was because of the strong community that gathered and everyday kept flags in their yards and yellow ribbons on their cars. We were certainly not forgotten back home.

A lot of mail was sent from brothers and some from companies thanking me for my service. Angela sent me some snacks and Tums for my stomach. A note was included in the package that made me sad, "God has a plan for all of us so if it's time to go then its time to go."

The room looked more cluttered with everyone packing up their sea bags. I sat down and organized my packages. A man who always writes me and sends me good things, John Neuhous is a true American. He lives in Kentucky, works at the lumberyard, and sounds like he has a good life. I thought about the sacrifice that I was making to keep them safe and it made me happy for a second.

Our dog Beans was causing quite a commotion back home. One of the news channels had a story about Beans making her famous, but the Marine Corps does not officially condone the fact that the dog is a health hazard. To their knowledge they said, "We never had a pet," and, "stray dogs are all over Iraq."

I tidied up my rack and sat down for a while to watch dumb movies everyone always watches and engrosses themselves in every time we come back. Just then, a large explosion shook the doors and windows. We quickly got accountability and ran out onto our balcony to see what the hell was going on. A huge cloud of smoke was coming up near CP 8 and no one knew what the explosion was. It was quite odd but soon everyone went back to what they were doing like it was nothing. The explosion sounded like a missile of some sort.

Later that night, Dan and I stayed up half the night watching the X-Files. "Skinner is such a bad ass!" I said, as I stumbled off to bed. It reminded me of how my brother and I religiously watched the X-Files every Friday night at 9:00.

AUGUST 23, 2005

A supply convoy arrived early in the morning and Sgt Carr was returned to us from al-Asad. They pretty much told him that his hearing problem was going to be permanent. We set out for our static positions again hoping that one day we wouldn't have to go out again and I could see my family. It was as if we were prisoners in an everlasting nightmare and could not wake up. We pulled up to a watey about a few clicks south of South Dam Road and Sgt Carr got out to clear it, because of the IED's placed there earlier when MAP 5 was hit. I saw him searching around from my helpless and vulnerable driver's seat position when he dug up something from under the bridge. It was a Motorola talk-on and looked as if someone had used it either to signal a triggerman or to blow the IED himself. A number was written on the battery pack, an Arabic number three.

Once we found the talk-on, we decided to stay near the watey to keep an eye on it. Cars rushed over the bridge, but then continuously moved around what looked like something in the road. Ross and I dismounted the vehicle once we were set into our OP's and went to check it out. It was extremely hot out and every step I took felt like I was going to pass out. We moved up to the bridge while kneeling to block cars and then continuing on. The bridge was clear all except for a few pieces of shrapnel shining in the sunlight where a previous IED went off.

It always worries me how easy it would be to put IED's on local highways back home. I could feel the real world slip away and reality seemed only to be this hellhole.

Another full moon tonight rose and fell almost like the sun. I was awake every three hours for watch. It all seemed useless. Like what I was doing was not helping anyone, just being here to watch over and babysat people so they didn't do anything bad. I started to hate being around people, I loved to be alone and not having people next to me, to do what I wanted when I wanted was the best feeling in the world.

AUGUST 24, 2005

I decided to try and get in shape today. I climbed to the fifth deck where it looked like a prison yard. Marines were working out and I saw Gunny Laden with his tattoos of tank rounds just below his elbow. He was lying down lifting what looked like 300 pounds. *Idol hands are the devil's play toy,* I kept thinking as I picked up weights. I quickly finished up, took a shower, and watched some TV for a while. It always reminds me of those mental hospitals or nursing homes where everyone is sitting around staring at the TV like it is a drug or something.

The best part of my day was when I got a chance to use the phone. I felt isolated, but I liked being by myself. I felt sick and didn't know why. I went outside to puke and then came back down to sit in the A/C they just put in at the phone center. I imagined what it was like to talk on my cell phone for three hours instead of thirty minutes. The walls felt like they were collapsing on me. I felt weak and dizzy. I finished my phone call and then went back downstairs to fall asleep.

33

This morning on our day off we were ordered at the last minute to do some VCP's. The main reason was to get us out of the Dam and keep us busy. Crazy 8 wasn't happy about it and we bitched up a storm until Sgt Carr came in and told us he didn't like going out any more then we did and that we would be scaring the shit out of the Hajjis today. Sgt Carr had something special planned and he probably had some time to think after his surgery. He told us to get all the cammie paint that we had and be down on the trucks in a half an hour.

Dan and I went downstairs together with our gear. We never really got to talk much because we were in different vehicles, he was in vehicle 4 and I was in vehicle 1. I tried to fix him up with my fiancée's friend but he just never got around to calling. I supposed that some people didn't have the patience I did to sit up in the Segovia for hours on end, waiting for one thirty minute phone call. For me I could wait forever and I didn't care, it wasn't like I had anything constructive to do.

I traded out my SAW for Dickason's M-16 like I always do and noticed Sgt Carr. He looked like something out of a KISS video, "That will definitely scare the shit out of them Sergeant!" I said surprised as I threw some sodas I stole from the chow hall into the cooler. Ross helped me with the usual ritual of going all the way up to the seventh deck, getting bags of ice in one of the freezers adjacent to the chow hall, carrying them back down, emptying the cooler, and then filling it with ice, water, and sodas. I noticed several other Marines were really getting into the face paint despite the fact that it was soon to warm up to 110 today. I almost pissed myself when I saw Stocker. He was wearing a bright, glittery, Uncle Sam hat, and red, white, and blue face paint. I couldn't help but joining in the madness so I took some of the black paint and put a big eight on my face. I guess we really lived up to our name today.

We got out to our stopping point and formed the vehicles for VCP's. On the way out to Bronze, I always hit the same potholes that were unavoidable in the destroyed road leading up to the Dam. Tinian was still doing some patrolling around CP 8 so we mostly stayed towards River Road and Phoenix to do VCP's. Vehicle 1 pulled up next to vehicle two to participate in the searches. Then the first car pulled up and Stocker yelled at it with his bullhorn to pull over. Two men came out of the vehicle and approached the search party. When they saw us, one of them laughed and Stocker yelled at them, "What are you laughing at fuckhead! Enso Mensiata mutha' fucka'!" All of us were trying not to burst out laughing and I went behind the truck to laugh so hard I almost cried. Crazy 8 hadn't had this much fun since we were in Hit.

I searched some of the vehicles and checked ID's for a while until about 1300. We decided to break for chow and then stop for the day after that. Most of us had home on our minds and there was nothing they could do to make that go away. It made it seem all better and I could still think of the time when we first landed here. Getting off the C130 and trying to come to grips with the fact that we still had seven months here. I drove us up to CP 8 where we would be staying for the night. It wasn't a real surprise to any of us and we all had our little routines. As soon as we stopped, I took off my flack and kevlar, laid my books out, grabbed a non-alcoholic Beck's and an MRE, and hung my feet out the unarmored window of the Humvee. If we weren't at war, things wouldn't have been that bad.

I fell asleep until nightfall and then hopped up into the turret. We had our usual conversation and Sgt Carr had some music on his mini-disc player. Glenn Miller, Sinatra, or something classic, usually Metallica was his favorite and I didn't mind it much either.

2300 rolled around and we got a call from Battalion, "You need to send Kaybar 8 back to the Dam ASAP." *Oh shit,* I thought, *whatever it is, it can't be good.* It could be either we are going out on another extended operation until God knows when or someone just got in the shit and we had to go in after them. I knew I wasn't going to like it. We just laid out our cots, sleeping bags, and the bug nets that kept the nats and the ants I had a run in with a few months back off us. I just shoved everything in the back and jumped in the Humvee. "Ready Sgt?" I fastened my NVG's to my kevlar and adjusted the focus, flipped the switch to turn on the infrared lights and started the engine. I was really wondering about what we could have to do when we got back. What kind of shitty assignment would we be going on now? I sighed and put the Humvee in reverse. We drove down the small incline leading up to CP 8 and then made our way out onto Bronze. The ride back was full of anticipation and complaining. I think we were really annoying Sgt Carr, but I think he was pretty pissed about going back in too. Those surface to air missile warnings were still in effect and I was wondering if we were moving because of that. So many questions rolled through my mind on the way back to the Dam I almost rolled off the road thinking about them.

When we got back, we parked the Humvees in the motor pool and then I went to the hooch. I was got settled in for God knows how long at the Dam. I changed my sweaty skive shirt, sat my rifle on my rack and then laid down for a minute. Just then, Sgt Carr came in and motioned for me to come out into the hall, "Hey Wojo you need to go up to the CoC right away," he whispered. I got ready and he walked up the steps with me. I thought for sure I was in trouble. You never go to the CoC unless you are in trouble. I walked up the stairs in heavy anticipation. Sgt Carr stopped off at S-4 to get something or other and I kept walking up to the seventh deck passed the Segovia room, passed the giant chess set someone donated to us set up in the dark boiler room. I was half running now, *what the hell could they want?* When I got in First Sergeant Sowers and Major Gardner were standing there looking at me and they didn't look happy. "Hey Wojtecki how's it going?" the Major asked,

"Not bad. We just got in from a patrol," I told him, still panting from walking up seven flights of steps.

"Do you know the reason we called you up here?" He said.

"No, not at all. What is it?"

"Its about your dad, he's not well. We just got a Red Cross message from your family. He is terminally ill with cancer and they need you home right away."

I could hardly breathe at this point. I was in shock and it took a few seconds for things to sink in. *What was he talking about? What was going on?*

"Here is a Sat-Phone, use this to call home. Your mom left the number to the hospital. She has been with him ever since he was admitted on Wednesday."

"Thank you, First Sergeant."

"Anything else we can get you?" Major Gardner asked,

"No, I'll be fine. I just need to talk to my family."

"Okay, take as long as you like and come back in here because we need to find you a flight out of here ASAP."

"Aye, First Sergeant."

The Sat-Phone felt heavy in my hands as I walked out on the balcony to get a signal. I frantically dialed the numbers. My hands were shaking. There was something about dialing 6117-1 and then the number, a ring, and then, "Hello?" I answered hesitantly,

"Mom?"

"Matt, oh my Gosh I'm so glad to hear your voice!"

"Is dad doing okay?"

My mom wasn't doing too well. She told me that my dad wasn't doing very well and they weren't sure how long it would be. "Can I talk to him?" I said in tears,

"Yes, hold on and I'll put him on."

"Matt?" I heard my dad say, "I'm so sorry I was going to wait for you but I don't know what happened..." My mom took the phone from him and said he wasn't feeling himself today. I couldn't take it any more and I thought for second about just throwing myself over this balcony and ending it all. *That would be stupid,* I thought, *after all I've been through.* I just wished that this wasn't happening to me.

I went back to the CoC and returned the phone. There, First Sergeant Sowers said that a CH53 was making a run from al-Asad to the Dam tomorrow at 0900 and I was to be on that bird. He explained how I had to have all my gear ready and packed. The shit I packed inside my sea bags had to be emptied out and put in my Molly pack. The only things going with me were two sea bags and my carry on.

I got back down to the hooch and everyone knew something was wrong. "What's wrong Wojo?" Dan said as I feverishly moved towards the balcony. I spent most of the night out there thinking. Dan and my friends for the last ten months were there to comfort me and tell me it would be okay. Truthan said that he lost his mom when he was young and he said it sucked for him too. I had been waiting, wanting, and dreaming about going home. Now I finally was, but the one person I wanted to see when I got home was terminally ill.

Dan helped me pack up my stuff. I packed some cookies and other food items in my carry on. Who knows how long I would be at al-Asad. The trunk full of goodies from care packages I left for the unit replacing us and left my bedspread and most of the amenities that made me feel like home with Dan. I guess he would just fall in on my rack after I was gone. That was okay, I didn't care. I was getting the fuck out of here, but I wasn't sure where I was going, or what kind of world I would come back to once I got there. I was scared and felt helpless.

It was 0200. I laid awake in my rack and couldn't sleep. I wondered out onto the porch, stared out onto the Euphrates one last time and then decided to lug my shit up to the tenth deck that way I wouldn't have to do it in the morning. It seemed like a good plan until I got to the fifth deck and almost killed myself carrying the two sea bags upstairs. A word to describe what I was feeling would be devastation.

AUGUST 26-29 MY EXPERIENCE AT CAMP RIPPER - AL-ASAD, IRAQ

My alarm was set for 0700. I wanted to eat chow before I left. Sleep was useless anyway and the morning came quickly. Dan rolled over on the top bunk, "Hey you leavin' Wojtecki?"

"Yea, I'll see ya later. See ya when you get home."

"Alright man. See ya."

Part of me wanted to reach over and hug him. He wasn't alive yet and neither was anyone else so I quietly slipped out and made my way upstairs.

Chow was sick and horrible as always. I was so used to complaining about my food. I'm not sure how I could get used to eating good food. I got up to the tenth deck and stared at my sea bags. *What the fuck are you doing? Where are you going?* I kept asking myself. *I'm going home,* I caught myself answering under my breath.

Marines, A Corpsman, and the Sergeant Major were standing 100m from the Hilo pad. I knew I was in the right place. I asked the guy if he was waiting to go to al-Asad and he said he was. I just remembered how I wanted so desperately to be alone and away from everyone and now all I wanted to do was go back down there and be with them. I felt alone and helpless. *What if I got on the wrong flight?* It was like the one time when I was four years old and got lost in the grocery store. I sat there for a good two hours waiting for this bird to land. As usual, it was late by about 45 minutes. Brooks ran up to me and said that someone was looking for me to make sure I got on the flight. He was assigned to check on me and wanted to make sure that I left all of my serialized gear downstairs, "I'll be fine," I said and he ran back downstairs.

The roaring sound of the rotors whooshed over us as the bird made a circle around the Dam then finally landed on the Hilo pad. The Sergeant Major was the first one to get on the enormous aircraft. It took us a while to get the manifests straightened out and everyone accounted for before we finally took off. I looked into one of the small round windows. I saw the Dam get smaller and smaller and then finally it disappeared into the desert. al-Asad was about a twenty-minute ride from the Dam, quite a short ride compared to the three hours it usually took us on the ground, dodging IED's and holes in the ground suspected to contain mines. My ears still bothered me and the loud high pitched sound didn't help them at all. When we exited the bird onto the tarmac of the airfield, I could still hear the rotors in my head. I was carrying all of my gear and it was rather difficult. The Sgt Major noticed me and asked if I needed any help. Of course, I was trying to be tough and because I didn't want someone of higher rank carrying my shit. That looks bad. After I dropped my sea bags twice on the way to God knows where, the Marine in front of me just grabbed one of my sea bags without asking and we kept on walking really fast to the edge of the airfield where the tarmac was swallowed up by dust and sand.

The Sgt Major told me if I needed anything that he would be over at the RAS building. He pointed to the large Red Cross marked on the building next to a bunch of others that looked exactly the same. After he left, I was on my own and I was supposed to report to the regimental headquarters to fill out paperwork.

The majority of the day I was stuck carrying my personal record and orders for emergency leave around with me. I went to chow and then came back and they said that there would be a flight going out tomorrow if I wanted to just take my gear over to one of the tents and sleep there for the night. I was so pissed right now. It wasn't like I was just going home for no reason and as many times as they looked at my paperwork they obviously knew that my dad was not doing well and it actually was a matter of life and death to get back to Ohio. It didn't matter how as long as I could get off this God forsaken hellhole of a base. As if that wasn't bad enough I went to look for my gear and it wasn't there! For the next three hours I spend looking for my gear, asking people where it was and their typical desk jockey, "I don't want to do shit" attitudes pissed me off even more. There were a few Marines that helped me, but when it came to turning my rifle into the armory, it was a real chore just to get someone to drive me down there. They were going to make me walk, which would have taken most of the day. A Marine that appeared to be on his lunch break, got into a white truck and motioned me to come with him. We talked on the way over and I told him about Hit and Hadithah and about life outside the wire. He just smiled at me. He was a nice guy, but I don't think he would understand what I went through. Just then, I realized how difficult it was to describe the events that took place over the last few months. How would I explain this to my family? If we kept things up the way they were going, I guess I would have a few days to think about it.

The small opening to the armory led me down to a dungeon like basement that looked like an old Iraqi bunker. A Marine reading last month's issue of Maxim asked me what I wanted in a nice way. "I just need to turn my rifle in," I said and he grabbed for it. After I turned it in, I felt weird, like I forgot something. I was ready to go back there and ask him to give it back to me. It was my rifle. I spent the last seven months taking care of it and now I was saying goodbye. It made me kind of sad, although it seemed like a burden was lifted from me. I didn't have to carry that piece of shit with me to the head, to chow, and pretty much everywhere that I went. I stepped into the truck and we went back to Camp Ripper where chow was just now being served.

I didn't mind the chow and for the first time in months, I got to eat food that didn't taste like human waste. Stepping into the hand washing station and then opening the doors of the chow hall to an air-conditioned room, I noticed a Marine that I thought looked familiar. He was sitting at a plastic white table with a clicker just clicking as people would enter. "Brett how the hell are 'ya?!" I yelled as he almost fell off his chair. His arm was in a sling because apparently he hurt it bad. The funniest part was the way he was injured. Dmytriw was in the turret and went to get down. He stepped on the hood and slipped on a pork rib MRE falling straight into LCpl Dinkelman and injuring his collarbone. Dmytriw always told him that he owed him one after that. After all it got Brett to al-Asad and eventually home. If you got passed al-Asad then you were home free, but people had a way of getting lost in the paperwork here and could stay here for months if you didn't play your cards right. Brett and I had a long conversation and I asked him where he was staying. They had him staying in a white trailer while he healed from his injuries and until our unit RIPed with 3/2. He would then catch up with them and fly home. I asked Brett if I could stay with him just until I left there tomorrow hopefully and he agreed. He told me to meet him outside in about an hour.

I ate chow and watched the TV as if it were my first time. I ate slowly so that I could taste every bite of food. I couldn't wait to meet Brett after chow. Honestly, I was getting kind of lonely and there was no one to complain to or talk to. Then there was the thought of my dad hooked up to wires and breathing tubes. As much as I wanted to get back right away, I was afraid to go into that room even in my mind. After all I had been through, I was still afraid.

Brett stood by the mob of Pakistani chow hall workers and POG's with their bicycles propped up against the fence. It was a hot day out today and the sun beat down on my face as I stepped out of the A/C. "Hey Matt!" Brett called to me from the shaded area. I finally found my gear and I told him I was going to get it. He said that his trailer number was 222-IB, right by the showers. I thanked him for letting me stay with him and I thought that maybe we could go to the PX later on to pick up some souvenirs.

My gear was hidden in a back room near supply. It sucked lugging all the gear around that I owned. It was like carrying my entire life with me. Eventually in a few days, I could walk around without having to worry about gear or rifles. I was almost home free.

Brett sat inside his air-conditioned trailer. He wasn't looking good and he had gone off the deep end. He locked his rifle up to his rack so he didn't have to carry it around with him and it wasn't like he needed it in this place. I tried not to mention the fact that I was getting out of here because it just made him more depressed. "So, you wanna go up to the PX?" I asked Brett.

"Sure, you wanna see all the stuff I bought so far?"

"Yea, sure," I said to him as he pulled out a big trunk full of stuff that looked like he had went to the PX almost everyday and bought something for the past several weeks. There were DVD's, food, Iraqi made rugs, t-shirts, and his favorite Folex watches. He said he worked at a jewelry company and everyone would just assume they were real anyway. He had a good point.

We started walking to the PX and I told Brett about my dad and how I was getting out of this place. He felt bad for me, but I could tell he wanted to get out of here more than anyone. He told me about what he was doing with himself at al-Asad since he got here. He would go to the PX, buy stuff, go to chow, walk around, watch TV, and maybe even go to the Salsa night they had at one of the nearby enlisted clubs. After a while, he said that he got so bored that he asked them to give him a job and so they gave him a position at the chow hall. He went from combat to chow hall clicker. I just laughed at him although it wasn't that funny to him.

When we got to the PX, I had a list of all the stuff I had to buy for my family and fiancée. I got two rugs, one for Angela, and one for me. I bought some Iraqi money and some other little things like an Iraqi flag that I could show to my brother. I tried to think of some other things that I might buy for souvenirs, but I only ended up getting a few things. *How do I want to remember this time that we had here? Would I want to remember it when I got back?* I asked myself as I picked out souvenirs.

Brett and I went to a Café by the PX they just built not to long ago. It reminded me of some of the Café's back home. Modern looking furniture filled the nice, clean room. I had an espresso and talked more with Brett about how this place really sucked. We finally caught a bus back to Camp Ripper and then I took a nap for about five hours in the A/C.

I woke up to one single booming sound. It sounded very far away. Sirens went off and I walked outside to see what was going on. Everyone was running for cover like it was the end of the world or we were being assaulted. *This was ridiculous,* I thought, *Fucking POG's.* Someone ran by me and told me to get my flack and kevlar on, but I just stood there looking at them like, "Why the fuck are you telling me to get my gear on. Do you know the shit I've been through? I've had mortars go off right next to me for Christ's sake!" People that had never seen a mortar explode or had ever experience a fun filled night where mortars went off all night, were now running for cover and scurrying to get accountability. Those words never seemed to come out. I walked back into the tin can and fell asleep.

I woke up around 2030 and took a shower. Brett had the next season of a sitcom that we used to watch back at the Dam and we decided to have a marathon. The problem was we had to watch it on a small little DVD screen. Everyone in the hooch, including some guys from Lima crowded around the screen and we watched it until we were tired. Between episodes, I would go outside and stare at the open desert while I talked with some of the Lima Guys. One guy I talked to got shot in the ass by a 7.62 round. It was pretty bad, but I couldn't help laughing my ass off, literally. We talked for about a half an hour and I told him I was part of a MAP platoon. He said that he really respected the MAP's because of what they had to put up with on the roads everyday. I told him that I really respected Lima Company because of all the shit they went through. He asked me if I thought that these Iraqi people really cared about us and I told him I didn't know. I would hope that they would and I told him it didn't really matter, that we are selfless and it would be wrong to keep freedoms we have in the U.S. all to ourselves. Although, we both agreed that this country was a shit hole and we would rather be back in the U.S. any day. We went back inside and watched the rest of our sitcom and then I tried to get to sleep.

All I could think about was trying to get home to my dad. Why was I not on a flight yet? I wanted to see him and tell him stories. I wanted him to be proud of me, because if he wasn't, who would be? I thought that being in the shit was hell, but this was even worse. Waiting to get out of here, but no matter what I did they keep saying that I would have to stay here longer.

⋘◆⋙

I got up early around 0600 when Dinkelman normally got up for his chow hall duty. Supposedly, today would be the day they would ship me out of here and they said my paperwork would be ready. Chow came and I ate another breakfast here and then lunch came and I was getting fed up. They said that the Colonel was in a meeting and had to sign off on my paperwork.

"Unless you wanted to interrupt the Colonel in his meeting," they said, "you will have to sit tight until he is done." I explained my situation again and they said they would put a rush on it, whatever that meant. It was the most frustrating thing and I was stuck in a difficult situation because I had nowhere to go and could not do anything about it.

The time came where everything had to be worked out, which took another day away from being home with my dad. I finally made it to the airfield in a holding room they called the "John Deere Ranch." It was a place where Marines came and sometimes never made it back to. Where they waited, slept, talked, had a taste of disgusting MRE's, and then waited some more. Independent contractors also waited around with their expensive high-speed gear that they purchased with their 100K salaries. I sat in the middle of the aisles on top of my sea bags. I fell asleep until late afternoon waiting. They said that there were some problems with the computers and they went down, therefore they couldn't process my flight out of there and I would have to wait until the next flight. I was furious and felt as helpless as when I was behind the wheel of a Humvee. I went outside to get some air and talked to an Army Specialist on his way to Tacrit. He said that he was a driver and had driven about as much as we did hauling supplies and other cargo to nearby bases in that part of Iraq. He agreed with me that this was ridiculous and we talked for a couple of hours. He said that he was just going back to the States for R&R and I never understood how the Army could do that, go back to the States for two weeks and then come back here to finish up. That would have driven me insane and I probably would never come back if I had a chance to have R&R.

Just then, a crowd full of Marines with new cammies flooded into The Ranch. It was a company of 3/1 Marines that were on their way to relieve our unit. They talked about things like what to do if an IED went off and the Gunny stood up their in front of everyone and motivated them. They seemed exited to get to Hadithah and relived us and that was probably fine with 3/25. "Now when 3/25 got engaged in an IED explosion what did they do wrong? They didn't watch for secondary fire," The Gunny said. I don't think that he knew there was someone in there watching him from 3/25. Otherwise, he wouldn't have said that because it was bullshit. I knew he was just saying it to drive the point home. The Marines needed to learn from our mistakes and hopefully they would not have to witness what we did. I sat there in the white lawn chair next to a JTAC, the company commander of 3/1, and the XO.

I talked with the Marines in charge at the desk and they said they had a flight for me leaving tonight in about another hour. I was so happy and I was finally getting the hell off this base. They printed off my itinerary and said I would be flying to Ali-Asalem. At first, I thought this was a person that I was going to go see, but later I found out that it was an airport in Kuwait. I would be flying to an Army base, where they would process me out and then I would be transported to a public airport and be on my way back to the CONUS, as our APL always liked to say.

Our bird finally landed a little after 1900. I grabbed all my gear and loaded it onto the bus that would shuttle us onto the tarmac. About six others and the Army specialist accompanied me to the C130. The ride was quick, but there was something I found particularly odd with some of the Marines on the bus. Half of them were in handcuffs. It was very weird and I mentioned it to the Specialist. He didn't have a clue either, but it kind of made you wonder what they did and why we were stuck riding with them. One Sergeant, who looked like he was in charge of them, made sure their handcuffs were fastened snuggly before exiting the bus to our flight. I got off the bus quickly and my new friend helped me with my sea bags. The wind almost blew me over coming from the aircraft's large rotors that made a loud hissing sound that didn't help my hearing at all. One by one, we filed off into the mouth of the large beast. I sat down in the flimsy red cloth seats that covered half of the aircraft and strapped myself in with a small piece of rope that I could never figure out how to fasten. We were now on our way to Kuwait. A feeling inside me that I can't describe came over me as I watched the stars through the small porthole. I made it.

The prisoners were allowed to take their cuffs off, which scared the shit out of me. I'm not sure what they would have done to us, maybe hi-jack the plane and take us on a trip to God knows where or just kill us all after coming this far. To my surprise, they were calm, although one of them was crazy. He was a large Marine and carried a SAW with him, which he proceeded to clean from barrel to butt stock. I found it funny when he thought he was a conductor of the Phil Harmonic orchestra. He started conducting with the operating rod of his M249. *God this guy was a nut job, why the hell did they stick us with him?* He continued waving his rod around like he knew what he was doing or that there was actually music, I'm not sure I knew which was scarier. I looked at the crazy guy and then to the Specialist. I could tell he agreed with me, but it was too loud to hear him and I was too tired to care.

We landed about three hours later and everyone filed off. The feeling of nothingness came over me again and all I could see was a field, some lights, and tents. I knew we were in Kuwait because there was something about it that made it feel empty. I followed the Specialist off the tarmac and guessed that maybe since he had been here that he knew where to go. We almost were lost until we were instructed to load onto buses with other soldiers going on R&R. I guess this was a regular thing around here and soldiers were rotated back to the States almost weekly. Another Marine from Arizona hooked up with us on our way there and he said his name was Zack. Zack was on emergency leave too because his Grandma was in the hospital and wasn't expected to live. He kept me company and talked about scorpions and the desert in Arizona. He says that it's almost the same as Iraq.

We were escorted by two police vehicles with their sirens on and we headed to the airport. It fell completely silent and everyone seemed to be zoned out or tuned out to the world. I was scrunched up between two soldiers and one of them kept saying, "Ohhhh its su' gunna be good to get some R&R!" I just looked at him with a thousand yard stare and then looked toward the window where I could see the Army base where everyone went to process out. It was the final step to getting to the airport and getting on a commercial flight back to the U.S.

When we got to the base, everyone scattered as if they had been there before and were familiar with where to go. We just stood there and the specialist pointed us toward a long trailer where we went to sign papers and get our itinerary. Zack and I stepped inside and caught a glimpse of the large Marine Corps flag hanging up under the cammie netting. We knew we were in the right place.

A very tall man in civilian attire called us over and I explained to him that I was going on emergency leave and handed him a stack of papers that had now accumulated to be about an inch thick. Documents, orders stamped and then stamped again, signed by the Colonel, the Regiment, and then by my command. He took a quick look at them and then said, "Okay well if you just want to wait over there while I process you in. Oh yea and get rid of those fucking uniforms! You think you're going to walk into the Kuwaiti international airport looking like that? You might as well put a bull's eye on your chest." While he was processing our papers, I quickly unlocked my sea bags, found the only pair of civi's I had, and then went outside to the Porta-Johns to change. I didn't argue with him about getting into civi's, I was looking forward to it and although they were pretty wrinkled from laying there for close to half a year, I was glad to wear them. It made sense what he was saying and I would believe that a lot of people were not happy to see Marines in uniform.

After changing, I went back inside. The Marine in civi's gave us our paperwork and then I made sure to hand him the three clips of ammo I still had and the two grenades I had strapped to my flack. For some reason I didn't think I needed them.

Chow opened on base after 0100 for mid rats. We were supposed to meet a bus at the station at 0300 for transport to the airport and then catch a flight around 0600 to Heathrow Airport in London. Zack and I had a lot of time to talk. He was a quiet guy and didn't say much, although I wasn't really talkative either and only had one thing on my mind, which was getting back and seeing my dad. We walked down to the Army chow hall, where if we still had weapons, would have made us pull the trigger into a clearing barrel. That never made sense to me, why would you pull the trigger on your weapon when you have already inspected it? I guess it was just another thing that I thought about, but the main thing I was thinking about now was getting some good food. I was starving and it seemed like I hadn't eaten in days. The small looking trailer, when I entered it opened up to a very large room filled with food and beverages. It was like heaven to me and I got some of everything. *The Army really had it great,* I thought as I woofed down salads, ice cream, pop, cake, and other good tasting items.

After eating so much I couldn't walk, I stumbled outside into the darkness and waited for Zack. He was finishing a Sunday he had craftily constructed out of vanilla and chocolate ice cream. By then it was already 0200 and we had to get to the bus stop with all of our gear.

As I was about to pick up my gear that now felt like it weighed a thousand pounds, the Marine in civi's offered to drive us to the bus stop. If we didn't get a ride it would have taken us well over an hour to get there with all our gear and we drove well over five minutes to get there in his brand new government issued SUV.

We waited there for an hour or so and drank the last few Mozn bottles we would ever see before departing for the airport. Now it was just us and the open world. We were no longer on the military base, but were now in the world of Arabia and we stuck out like sore thumbs.

Zack and I were unloaded at the airport gates with all of our belongings. A short Kuwaiti reached out and grabbed both of my sea bags. I was ready to break his arm and then I realized that he was just a baggage handler and was throwing my gear on a cart to take inside. As he kept the cart rolling, I looked around the airport. It was amazing! There were marble floors, very high ceilings, and very upscale shops everywhere. A large Kuwaiti flag hung off the balcony of the two-story mall and airport. We kept walking and I was thinking about which stores I wanted to go to first. There was a Starbucks, a CD store, newspaper stands, cigar shops, and restaurants everywhere. People in robes and Hajji Headdresses, indicating that a man had made a journey to Mecca and was now called a "Hajji" respectfully. One man walked around with what looked like his three wives who each carried a piece of designer luggage. It was obvious this country was in the money just by looking around its airport.

The baggage handler stopped at the front gate and held out his hand, "tip tip…," he said. What I was about to say was, "You piece of shit. We liberated your country and gave you all this wealth, the least you could do is respect us and give us a tip!" He knew we were American and wouldn't go away until we gave him one. These people have some nerve. I didn't have any cash on me and Zack reached into his pocket and pulled out a ten. Apparently, that wasn't enough because he just kept standing there. At first, I thought he was crazy, but then I remembered that the exchange rate here was 2.48 dollars per Kuwaiti Dinar at the time, so our money was less valuable than theirs was. Zack gave him twenty bucks and he finally went away. *That was the last time we let people carry our luggage.* We didn't really know what to do and were supposed to report to a consulate of some kind where we could get a printout of our final itinerary. Two guys waiting at the gate, probably Army R&R guys, pointed us in the right direction. We had to walk all the way back outside to a balcony outside, up a flight of steps to a second story to a secluding office that was well hidden from the airport. I wondered why that was for a second and then it became obvious to me.

We straightened out our flights. We were to catch a flight to London at 0600, then to Chicago, and then I was supposed to arrange a flight to Cleveland from there. That was comforting and I knew it was going to be a pain in the ass for the next twenty some hours we would be flying halfway across the world.

I walked around and explored with Zack. We stopped at a CD shop, "What's the best Arabic music?" I asked the clerk.

"Oh, any one of these are good, but I like this one," He pointed to a CD with Arabic writing on it and I agreed to buy it. There was no bargaining or anything. It was 7.99 KD. I didn't care because I was never going to see this country again and wanted to remember the short time I was here. The place still felt empty every time you walked outside. I went to Starbucks and bought a Latté then the pizza shop, the newsstand, and the cigar shop. This was my first experience shopping and I remembered why I loved doing it. I couldn't wait to get home and shop with Angela.

We didn't have much to do other than sleep until 0600 rolled around. I felt happy inside but every time I felt that way, I remembered what was happening. I tried to get some sleep on the chairs but it was useless. I couldn't sleep with all these Arabs around, *what if one of them had a gun or charged at us with a bomb?* We were not safe, not until we crossed over into the U.S.

The gates opened at 0605 and we went through a quick security check. Some Kuwaiti guards checked me over. They asked for an ID, which was probably the only thing they knew in English. I handed them my military ID and they smiled at me and then talked amongst each other. I heard them say something in Arabic and I caught a little bit of it they said, "Endoc Hawaea" which meant, Marine, so I knew they were talking about me. They were either insulting me or they were complimenting me. I wanted to think they were honoring me for the sacrifices that Americans gave to give them a country, but I doubt that's what they said. They motioned me to go ahead and I was through with Kuwait. A few minutes and I would be on a flight to London. My friend Zack from Arizona was caught up in customs. He had to get his ID out and I guess they conducted a search on him. I thought about waiting for him, but I really needed to get home and he was on the same flight as I was. I would probably never see him again, but it was nice to know him for this short time. It just made me wonder how many people I knew for such a short time and then never really remembered. The flight attendant ripped my ticket and I was almost home free.

The flight was long and boring. I tried to listen to some music, but I couldn't understand it. The flight attendant offered me wine and I gladly accepted. I wasn't going to complain about it and I was glad to have it, but it made me sleepy and I dozed off until I heard the Captain speaking letting us know that we were landing in London.

I made a quick half an hour stop in London and I don't even think it counted as being there. It was enough to get a few quick pictures, talk to some of the people, hear their accents, and then catch another connecting flight in a completely different terminal. I had to take a train and only had less than twenty minutes to get there. The airport was very large and it seemed like I was riding forever. Getting on trams in London really scared me, especially after what recently happened not far from here in the subway. My anticipation was high, I was hoping and praying that a miracle could happen and bring my dad back to health so he could drink a bottle of beer with me and we could talk about everything. At this point, I didn't even care what as long as I got to talk with him.

I took flight after flight. Hours of time seemed to slip away into thin air as I kept setting back my watch, "-8, -6, -5…" I got to Chicago and made a phone call there to my house. There was no answer. They must be at the hospital. I called Angela on her cell phone and she picked up. I told her to tell my family they arranged a flight closer at the Akron airport at 7:15pm that night and I would be there. I could hardly hold the phone I was shaking so much. Angela tried to calm me down, but I was so on edge I almost couldn't control myself.

I would be in Chicago for a few hours while they cleared my bags and I got my boarding pass to Akron / Canton. I was so close and I had come so far. I had to walk outside to my terminal. I looked out at the great windy city. A strong feeling came over me. *This is what I fought for. I can say this is mine. This is my home. I am home.* It was the greatest feeling I've ever had and it's the feeling of being gone for what seemed like forever in a foreign country and then coming back to my homeland. I loved this country. I walked back inside and tried to get something to eat before taking off again.

It was a short flight from Chicago to Akron. Everything was going in fast forward now. I wasn't sure what I would do when I saw everyone. We landed and taxied to the gate of the small airport and then it was time to get off.

35

I walked toward the gate and then walked slowly down the hallway. My heart was beating a mile a minute and then I saw them. My brothers Chris, Pat, and Tim, my mom, Angela's mom, my mom's friend Gloria, and Angela were all there waiting for me. My jaw dropped and I ran to them like something out of a movie. I could hug all of them for about an hour and I think I did. We talked in person, not over an Internet phone or email. It was great. I was home.

We went straight to the hospital from the airport. Angela held my hand the whole way there while I talked about everything, the long flight over here, the pain in the ass it was to get out of Iraq, and how it was so good to be back. For moments I tried to avoid talking about my dad, he was waiting for me too, and I couldn't wait to see him.

My brother told me that it would be kind of shocking to see my dad. He was hooked up to machines and cords and wires were all over. I tried to prepare myself for it, but the more I did, the more I felt worse. I wished that I could have come home and he would be okay and everything would be fine. We could go out to eat and he could say, "I'm proud of you son," but that's not the way it ended, not at all.

We all stood outside the Cuyahoga Falls General Hospital together talking and trying to laugh. My mom wasn't doing too well. We talked for a half an hour or so. From out of nowhere, a cat from the nearby alleyway came out and rubbed up against my feet. That was strange. He was so cute how he purred and meowed as if he wanted something eat. "I don't have anything kitty," I said. I picked him up and petted him. He put us at ease.

My brother Chris hugged me, my fiancée held my hand, my mom was right behind me, and my brothers were all around me. We went into the hospital and up to the second floor IC unit. I didn't know what would happen. At this point, I was totally at a loss for words. They had a bunch of food in the waiting room. Everyone was camped out and looked like they had spent several days there. Nothing really mattered. I just wanted to see my dad.

They showed me where he was. I saw him. He was hooked up to wires and cords. I wanted him to talk to me, but he couldn't talk. I sat down next to him and talked to him. I said, "I'm home dad you don't have to worry about me any more." *Why did God do this? Why is he doing this to me?* I sat there for a few more minutes and then couldn't take it any more. I walked down the hallway and found a door that connected to a balcony and stepped outside to get some air.

36

AUGUST 30, 2005

They said he wouldn't be around for much longer. The cancer just got worse and worse and made him weaker and weaker. He was a true warrior and my hero. I was proud of him for holding on as long as he did. They moved him to a nice quiet place, a hospice in Fairlawn. It was a quiet place surrounded by trees and beautiful flowers and shrubbery. His room was quiet and a door could be opened up to the outside. It was raining out so we opened it just a crack so that he could hear the sound of the rain. My dad always liked watching storms.

I cried some more and for the first time in almost a year, I felt emotions. We spent the day with him and in between things. I walked around the hospice center with my brother and fiancée. There were rooms where families could spend time with their loved ones. There was a room with a grand piano, a library, and a computer with Internet. I talked to my brother about how good it was to get back and for a second I think we pretended like nothing was wrong, that dad would be there right around the corner to sit down with us and join in the conversation.

For the first time in years, I sat down and played the piano. I got the hang of it after a few tries.

I went back to the room to visit with my dad. My unit requested that I check in as soon as I was at the hospital, so I gave them a quick call to let them know I had finally made it back alright. They said to take as much time as I needed. I turned off my phone and visited with everyone. My mom, brothers, and my fiancée were all in the room and a friend of the family, Jessie was there too. She went to get some coffee for all of us and I scouted out a place to sleep for the night. The couch looked like a good spot. It was great not to have to get up every four hours, although I still did, and it was great not have to wake up to explosions. I tried to spend the night there, afraid, scared, and sad. There were no bombs around, no Arabs to slit my throat in my sleep, and no gunfights going on tonight.

AUGUST 31, 2005

I woke up at 0800 and everyone was still sleeping. I tried to fall back asleep and as I was finding out, this sleep thing was very difficult for me to get used to. I just stared at the ceiling until 0900 and other people woke up. I was hoping to wake up at home and my dad would be there to say, "I wanna here those feet hit the floor!" I missed him. I walked into his room and talked to him again. I thanked him for all the letters he sent me and all he did for me. He is the best dad in the world.

Angela came to the hospice around 1100. We walked down the hallway and went out a door that opened up to a garden of various flowers and stones. It was tranquil and more vegetation than I had seen in a year. We walked slowly, talking about why this had to happen. *Why was my Dad dying? What would I do with my life?* "He would want me to continue on and go to school," I told Angela as we sat there next to the fountain overlooking the hospice. The rain cleared up and it was sunny out. The birds chirped and the breeze blew over my face. I was home.

Epilogue

My Dad wrote these words for his family shortly before he died on August 31, 2005. I hope they will inspire all who read them.

———⟢◈⟣———

Epilogue is defined as the speech given by an actor at the end of a play.

My wish is that these memoirs will help my family now as well as future generations to find happiness in their lives. I wish you all peace, joy, and love.

Don't work for money, if you do you will get what you deserve - an ulcer. Do what you have a passion to do and the money will take care of itself.

Do the work you can be excited about and love to do. Have a passion for what you do.

Build a strong religious foundation for your life. Consult your Creator often. Miracles occur when you least expect them.

Love people. Surround yourself with good people. Avoid those who are not.

Let people live up to your expectations. Don't fly with the buzzards, they will pick your bones dry and fly away. Soar with eagles.

Make your name your most valuable possession.

Keep a high level of honesty and integrity in everything you do.

Get your strength from your family. Give them credit for their support.

Enjoy people you love and who love you while you can. Don't be too busy.

Embrace good art and good music. It will refresh you. Reject that which is vulgar and degrading; don't waste your time with it.

Learn from others constantly. There are two kinds of people - those who will show you examples of how to and those who will show you examples of how not to...

Never quit learning. Learn something new everyday. Be eager to learn.

Maintain a sense of humor even when things don't go well and you feel down.

Don't try to be like the other person, be better. Know that you are unique and interesting, if everyone looked like they were part of a TV commercial this would be a boring and dumb world. We are all different and that makes the world beautiful.

Love your country, it is the best in the world, no other country even comes close. Don't totally embrace patrician politics, support what is right and reject what is wrong. John F. Kennedy said, *"Ask not what your country can do for you, but ask what you can do for your country."* Be part of your government at some level, after all it belongs to you (you pay for it).

Glossary

.50 cal- heavy machine gun

0311- basic infantry

0341- see mortarmen

155- 155 milometer mortar round manufactured by the South Africans

240- see 240G

240G- heavy machine gun

81's- 81mm mortars or an 81mm mortar platoon

AAV- amphibious assault vehicle

Abu-Ghraib- infamous prison known for excessive torture of Iraqi prisoners

ACOG- scope mounted on top of an M16-A4 service rifle

AFB- air force base

Agaaf- Stop in Arabic

AK- A Russian machine gun AK stands for Alexander Kalashnikov (maker) and 1947 or 47, and 1974 or 74 was the year it was released and manufactured.

Al-Anbar- province in Iraq where we were located

Ali-Asalem- Kuwaiti Airport / Airbase

Ali-Babba- bad guys, evil men, terrorists (see Mujahadeen)

Aljazeera- an Arabic news network reporting in some areas of Iraq and believed to be corrupted by terrorists

Amtrak- see AAV

Anicanda- 3/2's construction / heavy equipment unit

AO- area of operations

AP- all purpose

APL- assistant patrol leader

ASP- ammo supply point

AT-4- American made rocket

AZ- see Azerbaijani

Azerbaijani- country formerly part of the Soviet Union that has reclaimed parts of the Hadithah Dam in cooperation with U.S. forces. Azerbaijani's guarded the Dam

al-Asad- Iraqi Airbase taken over by the U.S. military

al-Qaeda- terrorist cell located in the majority of the Al-Anbar province. Believed to be linked to the 9/11 terrorists bombings

al-Qui'm- large city nearest to the Syrian border. 3/2's area of operations

BAS- battalion aid station

Baath Party- minority political party consisting of mostly Sunni Muslims and Sadaam Hussein led the group.

Balad- city in Iraq known for its medical facilities

Barwanah- Iraqi city near Hadithah

Bashio- 3/2's Forward Air Command / reconnaissance

BC- Battalion Commander

BDA- Battle Damage Assessment

Beiji- Small oil thriving city in the Al-Anbar province

BFT- see Blue Force Tracker

BIR- basic individual record

Bien- what Iraqi kids call a "pen."

Binos- Binoculars

Blue Force Tracker- small computer inside of Humvees for tracking friendlies and known hazardous areas on the battlefield

BOLO- be on the lookout for

Bonidari- city in Iraq

Box- procedure where Humvees will block the road to conduct a vehicle check point

Brass- Officers

Bulldog- call sign for the center of command

BZO- battle sight zero

C-4- explosives used to demolish obstructions in Iraq

C130- large military aircraft used for transport

CAAT- combined anti-armor team

CASEVAC- casualty evacuation

Cal- caliber

Cammies- camouflage uniforms worn by the Marines

CBR- counter battery radar

CH53- large helicopter used for transport of large vehicles and personnel

Charms- candy similar to Jolly Ranchers inside of MRE's. Believed to be bad luck

Chechnyan- small country that rebelled against Russia and fled to parts of Iraq

Chem-Light- glow stick filled with a chemical providing light for roughly seven hours

Civi's- civilian attire

CLU- command launch unit

Click- a little less than a kilometer

CO- commanding officer

COG- corporal of the guard. Usually a corporal that takes charge over fire watch for that night.

COM- communications

CONUS- continental United States

Coax- 7.62mm rounds shot through a tanks 240 which is remotely fired using an electrical signal

CoC- center of command

CP- check point

Cpl- corporal

Crypto- encryption for radios

Curbasa- very small town in Iraq

Debrief- meeting after a mission is complete to discuss shortcomings and positive things taken from the mission

Det- short for "Detonation." Cord used to detonate C-4

Det-Fac- detention facility

DIV- division

Dinar- money used in Iraq

Dulab- an Ammo Supply Point

Eitibhy'a- attention in Arabic

EMP- marksmanship program that prepared personnel for close engagements in combat

Endoc Hawaea- Marines in Arabic

Enso Mensiata- get out of the vehicle in Arabic

EOD- enemy ordinance disposal

EOF- escalation of force

FAC- forward air command

Fallen Angels- Marines killed in combat

Fallujah- very large city in Iraq

FDC- fire direction center

FO- forward observer

FOB- forward operating base

Folex- a fake Rolex that Iraqis would sell Americans as they came by nearby shops

FPF- final protective fire / last line of defense in an engagement.

Freedom Guard- Iraqi soldiers based at FOB Hit

Friendlies- alleys / coalition forces

Goat Rope- a completely unorganized mess

GPS- global positioning system

H&S- headquarters and support

Hadine- see Mujahadeen

Hadithah- city in Iraq near the Hadithah Dam where we were located

Hajji- term used to describe a Muslim male that has made a trip to Mecca. Considered to be a great honor.

Haqlaniyah- city in Iraq

Hawaea- see Endoc Hawaea

HE- high explosive mortar rounds

HESCO- huge barriers filled with sand and fortified large positions

HET- interrogation team

Head- Marine Corps term for a bathroom

High Back- a Humvee with an open back similar to a pickup. Used to transport groups of Marines and very lightly armored.

Highers- higher ranking military officials

Hive- a sniper position

Hooches- Marine Corps camp or small shelters that house Marines

Humvee- urban vehicle used for patrolling and light transport

Hushfah- very small town in Iraq about half the size of a city block

HVT- high value target

IDF- indirect fire

IED- improvised explosive device

IFF- Iraqi freedom fighters. See Freedom Fighters

ING- Iraqi national guard

IP- Iraqi police

IR- infrared

ISF- Iraqi security forces

Iso Mat- insolated mat put down before putting down a sleeping bag. Protects from moisture coming up from the ground.

JDAM- a 500 pound bomb

JTAC- a Marine, usually and Officer, that is licensed to talk to F-15's and other aircraft

K-3- oil refinery complex near Hadithah

Kaybar- call sign for Mobile Assault Platoons

KBR- Kellogg, Brown, and Root, independent contractors that provide the majority of supplies and services in Iraq.

Kevlar- light weight material used to protect against small arms fire and shrapnel. Usually a "kevlar" refers to a helmet in the Marine Corps.

KIA- killed in action

Kusay- one of Sadaam Hussein's brothers

LAV- light armored vehicles

LCpl- lance corporal or E-2 rank in the Marine Corps.

Lejeune- Marine Corps camp located in North Carolina
Little Beirut- small town in Iraq
LTC- Lieutenant Colonel
Lt- Lieutenant
LZ- landing zone
M16-A4- service rifle carried by the majority of Marines
M203- grenade launcher and M-16 rifle
M240G- see 240G
M249- see SAW
MAKO- call sign for snipers. Stands for Mako Shark, which an animal known for sneaking up on it's prey and devouring them.
MAM- military aged male
MAP- mobile assault platoon
MAR- marine
Mad-Max- maneuver done during Marine Corps training where all vehicles rush up on line and assault through the objective
Maj- Major
Maslow- Psychologist that developed a Hierarchy of needs
MEDEVAC- medical evacuation
Mechs- mechanics
Mensiata- see enso mensiata
MG42- an automatic anti-tank gun
Mid-Rats- meal between dinner and breakfast lasting from usually 2300-0200
MOS- occupation in the Marine Corps
MOUT- modern operations under urban terrain
Mod-Dues- see .50 cal
Mortarmen- personnel that specialize in firing mortars
Mozn- water shipped to Marine Corps camps from Saudi Arabia
MP- military police
MRE- meal ready to eat
MRK19- automatic grenade launcher mounted on Humvees and used for severe engagements
MSR- Iraqi interstate routes that run across Iraq
Muj- see Mujahadeen
Mujahadeen- terrorist cell located in the Al-Anbar province and other parts of Iraq
NCO- non-commissioned officer
NJP- Navy / Marine Corps judicial punishment under the articles of the UCMJ
NSTR- nothing significant to report

NVG's- night vision goggles
OP- observation post
Op-Sec- operational security
PAC2A- infrared laser mounted on the M16 that can only be seen with night vision
PAS13- scope that allows a Marine to see heat signatures and other objects at night
PE-4- enemy C-4 explosives sold on the black market to terrorists
PFC- private first class
PL- patrol leader
Playstation- video game system
POG- personnel other then grunt
POGy Bait- junk food
POO- point of origin
POS- position
Porta-Johns- portable toilets
PRC119- radios used in Humvees and rarely foot mobile patrols because of the bulkiness.
Promitherin- chemical sprayed on uniforms to keep away bugs
PSP- portable Playstation
Psy-Ops- psychological operations
PT- physical training
PTSD- post traumatic stress disorder
PVS14- A type of Night Vision scope
PX- Military supermarket
QRF- quick reaction force
Quad-Con- military storage units similar to a truck trailer but smaller
Qui'm- see al-Qui'm
R&R- relaxation and rehabilitation
RAS- regimental aid station
Raghead- offensive term for Arabic people
Ramadi- city in Iraq
Rankless- not wearing rank
RCAX- reserve combined arms exercise
REI tent- small tents not far from Iraqi pipelines sheltering Iraqi guards employed by the Ministry of Oil to watch over Iraq's oil pipelines to prevent destruction
Recon- reconnaissance
RF- radio frequency
RIPed- relief in place
ROE- rules of engagement

Roger- affirmative / yes

Rolled Up- to capture enemy personnel

RPG- rocket propelled grenade

RPK- enemy assault weapon

RTB- return to base

RTT- small radio for talking to unit commanders

SA- South Africa

SAC- strategic air command

SASO- stability and support operations

SASR- sniper rifle

SAW- M249 squad automatic weapon

Sadaam Hussein- Iraqi dictator and corrupt ruler responsible for the deaths of thousands of Iraqis and Kurds

Satchel Charge- one satchel= 1lb. of C-4

SE- southeast

SEAD- mortar movement; suppress enemy air defense

SESM- rounds full of paint used in training

Secondaries- Enemies that ambush after a mine strike or an IED attack

Segovia- European Phone Company specializing in Internet phone service

Sheik- elder and usually a town's leader or general religious leader / elder

Shock Tube- tube used in demolitions that are used to intensify the explosive effects of C-4

Shwaya- I don't know / not sure / I don't understand, in Arabic

SKS- Russian infantry rifle / bolt action

SOG- sergeant of the guard

SOI- school of infantry

SOP- standard operating procedures

Squawk Box- a speaker box used to listen to a military radio

STAX- sight target acquisition / snipers

Sunni Triangle- large area in Iraq shaped like a triangle mostly occupied by Sunni Muslims and believed to be the most dangerous area in Iraq

Syria- Arabic country bordering Iraq believed to harbor terrorists

TAC- alternate frequency

Tacrit- city near Ramadi, Iraq

Talk-On- a small radio CB manufactured by Motorola used by insurgents

Tasker- day where MAP's would complete miscellaneous tasks for the company

Terp- interpreter

Tight 360- movement where all Humvees in a MAP platoon will form a circle so that each vehicle faces a different direction and is most efficient at guarding against ambushes or enemies

Tinian- call sign for the line companies

TOW- a wire guided missile used by MAP platoons and mounted on Humvees and believed to be less accurate than a Javelin missile

Tray Rats- a larger MRE that will feed an entire company

TTP- training procedures

Tun Tavern- birthplace of the Marine Corps

Type 1- air strike made up of heavy bombs

Type 2- air strike made up of smaller arms such as mini-guns and small rockets

Ubaydi- small city near Al-Qui'm and fifteen miles south of Syria

Uday- Salaam's brother and top aid to the Republican Guard - Uday controlled the media in Iraq.

USD- U.S. dollars

UXO- unexploded ordinance

VBIED- vehicle born IED

VC- vehicle commander

VCP- vehicle check point

Victor- vehicle

Voluntolds- Marines volunteered to do a particular task as opposed to volunteering which is willingly doing something.

VX- deadly nerve agent believed to still be in Iraq and caused massive destruction among the Kurds during the first Gulf War.

Watey- ditch where water once was but has since dried up leaving a huge crevice

WIA- wounded in action

Wiley X's- protective glasses that are used to prevent shrapnel from entering the eyes during combat

WMD- weapons of mass destruction

XO- An Officer, usually a Captain that takes charge during the Commanding Officer's absence

Zarkowi- Terrorist leader of the Mujahadeen

A Dedication to Heroes

LCpl Daniel Chavez
Cpl Dustin Derga
Cpl Bryan Richardson
HM2 Jeffery Wiener
Sgt Aaron Cepeda
LCpl Jourdan Grez
HM3 Travis Youngblood
Cpl Michael Lindemuth
LCpl Dustin Birch
LCpl Ryan Kovacicek
LCpl Thomas Keeling
Cpl Joseph Tremblay
SSgt Kendall Ivy
LCpl Nicholas Erdy
LCpl Wesley Davids
LCpl Lance Graham
Sgt Jeffrey Boskovitch
LCpl Brian Montgomery
SSgt Joseph Goodrich
SSgt Anthony Goodwin
Sgt Nathaniel Rock
Sgt David Wimberg
Sgt James Graham
Maj Ricardo Crocker

LCpl Kevin Waruinge
Cpl David Stewart
Sgt Bradley Haper
The Arabic interpreter Neill
LCpl Daniel Deyarmin Jr.
Sgt David Coullard
LCpl Roger Castleberry Jr.
Cpl Andre Williams
LCpl Jonathan Grant
Sgt Michael Marzano
PFC Christopher Dixon
LCpl Devon Seymour
LCpl Christopher Lyons
LCpl Grant Fraser
LCpl Nicholas Bloem
LCpl Timothy Bell Jr.
LCpl William Wightman
Cpl David Kreuter
LCpl Michael Cifuentes
PFC Christopher Dyer
Sgt Justin Hoffman
LCpl Aaron Reed
LCpl Edward Schroeder II
LCpl Eric Bernholtz
Cpl Brad Squires

This journal pays special tribute to those of us brave men who did not make it home. I can assure families and friends that the heroes of 3/25 will not be forgotten and are now in a better place in heaven. There is not a day that goes by that I don't think about them. There is a special place in my heart for these

Marines. *In some way, I know I will see them again in time. Squires will be smoking a cigarette and joking, Keeling will be talking about college and always joking with Uzukawu about selling his Acura, Brian Montgomery will be at the Yacht club with me having a few drinks, Cpl Lindemuth will be wearing his aviator sunglasses and pretending that he is good at karaoke. Each one of these Marines, everyone knew in a special way, and I can just tell you that to honor the memory of these Marines who now guard the gates of heaven, think about those little things that you remember about them and keep those little memories in your hearts forever.*

-*Semper Fi*
Cpl Matthew Wojtecki
Weapons Co. 3/25 MAP 8

About the Author

Cpl. Matthew Wojtecki, 23, is a reservist at Weapons Company 3/25 based out of Akron, OH. Last year in January of 2005, Cpl. Wojtecki and the Marines of 3/25 were mobilized in support of Operation Iraqi Freedom III. Prior to deployment, Matthew attended Kent State University pursuing a finance and computer information systems degree. He is engaged to his Fiancé, Angela whom he left behind to fight in Iraq.

Although after returning home, the events of September 11th and the memories of war are still heavy on Matthew's mind, they serve as a constant reminder that freedom isn't free, and that the life he has, came with some sacrifice.

CPSIA information can be obtained
at www.ICGtesting.com
Printed in the USA
FFOW02n1846310518
46965737-49239FF

9 781425 954000